John Dewey

John Dewey

A CENTENNIAL BIBLIOGRAPHY
BY MILTON HALSEY THOMAS

THE UNIVERSITY OF CHICAGO PRESS

Library of Congress Catalog Card Number: 62-12638

THE UNIVERSITY OF CHICAGO PRESS, CHICAGO & LONDON
The University of Toronto Press, Toronto 5, Canada

JOHN DEWEY: A CENTENNIAL BIBLIOGRAPHY, *by Milton Halsey Thomas.* © *1962 by The University of Chicago Composed and printed by* THE UNIVERSITY OF CHICAGO PRESS, *Chicago, Illinois, U.S.A.*

First published as A BIBLIOGRAPHY OF JOHN DEWEY, *by Milton Halsey Thomas and Herbert Wallace Schneider Copyright 1929, 1957 by Columbia University Press.* A BIBLIOGRAPHY OF JOHN DEWEY, 1882–1939, *by Milton Halsey Thomas. Copyright 1939 by Columbia University Press*

Preface

This volume, undertaken in connection with the centenary tributes to John Dewey in 1959, lists his published writings from the earliest, in 1882, to the present time. The arrangement is chronological by date of publication, books and parts of books appearing immediately under the annual heading, followed by articles. Reviews and translations are listed with the original printings. This portion of the book is intended to be exhaustive. Public statements and appeals which Dewey merely signed as a member of a committee have, in general, been omitted, as well as brief newspaper reports of his addresses.

The second portion of this book, Writings about John Dewey, lists books, parts of books, and articles, exclusive of book reviews, which the writer has been able to locate through bibliographical channels and from suggestions and clues provided by Dewey scholars. If he has erred, it has been on the side of inclusiveness. The masters' and doctors' theses listed here are, for the most part, unpublished, except on microfilm, and available only at the institutions of their origin.

This bibliography was begun 17 March 1926 after a conversation with Mr. Dewey. The writer was then librarian of the Butler Library of Philosophy, a departmental library at Columbia University, and in daily contact with Dewey and his students. Frequent requests had indicated the need for a listing of Dewey's writings and the material relating to him. Dewey was kind and helpful, though nothing could have interested him less than the unearthing of his former writings. As soon as he had completed an article or a book and sent it off to the printer, he went on to something else, and the item was dismissed and forgotten unless it was answered or attacked, and further word was necessary. Copies of his books, sent to him by his publishers, were given away to his colleagues and friends, and reprints of his articles disappeared even faster. No institution or individual known to this writer has assembled a complete collection of Dewey's published writings, and the titles listed here have been gathered in person from many libraries and by means of extensive correspondence. The writer has not followed a career in philosophy, but it has been a pleasure and satisfaction for thirty-five years to keep up with the Dewey literature and to record it.

It is also a pleasure to point out that although the writings listed here place Dewey among the most prolific of modern authors, not a single item was written with anything less than his best efforts, or merely for money. After his first diffident offerings had been printed by William Torrey Harris, he never lacked media, and the time soon came when he was importuned by editors, publishers, and organizations. But most of his contributions seem to have originated with him, and they impress this writer as the work of a dedicated man focusing one of the greatest intellects of our day on some problem which came to his attention: a problem which may have troubled Aristotle, or an injustice encountered in his morning paper.

The difference in style and readability between Dewey's professional writings and his popular books and articles should not go unnoticed. In the former, his immense learning and the comprehensiveness of his thinking combined with intellectual honesty and a desire for exactitude of statement to produce a prose which is often difficult and baffling. He was fully aware of this, and quipped about it in his autobiographical article. It is impossible to resist quoting Justice Holmes's famous remark to Sir Frederick Pollock:

But although Dewey's book [*Experience and Nature*] is incredibly ill written, it seemed to me after several rereadings to have a feeling of intimacy with the inside of the cosmos that I found unequaled. So methought God would have spoken had He been inarticulate but keenly desirous to tell you how it was.

On the other hand, when Dewey became an advocate or an expositor or a critic, he wrote the agreeable English of the educated man of his day, based on early mastery of Latin and Greek and fostered by extensive youthful reading of the best nineteenth-century British writers and the King James Bible.

The present work was compiled in libraries and other repositories from Chicago to Rome, chiefly at Princeton and Columbia, but with fruitful sorties to Harvard, Yale, and Rutgers, the Bodleian and the British Museum, the Bibliothèque Nationale, the public libraries of Boston and New York, and the Library of Congress.

No book of this sort can be produced without the assistance and co-operation of others, and the writer takes pleasure in recording his indebtednesses. Many librarians have been helpful far beyond the call of duty, especially Miss Christine L. Reb (Chicago), Miss Agnes N. Tysse (Michigan), Miss Lila Chandra (Berkeley), Joseph Ruffier (Washington Square), Mrs. Frances G. K. Holbrook (U.C.L.A.), and Miss Katharine Standish Pearce (Princeton). Several Dewey scholars have taken a genuine interest in the book. Dr. Corliss Lamont has been most helpful in all three editions. Professor Herbert Wallace Schneider has continued to give valuable aid. Professor Sidney Ratner's erudition and wealth of bibliographical knowledge have been indispensable and freely drawn upon. Professor Francis Trowbridge Villemain has lent numerous remote and uncommon items. Dr. Joseph Ratner contributed some early titles unearthed since the 1939 edition. Julius Altman sought us out to give us the benefit of his studies. Professor Gérard Deledalle has given assistance on French material. Professor and Signora Nicola Abbagnano gave the compiler warm hospitality and invaluable help on Italian writings during a stay at Santa Margherita Ligure. Dr. Graziella Federici Vescovini sent us just in time an extremely useful article on the fortunes of John Dewey in Italy. Mrs. Dewey provided some very helpful information on translations of her husband's works. Much appreciation and credit must go to our assistants during the years this edition was in progress: Joan Morin Stevenson, Sue Levitt, Marjorie Thompson Bhavnani, and Diane Nester Rafuse.

In the month of the Dewey Centennial the writer changed his university affiliation from Columbia to Princeton; he records with gratitude that both institutions made substantial grants for the preparation of this book.

M. HALSEY THOMAS

PRINCETON UNIVERSITY
18 April 1962

Contents

Chronology of John Dewey

1859 Born at 186 South Willard Street, Burlington, Vermont, 20 October

1875 Graduate, Burlington High School

1879 A.B. University of Vermont; Phi Beta Kappa; Delta Psi

1879 Teacher of the classics, the sciences, and algebra, at the high school, Oil City, Pennsylvania, 1879–1881

1881 Teacher in Lake View Seminary, Charlotte, Vermont; private student of philosophy with Professor H. A. P. Torrey, 1881–1882

1882 Graduate student, Johns Hopkins University, 1882–1884

1883 Fellow of Johns Hopkins University, 1883–1884

1884 PH.D. Johns Hopkins University

1884 Instructor in Philosophy, University of Michigan, 1884–1886

1886 Married to [Harriet] Alice Chipman (PH.B. University of Michigan 1886) of Fenton, Michigan, 28 July

1886 Assistant Professor of Philosophy, University of Michigan, 1886–1888

1888 Professor of Philosophy, University of Minnesota, 1888–1889

1889 Professor of Philosophy, University of Michigan, 1889–1894

1894 Professor of Philosophy and Chairman of the Department of Philosophy, Psychology, and Education, University of Chicago, 1894–1904

1899 President of the American Psychological Association, 1899–1900

1902 Director of the School of Education, University of Chicago, 1902–1904

1904 Professor of Philosophy, Columbia University, 1904–1930

1905 President of the American Philosophical Association, 1905–1906

1906 Lecturer in Philosophy, Johns Hopkins University, 1906–1907

1910 Member of the National Academy of Sciences

1911 Member of the American Philosophical Society

1915 A founder and first president of the American Association of University Professors

1919 Lecturer at Imperial University, Tokyo, February–March

1919 Lecturer at National Universities of Peking and Nanking, 1919–1921

1923 Membre correspondant, section de philosophie, Académie des Sciences Morales et Politiques, Institut de France, 24 mars.

1924 Educational survey of Turkey

1926 Educational survey of Mexico

1927 Death of Alice Chipman Dewey, 14 July

1928 Educational survey of Soviet Russia

1929 Gifford Lecturer, University of Edinburgh

1930 Professor Emeritus of Philosophy in residence, Columbia University, 1930–1939; Professor Emeritus, 1939–1952

1930 William James Lecturer, Harvard University

1937 Chairman of the Commission of Inquiry into the Charges Made against Leon Trotsky in the Moscow Trials

1946 Married to Roberta (Lowitz) Grant of New York City, 11 December

1952 Died at his home, 1158 Fifth Avenue, New York City, 1 June, aged 92 years, 7 months, and 22 days

HONORARY DEGREES: LL.D. University of Wisconsin 1904, University of Vermont 1910, University of Michigan 1913, Johns Hopkins University 1915, Illinois College 1917, University of St. Andrews 1929, Harvard University 1932; LITT.D. Columbia University 1929, Yale University 1951; D.Sc. University of Pennsylvania 1946; HON.PH.D. National University of Peking 1920, University of Oslo 1946; DOCTEUR DE L'UNIVERSITÉ *honoris causa* Paris 1930. Mr. Dewey refused a proffered honorary degree from Charles University of Prague in 1948.

Writings of John Dewey

1882

THE METAPHYSICAL ASSUMPTIONS OF MATERIALISM. *Journal of Speculative Philosophy*, Apr. 1882, XVI, 208–213.

Abstracts in *Johns Hopkins University Circular*, Feb. 1883, II, 59; *Revue philosophique*, Jan. 1883, XV, 109.

THE PANTHEISM OF SPINOZA. *Journal of Speculative Philosophy*, July 1882, XVI, 249–257.

Abstract in *Johns Hopkins University Circular*, Feb. 1883, II, 59.

1883

KNOWLEDGE AND THE RELATIVITY OF FEELING. *Journal of Speculative Philosophy*, Jan. 1883, XVII, 56–70.

Read before the Metaphysical Club of Johns Hopkins University, 12 Dec. 1882.

1884

THE PSYCHOLOGY OF KANT.

Dissertation for the PH.D. degree at Johns Hopkins University. This was not published, and no copy is owned by the university. (Title from Johns Hopkins University, *List of Dissertations . . . 1878–1919*, p. 7.)

KANT AND PHILOSOPHIC METHOD. *Journal of Speculative Philosophy*, Apr. 1884, XVIII, 162–174.

THE NEW PSYCHOLOGY. *Andover Review*, Sept. 1884, II, 278–289.

Read before the Metaphysical Club of Johns Hopkins University, 11 Mar. 1884.

THE OBLIGATION TO KNOWLEDGE OF GOD. *The Monthly Bulletin*, Students' Christian Association, University of Michigan, Nov. 1884, VI, 23–25.

1885

EDUCATION AND THE HEALTH OF WOMEN. *Science*, 16 Oct. 1885, VI, 341–342.

1886

PSYCHOLOGY IN HIGH-SCHOOLS FROM THE STANDPOINT OF THE COLLEGE. Michigan Schoolmasters' Club, *Papers, 1886* (Lansing, Michigan: H. R. Pattengill [1886]). 4 pp.

"A paper read at the first meeting of the Michigan Schoolmasters' Club [in Ann Arbor, 1 May 1886], by Dr. John Dewey, of the University of Michigan."

Reproduced in facsimile by Edwards Brothers, Ann Arbor, 1947.

THE PLACE OF RELIGIOUS EMOTION. *The Monthly Bulletin*, Students' Christian Association, University of Michigan, Oct. 1886, VIII, 23–25.

THE PSYCHOLOGICAL STANDPOINT. *Mind*, Jan. 1886, XI, 1–19.

Reply to this article and PSYCHOLOGY AS PHILOSOPHIC METHOD (*ib.*, Apr. 1886), by Shadworth Holloway Hodgson, ILLUSORY PSYCHOLOGY, *ib.*, Oct. 1886, XI, 478–494. See Dewey's "ILLUSORY PSYCHOLOGY" (*ib.*, Jan. 1887), below.

Abstract in *Revue philosophique*, Apr. 1886, XXI, 436.

HEALTH AND SEX IN HIGHER EDUCATION. *Popular Science Monthly*, Mar. 1886, XXVIII, 606–614.

SOUL AND BODY. *Bibliotheca Sacra*, Apr. 1886, XLIII, 239–263.

PSYCHOLOGY AS PHILOSOPHIC METHOD. *Mind*, Apr. 1886, XI, 153–173.

See note under THE PSYCHOLOGICAL STANDPOINT, above.

INVENTORY OF PHILOSOPHY TAUGHT IN AMERICAN COLLEGES. *Science*, 16 Apr. 1886, VII, 353–355.

1887

PSYCHOLOGY. New York: Harper & Brothers, 1887 [°1886]. xii, 417 pp.

Contents. Introductory: Science and Method of Psychology—Mind and Modes of Activity. Part I, Knowledge: Elements of Knowledge —Processes of Knowledge—Stages of Knowledge-Perception—Memory—Imagination—Thinking—Intuition. Part II, Feeling: Introduction to Feeling—Sensuous Feeling—Formal Feeling—Development of Qualitative Feeling—Intellectual Feeling—Aesthetic Feeling—Personal Feeling. Part III, The Will: Sensuous Impulses—Development of Volition—Physical Control—Prudential Control—Moral Control—Will as the Source of Ideals and of Their Realization.

Reviewed in *American Journal of Psychology*, Nov. 1887, I, 154–159 [Granville Stanley Hall]; *Andover Review*, Apr. 1888, IX, 437–441 (Henry Augustus Pearson Torrey); *Bibliotheca Sacra*, Apr. 1888, XLV, 381–383; *Mind*, Apr. and July 1887, XII, 301–302, 439–443 [George Croom Robertson]; *New Englander and Yale Review*, Apr. 1887, XLVI, 387–390; *Revue philosophique*, Aug. 1887, XXIV, 202–203 (Théodule Ribot).

Abstract in *Johns Hopkins University Circular*, Aug. 1887, VI, 125. See edition of 1891.

"Illusory Psychology," *Mind*, Jan. 1887, XII, 83–88.

Reply to Shadworth Holloway Hodgson, Illusory Psychology, *ib.*, Oct. 1886, XI, 478–494. Rejoinder by Hodgson, "Illusory Psychology"—a Rejoinder, *ib.*, Apr. 1887, XII, 314–318.

Ethics and Physical Science. *Andover Review*, June 1887, VII, 573–591.

Abstract in *Johns Hopkins University Circular*, Aug. 1887, VI, 125.

Review of George Trumbull Ladd, *Elements of Physiological Psychology*. *New Englander and Yale Review*, June 1887, XLVI, 528–537.

Knowledge as Idealisation. *Mind*, July 1887, XII, 382–396.

1888

Leibniz's New Essays Concerning the Human Understanding. A Critical Exposition. (Griggs's Philosophical Classics, edited by George Sylvester Morris, No. 7.) Chicago: S. C. Griggs and Company, 1888. xvii, 272 pp.

Reprinted in 1902 by Scott, Foresman & Co., Chicago.

Contents. The Man—Sources of His Philosophy—The Problem and Its Solution—Locke and Leibniz, Innate Ideas—Sensation and Experience—The Impulses and the Will—Matter and Its Relation to Spirit—Material Phenomena and Their Reality—Some Fundamen-

tal Conceptions—The Nature and Extent of Knowledge—The Theology of Leibniz—Criticism and Conclusion.
Reviewed in *Mind*, Oct. 1888, XIII, 612; *New Englander and Yale Review*, Jan. 1889, L, 66–68; *Science*, 19 Oct. 1888, XII, 188.

THE ETHICS OF DEMOCRACY. (University of Michigan. Philosophical Papers. Second ser., No. 1.) Ann Arbor: Andrews & Company, 1888. 28 pp.
Lecture delivered at the University of Michigan.

1889

THE LATE PROFESSOR MORRIS. *The Palladium.* An Annual Edited by the College Fraternities at the University of Michigan, 1889, XXXI, 110–118.
Reprinted in part in Robert Mark Wenley, *The Life and Work of George Sylvester Morris* (New York, 1917), 308–313.

APPLIED PSYCHOLOGY. An Introduction to the Principles and Practice of Education. By J[ames] A[lexander] McLellan and John Dewey. Boston: Educational Publishing Company [n.d., pref. 1889]. xxxi, 317 pp.
Contents. Psychology and Its Relations to the Teacher: The Educational Importance of Psychology—The Educational Limitations of Psychology—The Treatment of Psychology Adopted. The Bases of Psychical Life: Sensation—Interest—Impulse. The Psychical Processes: Classification and Contents of Our Minds—Classification of Processes Corresponding to These Contents—Educational Principles —Apperception and Retention. Forms of Intellectual Development: Principles of Intellectual Development—Stages of Intellectual Development—Training of Perception, Memory, Imagination, Thought. The Forms of Emotional Development: Conditions of Interest— Principles of Emotional Growth—The Forms, or Stages, of Emotional Growth. Forms of Volitional Development: Factors of Volitional Development—Stages of Volitional Development or of Self Control. Mind and Body: Importance of Body for Soul—Structure of Nervous System in Man—Elementary Properties of Nerve Structures—Psychological Equivalents—Localization of Function—Educational Principles. Summary of Principles: Bases of Instruction—Ends of Instruction—Methods of Instruction—Relation of Knowledge, Feeling, and Will—Criticism of Maxims.

PSYCHOLOGY. Second edition. New York: Harper & Brothers, 1889. xii, 427 pp.
For Contents, see edition of 1887.

THE PHILOSOPHY OF THOMAS HILL GREEN. *Andover Review*, Apr. 1889, XI, 337–355.

THE LESSON OF CONTEMPORARY FRENCH LITERATURE. *Christian Union*, 11 July 1889, IX, 38–39.

GALTON'S STATISTICAL METHODS. *Publications of the American Statistical Association*, Sept. 1889, N.S. I, 331–334.
Review of Francis Galton, *Natural Inheritance*.

ETHICS IN THE UNIVERSITY OF MICHIGAN. *Ethical Record*, Oct. 1889, II, 145–148.
Describes courses in ethics to be given in 1889–1890.

1890

A COLLEGE COURSE. WHAT SHOULD I EXPECT FROM IT? *The Castalian*, Published by the Independents of the Senior Class, University of Michigan, 1890, V, 26–29.

ON SOME CURRENT CONCEPTIONS OF THE TERM "SELF." *Mind*, Jan. 1890, XV, 58–74.

IS LOGIC A DUALISTIC SCIENCE? *Open Court*, 16 Jan. 1890, III, 2040–2043.
Review and criticism of John Venn, *Empirical Logic*. See note to THE LOGIC OF VERIFICATION, below.

REVIEW of Edward Caird, *The Critical Philosophy of Immanuel Kant*. *Andover Review*, Mar. 1890, XIII, 325–327.

REVIEW of John Pentland Mahaffy and John Henry Bernard, *Kant's Critical Philosophy for English Readers*. *Andover Review*, Mar. 1890, XIII, 328.

REVIEW of Johann Eduard Erdmann, *A History of Philosophy* (English translation by Williston Samuel Hough). *Andover Review*, Apr. 1890, XIII, 453–454.

THE LOGIC OF VERIFICATION. *Open Court*, 24 Apr. 1890, IV, 2225–2228.
Reply and criticism of the position stated in IS LOGIC A DUALISTIC SCIENCE? above.

REVIEW of James MacBride Sterrett, *Studies in Hegel's Philosophy of Religion. Andover Review*, June 1890, XIII, 684–685.

PHILOSOPHICAL COURSES AT THE UNIVERSITY OF MICHIGAN. *Monist*, Oct. 1890, I, 150–151.

1891

OUTLINES OF A CRITICAL THEORY OF ETHICS. Ann Arbor: Register Publishing Company, 1891. viii, 253 pp.

Reprinted in facsimile, New York: Hillary House, 1957.

Contents. Introduction. Part I, Fundamental Ethical Notions: The Good—The Idea of Obligation—The Idea of Freedom. Part II, The Ethical World. Part III, The Moral Life of the Individual: The Formation and Growth of Ideals—The Moral Struggle, or the Realization of Ideals—Realized Morality, or the Virtues. Conclusion.

Reviewed in *Andover Review*, July 1891, XVI, 95–98 (James Hervey Hyslop); *Educational Review*, Oct. 1891, II, 297–298 (James Hervey Hyslop); *International Journal of Ethics*, July 1891, I, 503–505 (Josiah Royce); *Mind*, July 1891, XVI, 424; *Monist*, July 1891, I, 600–601; *New Englander and Yale Review*, Sept. 1891, LV, 275; *Philosophical Review*, Jan. 1892, I, 95–99 (Thomas Davidson); *Revue philosophique*, Jan. 1892, XXXIII, 97 (Georges Rodier).

See note under *The Study of Ethics* (1894).

PSYCHOLOGY. Third revised edition. New York: Harper & Brothers, 1891. xii, 427 pp.

For Contents, see edition of 1887.

Another issue of the third revised edition has the imprint: New York, American Book Company [1891].

Reviewed in *Revue de metaphysique et de morale*, II (Sup. to July 1894, p. 3).

LECTURES VS. RECITATIONS: A SYMPOSIUM. *The Castalian*, Published by the Independents of the Senior Class, University of Michigan, 1891, VI, 65.

MORAL THEORY AND PRACTICE. *International Journal of Ethics*, Jan. 1891, I, 186–203.

REVIEW of James Hutchins Baker, *Elementary Psychology, with Practical Applications to Education and the Conduct of Life. Educational Review*, May 1891, I, 495–496.

POETRY AND PHILOSOPHY. *Andover Review*, Aug. 1891, XVI, 105–116.

Commencement address at Smith College, 18 June 1890. Reports in *Northampton Herald*, 18 June 1890; *Springfield Republican*, 19 June 1890; and *Hampshire Gazette*, 24 June 1890. Also delivered as the Alumni Oration at the University of Vermont in the College Street Church (Congregational), Burlington, 24 June 1890. Reported in *University [of Vermont] Cynic*, 26 June 1890, VIII, iv, 57–59.

Reprinted in *Characters and Events* (1929), I, 3–17, with the title MATTHEW ARNOLD AND ROBERT BROWNING.

THE PRESENT POSITION OF LOGICAL THEORY. *Monist*, Oct. 1891, II, 1–17.

Summarized in *Philosophical Review*, Jan. 1892, I, 112–113.

HOW DO CONCEPTS ARISE FROM PERCEPTS? *Public School Journal*, Nov. 1891, XI, 128–130.

Comment by William Torrey Harris, *ib.*, Dec. 1891, XI, 179.

THE SCHOLASTIC AND THE SPECULATOR. *The Inlander* (University of Michigan), Dec. 1891, Jan. 1892, II, 145–148, 186–188.

1892

INTRODUCTION TO PHILOSOPHY. SYLLABUS OF COURSE 5. February, 1892. [Ann Arbor, 1892.] 24 pp. cover-title.

INTRODUCTION TO PHILOSOPHY. October, 1892. [Ann Arbor, 1892.] 14 pp. cover-title.

Copies of these syllabi may be found in the Michigan Historical Collections, University of Michigan; binder's title: PAMPHLETS, VOL. I, THE PHILOSOPHICAL DEPARTMENT, UNIVERSITY OF MICHIGAN.

REVIEW of Francis Howe Johnson, *What Is Reality? An Inquiry as to the Reasonableness of Natural Religion and the Naturalness of Revealed Religion*. The Inlander (University of Michigan), Mar. 1892, II, 282–283.

REVIEW of Alfred John Church, *The Story of the Odyssey*. The Inlander (University of Michigan), Mar. 1892, II, 286–287.

[THOMAS HILL] GREEN'S THEORY OF THE MORAL MOTIVE. *Philosophical Review*, Nov. 1892, I, 593–612.

TWO PHASES OF RENAN'S LIFE: THE FAITH OF 1850 AND THE
DOUBT OF 1890. *Open Court*, 29 Dec. 1892, VI, 3505–3506.

Reprinted in *Characters and Events* (1929), I, 18–23, with the title
ERNEST RENAN.

1893

CHRISTIANITY AND DEMOCRACY. In *Religious Thought at the University of Michigan* (Ann Arbor: The Inland Press, 1893),
62–69.

Address delivered before the Students' Christian Association, New-
berry Hall, University of Michigan, Sunday morning, 27 Mar. 1892.

THE RELATION OF PHILOSOPHY TO THEOLOGY. *The Monthly Bulletin*, Students' Christian Association, University of Michigan, Jan. 1893, XVI, 66–68.

REVIEW of Bernard Bosanquet, *A History of Aesthetic*. *Philosophical Review*, Jan. 1893, II, 63–69.

RENAN'S LOSS OF FAITH IN SCIENCE. *Open Court*, 5 Jan. 1893,
VII, 3512–3515.

Reprinted in *Characters and Events* (1929), I, 23–30, with the title
ERNEST RENAN.

THE SUPERSTITION OF NECESSITY. *Monist*, Apr. 1893, III, 362–
379.

Suggested by Charles Santiago Sanders Peirce, THE DOCTRINE OF
NECESSITY EXAMINED, *ib.*, Apr. 1892, II, 321–337.

Summarized in *Philosophical Review*, July 1893, II, 488 (Albert Ross
Hill).

ANTHROPOLOGY AND LAW. *The Inlander* (University of Michigan), Apr. 1893, III, 305–308.

TEACHING ETHICS IN THE HIGH SCHOOL. *Educational Review*,
Nov. 1893, VI, 313–321.

Summarized in *Sunday News Tribune* (Detroit), 5 Nov. 1893.

SELF-REALIZATION AS THE MORAL IDEAL. *Philosophical Review*,
Nov. 1893, II, 652–664.

WHY STUDY PHILOSOPHY? *The Inlander* (University of Michigan), Dec. 1893, IV, 106–109.

1894

THE STUDY OF ETHICS: A SYLLABUS. Ann Arbor: Register Publishing Company, 1894. iv, 151 pp.

Reprinted in 1897 with the imprint: Ann Arbor, George Wahr.

Contents. The Nature of Ethical Theory—The Factors of Moral Conduct—General Analysis of Conduct—The Moral Consciousness—Moral Approbation—Reflective Approbation, Conscience—Nature of Obligation—Freedom and Responsibility—Virtue and the Virtues.

From Prefatory Note: "The edition of my *Outlines of [a Critical Theory of] Ethics* having been exhausted, I have prepared the following pages, primarily for the use and guidance of my own students. . . . These present pages . . . are in no sense a second edition of the previous book."

Reviewed in *International Journal of Ethics*, Oct. 1895, VI, 110–113 (Josiah Royce); *Psychological Review*, July 1895, II, 430–431 (Roger Bruce Johnson); *Revue de métaphysique et de morale*, III (Sup. to Mar. 1895, p. 5); *Revue philosophique*, Mar. 1897, XLIII, 328–332 (François Pillon).

INTUITIONALISM. In *Johnson's Universal Cyclopædia* (New York: D. Appleton and Company [°1894, 1896, 1897]), IV, 657–659.

MORAL PHILOSOPHY. *Ib.*, V, 880–885.

Reprinted in 1900, *q.v.*

FRED NEWTON SCOTT. *The Oracle* [University of Michigan student publication], 1894.

THE PSYCHOLOGY OF INFANT LANGUAGE. *Psychological Review* Jan. 1894, I, 63–66.

ETHICAL. *Psychological Review*, Jan. 1894, I, 109–111.

Review of Josiah Royce, ON CERTAIN PSYCHOLOGICAL ASPECTS OF MORAL TRAINING (*International Journal of Ethics*, July 1893, III, 413–436); Georg Simmel, MORAL DEFICIENCIES AS DETERMINING INTELLECTUAL FUNCTIONS (*ib.*, 490–507); and Josiah Royce, THE KNOWLEDGE OF GOOD AND EVIL (*ib.*, Oct. 1893, IV, 48–80).

[JOHN] AUSTIN'S THEORY OF SOVEREIGNTY. *Political Science Quarterly*, Mar. 1894, IX, 31–52.

THE EGO AS CAUSE. *Philosophical Review*, May 1894, III, 337–341.

Reply by James Hervey Hyslop, THE EGO, CAUSALITY, AND FREEDOM, *ib.*, Nov. 1894, III, 717–722.

RECONSTRUCTION. *The Monthly Bulletin.* Students' Christian Association, University of Michigan, June 1894, XV, 149-156.

SOCIAL PSYCHOLOGY. *Psychological Review*, July 1894, I, 400-411.

Review of Lester Frank Ward, *The Psychic Factors of Civilization;* Benjamin Kidd, *Social Evolution;* George Burton Adams, *Civilization during the Middle Ages;* and Robert Flint, *History of the Philosophy of History.*

THE CHAOS IN MORAL TRAINING. *Popular Science Monthly*, Aug. 1894, XLV, 433-443.

THE THEORY OF EMOTION. I. Emotional Attitudes (*Psychological Review*, Nov. 1894, I, 553-569); II. The Significance of Emotions (*ib.*, Jan. 1895, II, 13-32).

Summarized in *Philosophical Review*, Mar. 1895, IV, 207-208 (David Irons); *Revue philosophique*, Mar. 1895, XXXIX, 344.

REVIEW of James Bonar, *Philosophy and Political Economy in Some of Their Historical Relations. Political Science Quarterly*, Dec. 1894, IX, 741-744.

1895

THE PSYCHOLOGY OF NUMBER AND ITS APPLICATIONS TO METHODS OF TEACHING ARITHMETIC. By James A[lexander] McLellan and John Dewey. (International Education Series, edited by William Torrey Harris, Vol. XXXIII.) New York: D. Appleton and Company, 1895. xv, 309 pp.

Published in London by Edwin Arnold, 1895.

Contents. What Psychology Can Do for the Teacher—The Psychical Nature of Number—The Origin of Number: Dependence of Number on Measurement, and of Measurement on Adjustment of Activity—The Origin of Number: Summary and Applications—The Definition, Aspects, and Factors of Numerical Ideas—The Development of Number; or, the Arithmetical Operations—Numerical Operations as External and as Intrinsic to Number—On Primary Number Teaching—Notation, Addition, Subtraction—Multiplication and Division—Measures and Multiples—Fractions—Decimals—Percentage and Its Applications—Evolution.

Reviewed in *American Journal of Psychology*, Jan. 1896, VII, 300-

301 (Granville Stanley Hall); *Mind*, Apr. 1896, N.s. V, 275; *Nation*, 28 Nov. 1895, LXI, 395; *Psychological Review*, July 1896, III, 434–437 (Alexander Ziwet); *Science*, 24 Jan. 1896, N.s. III, 134–136 (Henry Burchard Fine).

See Dewey's reply to Fine, PSYCHOLOGY OF NUMBER (*Science*, 21 Feb. 1896), below.

See also J. A. McLellan and A. F. Ames, *The Public School Arithmetic for Grammar Grades, based on McLellan and Dewey's "Psychology of Number"* (New York: The Macmillan Company, 1902). xii, 369 pp.; and letter of William Davis Mackintosh in *Nation*, 9 Jan. 1896, LXII, 32–33.

PLAN OF ORGANIZATION OF THE UNIVERSITY PRIMARY SCHOOL. [caption-title; n.p., n.d., Chicago? 1895]. 25 pp.

NOTE, p. [1]: "This is privately printed, not published, and is to be so treated. It will be understood to define the general spirit in which the work is undertaken, not to give a rigid scheme." (*See* Katherine Camp Mayhew and Anna Camp Edwards, *The Dewey School . . .* New York, 1936, p. 465.) Copy in the Library of the University of Chicago.

THE RESULTS OF CHILD-STUDY APPLIED TO EDUCATION. *Transactions of the Illinois Society for Child-Study*, Jan. 1895, Vol. I, No. 4, 18–19.

Answer to a questionnaire.

THE PHILOSOPHIC RENASCENCE IN AMERICA. *Dial*, 1 Feb. 1895, XVIII, 80–82.

Review of Paul Deussen, *The Elements of Metaphysics;* Friedrich Max Müller, *Three Lectures on the Vedanta Philosophy;* David Jayne Hill, *Genetic Philosophy;* Georg Wilhelm Friedrich Hegel, *Philosophy of Mind* (Translated by William Wallace); Herbert Nichols and William E. Parsons, *Our Notions of Number and Space;* Théodule Ribot, *Diseases of the Will;* Charles Van Norden, *An Outline of Psychology;* Alexander Thomas Ormond, *Basal Concepts in Philosophy;* and Paul Carus, *A Primer of Philosophy.*

REVIEW of *Johnson's Universal Cyclopædia*, Vols. I–V. *Psychological Review*, Mar. 1895, II, 186–188.

Review of the psychological articles in these volumes.

LETTER TO THE EDITOR. *Chicago Evening Post*, 19 Dec. 1895.

Argues that the Chicago Board of Education should accept the gift of the Cook County Normal School.

1896

INTEREST AS RELATED TO [THE TRAINING OF THE] WILL. *In* National Herbart Society, *Second Supplement to the Herbart Year Book for 1895* (Bloomington, Ill., 1896), 209–255.

Contents. The Original Paper on Interest by Dewey—The Discussion of the Paper at Jacksonville—A List of References to Articles and Books Treating the Subject of Interest.

Revised and republished in 1899, see below.

Reprinted in *Educational Essays* (1910), 73–132.

Reply by William Torrey Harris, *Educational Review*, May 1896, XI, 486–493.

INTERPRETATION OF THE CULTURE-EPOCH THEORY. *In* National Herbart Society, *Second Yearbook* (Bloomington, Ill., 1896), 89–95.

First published in the *Public School Journal*, Jan. 1896, XV, 233–236.

Discussion by Charles Alexander McMurry, *Public School Journal*, Feb. 1896, XV, 297–299; N. F. Daum, *ib.*, May 1896, XV, 509–510; Charles Cecil Van Liew, *ib.*, June 1896, XV, 546.

THE REFLEX ARC CONCEPT IN PSYCHOLOGY. *University of Chicago Contributions to Philosophy* (1896), [Vol. I], No. 1, 39–52.

Reprinted from *Psychological Review*, July 1896, III, 357–370.

Reprinted in *Philosophy and Civilization* (1931), 233–248, with the title THE UNIT OF BEHAVIOR.

Summarized in *Philosophical Review*, Nov. 1896, V, 649–650 (James Edwin Creighton); *Revue de métaphysique et de morale*, V (Sup. to July 1897, p. 14); *Revue philosophique*, June 1897, XLIII, 668 (Jean Philippe).

Reply by George Herbert Mead, SUGGESTIONS TOWARD A THEORY OF THE PHILOSOPHICAL DISCIPLINES, *Philosophical Review*, Jan. 1900, IX, 1–17.

INFLUENCE OF THE HIGH SCHOOL UPON EDUCATIONAL METHODS. *School Review*, Jan. 1896, IV, 1–12.

Paper read at the School and College Conference at the University of Chicago, 15 Nov. 1895.

PSYCHOLOGY OF NUMBER. Letter in *Science*, 21 Feb. 1896, N.S. III, 286–289.

Reply to Henry Burchard Fine's review of McLellan and Dewey's *Psychology of Number* (1895), above.

WRITINGS OF DEWEY, 1896

The Metaphysical Method in Ethics. *Psychological Review*, Mar. 1896, III, 181–188.

Discussion of Archbishop Charles Frederick D'Arcy, *A Short Study of Ethics*.

Review of Sophie Willock Bryant, *Studies in Character*, and John Watson, *Hedonistic Theories from Aristippus to Spencer*. *Psychological Review*, Mar. 1896, III, 218–222.

Review of Hiram Miner Stanley, *Studies in the Evolutionary Psychology of Feeling*. *Philosophical Review*, May 1896, V, 292–299.

Review of Levi Leonard Conant, *The Number Concept: Its Origin and Development*. *Psychological Review*, May 1896, III, 326–329.

[Remarks on the Study of History in Schools.] *School Review*, May 1896, IV, 272.

At the Meeting of the North Central Association of Colleges and Secondary Schools at the University of Chicago, 3 Apr. 1896.

A Pedagogical Experiment. *Kindergarten Magazine*, June 1896, VIII, 739–741.

The beginnings of the University of Chicago Elementary School.

Imagination and Expression. *Kindergarten Magazine*, Sept. 1896, IX, 61–69.

Address delivered at the Annual Meeting of the Western Drawing Teachers' Association in May, 1896.

Reprinted in *Teachers College Bulletin*, 1 Mar. 1919, Ser. 10, No. 10, 6–9; and in part in *Third Report of the Western Drawing Teachers' Association* (Chicago, 1896), 136–138.

Pedagogy as a University Discipline. *University [of Chicago] Record*, 18 and 25 Sept. 1896, I, 353–355, 361–363.

Review of James Sully, *Studies of Childhood*. *Science*, 2 Oct. 1896, n.s. IV, 500–502.

The University School. *University [of Chicago] Record*, 6 Nov. 1896, I, 417–419.

Report of an address before the Pedagogical Club, 31 Oct. 1896.

1897

ETHICAL PRINCIPLES UNDERLYING EDUCATION. *In* National
Herbart Society, *Third Yearbook* (Chicago, 1897), 7–34.

Reprinted by the University of Chicago Press, 1908, 34 pp., and in
Educational Essays (1910), 19–72.

See *Moral Principles in Education* (1909).

Spanish translation in *Obras de Dewey*, II (Madrid, 1926).

THE SIGNIFICANCE OF THE PROBLEM OF KNOWLEDGE. (University of Chicago Contributions to Philosophy, [Vol. I], No.
III.) Chicago: The University of Chicago Press, 1897. 20 pp.

Address of the honorary president before the Philosophical Club of
the University of Michigan in the winter of 1897.

"Reprinted with slight change" in *The Influence of Darwin on Philosophy* (1910), 271–304.

MY PEDAGOGIC CREED. New York: E. L. Kellogg & Co. [ᶜ1897].
36 pp.

Published with Albion Woodbury Small, *The Demands of Sociology
upon Pedagogy.*

Reprinted from *School Journal*, 16 Jan. 1897, LIV, 77–80; also published in Ossian Herbert Lang, *Educational Creeds of the Nineteenth
Century* (New York: E. L. Kellogg & Co., 1898), 5–20.

Republished at Chicago [1910?] by A. Flanagan Company with an
Introduction by Samuel Train Dutton. Reprinted in *Journal of the
National Education Association*, Dec. 1929, XVIII, 291–295, Jan.
1935, XXIV, 13–16; in Dewey's *Education Today* (1940), 3–17; in
Future Teachers of America, *Fourth Yearbook* (1944), 8–23; in Robert Ulich, ed., *Three Thousand Years of Educational Wisdom* (Cambridge: Harvard University Press, 1954); in *Dewey on Education*
(1959), 19–32; and separately by the Progressive Education Association (Washington [1929]), 17 pp.

Translations. French by Ou Tsuin Chen (Paris, 1931); German by
Rudolf Prantl, *Zeitschrift für christliche Erziehungswissenschaft*, XV
(1925), 465–476; Italian by Luigi Oliva (Rome, 1913); Polish by
Josef Pieter (Warsaw, 1933); Spanish in *Quaderns d'estudi* (Barcelona), in *Revista de pedagogía*, 1931, X, 1–5, 74–80, and in *El niño y el
programa escolar*, tr. Lorenzo Luzuriaga (Buenos Aires, 1954). See
Dewey's *Il mio credo pedagogico* (1954).

THE AESTHETIC ELEMENT IN EDUCATION. *In* National Education Association, *Addresses and Proceedings*, 1897, 329-330, and discussion, 346.

Delivered before the Association at Milwaukee in July 1897.

THE KINDERGARTEN AND CHILD-STUDY. *In* National Education Association, *Addresses and Proceedings*, 1897, 585-586.

Delivered before the Department of Kindergarten Education of the Association at Milwaukee in July 1897.

Extracts in *School Journal*, 14 Aug. 1897, LV, 112.

CRITICISMS, WISE AND OTHERWISE, ON MODERN CHILD-STUDY. *In* National Education Association, *Addresses and Proceedings*, 1897, 867-868.

Delivered before the Department of Child-Study of the Association at Milwaukee in July 1897.

THE PSYCHOLOGY OF EFFORT. *Philosophical Review*, Jan. 1897, VI, 43-56.

Summarized in *Psychological Review*, July 1897, 437-438 (Harry Norman Gardiner); *Revue de métaphysique et de morale*, V (Sup. to Mar. 1897, 10-11); *Revue philosophique*, Feb. 1898, XLV, 220.

THE PSYCHOLOGICAL ASPECT OF THE SCHOOL CURRICULUM. *Educational Review*, Apr. 1897, XIII, 356-369.

THE INTERPRETATION SIDE OF CHILD-STUDY. *Transactions of the Illinois Society for Child-Study*, July 1897, II, ii, 17-27.

1898

[SYLLABUS.] The University of Chicago. Pedagogy I B 19. Philosophy of Education. 1898-1899 Winter Quarter. [Chicago, 1898.] 11 pp.

REPORT OF THE COMMITTEE ON A DETAILED PLAN FOR A REPORT ON ELEMENTARY EDUCATION. *In* National Education Association, *Addresses and Proceedings*, 1898, 335-343.

Submitted at Washington in July 1898.

SOME REMARKS ON THE PSYCHOLOGY OF NUMBER. *Pedagogical Seminary*, Jan. 1898, V, 426-434.

Reply to Daniel Edward Phillips, NUMBER AND ITS APPLICATION PSYCHOLOGICALLY CONSIDERED, *ib.*, Oct. 1897, V, 221-281.

Rejoinder by Phillips, SOME REMARKS ON NUMBER AND ITS APPLICATION, *ib.*, Apr. 1898, V, 590-598.

EVOLUTION AND ETHICS. *Monist*, Apr. 1898, VIII, 321–341.

Summarized in *Philosophical Review*, July 1898, VII, 423–424.

Reprinted in *Scientific Monthly*, Feb. 1954, LXXVIII, 57–66.

THE PRIMARY-EDUCATION FETICH. *Forum*, May 1898, XXV, 315–328.

Reprinted in *Education Today* (1940), 18–35.

Editorial reply in *School Journal*, 28 May 1898, LVI, 629–630.

REVIEW of William Torrey Harris, *Psychologic Foundations of Education*. *Educational Review*, June 1898, XVI, 1–14.

REVIEW of James Mark Baldwin, *Social and Ethical Interpretations in Mental Development*. *Philosophical Review*, July 1898, VII, 398–409.

Discussion of this review by Baldwin, *ib.*, Nov. 1898, VII, 621–628, and reply by Dewey, *ib.*, 629–630.

REVIEW of James Mark Baldwin, *Social and Ethical Interpretations in Mental Development*. *New World*, Sept. 1898, VII, 504–522.

Another review.

THE SENSE OF SOLIDITY. Letter in *Science*, 11 Nov. 1898, N.S. VIII, 675.

1899

INTEREST AS RELATED TO [THE TRAINING OF THE] WILL. (Chicago: The Society, reprinted, 1899.) 40 pp.

Second supplement to the *Herbart Yearbook for 1895*; see 1896.

PSYCHOLOGY AND PHILOSOPHIC METHOD. Berkeley: The University Press. 1899. 23 pp.

The annual public address before the Philosophical Union of the University of California, 15 May 1899.

Reprinted from the *University [of California] Chronicle*, Aug. 1899, II, 159–179; reprinted "with slight verbal changes" in *The Influence of Darwin on Philosophy* (1910), 242–270, with the title "CONSCIOUSNESS" AND EXPERIENCE.

THE METHOD OF THE RECITATION. A Partial Report of a Course of Lectures Given at the University of Chicago. Privately Printed for the Use of Classes in Theory at the Oshkosh [Wisconsin] Normal School, 1899. 62 pp.

THE SCHOOL AND SOCIETY; being Three Lectures by John Dewey, Supplemented by a Statement of the University Elementary School. Chicago: The University of Chicago Press, 1899. 125 pp.

See under 1900.

PLAY AND IMAGINATION IN RELATION TO EARLY EDUCATION. *School Journal*, 27 May 1899, LVIII, 589; *Kindergarten Magazine*, June 1899, XI, 636–640.

Reports of a paper read by Dewey at the School of Psychology, held by the Kindergarten College, Chicago, in April 1899.

PRINCIPLES OF MENTAL DEVELOPMENT AS ILLUSTRATED IN EARLY INFANCY. *Transactions of the Illinois Society for Child-Study*, Oct. 1899, IV, 65–83.

1900

THE ELEMENTARY SCHOOL RECORD. A Series of Nine Monographs. Nos. 1–9, Feb.–Dec. 1900. Chicago: The University of Chicago Press, 1900.

John Dewey, Editor; Laura Louisa Runyon, Managing Editor.

Contents. 1. Art—2. Music—3. Textiles—4. Botany—5. Kindergarten—6. Science—7. Manual Training—8. History—9. Curriculum. *The following articles are by Dewey:* No. 1, Feb. 1900, General Principles of Work, Educationally Considered [Introduction to Group III], 12–15; Historical Development of Inventions and Occupations, General Principles [Introduction to Group IV], 21–23. No. 2, Mar. 1900, General Introduction to Groups V and VI, 49–52. No. 3, Apr. 1900, Psychology of Occupations, 82–85. No. 4, May 1900, Reflective Attention, 111–113. No. 5, June 1900, Froebel's Educational Principles, 143–151. No. 8, Nov. 1900, The Aim of History in Elementary Education, 199–203. No. 9, Dec. 1900, The Psychology of the Elementary Curriculum, 221–232.

Reprinted in part as *The "Dewey" School* (London: The Froebel Society [1913?]), 80 pp.; revised edition, 1929, 119 pp.

Reviewed in *Nation*, 26 July 1900, LXXI, 77–78.

Spanish translation in *Obras de Dewey*, I (Madrid, 1926).

See *The School and the Child* (1907); and *The School and Society* (1915).

THE SCHOOL AND SOCIETY; being Three Lectures by John Dewey, Supplemented by a Statement of the University Elementary School. Chicago: The University of Chicago Press, 1900. 129 pp.

Published also in London by P. S. King & Son, 1900.

Contents. The School and Social Progress—The School and the Life of the Child—Waste in Education—Three Years of the University Elementary School.

Revised edition, 1915, *q.v.*

Translations. Arabic by Dimitri Kandalaft [Cairo, 193–?]; Bengali by F. Rahman; Bohemian by Ján Mrazík (Praha, 1904); Bulgarian by Dobroslav Miletic (1935); Dutch by Tj. de Boer (Groningen, 1929); Finnish (Helsinki, 1957); French (in part, in *L'Éducation,* June 1909 and Dec. 1912); German by Elsie Gurlitt (1905); Italian by Giuseppina Di Laghi (Catania, 1915); Italian translation of Dewey's revised edition of 1915 by Ernesto Codignola and Lamberto Borghi (Firenze, 1947, 1949, 1954); Japanese by Seiichi Miyahara (Tokyo, 1954, 1959); Persian (Tehran, 1948); Polish by Marja Lisowska (Lemberg, 1924) and by Roza Czaplinska-Mutermilchowa (Warsaw, 1933); Russian by G. A. Luchinskii (Moscow [1924]); Serbo-Croatian by M. Vanlic (1935); Spanish by Domingo Barnés (Madrid, 1915, 1929); Turkish by B. Avni (Constantinople, 1924).

Reviewed in *Chautauquan,* Mar., 1900, XXX, 589–592 (Laura Louisa Runyon); *Dial,* 16 Aug. 1900, XXIX, 98; *Educational Review,* Oct. 1900, XX, 303–306 (William Seneca Sutton); *Review of Education,* June 1901, VI, 31 (Addison Webster Moore); *Transactions of the Illinois Society for Child-Study,* Oct. 1899, IV, 100–101; *University [of Chicago] Record,* 6 July 1900, V, 159–160.

INTUITIONALISM. In *The Universal Cyclopædia* edited by Charles Kendall Adams (New York: D. Appleton and Company, 1900), VI, 321–323.

MORAL PHILOSOPHY. *Ib.,* VIII, 240–245.

MENTAL DEVELOPMENT. [Chicago] ᶜ1900. 12 leaves.

At head of title: University of Chicago, Department of Philosophy and Pedagogy.

Mimeographed; copy in University of Chicago Library.

PSYCHOLOGY AND SOCIAL PRACTICE. *Psychological Review,* Mar. 1900, VII, 105–124 (abstract, 127–128); *Science,* 2 Mar. 1900, N.S. XI, 321–333.

Presidential address before the American Psychological Association, New Haven, Dec. 1899.

Summarized in *Philosophical Review,* May 1900, IX, 340–341; *Revue philosophique,* Sept. 1901, LII, 337.

Reprinted as University of Chicago Contributions to Education, No. II (Chicago: The University of Chicago Press, 1901), 42 pp.; also in *Educational Essays* (1910), 133–167.

Spanish translation in *Obras de Dewey*, II (Madrid, 1926).

REVIEW of Josiah Royce, *The World and the Individual* (Gifford Lectures), First Series: The Four Historical Conceptions of Being (*Philosophical Review*, May 1900, IX, 311–324); Second Series: Nature, Man, and the Moral Order (*ib.*, July 1902, XI, 392–407).

SOME STAGES OF LOGICAL THOUGHT. *Philosophical Review*, Sept. 1900, IX, 465–489.

Summarized in *Revue de métaphysique et de morale*, VIII (Sup. to Nov. 1900, 11); *Revue philosophique*, June 1901, LI, 674 (J. Segond).

Reprinted in *Essays in Experimental Logic* (1916), 183–219.

1901

DICTIONARY OF PHILOSOPHY AND PSYCHOLOGY, Edited by James Mark Baldwin. Vol. I. New York: The Macmillan Company, 1901.

John Dewey, Consulting Editor.

The following article is by Dewey: History of Philosophy (with Josiah Royce), 480–482.

THE SITUATION AS REGARDS THE COURSE OF STUDY. *In* National Education Association, *Addresses and Proceedings*, 1901, 332–348.

An address delivered before the Department of Superintendence of the Association at Chicago, 28 Feb. 1901.

Published also in *Educational Review*, June 1901, XXII, 26–49, and in *School Journal*, 20 and 27 Apr., and 4 May 1901, LXII, 421–423, 445–446, 454, 469–471. Quotations and comments in *Kindergarten Magazine*, June 1901, XIII, 574–577.

ARE THE SCHOOLS DOING WHAT THE PEOPLE WANT THEM TO DO? *Educational Review*, May 1901, XXI, 459–474; *Review of Education*, June 1901, VII, 10–11.

Reprinted in *Education Today* (1940), 36–52, with the title THE PEOPLE AND THE SCHOOLS.

THE PLACE OF MANUAL TRAINING IN THE ELEMENTARY COURSE OF STUDY. *Manual Training Magazine*, July 1901, II, 193–199. Reprinted in *Education Today* (1940), 53–61. Summarized in *School Journal*, 31 Aug. 1901, LXIII, 182–183.

1902

DICTIONARY OF PHILOSOPHY AND PSYCHOLOGY. Vol. II. New York: The Macmillan Company, 1902.

The following articles are by Dewey: Mind, in Philosophy (with James Mark Baldwin), 81–82—Natural Realism, 134—Naturalism, in Art (with James Hayden Tufts), 138—Nature, 138–141—Nature, Philosophy of, 142—Necessity, 143–145—Neo-Criticism, 149—Neo-Platonism, 150—Nescience, 167—Nexus, 176—Nisus, 178—Noetic, 178–179—Nominalism, 180—Non-Being, 180–181—Noölogy, 181–182—Norm and Normative, in the Moral Sciences, 182—Noumenon and Noumenal, 184–185—Nous, 185–186—Nullibrists, 186—Number, in Metaphysics, 189—Object and Objective, General and Philosophical, 191–192—Objectivism, 194—One, The, 201—Ontological Argument, 202–203—Ontologism (2.), 203—Ontology, 203–204—Opinion, 205—Optimism and Pessimism, 210–212—Organic, 213—Organism, 218–219—Outness, 251—Oversoul, 252—Palingenesis, 254—Panentheism, 255—Panlogism, 255—Panpneumatism, 256—Panpsychism, 256—Pantheism, 256–257—Panthelism, 257–258—Parousia, 263—Passion and Passive, 266–267—Peripatetics, 280—Permanence, 280—Phase, 288—Phenomenalism, 288—Phenomenology, 288–289—Phenomenon, 289—Philosophy, 290–296—Phoronomy, 297—Pleroma, 305—Pluralism, 306—Plurality, 306—Pneuma, 307–308—Pneumatology, 308—Posit, 310–311—Positive (3. Philosophical), 311—Pre-established Harmony, 329–330—Presentationism (2.), 333—Primary, Primitive, Primordial, 340—Primum Mobile, 341—Principle, 341–342—Quietism, 412—Rationalism, 415–416—Reals, 424—Relation, 439–443—Same, The; and The Other, 484–485—Scepticism, 489–490—Schema, 490—Schematism, 490–491—Scholasticism (The Schoolmen), 491–495—Schopenhauerism (or Schopenhauereanism), 499—Scotism, 503—Sensationalism, 515–517—Singularism, 533—Speculation, 568—Statue of Condillac, 601—Subject, Subjective, 607–608—Subjectivism, 611—Substantiality Theory, or Substantialism, 614—Sui Generis, 620—Summists, 620–621—Syncretism (1.), 655—System, 659—Tabula Rasa, 661—Transcendentalism, 711—Transient, 712—Ubication, 723—Understanding and Reason, 725–726—Unity and Plurality, 734–736—Universal and Universality (4. and 5.), 737–739—Universal Postulate 741—Universe, 742—Unthinkable, 743—Vacuum, 747–748—World, 821.

THE CHILD AND THE CURRICULUM. (University of Chicago Contributions to Education, No. V.) Chicago: The University of Chicago Press, 1902. 40 pp.

Translations. German in Dewey and Kilpatrick, *Der Projekt-Plan* (Weimar, 1935) 142–160; Portuguese by Anísio S. Teixeira (São Paulo, 1930, 1952); Russian; Spanish, with an introduction by Lorenzo Luzuriaga (Madrid, 1925; Buenos Aires, 1948), review of translation in *Revista de Filosofía*, May 1926, XXIII, 570–571 (Roberto A. Masciotra); Swedish by Agnes Jacobsson-Undén (Lund, 1912).

Reprinted in *The School and the Child* (1907), 17–47.

Reprinted as a paperback, with *The School and Society* and an introduction by Leonard Carmichael, Chicago: University of Chicago Press—Phoenix Books [1956], 31, 159 pp.; and in *Dewey on Education* (1959), 91–111.

THE EDUCATIONAL SITUATION. (University of Chicago Contributions to Education, No. III.) Chicago: The University of Chicago Press, 1902. 104 pp.

Contents. The Educational Situation: I. As Concerns the Elementary School; II. As Concerns Secondary Education; III. As Concerns the College.

Revision of three papers originally prepared as follows: I. For the Superintendents' Section of the National Education Association; II. For the Conference of Secondary Schools affiliated with the University of Chicago; III. For the Harvard Teachers' Association.

DISCUSSION. *In* National Education Association, *Addresses and Proceedings*, 1902, 719–720.

Discussion of Theodore B. Noss, WHAT OUR SCHOOLS OWE TO CHILD-STUDY, *ib.*, 716–719.

THE SCHOOL AS SOCIAL CENTER. *In* National Education Association, *Addresses and Proceedings*, 1902, 373–383.

Address delivered before the Association at Minneapolis in July 1902. Published also in *Elementary School Teacher*, Oct. 1902, III, 73–86.

ACADEMIC FREEDOM. *Educational Review*, Jan. 1902, XXIII, 1–14.

CURRENT PROBLEMS IN SECONDARY EDUCATION. *School Review*, Jan. 1902, X, 13–28.

Read at the Fifteenth Educational Conference of the Academies and High Schools affiliated with the University of Chicago, in Nov. 1901.

THE EVOLUTIONARY METHOD AS APPLIED TO MORALITY. I. Its Scientific Necessity (*Philosophical Review*, Mar. 1902, XI,

107-124); II. Its Significance for Conduct (*ib.*, July 1902, XI, 353-371).

Reply by Theodore de Leo de Laguna, EVOLUTIONARY METHOD IN ETHICAL RESEARCH, *Philosophical Review*, May 1904, XIII, 328-337.

Abstract in *Revue philosophique*, Nov. 1903, LVI, 553-554.

See Morton Gabriel White, DEWEY ON THE GENETIC METHOD, *Journal of Philosophy*, 7 June 1945, XLII, 328-331.

IN REMEMBRANCE: FRANCIS W. PARKER. *Journal of Education*, 27 Mar. 1902, LV, 199.

INTERPRETATION OF SAVAGE MIND. *Psychological Review*, May 1902, IX, 217-230.

Summarized by M. S. Macdonald, *Philosophical Review*, Sept. 1902, XI, 529-530; abstract in *Revue philosophique*, Mar. 1903, LV, 348.

Reprinted in William Isaac Thomas, *Sourcebook for Social Origins* (Chicago, 1909), 173-186, and in Dewey's *Philosophy and Civilization* (1931), 173-187.

REVIEW of Lightner Witmer, *Analytical Psychology*. *School Review*, May 1902, X, 412.

[IN MEMORIAM: COLONEL FRANCIS WAYLAND PARKER.] *Elementary School Teacher*, June 1902, II, 704-708.

Address delivered at the services held at the University of Chicago, 6 Mar. 1902. Printed from stenographic report.

Reprinted in *Characters and Events* (1929), I, 95-99.

THE BATTLE FOR PROGRESS. *Journal of Education*, 16 Oct. 1902, LVI, 249.

Abstract of an address.

THE UNIVERSITY OF CHICAGO SCHOOL OF EDUCATION. Editorial in *Elementary School Teacher*, Nov. 1902, III, 200-203.

1903

STUDIES IN LOGICAL THEORY, by John Dewey, with the Co-operation of Members and Fellows of the Department of Philosophy. (University of Chicago. The Decennial Publications, Second Series, Vol. XI.) Chicago: The University of Chicago Press, 1903. xiii, 388 pp.

Published also in London by T. Fisher Unwin, 1909.

Contents. Thought and Its Subject-Matter, by John Dewey—

Thought and Its Subject-Matter: The Antecedents of Thought, by John Dewey—Thought and Its Subject-Matter: The Datum of Thinking, by John Dewey—Thought and Its Subject-Matter: The Content and Object of Thought, by John Dewey—Bosanquet's Theory of Judgment, by Helen Bradford Thompson—Typical Stages in the Development of Judgment, by Simon Fraser MacLennan—The Nature of Hypothesis, by Myron Louis Ashley—Image and Idea in Logic, by Willard Clark Gore—The Logic of the Pre-Socratic Philosophy, by William Arthur Heidel—Valuation as a Logical Process, by Henry Waldgrave Stuart—Some Logical Aspects of Purpose, by Addison Webster Moore.

Reviewed in *Dial*, 16 May 1904, XXXVI, 328–329 (Arthur Kenyon Rogers); *Edinburgh Review*, Apr. 1909, CCIX, 363–388 [Bertrand Russell]; *Educational Review*, Oct. 1904, XXVIII, 310–313 (Edwin Lee Norton); *Journal of Philosophy*, 18 Feb. 1904, I, 100–105 (Wilmon Henry Sheldon); *Mind*, Jan. 1904, N.S. XIII, 100–106 (Ferdinand Canning Scott Schiller), July 1911, N.S. XX, 435 (Bernard Bosanquet); *Monist*, Jan. 1904, XVI, 312; *Nation*, 15 Sept. 1904, LXXIX, 219–220 [Charles Santiago Sanders Peirce]; *Philosophical Review*, Nov. 1904, XIII, 666–667 (Andrew Seth Pringle-Pattison); *Psychological Bulletin*, 15 Jan. 1904, I, 1–5 (William James); *Revue philosophique*, Dec. 1904, LVIII, 655–656 (Théodule Ribot).

Professor Seth Pringle-Pattison's review was reprinted in his book, *The Philosophical Radicals* (Edinburgh, 1907), 178–194; that of Professor James, THE CHICAGO SCHOOL, in his *Collected Essays and Reviews* (New York, 1920), 445–447; that of C. S. S. Peirce in his *Collected Papers* (Cambridge, 1958), VIII, 145–147; and that of Bertrand Russell in his *Philosophical Essays* (London, 1910), 87–126.

See Arthur Kenyon Rogers, THE STANDPOINT OF INSTRUMENTAL LOGIC, *Journal of Philosophy*, 14 Apr. 1904, I, 207–212; Clarence Edwin Ayres, DEWEY: MASTER OF THE COMMONPLACE, *New Republic*, 18 Jan. 1939, LXXXVII, 313–306; and William James's *Letters*, II, 201–202, for further discussion of this book.

See also *Essays in Experimental Logic* (1916).

LOGICAL CONDITIONS OF A SCIENTIFIC TREATMENT OF MORALITY. Chicago: The University of Chicago Press, 1903. 27 pp.

Reprinted from the Decennial Publications of the University of Chicago, First Series, Vol. III, 113–139.

Reprinted in *Problems of Men* (1946), 211–249.

ETHICS. In *The [Encyclopedia] Americana* (New York: Scientific American [ᶜ1903–1906]), VII [unpaged], *sub voce*.

Reprinted in the *Encyclopedia Americana*, New York [ᶜ1918], X, 540–546.

RELIGIOUS EDUCATION AS CONDITIONED BY MODERN PSYCHOLO-
GY AND PEDAGOGY. *Proceedings of the Religious Education
Association*, 1903, 60–66.

Read at the first annual convention at Chicago in Feb. 1903.

INTRODUCTION. *In* Irving Walter King, *The Psychology of Child
Development* (Chicago: The University of Chicago Press,
1903), xi–xx.

[REMARKS on Frank Louis Soldan, *Shortening the Years of Elementary Schooling, School Review*, Jan. 1903, XI, 4–17.] *Ib.*,
17–20.

Reprinted in *Junior College Journal*, Mar. 1933, VIII, 320.

PSYCHOLOGICAL METHOD IN ETHICS. *Psychological Review*, Mar.
1903, X, 158–160.

Summary of a paper read at the joint meeting of the American Philosophical Association and the American Psychological Association at
Columbian University, Washington, D.C., 31 Dec. 1902.

THE PSYCHOLOGICAL AND THE LOGICAL IN TEACHING GEOME-
TRY. *Educational Review*, Apr. 1903, XXV, 387–399.

THE ORGANIZATION AND CURRICULA OF THE [UNIVERSITY OF
CHICAGO] COLLEGE OF EDUCATION. *Elementary School Teacher*, May 1903, III, 553–562.

METHOD OF THE RECITATION. *Elementary School Teacher*, May
1903, III, 563.

Syllabus of a course to be given by Dewey in the summer quarter,
1903, at the University of Chicago.

REVIEW of Katharine Elizabeth Dopp, *The Place of Industries in
Elementary Education. Elementary School Teacher*, June 1903,
III, 727–728.

EMERSON—THE PHILOSOPHER OF DEMOCRACY. *International
Journal of Ethics*, July 1903, XIII, 405–413.

A paper read at the Emerson Memorial Meeting at the University
of Chicago, 25 May 1903.

Summarized in *Philosophical Review*, Sept. 1903, XII, 574 (George
Holland Sabine).

Reprinted in *Characters and Events* (1929), I, 69–77, with the title
RALPH WALDO EMERSON.

THE ST. LOUIS CONGRESS OF THE ARTS AND SCIENCES. Letter in *Science*, 28 Aug. 1903, N.S. XVIII, 275-278.
Discussion of Hugo Münsterberg, THE ST. LOUIS CONGRESS . . . *Atlantic Monthly*, May 1903, XCI, 671-684. Reply by Münsterberg, *Science*, 30 Oct. 1903, N.S. XVIII, 559-563. Rejoinder by Dewey, *ib.*, 20 Nov. 1903, 665. Reply by Münsterberg, *ib.*, 18 Dec. 1903, 788.

DEMOCRACY IN EDUCATION. *Elementary School Teacher*, Dec. 1903, IV, 193-204.
Report of the same with the title DEMOCRACY AND FREEDOM IN THE SCHOOL, *Kindergarten Magazine*, Dec. 1903, XVI, 212-214.
Reprinted in *Journal of the National Education Association*, Dec. 1929, XVIII, 287-290; in *Progressive Education*, Mar. 1931, VIII, 216-218; and in Dewey's *Education Today* (1940), 62-73.

TOTAL ISOLATION. *Journal of Education*, 24 Dec. 1903, LVIII, 433.
Abstract of an address.

1904

EDUCATION, DIRECT AND INDIRECT. [Chicago] 1904. 10 pp.
Address at the Francis W. Parker School, Chicago, in Jan. 1904.
Reprinted in *Progressive Journal of Education*, 15 Oct. 1909, II, 31-38.

THE RELATION OF THEORY TO PRACTICE IN EDUCATION. *In* National Society for the Scientific Study of Education, *Third Yearbook*, 1904, Part I, 9-30.

NOTES UPON LOGICAL TOPICS. I. A Classification of Contemporary Tendencies (*Journal of Philosophy*, 4 Feb. 1904, I, 57-62); II. The Meanings of the Term "Idea" (*ib.*, 31 Mar. 1904, I, 175-178).

THE PSYCHOLOGY OF JUDGMENT. *Psychological Bulletin*, 10 Feb. 1904, I, 44-45.
Abstract of a paper read at the Twelfth Annual Meeting of the American Psychological Association at St. Louis in Dec. 1903.

SIGNIFICANCE OF THE SCHOOL OF EDUCATION. *Elementary School Teacher*, Mar. 1904, IV, 441-453.
Paper read before the School of Education Parents' Association, Chicago, 28 Jan. 1904.

THE PHILOSOPHICAL WORK OF HERBERT SPENCER. *Philosophical Review*, Mar. 1904, XIII, 159-175.

Abstracts in *Revue de métaphysique et de morale*, XIV (Sup. to May 1906, 13); *Revue philosophique*, Apr. 1905, LIX, 439 (J. Segond).

Reprinted in *Characters and Events* (1929), I, 45-62.

REVIEW of Wayland Richardson Benedict, *World Views and their Ethical Implications*. *International Journal of Ethics*, Apr. 1904, XIV, 389-390.

INTRODUCTION OF THE ORATOR [Nicholas Murray Butler]. *University [of Chicago] Record*, May 1904, IX, 12-13.

At the dedication of Emmons Blaine Hall, the School of Education of the University of Chicago, 14 May 1904.

REVIEW of Ferdinand Canning Scott Schiller, *Humanism. Psychological Bulletin*, 15 Sept. 1904, I, 335-340.

1905

PHILOSOPHY AND AMERICAN NATIONAL LIFE. *In* University of Vermont, *Centennial Anniversary of the Graduation of the First Class, July Third to Seventh 1904* (Burlington, Vermont, 1905), 106-113.

Address delivered at the Alumni Conference on the Influence of the University in the World, 5 July 1904.

THE REALISM OF PRAGMATISM. *Journal of Philosophy*, 8 June 1905, II, 324-327.

Reply to Stephen Sheldon Colvin, IS SUBJECTIVE IDEALISM A NECESSARY POINT OF VIEW FOR PSYCHOLOGY? *ib.*, 27 Apr. 1905, II, 225-231.

THE POSTULATE OF IMMEDIATE EMPIRICISM. *Journal of Philosophy*, 20 July 1905, II, 393-399.

Summarized in *Philosophical Review*, May 1906, XV, 350 (Mattie Alexander Martin).

Reprinted in *The Influence of Darwin on Philosophy* (1910), 226-241.

Reply by Charles Montague Bakewell, AN OPEN LETTER TO PROFESSOR DEWEY CONCERNING IMMEDIATE EMPIRICISM, *Journal of Philosophy*, 14 Sept. 1905, II, 520-522. (See reply by Dewey, IMMEDIATE EMPIRICISM, below.)

Reply by Frederick James Eugene Woodbridge, OF WHAT SORT IS COGNITIVE EXPERIENCE? *Journal of Philosophy*, 12 Oct. 1905, II,

573–576; reprinted in his *Nature and Mind* (1937), 316–320. (See reply by Dewey, THE KNOWLEDGE EXPERIENCE AND ITS RELATIONSHIPS, below.)

Reply by Boyd Henry Bode, COGNITIVE EXPERIENCE AND ITS OBJECT, *Journal of Philosophy*, 23 Nov. 1905, II, 658–663. (See reply by Dewey, THE KNOWLEDGE EXPERIENCE AGAIN, below.)

See also Joseph Alexander Leighton, COGNITIVE THOUGHT AND "IMMEDIATE" EXPERIENCE, *Journal of Philosophy*, 29 Mar. 1906, III, 174–180.

IMMEDIATE EMPIRICISM. *Journal of Philosophy*, 26 Oct. 1905, II, 597–599.

Reply to Charles Montague Bakewell, AN OPEN LETTER TO PROFESSOR DEWEY CONCERNING IMMEDIATE EMPIRICISM, *ib.*, 14 Sept. 1905, II, 520–522. Rejoinder by Bakewell, THE ISSUE BETWEEN IDEALISM AND IMMEDIATE EMPIRICISM, *ib.*, 7 Dec. 1905, II, 687–691.

See Ferdinand Canning Scott Schiller, THOUGHT AND IMMEDIACY, *ib.*, 26 Apr. 1906, III, 234–237.

THE KNOWLEDGE EXPERIENCE AND ITS RELATIONSHIPS. *Journal of Philosophy*, 23 Nov. 1905, II, 652–657.

Reply to Frederick James Eugene Woodbridge, OF WHAT SORT IS COGNITIVE EXPERIENCE? *ib.*, 12 Oct. 1905, II, 573–576.

THE KNOWLEDGE EXPERIENCE AGAIN. *Journal of Philosophy*, 21 Dec. 1905, II, 707–711.

Reply to Boyd Henry Bode, COGNITIVE EXPERIENCE AND ITS OBJECT, *ib.*, 23 Nov. 1905, II, 658–663.

1906

CULTURE AND INDUSTRY IN EDUCATION. *Proceedings of the Joint Convention of the Eastern Art Teachers Association and the Eastern Manual Training Association*, 1906, 21–30.

Read 31 May 1906 before the Convention, at Horace Mann School, Teachers College, Columbia University.

Reprinted in *Educational Bi-Monthly*, 1 Oct. 1908, I, 1–9; and in *Teachers College Bulletin*, Ser. 10, No. 1, 1 Mar. 1919, 10–18.

THE TERMS "CONSCIOUS" AND "CONSCIOUSNESS." *Journal of Philosophy*, 18 Jan. 1906, III, 39–41.

REVIEW of George Santayana, *The Life of Reason* (Vols. I and II). *Science*, 9 Feb. 1906, n.s. XXIII, 223–225.

BELIEFS AND REALITIES. *Philosophical Review*, Mar. 1906, XV, 113-119.

Presidential address at the Fifth Annual Meeting of the American Philosophical Association, Emerson Hall, Harvard University, 28 Dec. 1905.

Abstracts in *Revue de métaphysique et de morale*, XVI (Sup. to Nov. 1908, p. 18); *Revue philosophique*, Apr. 1907, LXIII, 555.

Reprinted "with verbal revisions" in *The Influence of Darwin on Philosophy* (1910), 169-197, under the title BELIEFS AND EXISTENCES.

REALITY AS EXPERIENCE. *Journal of Philosophy*, 10 May 1906, III, 253-257.

THE EXPERIMENTAL THEORY OF KNOWLEDGE. *Mind*, July 1906, N.S. XV, 293-307.

Summarized in *Philosophical Review*, Jan. 1907, XVI, 107-108 (M. W. Sprague); *Revue philosophique*, Dec. 1906, LXII, 666.

Reprinted "with considerable change in the arrangement and in the matter of the latter portion" in *The Influence of Darwin on Philosophy* (1910), 77-111.

EXPERIENCE AND OBJECTIVE IDEALISM. *Philosophical Review*, Sept. 1906, XV, 465-481.

Reply by John Edward Russell, OBJECTIVE IDEALISM AND REVISED EMPIRICISM, *ib.*, Nov. 1906, XV, 627-633.

Summarized in *Psychological Bulletin*, 15 July 1907, IV, 230-232 (Grace Bruce); *Revue philosophique*, Apr. 1907 LXIII, 557-558 (J. Segond).

Reprinted "with slight verbal changes" in *The Influence of Darwin on Philosophy* (1910), 198-225.

1907

THE SCHOOL AND THE CHILD; being Selections from the Educational Essays of John Dewey. Edited by J[oseph] J[ohn] Findlay. London: Blackie & Son, Ltd. [1907? pref. 1906]. 128 pp. (The Little Library of Pedagogics.)

Contents. Introduction—The Child and the Curriculum—Essays from the *Elementary School Record*: No. 1, The Kindergarten. No. 2, General Principles of Work, Educationally Considered. No. 3, Historical Development of Inventions and Occupations. No. 4, Children of Eight Years of Age. No. 5, Psychology of Occupations. No. 6,

Reflective Attention. No. 7, The Aim of History in Elementary Education. No. 8, The Psychology of the Elementary Curriculum. *Translations*. Russian (Moscow, 1923); Spanish in *Obras de Dewey*, I (Madrid, 1926).

Review of A[rthur] S[idgwick] and E[leanor] M[ildred Balfour] S[idgwick], *Henry Sidgwick, A Memoir*. *Political Science Quarterly*, Mar. 1907, XXII, 133-135.

The Control of Ideas by Facts. I. (*Journal of Philosophy*, 11 Apr. 1907, IV, 197-203); II. (*Ib.*, 9 May 1907, 253-259); III. (*Ib.*, 6 June 1907, 309-319).

Reply by Roy Wood Sellars, Professor Dewey's View of Agreement, *ib.*, 1 Aug. 1907, IV, 432-435.

Summarized in *Philosophical Review*, Jan. 1908, XVII, 104-105 (C. H. Williams); *Psychological Bulletin*, Oct. 1908, V, 336-337 (Robert Morris Ogden).

Reprinted in *Essays in Experimental Logic* (1916), 230-249.

Review of *Studies in Philosophy and Psychology* by the Former Students of Charles Edward Garman. *Philosophical Review*, May 1907, XVI, 312-321.

Education as a University Study. *Columbia University Quarterly*, June 1907, IX, 284-290.

Reality and the Criterion for the Truth of Ideas. *Mind*, July 1907, n.s. XVI, 317-342.

Summarized in *Philosophical Review*, Jan. 1908, XVII, 103-104 (Gustavus Watts Cunningham); *Psychological Bulletin*, May 1908, V, 166-167 (M. S. Case); *Revue philosophique*, Dec. 1907, LXIV, 662.

Reprinted "with many changes" in *The Influence of Darwin on Philosophy* (1910), 112-153 with the title The Intellectualist Criterion for Truth.

Pure Experience and Reality: a Disclaimer. *Philosophical Review*, July 1907, XVI, 419-422.

Reply to Evander Bradley McGilvary, Pure Experience and Reality, *ib.*, May 1907, XVI, 266-284. Rejoinder by McGilvary, Pure Experience and Reality: a Reassertion, *ib.*, July 1907, XVI, 422-424.

Review of George Santayana, *The Life of Reason* (Vols. I-V). *Educational Review*, Sept. 1907, XXXIV, 116-129.

1908

ETHICS. New York: Columbia University Press, 1908. 26 pp.
A lecture delivered at Columbia University in the series on science, philosophy, and art, 25 Mar. 1908.
Reprinted in *The Influence of Darwin on Philosophy* (1910), 46–76, with the title INTELLIGENCE AND MORALS.

ETHICS, by John Dewey and James H[ayden] Tufts. (American Science Series.) New York: Henry Holt and Company, 1908. xiii, 618 pp.
Published also in London by G. Bell and Sons, 1909.
Revised edition, 1932, *q.v.*
Part I was written by Mr. Tufts, Part II by Mr. Dewey, and in Part III, Chapters XX [Social Organization and the Individual] and XXI [Civil Society and the Political State] are by Mr. Dewey, Chapters XXII–XXVI by Mr. Tufts.

Contents. Introduction. Part I, The Beginnings and Growth of Morality: Early Group Life—The Rationalizing and Socializing Agencies in Early Society—Group Morality, Customs or Mores—From Custom to Conscience; from Group Morality to Personal Morality—The Hebrew Moral Development—The Moral Development of the Greeks—The Modern Period—A General Comparison of Customary and Reflective Morality. Part II, Theory of Moral Life: The Moral Situation—Problems of Moral Theory—Types of Moral Theory—Conduct and Character—Happiness and Conduct, The Good and Desire—Happiness and Social Ends—The Place of Reason in the Moral Life, Moral Knowledge—The Place of Duty in the Moral Life, Subjection to Authority—The Place of Self in the Moral Life—The Virtues. Part III, The World of Action: Social Organization and the Individual—Civil Society and the Political State—The Ethics of the Economic Life—Some Principles in the Economic Order—Unsettled Problems in the Economic Order—The Family.

Translations. Chinese; Japanese by R. Nakashima (Tokyo, 1912).

Reviewed in *American Journal of Psychology*, Jan. 1909, XX, 151 (Evander Bradley McGilvary); *American Journal of Sociology*, Mar. 1909, XIV, 687–690 (Guy Allen Tawney); *American Journal of Theology*, Jan, 1909, XIII, 140–143 (Arthur Oncken Lovejoy); *Dial*, 1 Mar. 1909, XLVI, 146; *Economic Bulletin*, Dec. 1908, I, 335–336 (Charles Abram Ellwood); *Educational Review*, Apr. 1909, XXXVII, 413–416 (Walter Taylor Marvin); *Independent*, 5 Aug. 1909, LXVII, 310; *Journal of Philosophy*, 5 Nov. 1908, V, 636–639 (Norman Wilde); *Monist*, July 1910, XX, 478; *Nation*, 5 Nov. 1908, LXXXVII, 438; *Outlook*, 14 Nov. 1908, XC, 595–596; *Philosophical*

Review, Mar. 1909, XVIII, 221–229 (William Caldwell); *Psychological Bulletin*, 15 Jan. 1909, VI, 14 (Evander Bradley McGilvary); *Revue de philosophie*, Mar. 1909, XIV, 318–322 (E.D.); *Revue de métaphysique et de morale*, XVII (Sup. to Nov. 1909, 17); *Revue philosophique*, Nov. 1910, LXX, 533–535 (J. Segond); *Revue des sciences philosophiques et théologiques*, July 1909, III, 539–540 (Marie Stanislas Gillet); *School Review*, Mar. 1909, XVII, 204–206 (Irving Elgar Miller); *Science*, 16 July 1909, N.S. XXX, 89–92 (Frank Thilly); *Survey*, 1 May 1909, XXII, 217–218 (Frank Addison Manny).

DOES REALITY POSSESS PRACTICAL CHARACTER? In *Essays, Philosophical and Psychological*, in Honor of William James, Professor in Harvard University, by his Colleagues at Columbia University (New York: Longmans, Green, and Company, 1908), 53–80.

Reviewed in *Mind*, Jan. 1910, N.S. XIX, 97–105 (Horace Meyer Kallen); *Revue de métaphysique et de morale*, XVI (Sup. to Sept. 1908, 12–13).

See Dewey: A REPLY TO PROFESSOR MCGILVARY'S QUESTIONS (*Journal of Philosophy*, 4 Jan. 1912), below.

Reprinted in *Philosophy and Civilization* (1931), 36–55, with the title THE PRACTICAL CHARACTER OF REALITY.

WHAT DOES PRAGMATISM MEAN BY PRACTICAL? *Journal of Philosophy*, 13 Feb. 1908, V, 85–99.

Review of William James, *Pragmatism*.

Comments in *Revue neo-scolastique*, Aug. 1909, XVI, 454 (Léon Noël). Summarized in *Revue de métaphysique et de morale*, XVI (Sup. to Nov. 1908, 24–25).

Reprinted, except the last paragraph, as WHAT PRAGMATISM MEANS BY PRACTICAL in *Essays in Experimental Logic* (1916), 303–329.

RELIGION AND OUR SCHOOLS. *Hibbert Journal*, July 1908, VI, 796–809.

Reprinted in *Characters and Events* (1929), II, 504–516; in *Intelligence in the Modern World* (1939), 702–715, with the title THE SCHOOLS AND RELIGIONS; and in *Education Today* (1940), 74–86.

THE LOGICAL CHARACTER OF IDEAS. *Journal of Philosophy*, 2 July 1908, V, 375–381.

See James Bissett Pratt, TRUTH AND IDEAS, *ib.*, 27 Feb. 1908, V, 122–131, and Addison Webster Moore, PRAGMATISM AND SOLIPSISM, *ib.*, 8 July 1909, VI, 378–383.

Reprinted in *Essays in Experimental Logic* (1916), 220–229.

THE BEARINGS OF PRAGMATISM UPON EDUCATION. I. (*Progressive Journal of Education*, Dec. 1908, I, ii, 1–3); II. (*Ib.*, Jan. 1909, I, iii, 5–8); III. (*Ib.*, Feb. 1909, I, iv, 6–7).

1909

MORAL PRINCIPLES IN EDUCATION. (Riverside Educational Monographs, edited by Henry Suzzallo.) Boston: Houghton Mifflin Company [1909]. ix, 60 pp.

Reissued in a facsimile edition by Philosophical Library, New York, 1959.

Also published in London by J. Calder, 1959 (Wisdom Library).

Contents. Introduction—The Moral Purpose of the School—The Moral Training Given by the School Community—The Moral Training from Methods of Instruction—The Social Nature of the Course of Study—The Psychological Aspect of Moral Education—Outline.

Reviewed in *Elementary School Teacher*, Dec. 1909, X, 204 (Frank Addison Manny); and in [*Proceedings of the*] *Second International Moral Education Congress*, 1912, 184–187.

An elaboration of *Ethical Principles Underlying Education* (1897).

Translations. Bohemian by F. Pavlásek, with a preface by Miloslav Skořepa (Praha, 1934); Chinese.

PRAGMATISM. 3. In *philosophy* . . . In *Century Dictionary Supplement* (New York: The Century Company, 1909), II, 1050.

"Special mention should be made of the assistance of Professor John Dewey of Columbia University, in the defining of *pragmatism* and related terms." *Prefatory Note* by Benjamin Eli Smith, editor in chief (I, viii).

THE PRAGMATIC MOVEMENT OF CONTEMPORARY THOUGHT: A SYLLABUS. New York, 1909. 11 pp.

OBJECTS, DATA, AND EXISTENCES. *Journal of Philosophy*, 7 Jan. 1909, VI, 13–21.

Reply to Evander Bradley McGilvary, THE CHICAGO "IDEA" AND IDEALISM, *ib.*, 22 Oct. 1908, V, 589–597.

Summarized in *Revue de philosophie*, May 1909, XIV, 735.

HISTORY FOR THE EDUCATOR. *Progressive Journal of Education*, Mar. 1909, I, v, 1–4.

DISCUSSION ON REALISM AND IDEALISM. *Philosophical Review*, Mar. 1909, XVIII, 182–183.

At the Eighth Annual Meeting of the American Philosophical Association, Johns Hopkins University, Dec. 1908.

Symposium on the Purpose and Organization of Physics Teaching in Secondary Schools, XIII. *School Science and Mathematics*, Mar. 1909, IX, 291–292.

[Discussion on the Concept of a Sensation.] *Journal of Philosophy*, 15 Apr. 1909, VI, 211–212.

At a meeting of the section of anthropology and psychology of the New York Academy of Sciences.

Teaching That Does Not Educate. *Progressive Journal of Education*, June 1909, I, viii, 1–3.

Is Nature Good? A Conversation. *Hibbert Journal*, July 1909, VII, 827–843.

Reprinted in *The Influence of Darwin on Philosophy* (1910), 20–45, with the title Nature and Its Good: A Conversation.

Review of Albert Schinz, *Anti-pragmatisme*. *Philosophical Review*, July 1909, XVIII, 446–449.

Darwin's Influence upon Philosophy. *Popular Science Monthly*, July 1909, LXXV, 90–98.

Delivered in a course of lectures on "Charles Darwin and his Influence on Science," given at Columbia University in the winter and spring of 1909.

Reprinted in *The Influence of Darwin on Philosophy* (1910), 1–19.

The Dilemma of the Intellectualist Theory of Truth. *Journal of Philosophy*, 5 Aug. 1909, VI, 433–434.

Summarized in *Revue philosophique*, Sept. 1910, LXX, 322 (Guillaume L. Duprat).

The Moral Significance of the Common School Studies. Northern Illinois Teachers' Association, *Topics for General Sessions: Moral and Religious Training in the Public Schools, November 5th and 6th, 1909, Elgin, Illinois*, 21–27.

1910

How We Think. Boston: D. C. Heath & Co., 1910. vi, 224 pp.

Published also in London by Harrap.

Revised edition, 1933, *q.v.*

Contents. Part I, The Problem of Training Thought: What Is Thought—The Need for Training Thought—Natural Resources in the Training of Thought—School Conditions and the Training of

Thought—The Means and End of Mental Training, the Psychological and the Logical. Part II, Logical Considerations: The Analysis of a Complete Act of Thought—Systematic Inference, Induction and Deduction—Judgment, the Interpretation of Facts—Meaning, or Conceptions and Understanding—Concrete and Abstract Thinking —Empirical and Scientific Thinking. Part III, The Training of Thought: Activity and the Training of Thought—Language and the Training of Thought—Observation and Information in the Training of Mind—The Recitation and the Training of Thought—Some General Conclusions.

Translations. Chinese; French by O. Decroly (Paris, 1925); German by Alice Burgeni, Introduction by Leopold Deuel (Zürich, 1951); Italian by U. Monroy (Firenze, 1961); Japanese (Tokyo, 1950); Polish by Zofja Bastgenówna, Introduction by Zygmunt Myslakowski (Warsaw, 1934, new ed. 1957); Portuguese by Godofredo Rangel (São Paulo, 1933, 1953); Russian by N. M. Nikol'skaia (Berlin, 1922); Spanish by Alejandro A. Jascalevich (Boston [ᶜ1917]), another translation? (Madrid, 1928).

Reviewed in *Educational Review,* June, 1910, XL, 97–98 (F. A. Fitzpatrick); *Independent,* 4 Aug. 1910, LXIX, 246; *Journal of Philosophy,* 27 Apr. 1911, VIII, 244–248 (Max Eastman); *Nation,* 5 May 1910, XC, 464; *New York Times,* 5 Nov. 1910 (Henry Addington Bruce); *Philosophical Review,* July 1911, XX, 441–442 (Walter Bowers Pillsbury); *Quarterly Journal of the University of North Dakota,* July 1911, I, 388–392 (L. G. Whitehead); *Revue de philosophie,* July 1911, XIX, 86–87 (E. D.); *School Review,* Nov. 1910, XVIII, 642–645 (Boyd Henry Bode).

See Laurence Buermeyer, PROFESSOR DEWEY'S ANALYSIS OF THOUGHT, *Journal of Philosophy,* 2 Dec. 1920, XVII, 673–681.

THE INFLUENCE OF DARWIN ON PHILOSOPHY AND OTHER ESSAYS IN CONTEMPORARY THOUGHT. New York: Henry Holt and Company, 1910. vi, 309 pp.

Published also in London by G. Bell & Sons, Ltd., 1910.

Reprinted in facsimile by Peter Smith, New York, 1951.

Contents. The Influence of Darwinism on Philosophy—Nature and Its Good: A Conversation—Intelligence and Morals—The Experimental Theory of Knowledge—The Intellectualist Criterion for Truth— A Short Catechism concerning Truth—Beliefs and Existences—Experience and Objective Idealism—The Postulate of Immediate Empiricism—"Consciousness" and Experience—The Significance of the Problem of Knowledge.

With the exception of A SHORT CATECHISM CONCERNING TRUTH, a paper read in the spring of 1909 before the Philosophical Club of

Smith College, all the papers in this collection have been published previously.

Reviewed in *Dial*, 16 Sept. 1910, XLIX, 183–184; *Journal of Philosophy*, 29 Sept. 1910, VII, 557–559 (Henry Sturt); *New York Times*, 28 May 1910 (Joseph Jacobs); *Outlook*, 18 June 1910, XCV, 368; *Philosophical Review*, Mar. 1911, XX, 219–221 (James Edwin Creighton); *Revue de métaphysique et de morale*, XVIII (Sup. to Nov. 1910, 12–13) [Emmanuel Leroux].

See Mortimer Jerome Adler, *Problems for Thomists* (New York, 1940), 271–272.

EDUCATIONAL ESSAYS by John Dewey. Edited by J[oseph] J[ohn] Findlay. London: Blackie & Son, Ltd., 1910. 168 pp.

Contents. Introduction by J. J. Findlay—Ethical Principles Underlying Education—Interest in Relation to Training of the Will—Psychology and Social Practice.

Translations. Italian, with Introduction, by Maria Teresa Gentile (Firenze, 1950); Swedish by Malte Jacobssen (Lund, 1912).

SCIENCE AS SUBJECT MATTER AND AS METHOD. *Science*, 28 Jan. 1910, n.s. XXXI, 121–127.

Address of the Vice President, and Chairman of Sec. L (Education), at the meeting of the American Association for the Advancement of Science, Boston, 29 Dec. 1909.

Reprinted in *Journal of Education*, 14, 21 and 28 Apr. 1910, LXXI, 395–396, 427–428, 454; and in *Characters and Events* (1929), II, 765–775, with the title SCIENCE AND THE EDUCATION OF MAN.

Editorial comment in *New York Evening Post*, 5 Feb. 1910.

REVIEW of Hugo Münsterberg, *The Eternal Values*. *Philosophical Review*, Mar. 1910, XIX, 188–192.

VALID KNOWLEDGE AND THE "SUBJECTIVITY OF EXPERIENCE." *Journal of Philosophy*, 31 Mar. 1910, VII, 169–174.

Summarized in *Philosophical Review*, Sept. 1910, XIX, 563 (J. R. Tuttle).

SOME IMPLICATIONS OF ANTI-INTELLECTUALISM. *Journal of Philosophy*, 1 Sept. 1910, VII, 477–481.

Summarized in *Philosophical Review*, Mar. 1911, XX, 239 (J. Reese Lin); *Revue philosophique*, Apr. 1912, LXXIII, 439 (Guillaume L. Duprat).

WILLIAM JAMES. *Independent*, 8 Sept. 1910, LXIX, 533–536.

Reprinted in *Characters and Events* (1929), I, 111–117.

WILLIAM JAMES. *Journal of Philosophy*, 15 Sept. 1910, VII, 505–508.

Reprinted in *Characters and Events* (1929), I, 107–111.

THE SHORT-CUT TO REALISM EXAMINED. *Journal of Philosophy*, 29 Sept. 1910, VII, 553–557.

Discussion of THE PROGRAM AND FIRST PLATFORM OF SIX REALISTS [*i.e.*, Edwin Bissell Holt, Walter Taylor Marvin, William Pepperell Montague, Ralph Barton Perry, Walter Boughton Pitkin, Edward Gleason Spaulding], *ib.*, 21 July 1910, VII, 393–401.

Reply by Edward Gleason Spaulding, REALISM: A REPLY TO PROFESSOR DEWEY AND AN EXPOSITION, *ib.*, 3 Feb. 1911, VIII, 63–77. See Dewey's rejoinder (*ib.*, 3 Feb. 1911), below.

1911

A CYCLOPEDIA OF EDUCATION, Edited by Paul Monroe. Vol. I. New York: The Macmillan Company, 1911.

John Dewey, Departmental Editor for Philosophy of Education.

The following articles are by Dewey: Abstraction, 14—Accommodation, 24–25—Activity, Logical Theory and Educational Implication of, 33–34—Adaptation, 35—Adjustment, 38–39—Altruism and Egoism, 105–106—Analogy, Logic of, 116—Analysis and Synthesis, 117–119—Art in Education, 223–225—Causation, 553–554—Character, 569–572.

Ib., Vol. II, 1911.

The following articles are by Dewey: Comparison, 163—Conception, 171–172—Concrete and Abstract, 173—Conduct, 175—Conflict, 175 —Control, 196—Course of Study, Theory of, 218–222—Culture and Culture Values, 238–240—Culture Epoch Theory, 240–242—Custom, 243–244—Deduction, 275—Definition, 280–281—Democracy and Education, 293–294—Demonstration, 294—Determinism, 318— Development, 319–320—Dialectic, 321–322—Didactics, 327—Discipline, 336—Dualism, 374—Dynamic, 380—Education, 398–401— Education and Instruction, 414—Effort, 421–422—End in Education, 451—Environment and Organsim, 486–487—Epistemology, 491—Evidence, 528—Evolution: The Philosophical Concepts, 528– 529—Experience and the Empirical, 546–549—Experiment in Education, 550–551—Experimentation, Logic of, 554–555—Explanation, 555—External Object, 559—Fact, 567–568—Form and Content, 641–642—Freedom, Academic, 700–701—Freedom of Will, 705–706—Function, 723–724.

REJOINDER TO DR. SPAULDING. *Journal of Philosophy*, 3 Feb. 1911, VIII, 77–79.

Reply to Edward Gleason Spaulding, REALISM: A REPLY TO PROFESSOR DEWEY AND AN EXPOSITION, *ib.*, 63–77. Reply by Spaulding, A REPLY TO PROFESSOR DEWEY'S REJOINDER, *ib.*, 12 Oct. 1911, 566–574.

JOINT DISCUSSION, with Articles of Agreement and Disagreement, by Dewey and Spaulding, *ib.*, 574–579.

Summarized in *Revue de métaphysique et de morale*, XX (Sup. to Jan. 1912, 22–24); XXI (Sup. to Mar. 1913, 23).

THE PROBLEM OF TRUTH. I. Why Is Truth a Problem? (*Old Penn, Weekly Review of the University of Pennsylvania*, 11 Feb. 1911, IX, 522–528); II. Truth and Consequences (*ib.*, 18 Feb. 1911, 556–563); III. Objective Truths (*ib.*, 4 Mar. 1911, 620–625).

A course of lectures delivered on the George Leib Harrison Foundation at the University of Pennsylvania.

IS CO-EDUCATION INJURIOUS TO GIRLS? *Ladies Home Journal*, June 1911, XXVIII, 22, 60–61.

MAETERLINCK'S PHILOSOPHY OF LIFE. *Hibbert Journal*, July 1911, IX, 765–778.

Reprinted in *Characters and Events* (1929), I, 31–44, with the title MAURICE MAETERLINCK.

BRIEF STUDIES IN REALISM. I. Naïve Realism *vs.* Presentative Realism (*Journal of Philosophy*, 20 July 1911, VIII, 393–400); II. Epistemological Realism: the Alleged Ubiquity of the Knowledge Relation (*ib.*, 28 Sept. 1911, 546–554).

Summarized in *Philosophical Review*, Jan. 1912, XXI, 120–121 (Elijah Jordan).

Replies by Evander Bradley McGilvary, PROFESSOR DEWEY'S "BRIEF STUDIES IN REALISM," *Journal of Philosophy*, 20 June 1912, IX, 344–349; Durant Drake, WHAT KIND OF REALISM? *ib.*, 14 Mar. 1912, IX, 149–154. See Dewey's replies, IN RESPONSE TO PROF. McGILVARY (*ib.*, 26 Sept. 1912) and DUALITY AND DUALISM (*ib.*, 30 Aug. 1917), below.

Reprinted in *Essays in Experimental Logic* (1916), 250–280.

THE STUDY OF PHILOSOPHY. *Columbia Monthly*, Aug. 1911, VII, 367–368.

1912

A CYCLOPEDIA OF EDUCATION. Vol. III. New York: The Macmillan Company, 1912.

The following articles are by Dewey: Generalization, 15—Harmony, Harmonious Development, 217—Hedonism, 242–243—Humanism and Naturalism, 338–340—Humanities, The, 340—Hypothesis, 363–364—Idea and Ideation, 370–371—Idealism, 371–373—Idealism and Realism in Education, 373–375—Imitation in Education, 389–390 —Individuality, 421–422—Induction and Deduction, 422–424—Infancy, Theory of, in Education, 445–446—Inference, 455—Information, 455–456—Initiative, 457—Innate Idea, 458–459—Interest, 472–475—Intuition, 480—Isolation, 499—Judgment, 571–572— Knowledge, 611–613—Law, 655–656.

REPLY TO PROFESSOR ROYCE'S CRITIQUE OF INSTRUMENTALISM. *Philosophical Review*, Jan. 1912, XXI, 69–81.

Reply to Josiah Royce, THE PROBLEM OF TRUTH, in *William James, and Other Essays* (1911).

A REPLY TO PROFESSOR MCGILVARY'S QUESTIONS. *Journal of Philosophy*, 4 Jan. 1912, IX, 19–21.

Reply to Evander Bradley McGilvary, PROFESSOR DEWEY'S "ACTION OF CONSCIOUSNESS," *ib.*, 17 Aug. 1911, VIII, 458–460, a criticism of Dewey's essay, DOES REALITY POSSESS PRACTICAL CHARACTER? in *Essays . . . in Honor of William James* (1908).

A TRENCHANT ATTACK ON LOGIC. *Independent*, 25 July 1912, LXXIII, 203–205.

Review of Ferdinand Canning Scott Schiller, *Formal Logic, a Scientific and Social Problem.*

IN RESPONSE TO PROFESSOR MCGILVARY. *Journal of Philosophy*, 26 Sept. 1912, IX, 544–548.

Reply to Evander Bradley McGilvary, REALISM AND THE EGOCENTRIC PREDICAMENT, *Philosophical Review*, May 1912, XXI, 351–356; PROFESSOR DEWEY'S "AWARENESS," *Journal of Philosophy*, 23 May 1912, IX, 301–302; PROFESSOR DEWEY'S "BRIEF STUDIES IN REALISM," *ib.*, 20 June 1912, 344–349.

REVIEW of Hugh Samuel Roger Elliott, *Modern Science and the Illusions of Professor Bergson. Philosophical Review*, Nov. 1912, XXI, 705–707.

PERCEPTION AND ORGANIC ACTION. *Journal of Philosophy*, 21 Nov. 1912, IX, 645–668.

Bergson's ideas of perception.

Summarized in *Revue de métaphysique et de morale*, XXII (Sup. to Mar. 1914, pp. 30–31); *Revue philosophique*, July 1913, LXXVI, 107. Reprinted in *Philosophy and Civilization* (1931), 202–232.

L'ÉCOLE ET LA VIE DE L'ENFANT (Translated by J. Desfueille). *L'Éducation*, Dec. 1912, 457–472.

Summarized in *L'Année pedagogique*, 1912, 310.

See *The School and Society* (1900).

1913

L'ÉCOLE ET L'ENFANT. Traduit par L. S. Pidoux, avec une Introduction par Édouard Claparède. (Collection d'actualités pédagogiques, publiée sous les auspices de l'Institut J. J. Rousseau.) Neuchâtel: Delachaux & Niestlé [1913]. xxxii, 136 pp.

Fourth edition, 1947. 174 pp.

Contents. Introduction: La Pédagogie de M. John Dewey—L'Intérêt et l'effort—L'Enfant et les programmes d'étude—Le But de l'histoire dans l'instruction primaire—Morale et éducation.

Reviewed in *L'Année pédagogique*, 1913, 61–62; *Revue de métaphysique et de morale*, XXII (Sup. to July 1914, 20–21); *Revue de philosophie*, Jan. 1914, XXIV, 89 (G. Jeanjean); *Revue philosophique*, Aug. 1914, LXXVIII, 208–211 (L. Dugas).

Italian translation, *Saggi pedagogici*, by M. T. Gentile (Firenze, 1951).

L'ÉDUCATION AU POINT DE VUE SOCIAL. *L'Année pédagogique*, 1913, III, 32–48.

INTEREST AND EFFORT IN EDUCATION. (Riverside Educational Monographs, edited by Henry Suzzallo.) Boston: Houghton Mifflin Company [°1913]. ix, 101 pp.

Contents. Editor's Introduction, by Henry Suzzallo—Unified *versus* Divided Activity—Interest as Direct and Indirect—Effort, Thinking, and Motivation—Types of Educative Interest—Place of Interest in the Theory of Education.

Translations. Armenian by Aroos Asadian Freeman (Constantinople, 1931); Portuguese by Anísio S. Teixeira (São Paulo, 1930); Serbo-Croatian by M. Aersenijevic; Spanish by A. M. Aguayo, in *Obras de Dewey*, II (Madrid, 1926).

SHOULD MICHIGAN HAVE VOCATIONAL EDUCATION UNDER "UNIT" OR "DUAL" CONTROL? *In* National Society for the

Promotion of Industrial Education, *Bulletin 18* (Peoria, Ill. [1913]), 27–34.

Address at the Seventh Annual Meeting of the Society at Grand Rapids, Mich., 23 Oct. 1913.

INTRODUCTION. *In* [Isadore Gilbert Mudge], *A Contribution to a Bibliography of Henri Bergson* (New York: Columbia University Press, 1913), ix–xiii.

INTRODUCTION. *In* Henry Street Settlement, Committee on Vocational Scholarships, *Directory of the Trades and Occupations Taught at the Day and Evening Schools in Greater New York* (New York, 1913), 2–3.

A CYCLOPEDIA OF EDUCATION. Vol. IV. New York: The Macmillan Company, 1913.

> *The following articles are by Dewey:* Liberal Education, 4–6—Many-Sided Interest, 129—Materialism, 158—Metaphysics, 202—Method, 202–205—Monism, 296—Morality and Moral Sense, 314—Nativism, 386—Nature, 387–389—Neo-Humanism, 408—Opinion, 552—Optimism, 552–553—Pantheism, 598—Pedantry, 622–623—Personality, 649–650—Pessimism, 654–655—Philosophy of Education, 697–703 —Plato, 722–725—Play, 725–727—Pluralism, 730.

Ib., Vol. V, 1913.

> *The following articles are by Dewey:* Positivism, 18–19—Pragmatism, 22–24—Problem, 47—Process, 49—Progress, 51–52—Proposition, 54—Rationalism, 109—Scientific Method, 292–293—Self, 317–319—Self-Consciousness, 319–320—Sensationalism, 324–325—Stimulus and Response, 422—Subject, 446–447—Syllogism, 492–493—System, 496—Term, 566—Theism, 581—Theory and Practice, 606–607 —Tradition, 621—Transcendentalism, 622–623—Truth, 632–633—Universal, 651—Utilitarianism, 700—Validity, 703—Values, Educational, 704–705.

AN UNDEMOCRATIC PROPOSAL. *American Teacher*, Jan. 1913, II, 2–4; *Vocational Education*, May 1913, II, 374–377.

Industrial education in Illinois.

Noticed in *L'Année pédagogique*, 1913, 193.

> See SOME DANGERS IN THE PRESENT MOVEMENT FOR INDUSTRIAL EDUCATION and INDUSTRIAL EDUCATION AND DEMOCRACY, below.

SOME DANGERS IN THE PRESENT MOVEMENT FOR INDUSTRIAL EDUCATION. *Child Labor Bulletin*, Feb. 1913, I, iv, 69–74.

> Reprint, with revisions, of AN UNDEMOCRATIC PROPOSAL, above; also printed as *Pamphlet No. 190* of the National Child Labor Committee, New York, 1913.

Reply by Edwin Gilbert Cooley, PROFESSOR DEWEY'S CRITICISM OF THE CHICAGO COMMERCIAL CLUB AND ITS VOCATIONAL EDUCATION BILL, *Vocational Education*, Sept. 1913, III, 24–29; also *In Reply to Dr. John Dewey's "Some Dangers in the Present Movement for Industrial Education"* [Chicago, 1913?], 8 pp.

INDUSTRIAL EDUCATION AND DEMOCRACY. *Survey*, 22 Mar. 1913, XXIX, 870–871, 893.

Part I, An answer to H. E. Miles, WORK AND CITIZENSHIP: THE WISCONSIN EXPERIMENT IN INDUSTRIAL EDUCATION, *ib.*, 15 Feb. 1913, XXIX, 682–685. Part II, Reprinted from *American Teacher*, Jan. 1913, above.

THE PROBLEM OF VALUES. *Journal of Philosophy*, 8 May 1913, X, 268–269.

CUT-AND-TRY SCHOOL METHODS. *Survey*, 6 Sept. 1913, XXX, 691–692.

At Thomas A. Edison's laboratory, West Orange, N.J.

PROFESSIONAL SPIRIT AMONG TEACHERS. *American Teacher*, Oct. 1913, II, 114–116.

An address delivered at the organization meeting of the Teachers' League of New York, 28 Feb. 1913.

1914

REASONING IN EARLY CHILDHOOD. *Teachers College Record*, Jan. 1914, XV, 9–15.

Stenographic report of a paper read before the Department of Kindergarten Education, Teachers College Alumni Conference, 21 Feb. 1913.

REPORTS OF LECTURES by John Dewey. By Jenny B. Merrill. I. On Rousseau, Pestalozzi, Froebel and Montessori (*Kindergarten-Primary Magazine*, Mar. 1914, XXVI, 186); II. On Social Motives in School Life (*ib.*, Apr. 1914, 215); III. On Pestalozzi (*ib.*, May 1914, 251); IV. Comparison of Herbart and Froebel (*ib.*, 255–256).

REPORT ON THE FAIRHOPE [ALABAMA] EXPERIMENT IN ORGANIC EDUCATION. *Survey*, 16 May 1914, XXXII, 199.

PSYCHOLOGICAL DOCTRINE AND PHILOSOPHICAL TEACHING. *Journal of Philosophy*, 10 Sept. 1914, XI, 505–511.

Read at the joint discussion of the American Philosophical and American Psychological Associations on "The Standpoint and Method of Psychology," New Haven, 30 Dec. 1913.

Reports in *Journal of Philosophy*, 12 Feb. 1914, XI, 88–89 (Melvin Everett Haggerty), and *Psychological Bulletin*, 15 Jan. 1914, XI, 37–38.

Summarized in *Philosophical Review*, Jan. 1915, XXIV, 120–121 (C. C. Church).

NATURE AND REASON IN LAW. *International Journal of Ethics*, Oct. 1914, XXV, 25–32.

Summarized in *Philosophical Review*, Jan. 1915, XXIV, 116 (A. J. Thomas).

Reprinted in *Characters and Events* (1929), II, 790–797, and in *Philosophy and Civilization* (1931), 166–172.

A POLICY OF INDUSTRIAL EDUCATION. *New Republic*, 19 Dec. 1914, I, 11–12; *Manual Training*, Mar. 1915, XVI, 393–397.

1915

GERMAN PHILOSOPHY AND POLITICS. New York: Henry Holt and Company, 1915. 134 pp.

New edition, 1942, *q.v.*

Contents. German Philosophy: the Two Worlds—German Moral and Political Philosophy—The Germanic Philosophy of History.

Three lectures delivered in Feb. 1915 on the John Calvin McNair Foundation at the University of North Carolina.

Reviewed in *Independent*, 5 July 1915, LXXXIII, 24–25; *International Journal of Ethics*, Oct. 1915, XXVI, 131–133 (James Hayden Tufts); *Journal of Philosophy*, 25 Nov. 1915, XII, 645–649 (George Santayana); *Mind*, Apr. 1916, N.S. XXV, 250–255 (Ferdinand Canning Scott Schiller); *Nation*, 29 July 1915, CI, 152–153; *New York Times*, 18 July 1915; *Philosophical Review*, Sept. 1915, XXIV, 540–545 (Frank Thilly); *Review of Reviews*, Aug. 1915, LII, 248–249; *Springfield Republican*, 10 June 1915.

See Dewey, IN REPLY (*New Republic*, 2 Oct. 1915); and TRAFFIC IN ABSOLUTES (*ib.*, 17 July 1915), below.

THE SCHOOL AND SOCIETY. Revised edition. Chicago: The University of Chicago Press [1915, 1953]. xv, 164 pp.

Published also in England by the Cambridge University Press, 1917.

Reprinted as a paperback, with *The Child and the Curriculum* and an Introduction by Leonard Carmichael, Chicago: University of Chicago Press—Phoenix Books [1956], 31, 179 pp.; and in part in *Dewey on Education* (1959), 33–90.

Contents. The School and Social Progress—The School and the Life of the Child—Waste in Education—The Psychology of Elementary Education—Froebel's Educational Principles—The Psychology of Occupations—The Development of Attention—The Aim of History in Elementary Education.

For translations, see edition of 1900.

Reviewed in *Boston Transcript*, 25 Aug. 1915; *Elementary School Journal*, Oct. 1915, XVI, 67.

SCHOOLS OF TOMORROW, by John Dewey and Evelyn Dewey. New York: E. P. Dutton & Company [ᶜ1915]. 316 pp.

Published in London by J. M. Dent & Sons, Ltd., 1915.

Contents. Education as Natural Development—An Experiment in Education as Natural Development—Four Factors in Natural Growth—The Reorganization of the Curriculum—Play—Freedom and Individuality—The Relation of the School to the Community—The School as a Social Settlement—Industry and Educational Readjustment—Education through Industry—Democracy and Education.

Translations. French by R. Duthil (Paris, 1931); Rumanian by G. I. Simeon (Bucharest, 1938); Russian by R. Landsberg with Introduction by I. Gorbunova-Posadova (Berlin, 1922); Spanish by Lorenzo Luzuriaga (Madrid, 1918; Buenos Aires, 1950).

Reviewed in *Bookman*, Sept. 1915, XLII, 88–91 (Florence Finch Kelly); *Dial*, 15 Aug. 1915, LIX, 109–111 (Thomas Percival Beyer); *Independent*, 9 Aug. 1915, LXXXIII, 198; *Nation*, 9 Sept. 1915, CI, 326–327; *New Republic*, 26 June 1915, III, 210–211; *New York Times*, 15 Aug. 1915; *Outlook*, 11 Aug. 1915, CX, 875; *Quarterly Journal of the University of North Dakota*, Apr. 1916, VI, 272–275 (Adoniram Judson Ladd); *Review of Reviews*, Aug. 1915, LII, 248–249; *Survey*, 8 Jan. 1916, XXXV, 438 (Edward Caldwell Moore).

INTRODUCTORY ADDRESS. *Science*, 29 Jan. 1915, N.S. XLI, 147–151.

Delivered before the American Association of University Professors at the Chemists' Club, New York City, 1 Jan. 1915.

INDUSTRIAL EDUCATION—A WRONG KIND. *New Republic*, 20 Feb. 1915, II, 71–73.

On the Indiana law of 1913 for the promotion of vocational education.

STATE OR CITY CONTROL OF SCHOOLS? *New Republic*, 20 Mar. 1915, II, 178–180.

Conditions in New York City.

SPLITTING UP THE SCHOOL SYSTEM. *New Republic*, 17 Apr. 1915, II, 283–284.

In Chicago.

CONDITIONS AT THE UNIVERSITY OF UTAH. Letter in *Nation*, 6 May 1915, C, 491–492, and in *Science*, 7 May 1915, N.S. XLI, 685.

Signed by John Dewey, President of the American Association of University Professors; Arthur Oncken Lovejoy, Secretary; and Edwin Robert Anderson Seligman, Chairman of the Committee of Enquiry, 30 Apr. 1915.

EDUCATION *vs.* TRADE-TRAINING. Letter in *New Republic*, 15 May 1915, III, 42–43.

Reply to VOCATIONAL EDUCATION, letter by David Snedden, *ib.*, 40–42.

DR. DEWEY REPLIES. Letter in *New Republic*, 22 May 1915, III, 72.

Reply to PAROCHIAL SCHOOL EDUCATION, letter of Charles P. Megan, *ib.*, 72.

THE SUBJECT-MATTER OF METAPHYSICAL INQUIRY. *Journal of Philosophy*, 24 June 1915, XII, 337–345.

Reprinted in *John Dewey on Experience, Nature, and Freedom* (1960), 211–223.

Apropos of Ralph Stayner Lillie, THE PHILOSOPHY OF BIOLOGY: VITALISM VS. MECHANISM, *Science*, 11 Dec. 1914, N.S. XL, 840–846.

THE EXISTENCE OF THE WORLD AS A PROBLEM. *Philosophical Review*, July 1915, XXIV, 357–370.

Comments on Bertrand Russell, *Our Knowledge of the External World as a Field for Scientific Method in Philosophy*.

Reprinted in *Essays in Experimental Logic* (1916), 281–302.

"TRAFFIC IN ABSOLUTES." An Extract from John Dewey, with a Review by F[rancis] H[ackett] and a Footnote by Walter Lippmann. *New Republic*, 17 July 1915, III, 281–285.

The extract is from *German Philosophy and Politics* (1915), 123–132.

THE LOGIC OF JUDGMENTS OF PRACTICE. I. Their Nature; II. Judgments of Value (*Journal of Philosophy*, 16 Sept. 1915, XII, 505–523); III. Sense-Perception as Knowledge (*ib.*, 30 Sept. 1915, 533–543).

Reply by Ralph Barton Perry, DEWEY AND URBAN ON VALUE JUDG-

MENTS, *ib.*, 29 Mar. 1917, XIV, 169–181. See Dewey's reply, THE OBJECTS OF VALUATION (*ib.*, 9 May 1918), below.

Reprinted in *Essays in Experimental Logic* (1916), 335–442.

IN REPLY. Letter in *New Republic*, 2 Oct. 1915, IV, 236.

Reply to William Ernest Hocking, POLITICAL PHILOSOPHY IN GERMANY, comments on *German Philosophy and Politics* (1915), *ib.*, 234–236.

PROFESSORIAL FREEDOM. Letter in *New York Times*, 22 Oct. 1915.

Protest against editorial in *New York Times*, 10 Oct. 1915, on the dismissal of Professor Scott Nearing from the University of Pennsylvania. Written as President of the American Association of University Professors.

Reprinted in *School and Society*, 6 Nov. 1915, II, 673, with the title THE CONTROL OF UNIVERSITIES.

ANNUAL ADDRESS OF THE PRESIDENT. *Bulletin of the American Association of University Professors*, Dec. 1915, I, 9–13.

Delivered at Washington, 31 Dec. 1915.

1916

DEMOCRACY AND EDUCATION. An Introduction to the Philosophy of Education. (Text-Book Series in Education, edited by Paul Monroe.) New York: The Macmillan Company, 1916. xii, 434 pp.

Contents. Education as a Necessity of Life—Education as a Social Function—Education as Direction—Education as Growth—Preparation, Unfolding, and Formal Discipline—Education as Conservative and Progressive—The Democratic Conception in Education—Aims in Education—Natural Development and Social Efficiency as Aims—Interest and Discipline—Experience and Thinking—Thinking in Education—The Nature of Method—The Nature of Subject Matter—Play and Work in the Curriculum—The Significance of Geography and History—Science in the Course of Study—Educational Values—Labor and Leisure—Intellectual and Practical Studies—Physical and Social Studies, Naturalism and Humanism—The Individual and the World—Vocational Aspects of Education—Philosophy of Education—Theories of Knowledge—Theories of Morals.

Translations. Arabic by Matta Akrawi and Zakariah Mikhail; Chinese (1934); German by Erich Hylla (Breslau, 1930; Braunschweig, 1949); Italian by Enzo Enriques Agnoletti (Firenze, 1949);

Japanese by Riichiro Hoashi (Tokyo, 1952); Persian by A. Arianpour (Tabriz); Portuguese by Godofredo Rangel and Anísio S. Teixeira (São Paulo, 1930); Spanish by Lorenzo Luzuriaga (Buenos Aires, 1946, 1953); Swedish by Alf Ahlberg (Stockholm, 1948); Turkish by B. Avni with Introduction by Mehmed Emin (1928).

Reviewed in *Boston Transcript*, 15 Apr. 1916; *Dial*, 15 Aug. 1916, LXI, 101–103 (Thomas Percival Beyer); *Elementary School Journal*, 1916, XVII, 13–17; *Independent*, 5 June 1916, LXXXVI, 401; *International Journal of Ethics*, July 1916, XXVI, 547–550 (Addison Webster Moore); *Journal of Philosophy*, 5 July 1917, XIV, 384–389 (Ernest Carroll Moore); *Nation*, 4 May 1916, CII, 480–481; *New Republic*, 1 July 1916, VII, 231 (W[alter] L[ippmann]); *Philosophical Review*, Sept. 1916, XXV, 735–741 (James Edwin Creighton); *Revue philosophique*, Mar.-Apr. 1920, LXXXIX, 277–300 (André Lalande); *Scuola e città*, 1950, I, 95–96 (Aldo Visalberghi); *Springfield Republican*, 23 Apr. 1916; *Survey*, 26 Aug. 1916, XXXVI, 541–542.

See Denton Loring Geyer, THE WAVERING AIM OF EDUCATION IN DEWEY'S EDUCATIONAL PHILOSOPHY, *Education*, Apr. 1915, XXXVII, 484–491; Herman Harrell Horne, *The Democratic Philosophy of Education* (1932); James E. Wheeler, JOHN DEWEY'S *Democracy and Education*, *Social Education*, March 1952, XVI, 100–102; and Samuel Burkhard, *A Work Book in the Philosophy of Education, Based on Dewey's Democracy and Education* [Tempe, Arizona, 1950; Dubuque, Iowa, 1951], 1 vol. unpaged.

ESSAYS IN EXPERIMENTAL LOGIC. Chicago: The University of Chicago Press [ᶜ1916]. vii, 444 pp.

Published in England by the Cambridge University Press, 1916.

Facsimile reprint, cloth and paperback, New York: Dover Publications [1953]. Three chapters reprinted by the University of Chicago Press [1958], 58 pp., for Humanities 2 course.

The introductory chapter was written especially for this volume; chapters 2–5 are reprinted (with editorial revisions) from the author's *Studies in Logical Theory* (1903); "the other essays are in part reprinted and in part rewritten, with additions, from various contributions to philosophical periodicals."

Contents. Introduction—The Relationship of Thought and Its Subject-Matter—The Antecedents and Stimuli of Thinking—Data and Meanings—The Objects of Thought—Some Stages of Logical Thought—The Logical Character of Ideas—The Control of Ideas by Facts—Naïve Realism vs. Presentative Realism—Epistemological Realism: The Alleged Ubiquity of the Knowledge Relation—The Existence of the World as a Logical Problem—What Pragmatism Means by Practical—An Added Note as to the "Practical"—The Logic of Judgments of Practice.

Reviewed in *Boston Transcript*, 26 July 1916; *Journal of Philosophy*, 26 Apr. 1917, XIV, 246–248 (Harold Chapman Brown); *New Republic*, 2 Sept. 1916, VIII, 118–119 (Morris Raphael Cohen) reprinted in his *Preface to Logic* (1944), 196–202; *London Times Literary Supplement*, 11 Jan. 1917; *Mind*, Apr. 1917, n.s. XXVI, 217–222 (Alfred Sidgwick); *Philosophical Review*, July 1917, XXVI, 421–430 (Reinhold Friedrich Alfred Hoernlé); *School Review*, Dec. 1916, XXIV, 775 (Max Carl Otto).

See Harry Todd Costello, PROFESSOR DEWEY'S "JUDGMENTS OF PRACTICE," *Journal of Philosophy*, 12 Aug. 1920, XVII, 449–455; Bertrand Russell, PROFESSOR DEWEY'S *Essays in Experimental Logic*, *ib.*, 2 Jan. 1919, XVI, 5–26; and Daniel Sommer Robinson, AN ALLEGED NEW DISCOVERY IN LOGIC, *ib.*, 26 Apr. 1917, XIV, 225–237, and Dewey's reply, CONCERNING NOVELTIES IN LOGIC, *ib.*, 237–245.

NATIONALIZING EDUCATION. *In* National Education Association, *Addresses and Proceedings*, 1916, 183–189, *Journal of the National Education Association*, I, ii, 183–189.

Delivered at the 54th Annual Meeting, Madison Square Garden, New York City, 7 July 1916.

Reprinted in *Journal of Education*, 2 Nov. 1916, LXXXIV, 425–428, and in *Education Today* (1940), 112–121.

METHOD IN SCIENCE-TEACHING. *In* National Education Association, *Addresses and Proceedings*, 1916, 729–734.

Delivered before the Science Section of the Association, New York City, 6 July 1916.

Reprinted in *General Science Quarterly*, Nov. 1916, I, 3–9; *Journal of the National Education Association*, Mar. 1917, I, 725–730; in *Science Education*, Apr. 1945, XXIX, 119–123; and *Science Teacher*, Apr. 1955, XXII, 119–122. Condensed in *Education Digest*, Oct. 1955, XXI, 41–43.

FORCE, VIOLENCE, AND LAW. *New Republic*, 22 Jan. 1916, V, 295–297.

Reprinted in *The New Republic Book* (1916), 52–57, and in *Characters and Events* (1929), II, 636–641.

ON UNDERSTANDING THE MIND OF GERMANY. *Atlantic Monthly*, Feb. 1916, CXVII, 251–262.

Reprinted in *Characters and Events* (1929), I, 130–148, with the title THE MIND OF GERMANY.

THE NEED OF AN INDUSTRIAL EDUCATION IN AN INDUSTRIAL DEMOCRACY. *Manual Training*, Feb. 1916, XVII, 409–414.

Read 30 Dec. 1915 at George Washington University, Washington,

D.C., at the Joint Session of Subsections 1, 2, 8 and 9 of Section IV (Education) of the Second Pan-American Scientific Congress.

Reprinted in *Proceedings of the Second Pan-American Scientific Congress* (Washington, 1917), IV, 222–225.

ORGANIZATION IN AMERICAN EDUCATION. *Teachers College Record*, Mar. 1916, XVII, 127–141.

Address before the staff of Teachers College.

VOCATIONAL EDUCATION. *New Republic*, 11 Mar. 1916, VI, 159–160.

Review of John Augustus Lapp and Carl Henry Mote, *Learning To Earn*.

AMERICAN ASSOCIATION OF UNIVERSITY PROFESSORS. Letter in *Nation*, 30 Mar. 1916, CII, 357.

Reply to letter of "A Looker-On in Babylon," *Educational Review*, Mar. 1916, LI, 310–313.

PROGRESS. *International Journal of Ethics*, Apr. 1916, XXVI, 311–322.

Summarized in *Current Opinion*, June 1916, LX, 419–420.

Reprinted in *Characters and Events* (1929), II, 820–830.

FORCE AND COERCION. *International Journal of Ethics*, Apr. 1916, XXVI, 359–367.

Reprinted in *Characters and Events* (1929), II, 782–789.

OUR EDUCATIONAL IDEAL IN WARTIME. *New Republic*, 15 Apr. 1916, VI, 283–284.

Reprinted in *Characters and Events* (1929), II, 493–497, with the title OUR EDUCATIONAL IDEAL; and in *Education Today* (1940), 87–91.

UNIVERSAL SERVICE AS EDUCATION. *New Republic*, 22 and 29 Apr. 1916, VI, 309–310, 334–335.

Reprinted in *Characters and Events* (1929), II, 465–473, and in *Education Today* (1940), 92–100.

VOLUNTARISM IN THE ROYCEAN PHILOSOPHY. *Philosophical Review*, May 1916, XXV, 245–254.

Reprinted in *Papers in Honor of Josiah Royce on His Sixtieth Birthday* [n.p., n.d.], 17–26.

THE SCHOOLS AND SOCIAL PREPAREDNESS. *New Republic*, 6 May 1916, VII, 15–16.

Reprinted in *Characters and Events* (1929), II, 474–478, and in *Education Today* (1940), 101–105.

AMERICAN EDUCATION AND CULTURE. *New Republic*, 1 July 1916, VII, 215–216.

Reprinted in *The New Republic Book* (1916), 232–237; in *Essays Toward Truth: Studies in Orientation*, Selected by Kenneth Allan Robinson, William Benfield Pressey and James Dow McCallum (New York [ᶜ1924]), 65–71; in *Characters and Events* (1929), II, 498–503, and in *Education Today* (1940), 106–111.

PROFESSIONAL ORGANIZATION OF TEACHERS. *American Teacher*, Sept. 1916, V, 99–101.

From an address delivered at a mass meeting called by the American Federation of Teachers during the National Education Association convention, New York City, 6 July 1916.

THE HUGHES CAMPAIGN. *New Republic*, 28 Oct. 1916, VIII, 319–321.

THE TRAGEDY OF THE GERMAN SOUL. *New Republic*, 9 Dec. 1916, IX, 155–156.

Review of George Santayana, *Egotism in German Philosophy*.

THE PRAGMATISM OF PEIRCE. *Journal of Philosophy*, 21 Dec. 1916, XIII, 709–715.

Reprinted in Charles Santiago Sanders Peirce, *Chance, Love and Logic*, edited by Morris Raphael Cohen (New York, 1923; reprinted 1949, 1956; Italian translation by Nicola and Marian Abbagnano, Torino, 1956), 301–308. See Dewey's review of this book, *New Republic*, 25 June 1924.

1917

ENLISTMENT FOR THE FARM. (Columbia War Papers, Ser. I, No. 1.) New York: Division of Intelligence and Publicity of Columbia University, 1917. 10 pp.

PROSPECTIVE ELEMENTARY EDUCATION. *In* Louis Win Rapeer, *Teaching Elementary School Subjects* (New York: Charles Scribner's Sons [ᶜ1917]), 552–569.

THE NEED FOR A RECOVERY OF PHILOSOPHY. In *Creative Intelligence, Essays in the Pragmatic Attitude*, by John Dewey, Addison Webster Moore, Harold Chapman Brown, George Herbert Mead, Boyd Henry Bode, Henry Waldgrave Stuart, James Hayden Tufts, Horace Meyer Kallen (New York: Henry Holt and Company [ᶜ1917]), 3–69.

Reprinted in *John Dewey on Experience, Nature, and Freedom* (1960), 19–69.

Reviewed in *Bookman*, Apr. 1917, XLV, 181–182 (Florence Finch Kelly); *Catholic World*, June 1917, CV, 393; *Dial*, 19 Apr. 1917, LXII, 348–352 (Max Carl Otto); *Journal of Philosophy*, 14 Mar. 1918, XV, 149–157 (Delton Thomas Howard); *Mind*, Oct. 1917, N.S. XXVI, 466–474 (Ferdinand Canning Scott Schiller); *New York Times*, 15 Apr. 1917; *Philosophical Review*, Mar. 1919, XXVIII, 200–208 (Katherine Everett Gilbert); *Springfield Republican*, 3 Feb. and 19 Aug. 1917; *Survey*, 15 Dec. 1917, XXXIX, 326 (John Collier).

Translation. Italian by Lamberto Borghi (Firenze, 1957).

See Wendell T Bush, CONSTRUCTIVE INTELLIGENCE, *Journal of Philosophy*, 13 Sept. 1917, XIV, 505–520.

[GEORGE SYLVESTER MORRIS: AN ESTIMATE.] *In* Robert Mark Wenley, *The Life and Work of George Sylvester Morris* (New York: The Macmillan Company, 1917), 313–321.

ILL ADVISED. Letter in *American Teacher*, Feb. 1917, VI, 31.

Regarding a resolution adopted by the American Federation of Teachers at Chicago, as printed in the *American Teacher*, Jan. 1917, VI, 16.

EXPERIMENT IN EDUCATION. *New Republic*, 3 Feb. 1917, X, 15–16.

Reprinted in *Education Today* (1940), 122–125.

THE CONCEPT OF THE NEUTRAL IN RECENT EPISTEMOLOGY. *Journal of Philosophy*, 15 Mar. 1917, XIV, 161–163.

LEARNING TO EARN: THE PLACE OF VOCATIONAL EDUCATION IN A COMPREHENSIVE SCHEME OF PUBLIC EDUCATION. *School and Society*, 24 Mar. 1917, V, 331–335.

Also published in *Citizens of To-Morrow* . . . addresses delivered . . . by John Dewey, Samuel Gompers, Owen R. Lovejoy . . . New York: Public Education Association, 1917. 32 pp.

Address at the annual meeting of the Public Education Association, Hotel Biltmore, New York, 20 Feb. 1917.

Reprinted in *Education Today* (1940), 126–132.

CURRENT TENDENCIES IN EDUCATION. *Dial*, 5 Apr. 1917, LXII, 287–289.

FEDERAL AID TO ELEMENTARY EDUCATION. *Child Labor Bulletin*, May 1917, VI, 61–66.

Address at the 13th Annual Conference on Child Labor at Baltimore in Mar. 1917.

WRITINGS OF DEWEY, 1917

In a Time of National Hesitation. *Seven Arts Magazine*,
May 1917, II, 3–7.
> Reprinted in *Characters and Events* (1929), II, 443–446, with the
> title The Emergence of a New World.

The Need for Social Psychology. *Psychological Review*, July
1917, XXIV, 266–277.
> Address delivered on the occasion of the celebration of the twenty-
> fifth anniversary of the American Psychological Association, New
> York, 28 Dec. 1916.
> Reprinted in *Characters and Events* (1929), II, 709–720, with the title
> Social Psychology and Social Progress.

H. G. Wells, Theological Assembler. *Seven Arts Magazine*,
July 1917, II, 334–339.
> Comments on Herbert George Wells, *God, the Invisible King*.
> Reprinted in *Characters and Events* (1929), I, 78–82.

Conscience and Compulsion. *New Republic*, 14 July 1917, XI,
297–298.
> Reprinted in *Characters and Events* (1929), II, 576–580.
> Reply by Randolph Silliman Bourne, Conscience and Intelli-
> gence in War, *Dial*, 13 Sept. 1917, LXIII, 193–195. (Reprinted in
> his *The History of a Literary Radical & Other Papers*, New York:
> S. A. Russell, 1956, 197–204.)

The Future of Pacifism. *New Republic*, 28 July 1917, XI,
358–360.
> Replies by David Starr Jordan, An Appraisal of War Purposes,
> *ib.*, 25 Aug. 1917, XII, 104–105, and Robert Morss Lovett, A Task
> for Pacifists, *ib.*, 106–107.
> Reprinted in *Characters and Events* (1929), II, 581–586.

What America Will Fight For. *New Republic*, 18 Aug. 1917,
XII, 68–69.
> Editorial reply, "Motivation" of the War, in *New York Evening
> Post*, 20 Aug. 1917.
> Reprinted in *Characters and Events* (1929), II, 561–565, with the
> title America and War.

Duality and Dualism. *Journal of Philosophy*, 30 Aug. 1917,
XIV, 491–493.
> Comment on Durant Drake, What Kind of Realism? *ib.*, 14 Mar.
> 1912, IX, 149–154, and A Cul-de-Sac for Realism, *ib.*, 5 July 1917,
> XIV, 365–373. Reply by Drake, Dr. Dewey's Duality and Dual-
> ism, *ib.*, 22 Nov. 1917, 660–663.

CONSCRIPTION OF THOUGHT. *New Republic*, 1 Sept. 1917, XII, 128–130.

Reprinted in *Characters and Events* (1929), II, 566–570.

WAR ACTIVITIES FOR CIVILIANS. *New Republic*, 1 Sept. 1917, XII, 139–140.

Review of *National Service Handbook*.

FIAT JUSTITIA, RUAT CŒLUM [*sic*]. *New Republic*, 29 Sept. 1917, XII, 237–238.

Reprinted in *Characters and Events* (1929), II, 592–595.

THE PRINCIPLE OF NATIONALITY. *Menorah Journal*, Oct. 1917, III, 203–208.

Comment in *New York Evening Post*, 12 Oct. 1917.

[STATEMENT.] *New York Times*, 9 Oct. 1917.

On the resignation of Charles Austin Beard as Professor of Politics in Columbia University.

IN EXPLANATION OF OUR LAPSE. *New Republic*, 3 Nov. 1917, XIII, 17–18.

Regarding the exclusion of the *New York Call* and *Vorwaerts* from the mails.

Reprinted in *Characters and Events* (1929), II, 571–575.

THE CASE OF THE PROFESSOR AND THE PUBLIC INTEREST. *Dial*, 8 Nov. 1917, LXII, 435–437.

Comment on academic events at the University of Minnesota and at Columbia University.

DEMOCRACY AND LOYALTY IN THE SCHOOLS. *New York Evening Post*, 19 Dec. 1917; *American Teacher*, Jan. 1918, VII, 8–10.

Address delivered 15 Dec. 1917 at a meeting at the De Witt Clinton High School, New York City, called by the Teachers' Union to consider the cases of three teachers suspended from the school on charges of holding views "subversive of discipline."

PUBLIC EDUCATION ON TRIAL. *New Republic*, 29 Dec. 1917, XIII, 245–247.

In New York City; see preceding item.

Reprinted in *Education Today* (1940), 133–138.

1918

CONFIDENTIAL REPORT: CONDITIONS AMONG THE POLES IN THE UNITED STATES. By John Dewey. [Washington?] 1918. 80 pp.

Contents. Introduction—Occasion of Report—Sources of Information—General European Conditions as Affecting the Poles in the United States—European Developments during the War—The Paris Committee and Its Policies—Polish Conditions in the United States—Conclusions—The Detroit Convention—Specific Points of Friction and Discord—General Conclusions.

The only copy we have located is in the University of California Library at Berkeley, accessioned 1948. Because of the unusual character of this item, we quote at length from Dewey's Introduction; the order of these sections has been transposed.

SOURCES OF INFORMATION. Mr. Albert C. Barnes, of Philadelphia, spoke to me in New York City last April regarding the possibility of securing some well-trained post-graduate students from Columbia University to undertake a study during the summer months of conditions among an immigrant group in Philadelphia. The Poles were selected. The main object of the inquiry was to ascertain forces and conditions which operate against the development of a free and democratic life among the members of this group, to discover the influences which kept them under external oppression and control. To quote from a letter written by Mr. Barnes: "The idea would be to work out a practical plan, based upon first-hand knowledge, to eliminate forces alien to democratic internationalism and to promote American ideals in accordance with the principles announced by President Wilson in his various public communications." As to method, he emphasized simply the importance of competent scientific impartial inquiry. Neither then nor at any other time did Mr. Barnes give any instructions as to specific points to be investigated, much less as to any particular kind of results to be attained.

In accordance with his request the following persons were selected and after about a month's preliminary study on their part of conditions in Philadelphia the following assignment of topics made:

Mr. Brand Blanchard [sic], religious conditions and activity of the church; Miss Frances Bradshaw, educational conditions, including both public and parochial schools; Mrs. A. Levitas, conditions affecting family life and women; Mr. Irwin Edman began with a study of general intellectual, esthetic and neighborhood activities, but in connection with developments related below gradually diverted his energies to a study of conditions as affected by international politics. In May, Mr. Barnes asked me to act as adviser and general supervisor of the undertaking. The inquiry itself was set on foot on the fifteenth of May, 1918. In addition to the persons mentioned above one of whom, Mrs. Levitas, is herself a Polish immigrant, persons were engaged both permanently and for stated periods to act as interpreters and translators. Other persons have been engaged in library research from time to time. All of the active investigators lived in a house in the Polish district during the study of the immigrants.

OCCASION OF REPORT. I received a telegram signed General [Marlborough] Churchill on August 15, 1918, requesting me to come to Washington to place at the disposal of the Military Intelligence Bureau any information in my possession on conditions among the Poles in this country. At various conferences held on August 17 and some days of the ensuing week I met Captains Uterhart and Dalrymple and Lieutenant Horgan. During these conferences it appeared that the information which I had to report covered a variety of the branches of service and also a number of matters that fell primarily within the province of the State Department. Accordingly, Major Hunt asked me to make out a written report of the whole situation.

Two preliminary reports covering more urgent phases of the matter have been handed in, one on August 19, regarding the Detroit Convention, and another on August 23, on publicity for Polish affairs. It will be found necessary to traverse some of that material in the following report.

In preparing this report it has been necessary to choose between such condensation as might fail to bring out the significance of the material and restatement of historical and other facts which are already familiar as matter of record. In view of the diversity and complexity of interests concerned, it has seemed better to err, if at all, in the direction of undue explanation.

EDUCATION FOR DEMOCRACY. [n.p., n.d.] 2 pp.

Address delivered at the Detroit, Michigan, Open Forum, 3 Feb. 1918.

THE MOTIVATION OF HOBBES'S POLITICAL PHILOSOPHY. In *Studies in the History of Ideas*, by the Department of Philosophy of Columbia University, I (New York: Columbia University Press, 1918), 88–115.

Reviewed in *Dial*, 19 Sept. 1918, LXV, 218–219; *Philosophical Review*, Mar. 1919, XXVIII, 213–216 (Joseph Alexander Leighton); *Revue de métaphysique et de morale*, XXIX (Sup. to Jan.-Mar. 1922, pp. 12–13).

VOCATIONAL EDUCATION IN THE LIGHT OF THE WORLD WAR. (Vocational Education Association of the Middle West, *Bulletin No. 4*, Jan. 1918.) [Chicago, 1918.] 10 pp.

Read at their convention in Chicago, 25 Jan. 1918.

INTRODUCTORY WORD. *In* Frederick Matthias Alexander, *Man's Supreme Inheritance* (New York: E. P. Dutton & Co. [°1918]), xiii–xvii.

See Dewey's REPLY TO A REVIEWER (*New Republic*, 11 May 1918), below.

CONCERNING ALLEGED IMMEDIATE KNOWLEDGE OF MIND. *Journal of Philosophy*, 17 Jan. 1918, XV, 29–35.

AMERICA IN THE WORLD. *Nation*, 14 Mar. 1918, CVI, 287.

From an address delivered at Smith College, 22 Feb. 1918.

Reprinted in *Characters and Events* (1929), II, 642–644, with the title AMERICA AND THE WORLD.

MORALS AND THE CONDUCT OF STATESMEN. *New Republic*, 23 Mar. 1918, XIV, 232–234.

Reply to Salmon Oliver Levinson, THE LEGAL STATUS OF WAR, *New Republic*, 9 Mar. 1918, XIV, 171–173.

See Walter Lippmann, "THE OUTLAWRY OF WAR," *Atlantic Monthly*, Aug. 1923, CXXXII, 245–253, and Dewey's four articles on this subject: POLITICAL COMBINATION OR LEGAL COOPERATION? (*New Republic*, 21 Mar. 1923); IF WAR WERE OUTLAWED (*ib.*, 25 Apr. 1923); WHAT OUTLAWRY OF WAR IS NOT (*ib.*, 3 Oct. 1923); WAR AND A CODE OF LAW (*ib.*, 24 Oct. 1923), below.

Reprinted in *Characters and Events* (1929), II, 645–649, and in *Intelligence in the Modern World* (1939), 508–511, with the title PRECONDITIONS OF THE SECURITY OF NATIONS.

INTERNAL SOCIAL REORGANIZATION AFTER THE WAR. *Journal of Race Development*, Apr. 1918, VIII, 385–400.

Reprinted in *Characters and Events* (1929), II, 745–759, with the title ELEMENTS OF SOCIAL REORGANIZATION.

See THE ECONOMIC BASIS OF THE NEW SOCIETY in *Intelligence and the Modern World* (1939), 416–433.

A NEW SOCIAL SCIENCE. *New Republic*, 6 Apr. 1918, XIV, 292–294.

Reprinted in *Characters and Events* (1929), II, 733–738, with the title THE NEW SOCIAL SCIENCE.

EDUCATION AND SOCIAL DIRECTION. *Dial*, 11 Apr. 1918, LXIV, 333–335.

Reprinted in *Education Today* (1940), 139–143.

POLITICAL SCIENCE AS A RECLUSE. *New Republic*, 27 Apr. 1918, XIV, 383–384.

Reprinted in *Characters and Events* (1929), II, 728–732.

THE OBJECTS OF VALUATION. *Journal of Philosophy*, 9 May 1918, XV, 253–258.

Reply to Ralph Barton Perry, DEWEY AND URBAN ON VALUE JUDGMENTS, *ib.*, 29 Mar. 1917, XIV, 169–181, and Wendell T Bush,

VALUE AND CAUSALITY, *ib.*, 14 Feb. 1918, XV, 85–96. See Dewey, THE LOGIC OF JUDGMENTS OF PRACTICE (*ib.*, 16 and 30 Sept. 1915), above.

REPLY TO A REVIEWER. Letter in *New Republic*, 11 May 1918, XV, 55.

Reply to Randolph Bourne's review of Frederick Matthias Alexander, *Man's Supreme Inheritance*, *New Republic*, 4 May 1918, XV, 28–29. Rejoinder by Bourne, OTHER MESSIAHS, letter in *ib.*, 25 May, 1918, XV, 117.

WHAT ARE WE FIGHTING FOR? *Independent*, 22 June 1918, XCIV, 474, 480–483.

On America's aims and ideals in the war.

Reprinted in *Characters and Events* (1929), II, 551–560. with the title THE SOCIAL POSSIBILITIES OF WAR.

AUTOCRACY UNDER COVER. *New Republic*, 24 Aug. 1918, XVI, 103–106.

Nationalism in Poland.

THE APPROACH TO A LEAGUE OF NATIONS. *Dial*, 2 Nov. 1918, LXV, 341–342.

Reprinted in *Characters and Events* (1929), II, 602–605.

CREATIVE INDUSTRY. *New Republic*, 2 Nov. 1918, XVII, 20–23.

Review of Helen Marot, *Creative Impulse in Industry*.

THE CULT OF IRRATIONALITY. *New Republic*, 9 Nov. 1918, XVII, 34–35.

Reprinted in *Characters and Events* (1929), II, 587–591.

THE LEAGUE OF NATIONS AND THE NEW DIPLOMACY. *Dial*, 16 Nov. 1918, LXV, 401–403.

Reprinted in *Characters and Events* (1929), II, 606–609.

THE FOURTEEN POINTS AND THE LEAGUE OF NATIONS. *Dial*, 30 Nov. 1918, LXV, 463–464.

THE POST-WAR MIND. *New Republic*, 7 Dec. 1918, XVII, 157–159.

Reprinted in *Characters and Events* (1929), II, 596–601.

A LEAGUE OF NATIONS AND ECONOMIC FREEDOM. *Dial*, 14 Dec. 1918, LXV, 537–539.

Reprinted in *Characters and Events* (1929), II, 610–614.

THE NEW PATERNALISM. *New Republic*, 21 Dec. 1918, XVII, 216–217.

Intellectual paternalism stimulated by the war.

Reprinted in *Characters and Events* (1929), II, 517–521, with the title PROPAGANDA.

1919

THE PSYCHOLOGY OF DRAWING—IMAGINATION AND EXPRESSION —CULTURE AND INDUSTRY IN EDUCATION. (Teachers College Bulletin, Ser. 10, No. 10, 1 Mar. 1919.) New York: Teachers College, Columbia University, 1919. 18 pp.

Reprints of three articles, collected by Professor Patty Smith Hill. THE PSYCHOLOGY OF DRAWING, an address given before the Western Drawing Teachers Association at Indianapolis, was originally published in the primary drawing books of the Chicago public schools in 1897–1898.

PHILOSOPHY AND DEMOCRACY. *University [of California] Chronicle*, Jan. 1919, XXI, 39–54.

Address before the Philosophical Union of the University of California, 29 Nov. 1918.

Reprinted in *Characters and Events* (1929), II, 841–855.

THEODORE ROOSEVELT. *Dial*, 8 Feb. 1919, LXVI, 115–117.

Reprinted in *Characters and Events* (1929), I, 87–94.

REVIEW of Robert Mark Wenley, *Life and Work of George Sylvester Morris. Philosophical Review*, Mar. 1919, XXVIII, 212–213.

JAPAN AND AMERICA. *Dial*, 17 May 1919, LXVI, 501–503.

DEWEY'S LECTURES IN JAPAN. *Journal of Philosophy*, 19 June 1919, XVI, 357–364.

Outlines of eight lectures on "Problems of Philosophic Reconstruction," delivered at the Imperial University at Tokyo in Feb. and Mar. 1919. These lectures were published as *Reconstruction in Philosophy* (1920), *q.v.*

ON TWO SIDES OF THE EASTERN SEA. *New Republic*, 16 July 1919, XIX, 346–348.

Dated, Nanking, May 28.

Reprinted in *China, Japan and the U.S.A.* (1921), 3–9, and in *Characters and Events* (1929), I, 170–176.

THE STUDENT REVOLT IN CHINA. *New Republic*, 6 Aug. 1919, XX, 16–18.

Dated, Peking, June 24.

THE INTERNATIONAL DUEL IN CHINA. *New Republic*, 27 Aug. 1919, XX, 110–112.

Dated, Peking, July 8.

MILITARISM IN CHINA. *New Republic*, 10 Sept. 1919, XX, 167–169.

Dated, Peking, July 28.

LIBERALISM IN JAPAN. I. The Intellectual Preparation (*Dial*, 4 Oct. 1919, LXVII, 283–285); II. The Economic Factor (*ib.*, 18 Oct. 1919, 333–337); III. The Chief Foe (*ib.*, 1 Nov. 1919, 369–371).

Reprinted in *Characters and Events* (1929), I, 149–169.

THE DISCREDITING OF IDEALISM. *New Republic*, 8 Oct. 1919, XX, 285–287.

Reprinted in *Characters and Events* (1929), II, 629–635, with the title FORCE AND IDEALS.

TRANSFORMING THE MIND OF CHINA. *Asia*, Nov. 1919, XIX, 1103–1108.

Reprinted in *Characters and Events* (1929), I, 285–295.

CHINESE NATIONAL SENTIMENT. *Asia*, Dec. 1919, XIX, 1237–1242.

Reprinted in *Characters and Events* (1929), I, 222–236, with the title THE GROWTH OF CHINESE NATIONAL SENTIMENT.

THE AMERICAN OPPORTUNITY IN CHINA. *New Republic*, 3 Dec. 1919, XXI, 14–17.

Dated, Peking, Sept. 12.

Reprinted in *Characters and Events* (1929), I, 296–303, with the title AMERICA AND CHINA.

OUR SHARE IN DRUGGING CHINA. *New Republic*, 24 Dec. 1919, XXI, 114–117.

Dated, Peking, Oct. 6.

1920

RECONSTRUCTION IN PHILOSOPHY. New York: Henry Holt and Company, 1920. vii, 224 pp.

Published in London by the University of London Press, 1921.

Enlarged edition, 1948, *q.v.*
Lectures delivered at the Imperial University of Japan, in Tokyo, during Feb. and Mar. 1919. See DEWEY's LECTURES IN JAPAN (*Journal of Philosophy*, 19 June 1919), above.

Contents. Changing Conceptions of Philosophy—Some Historical Factors in Philosophical Reconstruction—The Scientific Factor in Reconstruction of Philosophy—Changed Conceptions of Experience and Reason—Changed Conceptions of the Ideal and the Real—The Significance of Logical Reconstruction—Reconstruction in Moral Conceptions—Reconstruction as Affecting Social Philosophy.

Translations. Arabic by Amīn Mursī Qindīl (Cairo, 1959); Bohemian by Josef Schützner (Praha, 1929); Chinese by Ch'ung-ch'ing Hsü (1933); Italian, with Introduction by Guido de Ruggiero (Bari, 1931); Japanese; Persian by S. A. Saeedi (Tehran), another translation by Mahmoud Fakhr-e Dāiy (Tehran [195—]); Portuguese by Eugenio Marcondes Rocha (São Paulo [1957]); Spanish (Madrid, 1930), another translation by Amanda L. Ríos (Buenos Aires, 1955, 1958); Urdu.

Reviewed in *Dial*, Apr. 1921, LXX, 454–457 (Ralph Barton Perry); *Freeman*, 20 Apr. 1921, III, 140–141 (Horace Meyer Kallen); *Grinnell Review*, Mar. 1921, XVI, 378 (Clara Millerd Smertenko); *Nation*, 8 Dec. 1920, CXI, 658–660 (Boyd Henry Bode); *New York Evening Post Literary Review*, 13 Nov. 1920 (Arthur S. McDowall); *Philosophical Review*, Sept. 1921, XXX, 519–523 (George Plimpton Adams); *Revue de métaphysique et de morale*, XXX (Sup. to Jan.-Mar. 1923, pp. 10–11); *Springfield Republican*, 20 Jan. 1921.

See Wilmon Henry Sheldon, PROFESSOR DEWEY, THE PROTAGONIST OF DEMOCRACY, *Journal of Philosophy*, 9 June 1921, XVIII, 309–320; and Victor S. Yarros, WHAT ARE THE PROBLEMS OF PHILOSOPHY?—TAKING STOCK, *Open Court*, Oct. 1923, XXXVII, 596–604.

LETTERS FROM CHINA AND JAPAN, by John Dewey and Alice Chipman Dewey. Edited by Evelyn Dewey. New York: E. P. Dutton Company [ᶜ1920]. vi, 311 pp.

Published in London by J. M. Dent & Sons, Ltd. [1920].

Reviewed in *Bookman*, Aug. 1920, LI, 631 (Raymond Melbourne Weaver); *Freeman*, 14 July 1920, I, 429–430; *Nation*, 24 July 1920, CXI, 103–104 (Irita Van Doren); *New York Evening Post Literary Review*, 5 June 1920 (John William Robertson Scott); *New York Times*, 30 May 1920 (Maurice Francis Egan); *Outlook*, 9 June 1920, CXXV, 281.

[DEWEY's SPEECHES IN FUKIEN. Fukien: Board of Education, 1920.] 126 pp.
In Chinese.

[FIVE LECTURES OF DEWEY. Peking: Morning Post, 1920.]
In Chinese.

THE SEQUEL OF THE STUDENT REVOLT. *New Republic*, 25 Feb. 1920, XXI, 380–382.
The Sino-Japanese fracas in Foochow.

SHANTUNG, AS SEEN FROM WITHIN. *New Republic*, 3 Mar. 1920, XXII, 12–17.
Dated, Peking, Jan. 5.
Reprinted in *China, Japan and the U.S.A.* (1921), 9–21.

OUR NATIONAL DILEMMA. *New Republic*, 24 Mar. 1920, XXII, 117–118.
Reprinted in *Characters and Events* (1929), II, 615–619.

THE NEW LEAVEN IN CHINESE POLITICS. *Asia*, Apr. 1920, XX, 267–272.
Reprinted in *Characters and Events* (1929), I, 244–254, with the title JUSTICE AND LAW IN CHINA.

WHAT HOLDS CHINA BACK. *Asia*, May 1920, XX, 373–377.
Reprinted in *Characters and Events* (1929), I, 211–221, with the title CHINESE SOCIAL HABITS.

FREEDOM OF THOUGHT AND WORK. *New Republic*, 5 May 1920, XXII, 316–317.
Reprinted in *Characters and Events* (1929), II, 522–525.

AMERICANISM AND LOCALISM. *Dial*, June 1920, LXVIII, 684–688.
Reprinted in *Characters and Events* (1929), II, 537–541.

CHINA'S NIGHTMARE. *New Republic*, 30 June 1920, XXIII, 145–147.
Reprinted in *Characters and Events* (1929), I, 193–198.

HOW REACTION HELPS. *New Republic*, 1 Sept. 1920, XXIV, 21–22.
Reprinted in *Characters and Events* (1929), II, 815–819.

A POLITICAL UPHEAVAL IN CHINA. *New Republic*, 6 Oct. 1920, XXIV, 142–144.
Reprinted in *Millard's Review of the Far East*, 4 Dec. 1920, XV, 9–10, and in *China, Japan and the U.S.A.* (1921), 27–32.

INDUSTRIAL CHINA. *New Republic*, 8 Dec. 1920, XXV, 39–41.
Reprinted in *Impressions of Soviet Russia* (1929), 237–251.

1921

AIMS AND IDEALS OF EDUCATION. I. [Nature of Aims and Ideals]; II. The Relation of Aims and Ideals to Existent Facts; III. Growth as an Aim and Ideal. In *Encyclopedia and Dictionary of Education*, edited by Foster Watson, Vol. I (London, 1921), 32–34.

> Reprinted in *Ideals, Aims and Methods of Education*, by John Dewey [and others] (London, 1922), 1–9.

CHINA, JAPAN AND THE U.S.A. Present-Day Conditions in the Far East and Their Bearing on the Washington Conference. (New Republic Pamphlet No. 1.) New York: Republic Publishing Co., Inc., 1921. 64 pp.

> *Contents.* On Two Sides of the Eastern Sea—Shantung as Seen from Within—Hinterlands in China—A Political Upheaval in China—Divided China—Federalism in China—A Parting of the Ways for America.
>
> Reprinted from the *New Republic.*

THE ALEXANDER-DEWEY ARITHMETIC, by Georgia Alexander. Edited by John Dewey. 3 vols. New York: Longmans, Green and Co., 1921.

> VOL. I, Elementary Book—VOL. II, Intermediate Book—VOL. III, Advanced Book.

FIRST INTRODUCTION. *In* Scudder Klyce, *Universe;* with three Introductions, by David Starr Jordan, John Dewey, and Morris Llewellyn Cooke (Winchester, Mass.: S. Klyce, 1921), iii–v.

RACIAL PREJUDICE AND FRICTION. *Chinese Social and Political Science Review*, VI [1921], 1–17.

> Paper read before the Chinese Social and Political Science Association in Peking.

IS CHINA A NATION? *New Republic*, 12 Jan. 1921, XXV, 187–190.

> Reprinted in *Impressions of Soviet Russia* (1929), 272–250; and in *Characters and Events* (1929), I, 237–243, with the title CONDITIONS FOR CHINA'S NATIONHOOD.

THE SIBERIAN REPUBLIC. *New Republic*, 19 Jan. 1921, XXV, 220–223.

> Reprinted in *Characters and Events* (1929), I, 185–192.

SOCIAL ABSOLUTISM. *New Republic*, 9 Feb. 1921, XXV, 315–318.

Reprinted in *Characters and Events* (1929), II, 721–727.

THE FAR EASTERN DEADLOCK. *New Republic*, 16 Mar. 1921, XXVI, 71–74.

THE CONSORTIUM IN CHINA. *New Republic*, 13 Apr. 1921, XXVI, 178–180.

OLD CHINA AND NEW. *Asia*, May 1921, XXI, 445–450, 454, 456.

Reprinted in *Characters and Events* (1929), I, 255–269, with the title YOUNG CHINA AND OLD.

NEW CULTURE IN CHINA. *Asia*, July 1921, XXI, 581–586, 642.

Reprinted in *Characters and Events* (1929), I, 270–284.

HINTERLANDS IN CHINA. *New Republic*, 6 July 1921, XXVII, 162–165.

Dated, Peking, May 24.

Reply by Dora Winifred Black, AMERICAN POLICY IN CHINA, *ib.*, 2 Nov. 1921, XXVIII, 297, and rejoinder by Dewey, *ib.*

Reprinted in *China, Japan and the U.S.A.* (1921), 21–27.

DIVIDED CHINA. I. (*New Republic*, 20 July 1921, XXVII, 212–215); II. (*Ib.*, 27 July 1921, 235–237).

Reprinted in *China, Japan and the U.S.A.* (1921), 33–44.

SHANTUNG AGAIN. *New Republic*, 28 Sept. 1921, XXVIII, 123–126.

TENTH ANNIVERSARY OF THE REPUBLIC OF CHINA: A MESSAGE. *China Review*, Oct. 1921, I, 171.

FEDERALISM IN CHINA. *New Republic*, 12 Oct. 1921, XXVIII, 176–178.

Reprinted in *China, Japan and the U.S.A.* (1921), 44–50.

CHINA AND DISARMAMENT. *Chinese Students' Monthly*, Nov. 1921, XVII, 16–17.

THE PARTING OF THE WAYS FOR AMERICA. I. (*New Republic*, 2 Nov. 1921, XXVIII, 283–286); II. (*Ib.*, 9 Nov. 1921, 315–317).

Reprinted in *China, Japan and the U.S.A.* (1921), 51–64.

THE ISSUES AT WASHINGTON. I. Causes of International Friction (*Baltimore Sun*, 14 Nov. 1921); II. The Anglo-Japanese Alliance and the United States (*ib.*, 15 Nov. 1921); III. China's

Interest (*ib.*, 16 Nov. 1921); IV. Suggested Measures (*ib.*, 17 Nov. 1921).

The Washington Conference on the Limitation of Armaments, Nov. 1921.

PUBLIC OPINION IN JAPAN. *New Republic*, 16 Nov. 1921, XXVIII (Sup. to No. 363, 15–18).

Reprinted in *Characters and Events* (1929), I, 177–184, with the title JAPAN REVISITED: TWO YEARS LATER.

SHREWD TACTICS ARE SHOWN IN CHINESE PLEA. *Baltimore Sun*, 18 Nov. 1921.

FOUR PRINCIPLES FOR CHINA REGARDED AS BUT FRAMEWORK. *Baltimore Sun*, 23 Nov. 1921.

CLASSICISM AS AN EVANGEL. *Journal of Philosophy*, 24 Nov. 1921, XVIII, 664–666.

UNDERGROUND BURROWS MUST BE DUG OPEN. Success or Failure of U.S. Policies Depends on Adequate Demand for Publicity. *Baltimore Sun*, 29 Nov. 1921.

ANGLES OF SHANTUNG QUESTION. *Baltimore Sun*, 5 Dec. 1921.

THE CONFERENCE AND A HAPPY ENDING. *New Republic*, 7 Dec. 1921, XXIX, 37–39.

CHINESE RESIGNATION SEEMS UNSPORTSMANLIKE TO AMERICANS BUT A MATTER OF HABIT WITH THEM. *Baltimore Sun*, 9 Dec. 1921.

THREE RESULTS OF TREATY. *Baltimore Sun*, 11 Dec. 1921.

A FEW SECOND THOUGHTS ON FOUR-POWER PACT. *Baltimore Sun*, 17 Dec. 1921.

EDUCATION BY HENRY ADAMS. *New Republic*, 21 Dec. 1921, XXIX, 102–103.

On the appropriateness of some passages in *The Education of Henry Adams* for the Washington Conference.

1922

HUMAN NATURE AND CONDUCT. An Introduction to Social Psychology. New York: Henry Holt and Company, 1922. vii, 336 pp.

Published in London by G. Allen & Unwin, 1922.

Three lectures delivered in the spring of 1918 on the Raymond F. West Memorial Foundation at Leland Stanford, Jr., University, rewritten and considerably expanded, with an introduction and conclusion added.

Reprinted with a new introduction in the Modern Library (New York, 1930).

See Armed Forces Edition, 1944.

Contents. Introduction. Part I, The Place of Habit in Conduct: Habits as Social Functions—Habits and Will—Character and Conduct— Custom and Habit—Custom and Morality—Habit and Social Psychology. Part II, The Place of Impulse in Conduct: Impulses and Change of Habits—Plasticity of Impulse—Changing Human Nature—Impulse and Conflict of Habits—Classification of Instincts— No Separate Instincts—Impulse and Thought. Part III, The Place of Intelligence in Conduct: Habit and Intelligence—The Psychology of Thinking—The Nature of Deliberation—Deliberation and Calculation—The Uniqueness of Good—The Nature of Aims—The Nature of Principles—Desire and Intelligence—The Present and Future. Part IV, Conclusion: The Good of Activity—Morals Are Human— What Is Freedom?—Morality Is Social.

Reviewed in *American Review*, May-June 1923, I, 360–364 (Morris Raphael Cohen); *Boston Transcript*, 18 Mar. 1922; *Dial*, May 1922, LXXII, 514–516 (James Harvey Robinson); *International Journal of Ethics*, Oct. 1922, XXXIII, 108–109 (C. F. T.); *Journal of Philosophy*, 17 Aug. 1922, XIX, 469–475 (Clarence Edwin Ayres); *London Times Literary Supplement*, 15 June 1922; *Mind*, Jan. 1923, N.S. XXXII, 79–86 (G. C. Field); *New York Evening Post Literary Review*, 3 June 1922 (Abraham Aaron Roback); *Nation*, 5 July 1922, CXV, 20–21 (Matthew Thompson McClure); *New Republic*, 24 May 1922, XXX, 379–382 (Horace Meyer Kallen); *New York Times*, 8 Oct. 1922 (Austin Hay); *Philosophical Review*, Mar. 1923, XXXII, 182–197 (James Seth); *Quarterly Journal of the University of North Dakota*, Nov. 1924, XV, 77–80 (John Morris Gillette); *Rivista di Filosofia*, Jan. 1960, LI, 108–109 (P.R.); *Survey*, 15 Apr. 1922, XLVIII, 81 (J[oseph] K[inmont] H[art]); *Yale Review*, Jan. 1923, N.S. XII, 407–410 (Harry Todd Costello).

Translations. German by Paul Sakmann (Stuttgart, 1931); Italian by Giulio Preti and Aldo Visalberghi, with introductory note by Lamberto Borghi (Firenze, 1958); Japanese by Takashi Tômiya (Tokyo, 1951); Persian by M. Hamedani (Tehran); Portuguese by Eugénio Marcondes Rocha and Jacob Rualdi (Bauru, 1956); Spanish; Swedish by Alf Ahlberg (Stockholm, 1936).

See George Plimpton Adams, ACTIVITY AND OBJECTS in Dewey's *Human Nature and Conduct*, *Journal of Philosophy*, 25 Oct. 1923, XX, 596–603; William McDougall, CAN SOCIOLOGY AND SOCIAL

PSYCHOLOGY DISPENSE WITH INSTINCTS? *American Journal of Sociology*, May 1924, XXIX, 657–670; discussion by L. L. Bernard, *ib.*, 670–673; and Victor S. Yarros, SOCIAL IDEALS AND HUMAN NATURE, *Open Court*, Oct. 1922, XXXVI, 586–593.

Excerpts in Willard Thorp and Margaret Farrand Thorp, eds., *Modern Writing* (New York: American Book Company [1944]), 323–331; Saxe Commins and Robert Newton Linscott, eds., *Man and Man: The Social Philosophers*, Vol. II of *The World's Great Thinkers*, excerpt entitled MORALS AND CONDUCT (New York: Random House, 1947), 449–485; George Mayberry, ed., *A Little Treasury of American Prose: The Major Writers from Colonial Times to the Present Day*, excerpt entitled INTRODUCTION TO SOCIAL PSYCHOLOGY (New York: Charles Scribner's Sons, 1949), 353–358.

IDEALS, AIMS, AND METHODS IN EDUCATION. By John Dewey [and others]. (The New Educator's Library.) London: Sir Isaac Pitman & Sons, Ltd., 1922. 110 pp.

Section I, AIMS AND IDEALS OF EDUCATION, 1–9, by Dewey.

SYLLABUS FOR PHILOSOPHY 191–192, Types of Philosophic Thought, Columbia University, 1922–1923. [New York, 1922?] 67 multigraphed leaves.

Copies in the Columbiana collection, Columbia University Library.

AS THE CHINESE THINK. *Asia*, Jan. 1922, XXII, 7–10, 78–79.

Reprinted in *Characters and Events* (1929), I, 199–210, with the title THE CHINESE PHILOSOPHY OF LIFE.

AN ANALYSIS OF REFLECTIVE THOUGHT. *Journal of Philosophy*, 19 Jan. 1922, XIX, 29–38.

AMERICA AND CHINESE EDUCATION. *New Republic*, 1 Mar. 1922, XXX, 15–17.

Reprinted in *Characters and Events* (1929), I, 303–309, with the title AMERICA AND CHINA.

PRAGMATIC AMERICA. *New Republic*, 12 Apr. 1922, XXX, 185–187.

Reprinted in *Characters and Events* (1929), II, 542–547, and in Gail Kennedy, ed., *Pragmatism and American Culture* (Boston: D. C. Heath & Co., 1950), 57–60.

REVIEW of Walter Lippmann, *Public Opinion*. *New Republic*, 3 May 1922, XXX, 286–288.

THE AMERICAN INTELLECTUAL FRONTIER. *New Republic*, 10 May 1922, XXX, 303–305.

Reprinted in *Characters and Events* (1929), II, 447–452.

MIND IN THE MAKING. Letter in *New Republic*, 7 June 1922, XXXI, 48.

> Regarding LIBERALISM AND IRRATIONALISM, editorial on James Harvey Robinson, *The Mind in the Making, ib.*, 17 May 1922, XXX, 333–334.
>
> Dewey's letter is accompanied by editorial comment.

REALISM WITHOUT MONISM OR DUALISM. I. Knowledge Involving the Past (*Journal of Philosophy*, 8 June 1922, XIX, 309–317); II. (*Ib.*, 22 June 1922, 351–361).

> Reply to Arthur Oncken Lovejoy, PRAGMATISM *vs.* THE PRAGMATIST, in *Essays in Critical Realism* (1920), 35–81.
>
> Replies by Lovejoy, TIME, MEANING AND TRANSCENDENCE: I. THE ALLEGED FUTURITY OF YESTERDAY (*Journal of Philosophy*, 14 Sept. 1922, XIX, 505–515); II. PROFESSOR DEWEY'S *Tertium Quid* (*ib.*, 28 Sept. 1922, XIX, 533–541); and Sterling Power Lamprecht, A NOTE ON PROFESSOR DEWEY'S THEORY OF KNOWLEDGE, *ib.*, 30 Aug. 1923, XX, 488–494.
>
> See Dewey, SOME COMMENTS ON PHILOSOPHICAL DISCUSSION (*ib.*, 10 Apr. 1924), below.

VALUATION AND EXPERIMENTAL KNOWLEDGE. *Philosophical Review*, July 1922, XXXI, 325–351.

> Reply by David Wight Prall, IN DEFENSE OF A *Worthless* THEORY OF VALUE, *Journal of Philosophy*, 1 Mar. 1923, XX, 128–137.
>
> See Dewey, VALUES, LIKING, AND THOUGHT (*ib.*, 8 Nov. 1923), below.

NOTABLES AND COMMON PEOPLE. *New Republic*, 2 Aug. 1922, XXXI, 285–286.

> Review of Charles Hitchcock Sherrill, *Prime Ministers and Presidents*, and Frazier Hunt, *The Rising Temper of the East.*

EVENTS AND MEANINGS. *New Republic*, 30 Aug. 1922, XXXII, 9–10.

> Reprinted in *Characters and Events* (1929), I, 125–129.

EDUCATION AS A RELIGION. *New Republic*, 13 Sept. 1922, XXXII, 63–65.

> Editorial comment in *New York Times*, 13 Sept. 1922.
>
> Reprinted in *Education Today* (1940), 144–149.

EDUCATION AS ENGINEERING. *New Republic*, 20 Sept. 1922, XXXII, 89–91.

> Editorial comment in *New York Times*, 22 Sept. 1922.
>
> Reprinted in *Education Today* (1940), 150–156.

LE DÉVELOPPEMENT DU PRAGMATISME AMÉRICAIN. *Revue de métaphysique et de morale*, Oct. 1922, XXIX, 411-430.

Re-translated into English and published as THE DEVELOPMENT OF AMERICAN PRAGMATISM in *Studies in the History of Ideas*, Vol. II (1925), Supplement, 353-377, *q.v.*

EDUCATION AS POLITICS. *New Republic*, 4 Oct. 1922, XXXII, 139-141.

Editorial comment in *New York Times*, 3 Oct. 1922.

Reprinted in *Characters and Events* (1929), II, 776-781, and in *Education Today* (1940), 157-163.

KNOWLEDGE AND SPEECH REACTION. *Journal of Philosophy*, 12 Oct. 1922, XIX, 561-570.

INDUSTRY AND MOTIVES. *World Tomorrow*, Dec. 1922, V, 357-358.

Reprinted in *Characters and Events* (1929), II, 739-744.

MEDIOCRITY AND INDIVIDUALITY. *New Republic*, 6 Dec. 1922, XXXIII, 35-37.

Reprinted in *Characters and Events* (1929), II, 479-485, and in *Education Today* (1940), 164-170.

INDIVIDUALITY, EQUALITY AND SUPERIORITY. *New Republic*, 13 Dec. 1922, XXXIII, 61-63.

Reprinted in *Characters and Events* (1929), II, 486-492, and in *Education Today* (1940), 171-177.

1923

CULTURE AND PROFESSIONALISM IN EDUCATION. [New York, 1923.] 7 pp.

Address delivered at the opening exercises of Columbia University, 26 Sept. 1923.

Published also in *Fortnightly Bulletin of the Institute of Arts and Sciences, Columbia University*, 9 Nov. 1923, XI, iii, [iii-vi]; in *Journal of the National Education Association*, Dec. 1923, XII, 397-398; in *School and Society*, 13 Oct. 1923, XVIII, 421-424; and in Dewey's *Education Today* (1940), 178-183.

SYLLABUS FOR PHILOSOPHY 131-132, Social Institutions and the Study of Morals, Columbia University, 1923-[1924]. [New York, 1923?]. 57 multigraphed leaves.

Copies in the Columbiana collection, Columbia University Library.

FUTURE TRENDS IN THE DEVELOPMENT OF SOCIAL PROGRAMS THROUGH THE SCHOOLS. The School as a Means of Developing a Social Consciousness and Social Ideals in Children. In *Proceedings of the National Conference of Social Work, Washington, May 16–23, 1923* (Chicago [1923]), 449–453.

Reprinted in *Journal of Social Forces*, Sept. 1923, I, 513–517.

INTRODUCTION. In Frederick Matthias Alexander, *Constructive Conscious Control of the Individual* (New York: E. P. Dutton & Co. [ᶜ1923]), xxi–xxxiii.

SOCIAL PURPOSES IN EDUCATION. *General Science Quarterly*, Jan. 1923, VII, 79–91.

Read at the State Conference of Normal School Instructors at Bridgewater, Mass., in Sept. 1922.

A SICK WORLD. *New Republic*, 24 Jan. 1923, XXXIII, 217–218.

Reprinted in *Characters and Events* (1929), II, 760–764.

CHINA AND THE WEST. *Dial*, Feb. 1923, LXXIV, 193–196.

Review of Bertrand Russell, *The Problems of China*.

INDIVIDUALITY IN EDUCATION. *General Science Quarterly*, Mar. 1923, VII, 157–166.

Read at the State Conference of Normal School Instructors at Bridgewater, Mass., 5 Sept. 1922.

SHALL WE JOIN THE LEAGUE? *New Republic*, 7 Mar. 1923, XXXIV, 36–37.

Reply by Arthur Oncken Lovejoy, SHALL WE JOIN THE LEAGUE OF NATIONS? letter in *ib.*, 28 Mar. 1923, XXXIV, 138–139, and reply by Dewey, *ib.*, 139–140.

Reprinted in *Characters and Events* (1929), II, 620–624, with Dewey's reply, 625–628; reprinted in part in *Intelligence in the Modern World* (1939), 499–503, with the title ON INTERNATIONAL COÖPERATION.

ETHICS AND INTERNATIONAL RELATIONS. *Foreign Affairs*, 15 Mar. 1923, I, 85–95.

Reprinted in *Characters and Events* (1929), II, 804–814.

"WHAT IS A SCHOOL FOR?" *New York Times*, 18 Mar. 1923.

Answer to this question; part of a symposium.

POLITICAL COMBINATION OR LEGAL COÖPERATION? *New Republic*, 21 Mar. 1923, XXXIV, 89–91.

Reprinted in *Characters and Events* (1929), II, 666–671, with the title WHY NOT OUTLAW WAR?

IN BEHALF OF CULTURE. Letter to the Editors. *Freeman*, 21 Mar. 1923, VII, 38–39.

An appeal for funds for the Emergency Society for German Science and Art; signed also by John Grier Hibben and William Allan Neilson.

TRADITION, METAPHYSICS AND MORALS. *Journal of Philosophy*, 29 Mar. 1923, XX, 187–192.

Reply to Daniel Sommer Robinson, THE CHIEF TYPES OF MOTIVATION TO PHILOSOPHIC REFLECTION, *ib.*, 18 Jan. 1923, XX, 29–41.

IF WAR WERE OUTLAWED. *New Republic*, 25 Apr. 1923, XXXIV, 234–235.

Reprinted in *Characters and Events* (1929), II, 672–676.

REVIEW of George Santayana, *Scepticism and Animal Faith. New Republic*, 8 Aug. 1923, XXXV, 294–296.

WHAT OUTLAWRY OF WAR IS NOT. *New Republic*, 3 Oct. 1923, XXXVI, 149–152.

This article and WAR AND A CODE OF LAW (*ib.*, 24 Oct. 1923) constitute a reply to Walter Lippmann, THE OUTLAWRY OF WAR, *Atlantic Monthly*, Aug. 1923, CXXXII, 245–253. The articles were reprinted in pamphlet form with the title *Outlawry of War: What It Is and Is Not* (Chicago: American Committee for the Outlawry of War [1923]). 16 pp.

See Robert Lee Hale, LAW AND WAR, *American Bar Association Journal*, July 1924, X, 503–504.

Extract in *Congressional Digest*, Mar. 1928, VII, 94.

Reprinted in *Characters and Events* (1929), II, 677–684.

SHALL THE UNITED STATES JOIN THE WORLD COURT? *Christian Century*, 18 Oct. 1923, XL, 1329–1334.

An address in debate with Manley Ottmer Hudson under the auspices of the Unitarian Laymen's League, Unity House, Boston, 21 May 1923. Reported in *Christian Register*, 31 May 1923, CII, 511–512.

Reprinted in *Characters and Events* (1929), II, 650–655, with the title WHICH WORLD COURT SHALL WE JOIN? and in *Intelligence in the Modern World* (1939), 511–525, with the title INTERNATIONAL LAW AND THE WAR-SYSTEM.

WAR AND A CODE OF LAW. *New Republic*, 24 Oct. 1923, XXXVI, 224–226.

See note under WHAT OUTLAWRY OF WAR IS NOT, above.

Reprinted in *Characters and Events* (1929), II, 685–690.

VALUES, LIKING, AND THOUGHT. *Journal of Philosophy*, 8 Nov. 1923, XX, 617–622.

Reply to David Wight Prall, IN DEFENSE OF A *Worthless* THEORY OF VALUE, *ib.*, 1 Mar. 1923, XX, 128–137. See Dewey, VALUATION AND EXPERIMENTAL KNOWLEDGE (*Philosophical Review*, July 1922), above.

Rejoinder by Prall, VALUES AND THOUGHT-PROCESS, *Journal of Philosophy*, 28 Feb. 1924, XXI, 117–125, and reply by Dewey, THE MEANING OF VALUE (*ib.*, 26 Feb. 1925), below.

1924

REPORT AND RECOMMENDATION UPON TURKISH EDUCATION. Submitted by John Dewey.

Typewritten manuscript, 34 pages, undated, in Columbiana, Columbia University. No printed version in English has been found. The Library of Congress has a copy in Turkish, *Türkiye Maarifi Hakkinda Rapor* [Istanbul, Devlet Basimevi, 1939; vi, 30 pp.], but it was probably printed first in that language soon after Dewey's visit in 1924. The *Index Translationum* lists another edition or printing at Istanbul in 1952.

FUNDAMENTALS. *New Republic*, 6 Feb. 1924, XXXVII, 275–276.

Reprinted in *Characters and Events* (1929), II, 453–458.

THE CLASS ROOM TEACHER. *General Science Quarterly*, Mar. 1924, VII, 463–472.

Read at the State Conference of Normal School Instructors at Bridgewater, Mass., 5 Sept. 1922.

SCIENCE, BELIEF AND THE PUBLIC. *New Republic*, 2 Apr. 1924, XXXVIII, 143–145.

Reprinted in *Characters and Events* (1929), II, 459–464.

SOME COMMENTS ON PHILOSOPHICAL DISCUSSION. *Journal of Philosophy*, 10 Apr. 1924, XXI, 197–209.

Reply to Arthur Oncken Lovejoy and Sterling Power Lamprecht. Rejoinder by Lovejoy, PASTNESS AND TRANSCENDENCE, *ib.*, 23 Oct. 1924, XXI, 601–611. See note under REALISM WITHOUT MONISM OR DUALISM (*ib.*, 8 June 1922), above.

THE PROSPECTS OF THE LIBERAL COLLEGE. *Independent*, 26 Apr. 1924, CXII, 226–227.

Reprinted in *Education Today* (1940), 184–189.

KANT AFTER TWO HUNDRED YEARS. *New Republic*, 30 Apr. 1924, XXXVIII, 254–256.

Reprinted in *Characters and Events* (1929), I, 63–68, with the title IMMANUEL KANT.

THE LIBERAL COLLEGE AND ITS ENEMIES. *Independent*, 24 May 1924, CXII, 280–282.

Reprinted in *Education Today* (1940), 190–197.

REVIEW of Charles Kay Ogden and Ivor Armstrong Richards, *The Meaning of Meaning*. *New Republic*, 11 June 1924, XXXIX, 77–78.

REVIEW of Charles Santiago Sanders Peirce, *Chance, Love, and Logic*. *New Republic*, 25 June 1924, XXXIX, 136–137.

SECULARIZING A THEOCRACY: YOUNG TURKEY AND THE CALIPHATE. *New Republic*, 17 Sept. 1924, XL, 69–71.

Dated, Constantinople, Aug. 1924.

Reprinted in *Characters and Events* (1929), I, 324–329, and in *Impressions of Soviet Russia* (1929), 220–234.

ANGORA, THE NEW. *New Republic*, 15 Oct. 1924, XL, 169–170.

Reprinted in *Characters and Events* (1929), I, 330–334, and in *Impressions of Soviet Russia* (1929), 208–219.

DEWEY AIDS LA FOLLETTE. *New York Times*, 23 Oct. 1924.

Statement in praise of Robert Marion La Follette, candidate for President of the United States.

LOGICAL METHOD AND LAW. *Philosophical Review*, Nov. 1924, XXXIII, 560–572; *Cornell Law Quarterly*, Dec. 1924, X, 17–27.

Reprinted in *Philosophy and Civilization* (1931), 126–140; and in Jerome Hall, ed., *Readings in Jurisprudence* (Indianapolis, 1938), 343–355.

See comment by Jerome Frank in *Law and the Modern Mind* (1949), 337; and *Notre Dame Lawyer*, Spring 1950, XXV, 460 f.

THE TURKISH TRAGEDY. *New Republic*, 12 Nov. 1924, XL, 268–269.

Reprinted in *Characters and Events* (1929), I, 335–339, and in *Impressions of Soviet Russia* (1929), 197–207.

FOREIGN SCHOOLS IN TURKEY. *New Republic*, 3 Dec. 1924, XLI, 40–42.

Reprinted in *Characters and Events* (1929), I, 346–351, with the title AMERICA AND TURKEY.

1925

EXPERIENCE AND NATURE. (Lectures upon the Paul Carus Foundation, First Series.) Chicago, London: Open Court Publishing Company, 1925. xi, 443 pp.

Contents. Experience and Philosophic Method—Existence as Precarious and as Stable—Nature, Ends, and Histories—Nature, Means, and Knowledge—Nature, Communication, and as Meaning —Nature, Mind, and the Subject—Nature, Life, and Body-Mind— Existence, Ideas, and Consciousness—Experience, Nature, and Art —Existence, Value, and Criticism.
See edition of 1929.

Translations. Italian, (abridged) with Introduction and notes by Nicola Abbagnano (Torino, 1949); Japanese by Riichiro Hoashi (Tokyo [196—]); Spanish, with Introduction by José Gaos (México-Buenos Aires, 1948).

Reviewed in *Boston Transcript,* 9 May 1925; *Cuadernos Americanos,* Sept.-Oct. 1949, VIII, v, 131–142 (Augusto Salazar Bondy); *Dial,* May 1925, LXXVIII, 429; *Independent,* 3 Oct. 1925, CXV, 396; *International Journal of Ethics,* Jan. 1926, XXXVI, 201–205 (George Plimpton Adams); *Forum,* Aug. 1926, LXXVI, 316 (Joseph Jastrow); *Mind,* Oct. 1925, XXXIV, 476–482 (John Laird); *Nation,* 14 Oct. 1925, CXXI, Sup. 430–432 (Matthew Thompson McClure); *Nation and Athenaeum,* 5 Sept. 1925, XXXVII, 682–684 (Cyril Edwin Mitchinson Joad); *New Republic,* 25 Mar. 1925, XLII, 129–131 (Clarence Edwin Ayres); *New York Times,* 3 May 1925 (Robert Luther Duffus); *New York Herald Tribune Books,* 3 May 1925 (Irwin Edman); *Outlook,* 17 June 1925, CXL, 267–268; *Philosophical Review,* Jan. 1926, XXXV, 64–68 (Herbert Wildon Carr); *Quarterly Journal of the University of North Dakota,* May 1925, XV, 363–366 (Norborne Harris Crowell); *Revue de métaphysique et de morale,* XXXV (Sup. to Jan.-Mar. 1928, pp. 10–12); *Rassegna di pedagogia,* July-Aug. 1950 (F. Centineo); *Review of Reviews,* Nov. 1925, LXXII, 560; *Saturday Review of Literature,* 4 July 1925, I, 874–875 (Ralph Barton Perry); *Scuola e città,* 1950, I, 95–96 (Aldo Visalberghi); *Sewanee Review,* Oct. 1925, XXXIII, 496–499 (Hugh W. Sanford); *Social Forces,* June 1927, V, 686–687 (M. O.); *Spectator,* 26 Sept. 1925, CXXXV, 494–497 (Ferdinand Canning Scott Schiller); *Springfield Republican,* 20 Sept. 1925 (George Brown); Survey, 15 Nov., 15 Dec. 1925, 15 Jan., 15 Feb., 15 Mar., 15 Apr., 15 May, 15 June, 15 July, 15 Aug., 15 Sept. 1926, LV, 239–240, 377, 509–510, 570 *bis,* 697, LVI, 103–104, 266, 387, 471, 551, 642 (Joseph Kinmont Hart); *Welfare Magazine,* Oct. 1927, XVIII, 1401–1402 (Thomas Dawes Eliot); *World Tomorrow,* Dec. 1925, VIII, 383 (Paul Jones).

See Clarence Edwin Ayres, JOHN DEWEY: NATURALIST. A REPORT OF THE CARUS LECTURES FOR 1922, *New Republic*, 4 Apr. 1923, XXXIV, 158–160; Richard Burdon Haldane, *Human Experience: A Study of Its Structure* (London: John Murray, 1926); Everett W. Hall, SOME MEANINGS OF MEANING IN DEWEY'S *Experience and Nature*, *Journal of Philosophy*, 29 Mar. 1928, XXV, 169–181, and Dewey's reply, MEANING AND EXISTENCE, (*ib.*, 21 June 1928); Joseph Kinmont Hart, *Inside Experience: A Naturalistic Philosophy of Life and the Modern World* (New York: Longmans, Green and Co., 1925), a revision of the reviews in the *Survey*, above; George Santayana, DEWEY'S NATURALISTIC METAPHYSICS, *Journal of Philosophy*, 3 Dec. 1925, XXII, 673–688, and Dewey's reply, "HALF-HEARTED NATURALISM" (*ib.*, 3 Feb. 1927); Henry Nelson Wieman, RELIGION IN DEWEY'S *Experience and Nature*, *Journal of Religion*, Sept. 1925, V, 519–542; Victor S. Yarros, EMPIRICISM AND PHILOSOPHIC METHOD: PROFESSOR DEWEY'S VIEWS, *Open Court*, Oct. 1925, XXXIX, 586–592, METAPHYSICS, PSYCHOLOGY, AND PHILOSOPHY: PROFESSOR DEWEY'S VIEWS, *ib.*, Nov. 1925, 669–675, THE PROVINCE AND ISSUES OF PHILOSOPHY: PROFESSOR DEWEY'S VIEWS, *ib.*, Dec. 1925, 755–766.

See the comment by Justice Holmes in *Holmes-Pollock Letters*, II, 287, and numerous references in *Holmes-Laski Letters*.

THE "SOCRATIC DIALOGUES" OF PLATO. In *Studies in the History of Ideas*, by the Department of Philosophy of Columbia University, II (New York: Columbia University Press, 1925), 1–23.

Reviewed in *Journal of Philosophy*, 27 May 1926, XXIII, 300–303 (George Plimpton Adams); *Spectator*, 26 Sept. 1925, CXXXV, 494–497 (Ferdinand Canning Scott Schiller).

THE DEVELOPMENT OF AMERICAN PRAGMATISM. In *Studies in the History of Ideas*, by the Department of Philosophy of Columbia University, II (New York: Columbia University Press, 1925), Supplement, 353–377.

Retranslated from the French, LE DÉVELOPPEMENT DU PRAGMA-TISME AMÉRICAIN, in *Revue de métaphysique et de morale*, Oct. 1922, XXIX, 411–430 [by Herbert Wallace Schneider].

Chinese translation by Tung-yeh Hu (Taipei, 1950).

Reprinted in Daniel Sommer Robinson, *An Anthology of Recent Philosophy* (New York [°1929]), 431–445, in Dewey's *Philosophy and Civilization* (1931), 13–35; and in Dagobert D. Runes, *Twentieth Century Philosophy* (New York [°1943]), 451–468.

THE PROBLEM OF TURKEY. *New Republic*, 7 Jan. 1925, XLI, 162–163.

Reprinted in *Characters and Events* (1929), I, 340–345.

THE MEANING OF VALUE. *Journal of Philosophy*, 26 Feb. 1925, XXII, 126–133.

Reply to David Wight Prall, VALUES AND THOUGHT-PROCESS, *ib.*, 28 Feb. 1924, XXI, 117–125. See Dewey's original article, VALUATION AND EXPERIMENTAL KNOWLEDGE (*Philosophical Review*, July 1922), above.

HIGHLY-COLORED WHITE LIES. *New Republic*, 22 Apr. 1925, XLII, 229–230.

Reprinted in *Characters and Events* (1929), I, 312–316, with the title THE WHITE PERIL.

DEDICATION ADDRESS. *Journal of the Barnes Foundation*, May 1925, I, ii, 3–6.

Delivered at the dedication ceremonies of the Barnes Foundation, Merion, Pa., 19 Mar. 1925.

LITERATURE OR MATHEMATICS? *School and Society*, 27 June 1925, XXI, 786.

Note on Raymond Weeks, *Boy's Own Arithmetic*.

VALUE, OBJECTIVE REFERENCE, AND CRITICISM. *Philosophical Review*, July 1925, XXXIV, 313–332.

WHAT IS THE MATTER WITH TEACHING? *Delineator*, Oct. 1925, CVII, iv, 5–6, 78.

EXPERIENCE AND NATURE AND ART. *Journal of the Barnes Foundation*, Oct. 1925, I, iii, 4–10.

"Adapted from *Experience and Nature*."

Reprinted in *Art and Education*, by John Dewey [and others] ([Merion, Pa.] Barnes Foundation Press [ᶜ1929]), 3–12.

THE NATURALISTIC THEORY OF PERCEPTION BY THE SENSES. *Journal of Philosophy*, 22 Oct. 1925, XXII, 596–605.

Reprinted in *Philosophy and Civilization* (1931), 188–201, with the title, A NATURALISTIC THEORY OF SENSE PERCEPTION.

IS CHINA A NATION OR A MARKET? *New Republic*, 11 Nov. 1925, XLIV, 298–299.

Reprinted in *Characters and Events* (1929), I, 316–321, with the title THE WHITE PERIL.

PRACTICAL DEMOCRACY. *New Republic*, 2 Dec. 1925, XLV, 52–54.

Review of Walter Lippmann, *The Phantom Public*.

1926

FOREWORD. *In* William James Durant, *The Story of Philosophy*. (New York: Simon & Schuster, 1926), v.

After the first printing, this was taken out and thereafter printed on the jacket.

INDIVIDUALITY AND EXPERIENCE. *Journal of the Barnes Foundation*, Jan. 1926, II, i, 1–6.

Reprinted in *Art in Education*, by John Dewey [and others] ([Merion, Pa.:] Barnes Foundation Press [°1929]), 175–183, and in *Intelligence in the Modern World* (1939), 619–627, with the title, INDIVIDUALITY AND FREEDOM.

SUBSTANCE, POWER, AND QUALITY IN LOCKE. *Philosophical Review*, Jan. 1926, XXXV, 22–38.

Reprinted in Sidney Hook and Milton Ridvas Konvitz, eds., *Freedom and Experience: Essays Presented to Horace M. Kallen* (Ithaca: Cornell University Press, 1947), 205–220.

Summarized in *Revue d'histoire de la philosophie*, Jan.-Mar. 1927, I, 122–123.

THE CHANGING INTELLECTUAL CLIMATE. *New Republic*, 17 Feb. 1926, XLV, 360–361.

Review of Alfred North Whitehead, *Science and the Modern World*. See the next item.

ART IN EDUCATION—AND EDUCATION IN ART. *New Republic*, 24 Feb. 1926, XLVI, 11–13.

Further considerations of Whitehead's *Science and the Modern World*.

AFFECTIVE THOUGHT IN LOGIC AND PAINTING. *Journal of the Barnes Foundation*, Apr. 1926, II, ii, 3–9.

Reprinted in *Art and Education* (1929), 63–73; and in *Philosophy and Civilization* (1931), 117–125, with the title AFFECTIVE THOUGHT.

THE HISTORIC BACKGROUND OF CORPORATE LEGAL PERSONALITY. *Yale Law Journal*, Apr. 1926, XXXV, 655–673.

Reprinted in *Philosophy and Civilization* (1931), 141–165, with the title CORPORATE PERSONALITY.

WE SHOULD DEAL WITH CHINA AS NATION TO NATION. *Chinese Students' Monthly*, May 1926, XXI, 52–54.

AMERICA AND THE FAR EAST. *Survey*, 1 May 1926, LVI, 188.

Reprinted in *Characters and Events* (1929), I, 309–311, with the title AMERICA AND CHINA.

EVENTS AND THE FUTURE. *Journal of Philosophy*, 13 May 1926, XXIII, 253–258.

Discussion of Charlie Dunbar Broad, *Scientific Thought*.

Reprinted in Sidney Ratner, ed., *Vision and Action: Essays in Honor of Horace M. Kallen on his 70th Birthday* (New Brunswick: Rutgers University Press, 1953), 184–191.

A KEY TO THE NEW WORLD. *New Republic*, 19 May 1926, XLVI, 410–411.

Review of Bertrand Russell, *Education and the Good Life*.

WILLIAM JAMES IN 1926. *New Republic*, 30 June 1926, XLVII, 163–165.

Review of *The Philosophy of William James*, edited by Horace Meyer Kallen.

Reprinted in *Characters and Events* (1929), I, 117–122.

REVIEW of Graham Wallas, *The Art of Thought. New Republic*, 16 June 1926, XLVII, 118–119.

See Victor S. Yarros, SOCIAL SCIENCE, SUBJECTIVISM, AND THE ART OF THINKING, *Open Court*, Sept. 1926, XL, 537–547.

CHURCH AND STATE IN MEXICO. *New Republic*, 25 Aug. 1926, XLVIII, 9–10.

Reprinted in *Characters and Events* (1929), I, 352–357, and in *Impressions of Soviet Russia* (1929), 137–149.

THE ETHICS OF ANIMAL EXPERIMENTATION. *Atlantic Monthly*, Sept. 1926, CXXXVIII, 343–346.

Read at a hearing before a subcommittee of the 69th Congress, 1st Session, on Senate Bill No. 2975, to prohibit experiments on living dogs in the District of Columbia, etc., in May 1926; also published in the report of this hearing (Washington: Government Printing Office, 1926).

Reprinted in *Hygeia*, Feb. 1931, IX, 118–120.

MEXICO'S EDUCATIONAL RENAISSANCE. *New Republic*, 22 Sept. 1926, XLVIII, 116–118.

Editorial reply in *New York Times*, 22 Sept. 1926.

Reprinted in *Characters and Events* (1929), I, 364–371, and in *Impressions of Soviet Russia* (1929), 150–167.

FROM A MEXICAN NOTE-BOOK. *New Republic*, 20 Oct. 1926, XLVIII, 239–241.

Reprinted in *Characters and Events* (1929), I, 358–363, with the title THE NEW AND OLD IN MEXICO, and in *Impressions of Soviet Russia* (1929), 168–180.

BISHOP BROWN: A FUNDAMENTAL MODERNIST. *New Republic*, 17 Nov. 1926, XLVIII, 371–372.

Comments on William Montgomery Brown, *My Heresy*.

Reprinted in *Characters and Events* (1929), I, 83–86.

AMERICA'S RESPONSIBILITY. *Christian Century*, 23 Dec. 1926, XLIII, 1583–1584.

Editorial reply, "which missed the point altogether" (J. D.), in *New York Times*, 3 Jan. 1927.

Reprinted in *Characters and Events* (1929), II, 691–696, and in *Intelligence in the Modern World* (1939), 503–508.

1927

THE PUBLIC AND ITS PROBLEMS. New York: Henry Holt and Company [°1927]. vi, 224 pp.

Published also in London by G. Allen & Unwin, Ltd.

Reprinted as *The Public and Its Problems: An Essay in Political Inquiry*, with a new introduction by the author (Chicago: Gateway Books, 1946), xii, 224 pp.; also as a paperback (Denver: Alan Swallow, 1957 [°1927, 1954]), vi, 224 pp. See edition of 1946.

Lectures delivered during Jan. 1926 on the Larwill Foundation of Kenyon College, Gambier, Ohio. The lectures have been fully revised and expanded.

Contents. Search for the Public—Discovery of the State—The Democratic State—Eclipse of the Public—Search for the Great Community—The Problem of Method.

Spanish translation by Mario H. Calicchio (Buenos Aires, 1958).

Reviewed in *Les Études philosophiques* (Paris), July-Sept. 1958, 367–368 (Gérard Deledalle); *Journal of Philosophy*, 6 June 1929, XXVI, 329–335 (William Ernest Hocking); *Mind*, July 1928, XXXVII, 368–370 (O. de Selincourt); *New Republic*, 24 Aug. 1927, LII, 22–23 (Robert Morss Lovett); *New Scholasticism*, Apr. 1928, II, 210–212 (Virgil Michel); *New York Herald Tribune Books*, 27

Nov. 1927 (Sterling Power Lamprecht); *New York Times*, 23 Oct. 1927 (Robert Luther Duffus); *Philosophical Review*, Mar. 1929, XXXVIII, 177–180 (Thomas Vernor Smith); *Saturday Review of Literature*, 15 Oct. 1927, IV, 198–199 (Harold Joseph Laski); *Yale Review*, Apr. 1928, N.S. XVII, 610–612 (William Bennett Munro). A selection from this book entitled GOVERNMENT IN THE MACHINE AGE was reprinted in Walter Lippmann and Allan Nevins, ed., *A Modern Reader* (New York: D. C. Heath and Company [°1936]), 25–36. Excerpts in Waldo Ralph Browne, ed., *Leviathan in Crisis: An International Symposium on the State* (New York: The Viking Press, 1946), 3–13, and in Richard Carlton Snyder and H. Hubert Wilson, eds., *Roots of Political Behavior* (New York: American Book Company, 1949), 90–97.

THE RÔLE OF PHILOSOPHY IN THE HISTORY OF CIVILIZATION. In *Proceedings of the Sixth International Congress of Philosophy*, edited by Edgar Sheffield Brightman (New York: Longmans, Green & Co., 1927), 536–542.

Read at the Sixth International Congress of Philosophy, Harvard University, 15 Sept. 1926.

Reprinted from *Philosophical Review*, Jan. 1927, XXXVI, 1–9; also published in Daniel Sommer Robinson, *An Anthology of Recent Philosophy* (New York [°1929]), 47–54; and in *Philosophy and Civilization* (1931), 3–12. Summarized in *Journal of Philosophical Studies*, Apr. 1927, II, 270–271. See Horace Leland Friess, THE SIXTH INTERNATIONAL CONGRESS OF PHILOSOPHY, *Journal of Philosophy*, 11 Nov. 1926, XXIII, 617–638.

ANTHROPOLOGY AND ETHICS. In *The Social Sciences and Their Interrelations*, edited by William Fielding Ogburn and Alexander Goldenweiser (Boston: Houghton Mifflin Company [°1927]), 24–36.

INTRODUCTION. *In* Roswell P. Barnes, *Militarizing Our Youth: The Significance of the Reserve Officers' Training Corps in Our Schools and Colleges* (New York: Committee on Militarism in Education, 1927), 3–4.

INTRODUCTORY NOTE. *In* Joseph Kinmont Hart, *Inside Experience: A Naturalistic Philosophy of Life and the Modern World* (New York: Longmans, Green and Co., 1927), xxi–xxvi.

INTRODUCTORY WORD. *In* Sidney Hook, *The Metaphysics of Pragmatism* (Chicago: Open Court Publishing Co., 1927), 1–5.

FOREWORD. *In* Charles Clayton Morrison, *The Outlawry of War: A Constructive Policy for World Peace* (Chicago: Willett, Clark & Colby, 1927), vii–xxv.

FOREWORD. *In* Paul Radin, *Primitive Man as Philosopher* (New York: D. Appleton and Company, 1927), xv–xviii.

THE PRAGMATIC ACQUIESCENCE. *New Republic*, 5 Jan. 1927, XLIX, 186–189.

In answer to Lewis Mumford on Pragmatism in *The Golden Day*. Reply by Mumford, letter in *New Republic*, 19 Jan. 1927, XLIX, 250–251. All three items reprinted in Gail Kennedy, ed., *Pragmatism and American Culture* (Boston: D. C. Heath & Co., 1950), 36–57.

Reprinted in *Characters and Events* (1929), II, 435–442, with the title PHILOSOPHY AND THE SOCIAL ORDER.

"HALF-HEARTED NATURALISM." *Journal of Philosophy*, 3 Feb. 1927, XXIV, 57–64.

Reply to George Santayana, DEWEY'S NATURALISTIC METAPHYSICS, *ib.*, 3 Dec. 1925, XXII, 673–688, and Frank Thilly, CONTEMPORARY AMERICAN PHILOSOPHY, *Philosophical Review*, Nov. 1926, XXXV, 522–538.

POLITICS AND HUMAN BEINGS. *New Republic*, 16 Mar. 1927, L, 114–115.

Review of William Ernest Hocking, *Man and the State*, and George Edward Gordon Catlin, *The Science and Method of Politics*.

IMPERIALISM IS EASY. *New Republic*, 23 Mar. 1927, L, 133–134.

Reprinted in *Characters and Events* (1929), I, 372–377, with the title MEXICO AND THE MONROE DOCTRINE; and in *Impressions of Soviet Russia* (1929), 181–194.

THE REAL CHINESE CRISIS. *New Republic*, 27 Apr. 1927, L, 269–270.

THE INTEGRATION OF A MOVING WORLD. *New Republic*, 25 May 1927, LI, 22–24.

Review of Edmund Noble, *Purposive Evolution: The Link between Science and Religion*.

BANKRUPTCY OF MODERN EDUCATION. *Modern Quarterly*, June–Sept., 1927, IV, 102–104.

Review of John Ervin Kirkpatrick, *The American College and Its Rulers*.

Reprinted in part in *School and Society*, 7 Jan. 1928, XXVII, 21–23.

AN EMPIRICAL ACCOUNT OF APPEARANCE. *Journal of Philosophy*, 18 Aug. 1927, XXIV, 449–463.

Summarized in *Journal of Philosophical Studies*, Oct. 1927, II, 592–593.

Reprinted as APPEARING AND APPEARANCE in *Philosophy and Civilization* (1931).

THE FRUITS OF NATIONALISM. *World Tomorrow*, Nov. 1927, X, 454–456.

Reprinted in *Characters and Events* (1929), II, 798–803, with the title NATIONALISM AND ITS FRUITS.

SCIENCE, FOLK-LORE, AND THE CONTROL OF FOLKWAYS. *New Republic*, 9 Nov. 1927, LII, 316–317.

Review of Clarence Edwin Ayres, *Science, the False Messiah*.

PSYCHOLOGY AND JUSTICE. *New Republic*, 23 Nov. 1927, LIII, 9–12.

Discussion of the report of the Fuller Advisory Committee in the Sacco-Vanzetti case.

Reprinted in *Characters and Events* (1929), II, 526–536.

1928

THE PHILOSOPHY OF JOHN DEWEY. Selected and edited by Joseph Ratner. New York: Henry Holt and Company [ᶜ1928]. xii, 560 pp.

Published also in London by G. Allen and Unwin, Ltd., 1929.

Contents. Philosophic Method—Foundations of a Naturalistic Metaphysics—The Origin and Nature of the Human Mind—Mind and Consciousness—Consciousness, Meaning and Perception—The Instrumental Theory of Knowledge—The Instrumental Theory of Truth—Instrumentalism and Science—The Psychology of Habit and Impulse—Intelligence in Human Behavior—Morals and Science—Human Behavior and Moral Ideals—Elements of Education—Education and Human Progress—The Public and the State—Human Progress and Social Organization—Art and Religion in Human Life—Philosophy and Civilization.

Reviewed in *Catholic World*, Feb. 1929, CXXVIII, 624; *Journal of Philosophy*, 18 July 1929, XXVI, 407–409 (Mary Shaw Kuypers); *Nation*, 31 Oct. 1928, CXXVII, 457–458 (Eliseo Vivas); *New Scholasticism*, Oct. 1928, II, 387–388 (Virgil Michel); *New Statesman*, 16 Feb. 1929, XXXII, 612; *New York Herald Tribune Books*, 5 Aug. 1928 (Irwin Edman); *Philosophical Review*, May 1931, XL, 276–

281 (Donald Ayres Piatt); *Survey*, 1 Jan. 1929, LXI, 454–455 (Joseph Kinmont Hart); *Time*, 10 Sept. 1928, XII, xi, 45.

Professor Edman's review, JOHN DEWEY, AMERICAN, was reprinted in his book *Adam, the Baby, and the Man from Mars* (New York, 1929), 68–79.

Translations. Spanish by J. Mendez Herrera (Madrid, 1930).

PROGRESSIVE EDUCATION AND THE SCIENCE OF EDUCATION. [Washington: Progressive Education Association, ᶜ1928.] 14 pp.

Address at the Eighth Annual Conference of the Progressive Education Association, 8 Mar. 1928.

Reprinted from *Progressive Education*, July-Aug.-Sept. 1928, V, 197–204.

Reprinted in *Dewey on Education* (1959), 113–126.

A CRITIQUE OF AMERICAN CIVILIZATION. In *Recent Gains in American Civilization*, edited by Kirby Page (New York: Harcourt, Brace and Co. [ᶜ1928]), 253–276.

Reprinted, with additions, from *World Tomorrow*, Oct. 1928, XI, 391–395.

PHILOSOPHY. In *Whither Mankind: A Panorama of Modern Civilization*, edited by Charles Austin Beard (New York: Longmans, Green and Co., 1928), 313–331.

PHILOSOPHIES OF FREEDOM. In *Freedom in the Modern World*, edited by Horace Meyer Kallen (New York: Coward-McCann, 1928), 236–271.

Reprinted in *Philosophy and Civilization* (1931), 271–298, and in *John Dewey on Experience, Nature, and Freedom* (1960), 261–287.

AN APPRECIATION OF HENRY GEORGE. In *Significant Paragraphs from Henry George's* Progress and Poverty, edited by Harry Gunnison Brown (Garden City, N.Y.: Published for the Robert Schalkenbach Foundation by Doubleday, Doran & Co., Inc., 1928), v, 1–3.

Reprinted in pamphlet form with the title *John Dewey on Henry George, and What Some Others Say* (New York: Robert Schalkenbach Foundation [1928]), 8 pp.

[ADDRESS.] In *A Tribute to Professor Morris Raphael Cohen, Teacher and Philosopher* (New York, 1928), 17–20.

Delivered at the testimonial dinner to Professor Cohen at the Hotel Astor, New York City, 15 Oct. 1927.

Why I Am a Member of the Teachers' Union. *American Teacher*, Jan. 1928, XII, v, 3–6.

Address delivered at the membership meeting of the Teachers' Union of New York City, Local No. 5, American Federation of Teachers, on 18 Nov. 1927.

Body and Mind. *Bulletin of the New York Academy of Medicine*, Jan. 1928, IV, 3–19; *Mental Hygiene*, Jan. 1928, XII, 1–17.

Anniversary discourse, delivered before the New York Academy of Medicine, 17 Nov. 1927.

Reprinted in *Philosophy and Civilization* (1931), 299–317.

Justice Holmes and the Liberal Mind. *New Republic*, 11 Jan. 1928, LIII, 210–212.

Reprinted in *Characters and Events* (1929), I, 100–106, with the title Oliver Wendell Holmes.

Review of Robert Harry Lowie, *The Origin of the State*. *Columbia Law Review*, Feb. 1928, XXVIII, 255.

The Manufacturers' Association and the Public Schools. *Journal of the National Education Association* Feb. 1928, XVII, 61–62.

Delivered before the National Consumers' League, 28 Nov. 1927.

Philosophy as a Fine Art. *New Republic*, 15 Feb. 1928, LIII, 352–354.

Review of George Santayana, *The Realm of Essence*.

To the Chinese Friends in the United States. *Chinese Student Bulletin*, Mar. 1928, I, 4.

"As an Example to Other Nations." *New Republic*, 7 Mar. 1928, LIV, 88–89.

On the proposals for the outlawry of war.

See reply by James Thomson Shotwell, Divergent Paths to Peace, *ib.*, 28 Mar. 1928, LIV, 194, and rejoinder by Dewey, *ib.*, 194–196.

Reprinted in *Characters and Events* (1929), II, 697–702.

Social as a Category. *Monist*, Apr. 1928, XXXVIII, 161–177.

Delivered at a meeting of the Eastern Division of the American Philosophical Association at the University of Chicago in Dec. 1927.

Reprinted as The Inclusive Philosophic Idea in *Philosophy and Civilization* (1931), 77–92, and in part as The Social in *Intelligence in the Modern World* (1939), 1059–1069.

Discussion in *Journal of Philosophy*, 16 Feb. 1928, XXV, 100–102.

PERSONAL IMMORTALITY: WHAT I BELIEVE. *New York Times*, 8 Apr. 1928.

Brief statement in a symposium on the subject.

THINGS, THOUGHT, CONVERSATION. *Nation*, 18 Apr. 1928, CXXVI, 449–450.

Review of Scott Buchanan, *Possibility*, and Mortimer Adler, *Dialectic*.

THE DIRECTION OF EDUCATION. *School and Society*, 28 Apr. 1928, XXVII, 493–497; *Teachers College Record*, Oct. 1928, XXX, 7–12.

Address delivered at the installation of William Fletcher Russell as Dean of Teachers College, Columbia University, 10 Apr. 1928.
Reprinted in *Education Today* (1940), 198–202.

CHINA AND THE POWERS: II. Intervention a Challenge to Nationalism. *Current History*, May 1928, XXVIII, 212–213.

Reply to Major General William Crozier, U.S.A. (RET.), WHAT HOPE FOR CHINA? *ib.*, 205–212.
Reprinted in *Characters and Events* (1929), I, 321–323, with the title THE WHITE PERIL.

OUTLAWING PEACE BY DISCUSSING WAR. *New Republic*, 16 May 1928, LIV, 370–371.

Reprinted in *Characters and Events* (1929), II, 703–706.

REVIEW of Carleton Kemp Allen, *Law in the Making*. *Columbia Law Review*, June 1928, XXVIII, 832–833.

Response by the author in his fifth edition (Oxford, 1951), 145.

MEANING AND EXISTENCE. *Journal of Philosophy*, 21 June 1928, XXV, 345–353.

Reply to Everett W. Hall, SOME MEANINGS OF MEANING IN DEWEY'S EXPERIENCE AND NATURE, *ib.*, 29 Mar. 1928, XXV, 169–181.

BRAVE GOSPEL. *Saturday Review of Literature*, 7 July 1928, IV, 1016.

Review of Mary Hammett Lewis, *An Adventure with Children*.

WHY I AM FOR SMITH. *New Republic*, 7 Nov. 1928 [published 1 Nov.], LVI, 320–321.

See TWO GALLANT FIGURES, editorial in *New York World*, 3 Nov. 1928, on the meeting of Professor Dewey and Governor Smith.

IMPRESSIONS OF SOVIET RUSSIA. I. Leningrad Gives the Clue (*New Republic*, 14 Nov. 1928, LVI, 343–344); II. A Country in a State of Flux (*ib.*, 21 Nov. 1928, LVII, 11–14); III. A New World in the Making (*ib.*, 28 Nov. 1928, 38–42); IV. What Are the Russian Schools Doing? (*ib.*, 5 Dec. 1928, 64–67); V. New Schools for a New Era (*ib.*, 12 Dec. 1928, 91–94); VI. The Great Experiment and the Future (*ib.*, 19 Dec. 1928, 134–137).

Reprinted in *Impressions of Soviet Russia* (1929), 3–133; and in *Characters and Events* (1929), I, 378–431.

Reviewed in *Nation*, 19 June 1929, CXXVIII, 744 (Jessica Smith).

See George Olshausen, DEWEY, SPENGLER, AND RUSSIA, letter in *New Republic*, 19 Dec. 1928, LVII, 142.

THE WAY TO THINK. *Saturday Review of Literature*, 1 Dec. 1928, V, 423.

Review of Ernest Dimnet, *The Art of Thinking*.

1929

CHARACTERS AND EVENTS. Popular Essays in Social and Political Philosophy. Edited by Joseph Ratner. New York: Henry Holt and Company [ᶜ1929]. 2 vols.

Contents. VOL. I. Book One, Characters: Matthew Arnold and Robert Browning—Ernest Renan—Maurice Maeterlinck—Herbert Spencer—Immanuel Kant—Ralph Waldo Emerson—H. G. Wells— William Montgomery Brown—Theodore Roosevelt—Francis W. Parker—Oliver Wendell Holmes—William James. Book Two, Events and Meanings: Events and Meanings—The Mind of Germany—Liberalism in Japan—On the Two Sides of the Eastern Sea— Japan Revisited, Two Years Later—The Siberian Republic—China's Nightmare—The Chinese Philosophy of Life—Chinese Social Habits—The Growth of Chinese National Sentiment—Conditions for China's Nationhood—Justice and Law in China—Young China and Old—New Culture in China—Transforming the Mind of China— America and China—The White Peril—Young Turkey and the Caliphate—Angora, the New—The Turkish Tragedy—The Problem of Turkey—America and Turkey—Church and State in Mexico —The New and Old in Mexico—Mexico's Educational Renaissance —Mexico and the Monroe Doctrine—Leningrad Gives the Clue—A Country in a State of Flux—A New World in the Making—What

Are the Russian Schools Doing?—New Schools for a New Era—The Great Experiment and the Future.

Vol. II. Book Three, America: Philosophy and the Social Order—The Emergence of a New World—The American Intellectual Frontier—Fundamentals—Science, Belief, and the Public—Universal Service as Education—The Schools and Social Preparedness—Mediocrity and Individuality—Individuality, Equality, and Superiority—Our Educational Ideal—American Education and Culture—Religion and Our Schools—Propaganda—Freedom of Thought and Work—Psychology and Justice—Americanism and Localism—Pragmatic America. Book Four, War and Peace: The Social Possibilities of War—America and War—Conscription of Thought—In Explanation of Our Lapse—Conscience and Compulsion—The Future of Pacifism—The Cult of Irrationality—Fiat Justitia, Ruat Coelum—The Post-War Mind—The Approach to a League of Nations—The League of Nations and the New Diplomacy—A League of Nations and Economic Freedom—Our National Dilemma—Shall We Join the League?—Force and Ideals—Force, Violence, and Law—America and the World—Morals and the Conduct of States—Which World Court Shall We Join?—Why Not Outlaw War?—If War Were Outlawed—What Outlawry of War Is Not—War and a Code of Law—America's Responsibility—"As an Example to Other Nations"—Outlawing Peace by Discussing War. Book Five, Towards Democracy: Social Psychology and Social Progress—Social Absolutism—Political Science as a Recluse—The New Social Science—Industry and Motives—Elements of Social Reorganization—A Sick World—Science and the Education of Man—Education as Politics—Force and Coercion—Nature and Reason in Law—Nationalism and Its Fruits—Ethics and International Relations—How Reaction Helps—Progress—Philosophy and Internationalism—Philosophy and Democracy.

Reviewed in *American Mercury*, July 1929, Vol. XVII, No. 67, pp. xiv, xviii; *Boston Transcript*, 15 June 1929; *Chicago Tribune*, 14 Dec. 1929 (James Hayden Tufts); *Christian Science Monitor*, 7 June 1930; *London Times Literary Supplement*, 17 Oct. 1929; *New York Evening Post*, 18 May 1929 (John Herman Randall, Jr.); *New York Times*, 14 July 1929 (William MacDonald); *New York World*, 20 Oct. 1929 (Harry Hansen); 27 Oct. 1929 (C. Hartley Grattan); *Outlook*, 29 May 1929, CLII, 187 (Gorham B. Munson); *Saturday Review of Literature*, 26 Oct. 1929, VI, 310 (Ralph Barton Perry); *The Symposium*, Jan. 1930, I, 128-132 (Laurence Buermeyer); *World Tomorrow*, Nov. 1929, XII, 472.

EXPERIENCE AND NATURE. New York: W. W. Norton & Co., Inc. [°1929]. ix, 1a-4a, 1-443 pp.

Published also in London by G. Allen & Unwin, 1929; this edition reviewed in *London Times Literary Supplement*, 23 Jan. 1930, and in *Mind*, Oct. 1929, XXXVIII, 527–528 (E. M. Whitnall).

For contents, see edition of 1925.

Another issue of this edition has the imprint: Chicago, Open Court Publishing Co., 1926 [°1929].

Reprinted as a facsimile paperback by Dover Publications (New York, [1958]). "An unabridged and unaltered republication of the second edition."

This edition contains a new preface; the first chapter has been completely rewritten, and a few minor corrections have been made throughout the volume.

Reviewed in *New York World*, 27 Oct. 1929 (C. Hartley Grattan).

IMPRESSIONS OF SOVIET RUSSIA AND THE REVOLUTIONARY WORLD, MEXICO—CHINA—TURKEY. (The New Republic's Dollar Books.) New York: New Republic, Inc., 1929. 270 pp.

Reprinted in January 1932.

Contents. Soviet Russia, 1928: Leningrad Gives the Clue—A Country in a State of Flux—A New World in the Making—What Are the Russian Schools Doing?—New Schools for a New Era—The Great Experiment and the Future. Mexico, 1926: Church and State in Mexico—Mexico's Educational Renaissance—From a Mexican Note-Book—Imperialism Is Easy. Turkey, 1924: The Turkish Tragedy—Angora, the New—Secularizing a Theocracy. China, 1920: Industrial China—Is China a Nation?

Reprinted from the *New Republic;* certain essays also appear in *Characters and Events* (1929).

Reviewed in *American Mercury*, July 1929, Vol. XVII, No. 67, p. xviii; *Boston Transcript*, 3 Apr. 1929; *Christian Science Monitor*, 5 June 1929; *Nation*, 19 June 1929, CXXVIII, 744 (Jessica Smith); *New York Herald Tribune Books*, 31 Mar. 1929; *New York Times*, 21 Apr. 1929; *New York World*, 3 Mar. 1929 (Bernard Smith); *Saturday Review of Literature*, 4 May 1929, V, 971 (Norah Meade).

Translations. Japanese by Tokuji Yashamita (1935).

ART AND EDUCATION. By John Dewey, Albert C. Barnes, Laurence Buermeyer, Thomas Munro, Paul Guillaume, Mary Mullen, Violette de Mazia. [Merion, Pa.:] Barnes Foundation Press [°1929]. x, 349 pp.

The following articles in this volume are by Dewey: EXPERIENCE AND NATURE AND ART, 3–12; AFFECTIVE THOUGHT IN LOGIC AND PAINTING, 63–73; and INDIVIDUALITY AND EXPERIENCE, 175–183.

Second edition, 1947, *q.v.*

THE QUEST FOR CERTAINTY. New York: Minton, Balch & Co., 1929. 318 pp.; London: George Allen & Unwin, Ltd. [1930]. 302 pp.

Paperback edition, New York: Capricorn Books–G. P. Putnam's Sons, 1960.

Gifford Lectures, delivered at the University of Edinburgh, 1929.

Contents. Escape from Peril—Philosophy's Search for the Immutable—Conflict of Authorities—The Art of Acceptance and the Art of Control—Ideas at Work—The Play of Ideas—The Seat of Intellectual Authority—The Naturalization of Intelligence—The Supremacy of Method—The Construction of Good—The Copernican Revolution.

Translations. Arabic by A. F. Ahwani; Greek by Manōlēs Kornēlios (Athens, 1959); Japanese by Seiji Uyeda (Tokyo, 1950); Spanish, with Introduction by Eugenio Imaz (México–Buenos Aires, 1952).

Reviewed in *Boston Transcript,* 16 Nov. 1929; *Columbia Varsity,* Jan. 1930, XII, iii, 27–28 (J. G.); *Christian Century,* 8 Jan. 1930, XLVII, 48–49 (Ewart Edmund Turner); *Current History,* Jan. 1930, XXXI, 821–822 (S. B.); *Harvard Theological Review,* July 1930, XXIII, 213–233 (Julius Seelye Bixler); *International Journal of Ethics,* Apr. 1930, XL, 425–433 (Clarence Edwin Ayres); *Journal of Philosophy,* 2 Jan. 1930, XXVII, 14–25 (Clarence Irving Lewis); *London Times Literary Supplement,* 17 Apr. 1930; *Methodist Review,* Sept. 1930, CXIII, 724–734 (John Wright Buckham); *Mind,* July 1930, XXXIX, 372–375 (Ferdinand Canning Scott Schiller); *Nation,* 22 Jan. 1930, CXXX, 100–101 (Henry Hazlitt); *New Republic,* 3 Sept. 1930, LXIV, 77–79 (Kenneth Burke) also in his *Philosophy of Literary Form* (1941), 382–388; *New Statesman,* 15 Mar. 1930, XXXIV, 748; *New York Evening Post,* 19 Oct. 1929 (Irwin Edman); *New York Herald Tribune Books,* 20 Oct. 1929 (Joseph Wood Krutch); *New York Times,* 20 Oct. 1929 (Percy Hutchison); *New York World,* 27 Oct. 1929 (Clinton Hartley Grattan); *Open Court,* Aug. 1930, XLIV, 499–501 (Victor S. Yarros); *Philosophical Review,* Jan. 1931, XL, 79–89 (Max Carl Otto); *Religious Education,* Jan. 1930, XXV, 71–73 (Thomas Vernor Smith), 74–76 (Edgar Sheffield Brightman), 76–79 (Frank N. Freeman); *Saturday Review of Literature,* 21 Dec. 1929, VI, 585 (Ralph Barton Perry); *Spectator,* 12 Apr. 1930, CXLIV, sup. 619 (Cyril Edwin Mitchinson Joad); *The Symposium,* Apr. 1930, I, 263–268 (George Boas); *World Tomorrow,* Feb. 1930, XIII, 89–90 (Howard Y. Williams).

See Herman Harrell Horne, *John Dewey's Philosophy, Especially* The Quest for Certainty (Boston [1931]), and Gertrude A. Trageser, Criticism of John Dewey's *Quest for Certainty* (PH.D. thesis, Fordham University, 1934).

PHILOSOPHY. In *Research in the Social Sciences*, edited by Wilson Gee (New York: The Macmillan Company, 1929), 241–265.

THE SOURCES OF A SCIENCE OF EDUCATION. New York: Horace Liveright, 1929. 77 pp.

The Kappa Delta Pi lectures.

Translations. Chinese; German in Dewey and Kilpatrick, *Der Projekt-Plan* (Weimar, 1935), 102–141; Italian by M. Tioli Gabrieli (Firenze, 1950); Spanish in *La ciencia de la educación*, by Lorenzo Luzuriaga (Buenos Aires, 1941, 1948, 1951).

Reviewed in *Boston Transcript*, 30 Nov. 1929; Nation, 22 Jan. 1930, CXXX, 100–101 (Henry Hazlitt); *New York World*, 27 Oct. 1929 (Clinton Hartley Grattan); *Scuola e città*, 5 June 1951, II, 211–212 (F. De Bartolomeis).

FOREWORD. *In* Helen Edna Davis, *Tolstoi and Nietzsche, a Problem in Biographical Ethics* (New York: New Republic, Inc., 1929), ix–xiv.

SOVIET EDUCATION. In *Am I Getting an Education?* edited by Sherwood Eddy (Garden City, N.Y.: Doubleday, Doran & Co. [ᶜ1929]), 39–46.

FOREWORD. *In* Eastern Commercial Teachers Association, *First Yearbook*, 1929, xiii–xiv.

INTRODUCTION. *In* Henry Evelyn Bliss, *The Organization of Knowledge and the System of the Sciences* (New York: Henry Holt and Company [ᶜ1929]), vii–ix.

INTRODUCTION. *In* Maurice Hindus, *Humanity Uprooted* (New York: Jonathan Cape and Harrison Smith [1929]), [xv]–xix.

FOREWORD. In Feiwel Schneersohn, *Studies in Psycho-Expedition* (New York: The Science of Man Press, 1929), vii–viii.

INTRODUCTION: Group Action and Group Learning. *In* Alfred Dwight Sheffield, ed., *Training for Group Experience: A Syllabus of Materials from a Laboratory Course for Group Leaders Given at Columbia University in 1927* (New York: The Inquiry, 1929), ix–xv.

FREEDOM IN WORKERS' EDUCATION. *American Teacher*, Jan. 1929, XIII, v, 1–4.

Address delivered at a meeting under the auspices of Local 5, American Federation of Teachers, to discuss the action of the American Federation of Labor on Brookwood Labor College, held in New York, 9 Nov. 1928.

LABOR POLITICS AND EDUCATION. *New Republic*, 9 Jan. 1929, LVII, 211–214.

A comment on the activities of Matthew Woll in bringing about the censure of the Brookwood Labor College by the American Federation of Labor.

Excerpts in *School and Society*, 19 Jan. 1929, XXIX, 92–93.
Reply by Woll, *New Republic*, 20 Feb. 1929, LVIII, 19–20, and rejoinder by Dewey, *ib.*, 20.
See letter of Daniel Chase, *ib.*, 6 Mar. 1929, LVIII, 73.
See R. E. Woodmansee, DR. DEWEY AND THE I[NTERNATIONAL] L[ABOR] P[RESS], *ib.*, 27 Feb. 1929, LVIII, 46; DR. DEWEY AND THE COMMUNISTS, editorial in *New York World*, 30 Nov. 1928; and *Matthew Woll Takes Issue with Prof. John Dewey* . . . Washington, D.C., International Labor News Service, 12 Jan. 1929. 2 pp.
See letter of Dewey, MR. WOLL AS A COMMUNIST CATCHER, *New Republic*, 13 Mar. 1929, LVIII, 99.

GENERAL PRINCIPLES OF EDUCATIONAL ARTICULATION. *School and Society*, 30 Mar. 1929, XXIX, 399–406.

Address delivered before the Department of Superintendence of the National Education Association, Cleveland, 26 Feb. 1929; published also in their *Official Report*, 1929, 51–60; in National Education Association, *Addresses and Proceedings*, 1929, 674–683; and in *Education Today* (1940), 203–215.

REVIEW of George Sylvester Counts, *School and Society in Chicago*. *New Republic*, 10 Apr. 1929, LVIII, 231–232.

THE HOUSE DIVIDED AGAINST ITSELF. *New Republic*, 24 Apr. 1929, LVIII, 270–271.

Comments on Robert Staughton Lynd and Helen Merrell Lynd, *Middletown*.

Reprinted, with revisions, in *Individualism, Old and New* (1930), 9–18.
Reply by Mrs. Pearl Weber, *New Republic*, 8 May 1929, LVIII, 335.

"AMERICA"—BY FORMULA. *New Republic*, 18 Sept. 1929, LX, 117–119.

Comments on Mueller Freienfels, *Mysteries of the Soul*, translated from the German by Bernard Miall.

Reprinted in *Individualism, Old and New* (1930), 19–34.

WHAT DO LIBERALS WANT? Editorial in *Outlook and Independent*, 16 Oct. 1929, CLIII, 261.

REVIEW of Alfred North Whitehead, *Process and Reality*. New York *Sun*, 26 Oct. 1929.

JUVENILE READING. *Saturday Review of Literature*, 16 Nov. 1929, VI, 398.

Contribution to a symposium.

[ADDRESS.] *American Hebrew*, 29 Nov. 1929, CXXVI, 125.

At the semi-centennial banquet of the *American Hebrew*, Hotel Astor, New York, 21 Nov. 1929; printed in part.

THE SPHERE OF APPLICATION OF THE EXCLUDED MIDDLE. *Journal of Philosophy*, 19 Dec. 1929, XXVI, 701–705.

Reply by Ernest Nagel, CAN LOGIC BE DIVORCED FROM ONTOLOGY? *ib.*, 705–712.

1930

INDIVIDUALISM, OLD AND NEW. New York: Minton, Balch and Company, 1930. 171 pp.

Published also in London by G. Allen and Unwin, Ltd., 1931.

Contents. The House Divided against Itself—"America"–By Formula—The United States, Incorporated—The Lost Individual—Toward a New Individualism—Capitalistic or Public Socialism?—The Crisis in Culture—Individuality in Our Day.

Eight articles reprinted, with considerable new matter, from the *New Republic*.

Reviewed in *Mind*, Jan. 1932, XLI, 131–132 (Ferdinand Canning Scott Schiller); *Nation*, 22 Oct. 1930, CXXXI, 446–447 (Henry Hazlitt); *New York Herald Tribune Books*, 23 Nov. 1930 (André Maurois); *New York Times*, 21 Dec. 1930 (John Chamberlain); *New York World*, 19 Oct. 1930; *Società*, 1949, V, 174–175 (Nicola Badaloni); *World Unity*, Dec. 1930, VII, 193–201 (John Herman Randall, Jr.).

See Lewis Mumford, A MODERN SYNTHESIS, *Saturday Review of Literature*, 12 Apr. 1930, VI, 920–921, and replies by James T. Farrell and Joseph Ratner in *ib.*, 12 July 1930, 1194.

Reprinted in part in Donald Owen Wagner, ed., *Social Reformers: Adam Smith to John Dewey* (New York: The Macmillan Company, 1934), 730–739.

Translations. Arabic by K. Hammad; Italian, with Introduction by Felice Villani (Firenze, 1948). See Fortunato Brancatisano, JOHN DEWEY: INDIVIDUALISMO VECCHIO E NUOVO, *Italia intellettuale* (Reggio Calabria), Apr. 1950, III, 3–24.

HUMAN NATURE AND CONDUCT; AN INTRODUCTION TO SOCIAL PSYCHOLOGY. With a New Introduction. New York: The Modern Library [ᶜ1930]. ix, vii, 336 pp.

Reviewed in *New York Herald Tribune*, 27 Jan. 1931; *New York Times*, 20 July 1930.

CONSTRUCTION AND CRITICISM. New York [Columbia University Press], 1930. 25 pp.

The first Milton Judson Davies Memorial Lecture, delivered before the Institute of Arts and Sciences, Columbia University, 25 Feb. 1930.

Reviewed in *The New Scholasticism*, Jan. 1932, p. 78 (Virgil Michel); *United India and Indian States* (Delhi), 25 Oct. 1930.

CONDUCT AND EXPERIENCE. *In* Carl Murchison, ed., *Psychologies of 1930* (Worcester, Mass.: Clark University Press, 1930), 409–422.

Reprinted in *Philosophy and Civilization* (1931), 249–270.

See the comment by Arthur Fisher Bentley in his *Behavior, Knowledge, Fact* (Bloomington, Ind., 1935), 74–81.

FROM ABSOLUTISM TO EXPERIMENTALISM. *In* George Plimpton Adams and William Pepperell Montague, eds., *Contemporary American Philosophy: Personal Statements* (New York: The Macmillan Company, 1930), II, 13–27.

Reprinted in *John Dewey on Experience, Nature, and Freedom* (1960), 3–18; in Charles Frankel, *The Golden Age of American Philosophy* (New York: George Braziller, Inc., 1960), 385–395, in Robert Ulich, ed., *Three Thousand Years of Educational Wisdom* (Cambridge: Harvard University Press, 1954), and in part as THE PHILOSOPHER-IN-THE-MAKING, *Saturday Review of Literature*, 22 Oct. 1949, XXXII, xliii, 9–10, 39–44, and in *Saturday Review Treasury* (New York, 1957), 438–449.

Translations. Italian by Carlo Coardi (Milano, 1939); Spanish in Unión Panamericana, *John Dewey en sus noventa años* (Washington, 1949), 15–26.

IN RESPONSE. In *John Dewey, the Man and His Philosophy: Addresses Delivered in New York in Celebration of His Seventieth Birthday* (Cambridge: Harvard University Press, 1930), 173–181.

Remarks at the luncheon given in his honor at the Hotel Astor, 19 Oct. 1929.

PHILOSOPHY AND EDUCATION. *In* University of California, Southern Branch, Los Angeles, *Addresses Delivered at the Dedication of the New Campus*, 1930, 46–56.

Reprinted in Paul Arthur Schilpp, ed., *Higher Education Faces the Future; a Symposium on College and University Education in the United States* (New York: Horace Liveright, 1930), 273–282.

QUALITATIVE THOUGHT. *The Symposium*, Jan. 1930, I, 5–32.

Reprinted in *Philosophy and Civilization* (1931), 93–116, and in *John Dewey on Experience, Nature, and Freedom* (1960), 176–198.

THE UNITED STATES, INCORPORATED. (Individualism, Old and New, I.) *New Republic*, 22 Jan. 1930, LXI, 239–241.

Revised and expanded in *Individualism, Old and New* (1930), 35–50; reprinted in Charles Wright Thomas, ed., *Essays in Contemporary Civilization* (New York: The Macmillan Company, 1931), 598–612.

PSYCHOLOGY AND WORK. *Personnel Journal*, Feb. 1930, VIII, 337–341.

Address before the Personnel Research Foundation, New York City, 15 Nov. 1929.

THE LOST INDIVIDUAL. (Individualism, Old and New, II). *New Republic*, 5 Feb. 1930, LXI, 294–296.

Revised and expanded in *Individualism, Old and New* (1930), 51–73.

TOWARD A NEW INDIVIDUALISM. (Individualism, Old and New, III). *New Republic*, 19 Feb. 1930, LXII, 13–16.

Revised and expanded in *Individualism, Old and New* (1930), 74–100.

Comment by James Oppenheim, *New Republic*, 23 Apr. 1930, LXII, 275.

WHAT I BELIEVE. *Forum*, Mar. 1930, LXXXIII, 176–182.

Separately published with the title, *A Credo*, New York: Simon and Schuster [1931].

Reprinted in *Living Philosophies* [*a Series of Intimate Credos*, by Twenty-two Modern Thinkers] (New York: Simon and Schuster, 1931), 21–35, and in Gail Kennedy, ed., *Pragmatism and American Culture* (Boston: D. C. Heath & Co., 1950), 23–31.

A revision of this statement appears in Clifton Fadiman, ed., *I Believe* (New York: Simon and Schuster, 1939), 347–354. Reprinted in Gail Kennedy, *op. cit.*, 31–35.

CAPITALISTIC OR PUBLIC SOCIALISM? (Individualism, Old and New, IV). *New Republic*, 5 Mar. 1930, LXII, 64–67.

Revised and expanded in *Individualism, Old and New* (1930), 101–120.

THE CRISIS IN CULTURE. (Individualism, Old and New, V.) *New Republic*, 19 Mar. 1930, LXII, 123–126.

Revised and expanded in *Individualism, Old and New* (1930), 121–145.

THE APPLICABILITY OF LOGIC TO EXISTENCE. *Journal of Philosophy*, 27 Mar. 1930, XXVII, 174–179.

A reply to Ernest Nagel, CAN LOGIC BE DIVORCED FROM ONTOLOGY? *ib.*, XXVI, 705–712.

RELIGION IN THE SOVIET UNION: AN INTERPRETATION OF THE CONFLICT. *Current History*, Apr. 1930, XXXII, 31–36.

INDIVIDUALITY IN OUR DAY. (Individualism, Old and New, VI). *New Republic*, 2 Apr. 1930, LXII, 184–188.

Reprinted in *Individualism, Old and New* (1930), 146–171.

Translations. German by Olga Knopf in *Internationale Zeitschrift für Individualpsychologie*, Nov.-Dec. 1930, VIII, 567–576.

IN REPLY TO SOME CRITICISMS. *Journal of Philosophy*, 8 May 1930, XXVII, 271–277.

Reply to William Ernest Hocking, ACTION AND CERTAINTY (*ib.*, 225–238); Clarence Irving Lewis, PRAGMATISM AND CURRENT THOUGHT (*ib.*, 238–246); and Frederick James Eugene Woodbridge, EXPERIENCE AND DIALECTIC (*ib.*, 264–271).

WHAT HUMANISM MEANS TO ME. *The Thinker*, June 1930, II, ii, 9–12.

HOW MUCH FREEDOM IN NEW SCHOOLS? *New Republic*, 9 July 1930, LXIII, 204–206.

Contribution to a symposium on "The New Education Ten Years After."

Reprinted in *Education Today* (1940), 216–223.

German translation in Dewey and Kilpatrick, *Der Projekt-Plan* (Weimar, 1935), 199–205.

OUR ILLITERACY PROBLEM. *Pictorial Review*, Aug. 1930, XXXI, xi, 28, 65, 73.

THE DUTIES AND RESPONSIBILITIES OF THE TEACHING PROFESSION. *School and Society*, 9 Aug. 1930, XXXII, 188–191.

Used as a basis for discussion at the meeting of the National Council of Education, 28 June 1930.

Reprinted in *Education Today* (1940), 224–229.

TROIS FACTEURS INDÉPENDENTS EN MATIÈRE DE MORALE. *Bulletin de la société française de philosophie*, Oct.-Dec. 1930, XXX, 118–127 (Discussion, 127–135).

Read in English before the society, in Paris, 7 Nov. 1930; translated into French by Charles Cestre.

SOCIAL CHANGE AND ITS HUMAN DIRECTION. *Modern Quarterly*, Winter 1930–1931, V, 422–425.

Contribution to a symposium on "Marxism and Social Change."

[LETTER TO SENATOR GEORGE WILLIAM NORRIS.] *New York Times*, 26 Dec. 1930.

An invitation to Senator Norris to withdraw from the Republican Party and help form a new third party; written by Dewey as national chairman of the League for Independent Political Action.

Editorial comment in *ib.*, 27 Dec. 1930 and *Troy Record*, 27 Dec. 1930.

See THE NEED FOR A NEW PARTY, *New Republic*, 7 Jan. 1931, LXV, 203–205, and letter of George W. Coleman, DR. DEWEY'S ASTUTENESS, in *ib.*, 15 Apr. 1931, LXVI, 238.

1931

PHILOSOPHY AND CIVILIZATION. New York: Minton, Balch and Company, 1931. vii, 334 pp.

Published in London by G. P. Putnam's Sons, Ltd., 1933.

Contents. Philosophy and Civilization—The Development of American Pragmatism—The Practical Character of Reality—Appearing and Appearance—The Inclusive Philosophic Idea—Qualitative Thought—Affective Thought—Logical Method and Law—Corporate Personality—Nature and Reason in Law—Interpretation of the Savage Mind—A Naturalistic Theory of Sense Perception—Perception and Organic Action—The Unit of Behavior [i.e., The Reflex Arc Concept in Psychology]—Conduct and Experience in Psychology—Philosophies of Freedom—Body and Mind—Science and Society.

Translation. Polish by Stefan Purman (Warsaw, 1938).

Reviewed in *Boston Transcript*, 31 Oct. 1931 (E. N.); *Commonweal*, 16 Mar. 1932 (Gerald B. Phelan); *Journal of Philosophy*, 21 July 1932, XXIX, 412–415 (Thomas Vernor Smith); *London Times Literary Supplement*, 9 Mar. 1933; *Manchester Guardian*, 27 Apr. 1933 (Samuel Alexander); *Mind*, Apr. 1932, XLI, 265 (Ferdinand Canning Scott Schiller); *New Republic*, 4 Nov. 1931, LXVIII, 330–331 (Sidney Hook); *New York Evening Post*, 15 Oct. 1931 (Rudolf Kagey); *New York Herald Tribune Books*, 8 Nov. 1931 (Ernest Sutherland Bates); *Outlook and Independent*, 14 Oct. 1931, CLIX, 218–219 (N. L. Rothman); *Philosophical Review*, May 1932, XLI, 324 (Gustavus Watts Cunningham); *The Thinker*, Dec. 1931, IV, v, 82–84 (Horace Meyer Kallen).

See Francis Sydney Marvin, SCIENCE AND SOCIETY, *Nature*, 5 Mar. 1932, CXXIX, 329–331.

THE WAY OUT OF EDUCATIONAL CONFUSION. Cambridge: Harvard University Press, 1931. 41 pp.

The Inglis Lecture on Secondary Education, delivered at Harvard in 1931.

German translation in Dewey and Kilpatrick, *Der Projekt-Plan* (Weimar, 1935), 85–101.

Reviewed in *Boston Transcript*, 18 July 1931; *New York Times*, 31 May 1931.

CONTEXT AND THOUGHT. (University of California Publications in Philosophy, XII, iii, 203–224.) Berkeley: University of California Press, 1931.

Also published separately. Published in London by the Cambridge University Press, 1932.

Reprinted in *John Dewey on Experience, Nature, and Freedom* (1960), 88–110.

The George Holmes Howison Lecture for 1930.

AMERICAN EDUCATION PAST AND FUTURE. [Chicago], University of Chicago Press [ᶜ1931]. 14 pp.

Second address in the "Men of America" series of radio lectures sponsored by the National Advisory Council on Radio in Education, delivered from Station WEAF over a nation-wide network of the National Broadcasting Company, 25 Oct. 1931.

Printed in *School and Society*, 31 Oct. 1931, XXXIV, 579–584, with the title SOME ASPECTS OF MODERN EDUCATION. Printed in part in *New York Times*, 26 Oct. and 1 Nov. 1931. Excerpts in *Ohio Schools*, Jan. 1932, X, 15 and in *Educational Review* (China), Jan. 1932, XXIV, 6–8. Condensed in *School Management*, Mar. 1932, I, 12–15.

Translations. Spanish in *Revista de pedagogia*, 1931, X, 554–560.

See David Snedden, DIRECTIVE AIMS IN EDUCATION, *School and Society*, 5 Dec. 1931, XXXIV, 745–748.

JUSTICE HOLMES AND THE LIBERAL MIND. *In* Felix Frankfurter, ed., *Mr. Justice Holmes* (New York: Coward-McCann, Inc. [ᶜ1931]), 33–45.

THE CURRICULUM FOR THE LIBERAL ARTS COLLEGE, Being the Report of the Curriculum Conference Held at Rollins College, January 19–24, 1931. John Dewey, Chairman. Winter Park, Florida: Rollins College [1931]. 40 pp.

Remarks of Dewey, p. [7].

INTRODUCTION. *In* Jagadish Chandra Chatterji, *India's Outlook on Life: The Wisdom of the Vedas* (New York: Kailas Press, 1931), 7.

COLLEGE SONS—AND PARENTS. *New Republic*, 4 Feb. 1931.

Review of Christian Gauss, *Life in College.*

DEMOCRACY FOR THE TEACHER. *Progressive Education*, Mar. 1931, VIII, 216–218.

THE NEED FOR A NEW PARTY: I. The Present Crisis (*New Republic*, 18 Mar. 1931, LXVI, 115–117); II. The Breakdown of the Old Order (*ib.*, 25 Mar., 150–152); III. Who Might Make a New Party? (*ib.*, 1 Apr., 177–179); IV. Policies for a New Party (*ib.*, 8 Apr., 202–205).

Editorial comment in *ib.*, 18 Mar. and 8 Apr. 1931, LXVI, 111–113, 191.

APPRECIATION AND CULTIVATION. *Harvard Teachers Record*, Apr. 1931, I, 73–76.

"SURPASSING AMERICA." *New Republic*, 15 Apr. 1931, LXVI, 241–243.

Review of Sherwood Eddy, *The Challenge of Russia;* George Sylvester Counts, *The Soviet Challenge to America;* and William Chapman White, *These Russians.*

A PHILOSOPHY OF SCIENTIFIC METHOD. *New Republic*, 29 Apr. 1931, LXVI, 306–307.

Review of Morris Raphael Cohen, *Reason and Nature, an Essay on the Meaning of Scientific Method.*

Reply by Cohen and rejoinder by Dewey, *New Republic*, 17 June 1931, LXVII, 126–127.

IS THERE HOPE FOR POLITICS? *Scribner's Magazine*, May 1931, LXXXIX, 483–487.

FULL WAREHOUSES AND EMPTY STOMACHS. *People's Lobby Bulletin*, May 1931, I, i, 1–3.

An address broadcast by the National Broadcasting Company in April.

THE PRESIDENT AND THE SPECIAL SESSION. *People's Lobby Bulletin*, June 1931, I, ii, 1.

Regarding President Hoover's refusal to call an extra session of Congress to deal with the unemployment situation.

SECRETARY KLEIN ASKED BASIS OF OPTIMISM. *People's Lobby Bulletin*, June 1931, I, ii, 3–4.

Letter to Julius Klein, Assistant Secretary of Commerce.

Reply by Klein, *ib.*, Aug. 1931, I, iv, 3–4, and rejoinder by Dewey, 4–5.

CHALLENGE TO PROGRESSIVE SENATORS TO ACT FOR RELIEF. *People's Lobby Bulletin*, June 1931, I, ii, 5.

Open letter to Senators Norris, La Follette, Cutting, Wheeler and Costigan.

GEORGE HERBERT MEAD. *Journal of Philosophy*, 4 June 1931, XXVIII, 309–314.

Remarks at the funeral of Professor Mead in Chicago, 30 Apr. 1931. Also published separately [Chicago? 1931?] with the remarks of Edward Scribner Ames and James Hayden Tufts. (Copy at Yale University Library.)

See also Dewey's GEORGE HERBERT MEAD AS I KNEW HIM, *University of Chicago Record*, 1931, XVII, 174–175.

REVIEW of George Herbert Palmer, *The Autobiography of a Philosopher;* Ralph Barton Perry, *A Defense of Philosophy;* and George Santayana, *The Genteel Tradition at Bay. New England Quarterly*, July 1931, IV, 529–531.

SCIENCE AND SOCIETY. *Lehigh Alumni Bulletin*, July, 1931, XVIII, x, 6–7.

Commencement address delivered at Lehigh University, Bethlehem, Pennsylvania, 9 June 1931.

Revised and reprinted in *Philosophy and Civilization* (1931), 318–330, and in M. David Hoffman and Ruth Wanger, eds., *Leadership in a Changing World* (New York: Harper & Brothers, 1935), 266–276.

THE KEY TO HOOVER'S KEYNOTE SPEECH. *People's Lobby Bulletin*, July 1931, I, iii, 3–6.

Criticism of President Hoover's Indianapolis speech.

CONTRADICTS BORAH ON DEBT REVISIONS. *New York Times*, 15 July 1931.

Letter to Senator Borah favoring a complete readjustment of the interallied debts. Written as president of the People's Lobby.

SOCIAL SCIENCE AND SOCIAL CONTROL. *New Republic*, 29 July 1931, LXVII, 276–277.

Reprinted in *Intelligence in the Modern World* (1939), 949–954, and in Hillman Metcalf Bishop and Samuel Hendel, eds., *Basic Issues of American Democracy*, second edition (New York: Appleton-Century-Crofts, Inc. [1951]), 11–14.

SHOULD AMERICA ADOPT A SYSTEM OF COMPULSORY UNEMPLOYMENT INSURANCE? *Congressional Digest*, Aug. 1931, X, 212.

THE PEOPLE'S LOBBY. *New Republic*, 26 Aug. 1931, LXVIII, 48.

Letter to the editor.

TEACHERS AS CITIZENS. *American Teacher*, Oct. 1931, XVI, i, 7.

Report by Anna L. P. Collins of an address by Dewey before Local 195 of the American Federation of Teachers at Cambridge, Massachusetts, 9 Apr. 1931.

SOME ASPECTS OF MODERN EDUCATION. *School and Society*, 31 Oct. 1931, XXXIV, 579–584.

Radio address in the Men of America series, given over the NBC network, 25 Oct. 1931.

SETTING NEW GOALS AT SEVENTY. *New York World-Telegram*, 4 Nov. 1931.

Interview with William Engle.

1932

ETHICS. Revised edition. By John Dewey . . . and James H[ayden] Tufts. New York: Henry Holt and Company [ᶜ1932]. xiii, 528 pp.

Originally published in 1908. "About two-thirds of the present edition has been newly rewritten, and frequent changes in detail will be found in the remainder."

Contents. Introduction. Part I, The Beginnings and Growth of Morality: Early Group Life—Basic Activities and Agencies—Group

Morality, Customs or Mores—From Custom to Conscience; from Group Morality to Personal Morality—The Hebrew Moral Development—The Moral Development of the Greeks—The Roman Contribution to the Modern Moral Consciousness—Factors and Trends in the Modern Moral Consciousness. Part II, Theory of the Moral Life: The Nature of Moral Theory—Ends, the Good and Wisdom—Right, Duty and Loyalty—Approbation, the Standard and Virtue—Moral Judgment and Knowledge—The Moral Self. Part III, The World of Action: Morals and Social Problems—Morals and the Political Order —Ethical Problems of the Economic Life—Collective Bargaining and the Labor Union—Moral Problems of Business—Social Control of Business and Industry—Toward the Future—Marriage and the Family.

Part II was reissued as *Theory of the Moral Life*, with an Introduction by Arnold Isenberg; New York: Holt, Rinehart and Winston [1960], 179 pp.

Reviewed in *Boston Transcript*, 14 Dec. 1932; *Crozer Quarterly*, Jan. 1933, X, 125 (A. S. Woodburne); *International Journal of Ethics*, Oct. 1933, XLIV, 155–160 (Frank Chapman Sharp); *Philosophical Review*, Sept. 1934, XLIII, 523–525 (DeWitt Henry Parker).

THE PLACE OF MINOR PARTIES IN THE AMERICAN SCENE. (Government series, Lecture No. 13.) Chicago: University of Chicago Press, 1932.

PREFATORY REMARKS. *In* George Herbert Mead, *The Philosophy of the Present*, edited by Arthur Edward Murphy. Lectures upon the Paul Carus Foundation, Third Series. (Chicago: Open Court Publishing Company, 1932), xxxvi–xl.

INTRODUCTION. *In* Frederick Matthias Alexander, *The Use of the Self: Its Conscious Direction in Relation to Diagnosis, Functioning and the Control of Reaction* (New York: E. P. Dutton and Company [°1932]), xiii–xix.

FOREWORD. *In* Paul Howard Douglas, *The Coming of a New Party* (New York: Whittlesey House, 1932), vii–[viii].

HUMAN NATURE. *Encyclopaedia of the Social Sciences*, VIII (New York: The Macmillan Company, 1932), 531–536.

CHARLES SANDERS PEIRCE. *New Republic*, 6 Jan. 1932, LXVIII, 220–221.

Review of *Collected Papers of Charles Sanders Peirce*, edited by Charles Hartshorne and Paul Weiss, Vol. I, Principles of Philosophy.

EDUCATION AND BIRTH CONTROL. *Nation*, 27 Jan. 1932, CXXXIV, 112.

MONASTERY, BARGAIN COUNTER, OR LABORATORY IN EDUCATION? *Barnwell Bulletin* (Central High School, Philadelphia), Feb. 1932, IX, xl, 51–62.

Reprinted in *Education Today* (1940), 230–243.

POLITICAL INTERFERENCE IN HIGHER EDUCATION AND RESEARCH. *School and Society*, 20 Feb. 1932, XXXV, 243–246.

"Presented as part of the symposium program under the Committee of One Hundred on Scientific Research at the New Orleans meeting of the American Association for the Advancement of Science."

Reprinted in *Education Today* (1940), 244–249.

A THIRD PARTY PROGRAM. *New Republic*, 24 Feb. 1932, LXX, 48–49.

In regard to the program of the League for Independent Political Action. See PROSPECTS FOR A THIRD PARTY, below.

MARX INVERTED. *New Republic*, 24 Feb. 1932, LXX, 52.

Review of Gerald Heard, *The Emergence of Man*.

THE SCHOOLS AND THE WHITE HOUSE CONFERENCE. *American Teacher*, Feb.-Mar. 1932, XVI, v, 3–4.

THE ONLY WAY TO STOP HOARDING. *People's Lobby Bulletin*, Mar. 1932, I, xi, 1.

TO REPLACE JUDGE CARDOZO. *New Republic*, 9 Mar. 1932, LXX, 102.

Letter to the editor endorsing Walter Pollak for the vacancy on the New York State Supreme Court bench.

SELF-SAVER OR FRANKENSTEIN? *Saturday Review of Literature*, 12 Mar. 1932, VIII, 581–582.

Review of Oswald Spengler, *Man and Technics*.

PEACE—BY PACT OR COVENANT? *New Republic*, 23 Mar. 1932, LXX, 145–147.

PROSPERITY DEPENDENT ON BUILDING FROM BOTTOM UP. *People's Lobby Bulletin*, Apr. 1932, I, xii, 1.

DEWEY DESCRIBES CHILD'S NEW WORLD. *New York Times*, 10 Apr. 1932.

Apropos of the White House Conference on Child Health and Protection.

BENDING THE TWIG. *New Republic*, 13 Apr. 1932, LXX, 242–244.
Review of Albert Jay Nock, *The Theory of Education in the United States.*

THE COLLAPSE OF A ROMANCE. *New Republic*, 27 Apr. 1932, LXX, 292–294.
A plea for a realistic view of the business depression.
Reprinted in *The New Republic Anthology, 1915–1935* (New York: Dodge Publishing Company, 1936), 418–423.

POLITICS AND CULTURE. *Modern Thinker*, May 1932, I, 168–174, 238.
A lecture at the Rand School, New York City.

A RÉSUMÉ OF FOUR LECTURES ON COMMON SENSE, SCIENCE AND PHILOSOPHY. *Bulletin of the Wagner Free Institute of Science of Philadelphia*, May 1932, VII, ii, 12–16.
Delivered on the Richard B. Westbrook Foundation at the Wagner Institute, Philadelphia, 2, 8 and 9 Apr. 1932.

YOU MUST ACT TO GET CONGRESS TO ACT. *People's Lobby Bulletin*, May 1932, II, i, 1.

THE SENATE BIRTH CONTROL BILL. *People's Lobby Bulletin*, May 1932, II, i, 1–2.

ARE SANCTIONS NECESSARY TO INTERNATIONAL ORGANIZATION? YES [by] Raymond Leslie Buell. No [by] John Dewey. [Foreign Policy Association. Pamphlet No. 82–83. Series 1931–1932. June, 1932.] New York: Foreign Policy Association [1932.] 39 pp.
Reprinted in *Intelligence in the Modern World* (1939), 566–602, with the title SANCTIONS AND THE SECURITY OF NATIONS.

VOTERS MUST DEMAND CONGRESS TAX WEALTH INSTEAD OF WANT. *People's Lobby Bulletin*, June 1932, II, ii, 1.

THE ECONOMIC SITUATION: A CHALLENGE TO EDUCATION. *Journal of Home Economics*, June 1932, XXIV, 495–501.
Read before the Department of Supervisors and Teachers of Home Economics of the National Education Association at Washington, 22 Feb. 1932.
Reprinted in *Education Today* (1940), 260–268.

MAKING SOVIET CITIZENS. *New Republic*, 8 June 1932, LXXI, 104.
Review of Thomas Woody, *New Minds: New Men?* and Nicholas Hans, *History of Russian Educational Policy.*

John Dewey Surveys the Nation's Ills. *New York Times*,
10 July 1932.

Interview with Samuel Johnson Woolf.

Prospects for a Third Party. *New Republic*, 27 July 1932,
LXXI, 278–280.

Discussion of the conference of the League for Independent Political
Action held at Cleveland, 9–10 July 1932, with Dewey as president.
Editorial comment in *New York Times*, 24 July 1932.
See Robert Morss Lovett, Progressives at Cleveland, *New Republic*, 20 July 1932, LXXI, 258–259.

The Meiklejohn Experiment. *New Republic*, 17 Aug. 1932,
LXXII, 23–24.

Review of Alexander Meiklejohn, *The Experimental College*.

Get Mayor and Governor To Demand Relief. *People's Lobby
Bulletin*, Nov. 1932, II, vii, 1.

Funds for Brookwood College. *New Republic*, 7 Dec. 1932,
LXXIII, 101; *Nation*, 14 Dec. 1932, CXXXV, 592.

An appeal for contributions.

1933

How We Think. A Restatement of the Relation of Reflective
Thinking to the Educative Processes. Boston: D. C. Heath
and Company, 1933. x, 301 pp.

How We Think (1910) has been considerably expanded, revised, rewritten and clarified in this edition.

Contents. Part I, The Problem of Training Thought. What Is Think-
ing?: Different Meanings of Thought—The Central Factor in Thinking—Phases of Reflective Thinking—Summary. Why Reflective
Thinking Must Be an Educational Aim: The Values of Thinking—
Tendencies Needing Constant Regulation. Native Resources in
Training Thought: Curiosity—Suggestion—Orderliness—Some Educational Conclusions. School Conditions and the Training of
Thought: Introductory: Methods and Conditions—The Influence
of the Habits of Others—The Influence of the Nature of Studies—
The Influence of Current Aims and Ideals. Part II, Logical Considerations. The Process and Product of Reflective Activity: Psychological Process and Logical Form: Thinking as a Formal and as an Actual Occurrence—Education in Relation to Form—Discipline and
Freedom. Examples of Inference and Testing: Illustrations of Reflective Activity—Inference to the Unknown—Thinking Moves from

a Doubtful to a Settled Situation. Analysis of Reflective Thinking: Facts and Ideas—The Essential Functions of Reflective Activity. The Place of Judgment in Reflective Activity: Three Factors in Judging—Analysis and Synthesis: The Two Functions of Judgment. Understanding: Ideas and Meanings: Ideas as Suggestions and Conjectures—Things and Meanings—The Process by Which Things Acquire Meaning. Understanding: Conception and Definition: The Nature of Conceptions—How Conceptions Arise—Definition and Organization of Meanings. Systematic Method: Control of Data and Evidence: Method as Deliberate Testing of Facts and Ideas—The Importance of Method in Judging Data. Systematic Method: Control of Reasoning and Concepts: The Value of Scientific Conceptions —Significant Applications to Education: Characteristic Inadequacies. Empirical and Scientific Thought: What Is Meant by Empirical—Scientific Method. Part III, The Training of Thought. Activity and the Training of Thought: The Early Stage of Activity— Play, Work, and Allied Forms of Activity—Constructive Occupations. From the Concrete to the Abstract: What Is the Concrete?— What Is the Abstract? Language and the Training of Thought: Language as the Tool of Thinking—The Abuse of Linguistic Methods in Education—The Use of Language in its Educational Bearings. Observation and Information in the Training of Mind: The Nature and Value of Observation—Methods and Materials of Observation in the Schools—Communication of Information. The Recitation and the Training of Thought: False Ideas about the Recitation—The Functions of the Recitation—The Conduct of the Recitation—The Function of the Teacher—Appreciation. Some General Conclusions: The Unconscious and the Conscious—Process and Product—The Far and the Near.

Reviewed in *Boston Transcript*, 21 June 1933; *New Republic*, 21 Mar. 1934, LXXVIII, 165 (Sidney Hook); *Saturday Review of Literature*, 1 July 1933, IX, 682.

THE EDUCATIONAL FRONTIER. Written in Collaboration by William Heard Kilpatrick, Editor; Boyd Henry Bode, John Dewey, John Lawrence Childs, Robert Bruce Raup, Henry Gordon Hullfish and Vivian Trow Thayer. New York, London: The Century Company [ᶜ1933]. vi, 235 pp. Also published as *Yearbook* XXI of the National Society of College Teachers of Education, Chicago: University of Chicago Press, 1933.

Chapters II and IX are "a joint product of thought" of Dewey and J. L. Childs, written out by Dewey.

Reviewed in *New Republic*, 24 May 1933, LXXV, 49–50 (Sidney Hook).

NEW YORK AND THE SEABURY INVESTIGATION. A Digest and Interpretation of the Reports by Samuel Seabury concerning the Government of New York City, prepared by a Committee of Educators and Civic Workers under the Chairmanship of John Dewey. [New York]: The City Affairs Committee of New York [°1933]. 48 pp.

A HUMANIST MANIFESTO. *In* Charles Francis Potter, *Humanizing Religion* (New York: Harper and Brothers, 1933), 6–15.

Signed by John Dewey and thirty-three leading United States philosophers, writers, and clergymen.

LOGIC. *Encyclopaedia of the Social Sciences*, IX (New York: The Macmillan Company, 1933), 598–603.

OUTLAWRY OF WAR. *Ib.*, 508–510.

PRÉFACE À L'ÉDITION ANGLAISE PAR JOHN DEWEY. *In* Comité des Jeunes Révolutionnaires Cubains, *La Terreur a Cuba.* Préfaces de Henri Barbusse, à l'édition française, John Dewey à l'édition anglaise. I. les Assassinats du 27 Septembre. II. L'Histoire d'une Tyrannie. Adhésions Individuelles—Adhésions Collectives—Appendice. Édition française. Paris [Courbevoie, la Cootypographie], 1933. 98 pp. plates, portraits.

Copy in Bibliothèque Nationale. Dewey's preface (in French) is on pp. 9–10. No copy of an English edition has been found.

STEPS TO ECONOMIC RECOVERY. (Pamphlets on the Economic Crisis of 1929, Vol. 9, No. 9.) New York: Robert Schalkenbach Foundation [1933?]. 15 pp.

Address on Henry George *et al.* delivered over radio station WEVD. Copy in Yale University Library.

FOREWORD. *In* George Raymond Geiger, *The Philosophy of Henry George* (New York: The Macmillan Company, 1933), ix–xiii.

UNEMPLOYED AND UNDERPAID CONSUMERS SHOULD NOT PAY BILLION DOLLAR SUBSIDY TO SPECULATORS. *People's Lobby Bulletin*, Jan. 1933, II, viii, 1–2.

In regard to the farm allotment plan.

THE FUTURE OF RADICAL POLITICAL ACTION. *Nation*, 4 Jan. 1933, CXXXVI, 8–9.

Apropos of Norman Thomas, THE FUTURE OF THE SOCIALIST PARTY, in *ib.*, 14 Dec. 1932, CXXXV, 584–586.

A GOD OR THE GOD? *Christian Century*, 8 Feb. 1933, L, 193–196.

Review of *Is There a God?—A Conversation by Henry Nelson Wieman, Douglas Clyde Macintosh and Max Carl Otto*. Reply, MR. WIEMAN AND MR. MACINTOSH "CONVERSE" WITH MR. DEWEY, *Christian Century*, 1 Mar. 1933, L, 299–302. Rejoinder, DR. DEWEY REPLIES, *ib.*, 22 Mar. 1933, L, 394–395.

RELIEF IS VITAL. *People's Lobby Bulletin*, Feb. 1933, II, ix, 1–2.

OPINIONS REGARDING THE SIX-YEAR HIGH SCHOOL. *Junior College Journal*, Mar. 1933, VIII, 320.

UNITY AND PROGRESS. *World Tomorrow*. 8 Mar. 1933, XVI, 232–233.

In response to Reinhold Niebuhr, AFTER CAPITALISM—WHAT? *ib.*, 1 Mar. 1933, XVI, 203–205.

THE BANKING CRISIS. *People's Lobby Bulletin*, Mar. 1933, II, x, 1–2.

THE DRIVE AGAINST HUNGER. *New Republic*, 29 Mar. 1933, LXXIV, 190.

Letter to the editor, signed as chairman of the National Committee of the League for Independent Political Action.

THE CRISIS IN EDUCATION. *American Teacher*, Apr. 1933, XVII, 5–9.

Address before Yale Local No. 204, American Federation of Teachers, and the New Haven Teachers Association, Hotel Taft, New Haven, 29 Jan. 1933.

Also printed separately [n.p., n.d.]. 16 pp.

Excerpts in *Bulletin of the American Association of University Professors*, May 1933, XIX, 318–319.

CONGRESS FACES ITS TEST ON TAXATION. *People's Lobby Bulletin*, Apr. 1933, II, xii, 1–2.

EDUCATION AND OUR PRESENT SOCIAL PROBLEMS. *School and Society*, 15 Apr. 1933, XXXVII, 473–478; *Educational Method*, Apr. 1933, XII, 385–390.

Address before the Department of Supervisors and Directors of Instruction of the National Education Association, Minneapolis, 1 Mar. 1933.

Reprinted in National Education Association, *Addresses and Proceedings*, 1933, pp. 687–689; and in *Education Today* (1940), 250–259.

Translations. Spanish in *Revista de pedagogia*, 1933, XII, 337–344.

THE ADVENTURE OF PERSUASION. *New Republic*, 19 Apr. 1933, LXXIV, 285–286.

Review of Alfred North Whitehead, *Adventures of Ideas*.

DEWEY OUTLINES UTOPIAN SCHOOLS. *New York Times*, 23 Apr. 1933.

Address before the conference on the Educational Status of the Four- and Five-Year Old Child Held at Teachers College, Columbia, in Apr. 1933; printed in part.

THE REAL TEST OF THE NEW DEAL. *People's Lobby Bulletin*, May 1933, III, i, 1.

In regard to the Revenue Act.

ON THE GRIEVANCE COMMITTEE'S REPORT. *Union Teacher* (Teachers Union of the City of New York), May 1933, X, ix, 2–4.

SHALL WE ABOLISH SCHOOL "FRILLS"? No. *Rotarian*, May 1933, XLII, v, 18–19, 49.

Reply to Henry Louis Mencken's YES in *ib.*, 16–17, 48.

Reprinted in *Modern Thinker*, June 1933, III, 149–153; abridged in *School Management*, June 1933, II, v, 5, 16.

SUPERFICIAL TREATMENT MUST FAIL. *People's Lobby Bulletin*, June 1933, III, ii, 1–3.

Problems of recovery from the depression; reprinted in *ib.*, July 1938, VIII, iii, 1–3.

INFLATIONARY MEASURES INJURE THE MASSES. *People's Lobby Bulletin*, July 1933, III, iii, 1–2.

An open letter to President Franklin Delano Roosevelt, written early in May 1933.

WHY HAVE PROGRESSIVE SCHOOLS? *Current History*, July 1933, XXXVIII, 441–448.

Reprinted in *Education Today* (1940), 269–281.

TO SAVE THE RAND SCHOOL. *Nation*, 12 July 1933, CXXXVII, 47.

Letter to the editor, requesting contributions.

A CHALLENGE TO CRITICISM. *New Republic*, 16 Aug. 1933, LXXVI, 24–25.

Review of Martin Schütze, *Academic Illusions in the Field of Letters and the Arts.*

PLENTY *vs.* SCARCITY. *Commerce and Finance*, 30 Aug. 1933, XXII, 751–752.

An address delivered over radio station WEVD.

THE IMPERATIVE NEED FOR A NEW RADICAL PARTY. *Common Sense*, Sept. 1933, II, iii, 6–7.

Reprinted in Alfred Mitchell Bingham and Selden Rodman, eds., *Challenge to the New Deal* (1934), 269–273.

WILD INFLATION WOULD PARALYZE NATION. *People's Lobby Bulletin*, Sept. 1933, III, v, 1–2.

FARM PROCESSING AND OTHER CONSUMPTION TAXES MUST BE REPEALED. *People's Lobby Bulletin*, Nov. 1933, III, vii, 1.

Open letter to President Roosevelt.

THE NEXT SESSION [OF CONGRESS] AND THE PEOPLE'S LOBBY. *People's Lobby Bulletin*, Dec. 1933, III, viii, 1.

1934

ART AS EXPERIENCE. New York: Minton, Balch & Company [ᶜ1934]. vii, 355 pp.

Published also in London by G. Allen and Unwin, 1934.

Paperback reprint, New York: Capricorn Books–G. P. Putnam's Sons, 1959.

The William James Lectures, delivered at Harvard University in the winter and spring of 1931, "are the origin of the present volume."

Contents. The Live Creature—The Live Creature and "Etherial Things"—Having an Experience—The Act of Expression—The Expressive Object—Substance and Form—The Natural History of Form—The Organization of Energies—The Common Substance of the Arts—The Varied Substance of the Arts—The Human Contribution—The Challenge to Philosophy—Criticism and Perception—Art and Civilization.

Translations. Italian, with Introduction, by Corrado Maltese (Firenze, 1951); Japanese by Yasushi Suzuki (Tokyo, 1952); Spanish, with Introduction, by Samuel Ramos (México–Buenos Aires, 1949).

Reviewed in *American Mercury*, Oct. 1934, XXXIII, 253–255 (Ernest Sutherland Bates); *Apollo*, Dec. 1934, XX, 337–338; *Aut Aut*

5, Sept. 1951, 468–469 (Enzo Paci); *Boston Transcript*, 13 June 1934 (E. N.); *Chicago Tribune*, 25 Aug. 1934 (D. C. Rich); *Christian Century*, 26 Sept. 1934, LI, 1211–1212 (Edwin Theophil Buehrer); *Christian Science Monitor*, 25 Apr. 1934; *Current History*, June 1934, XL, xii; *Journal of Philosophy*, 10 May 1934, XXXI, 275–276 (Irwin Edman); *London Studio*, Aug. 1936, XII, 111 (Reginald Howard Wilenski); *Nation*, 20 June 1934, CXXXVIII, 710–711 (Robert J. Goldwater); *New Republic*, 25 Apr. 1934, LXXVIII, 315–316 (Kenneth Burke); *New York Herald Tribune*, 6 May 1934 (Horace Gregory); *New York Times*, 8 Apr. 1934 (Dino Ferrari); *Spectator*, 23 Nov. 1934, CLIII, sup. 6 (Wyndham Lewis); *Yale Review*, Sept. 1934, XXIV, 188 (Samson Lane Faison).

See also Edna Aston Shearer, DEWEY'S ESTHETIC THEORY, *Journal of Philosophy*, 7 and 21 Nov. 1935, XXXII, 617–627, 650–664; Georgiana Melvin, THE SOCIAL PHILOSOPHY UNDERLYING DEWEY'S THEORY OF ART, *Mills College Faculty Studies*, 1937, I, 124–136; John M. Warbeke, FORM IN EVOLUTIONARY THEORIES OF ART, *Journal of Philosophy*, 22 May 1941, XXXVIII, 293–300; the entries under Benedetto Croce in Part II of this book; James L. Jarrett, ART AS COGNITIVE EXPERIENCE, *Journal of Philosophy*, 5 Nov. 1953, L, 681–688; Edward Goodwin Ballard, AN ESTIMATE OF JOHN DEWEY'S *Art as Experience*, *Tulane Studies in Philosophy*, 1955, IV, 5–18, reviewed by Douglas N. Morgan in *Journal of Aesthetics and Art Criticism*, Dec. 1956, XV, 261.

Comments in Charles Austin Beard and Mary Ritter Beard, *America in Midpassage* (1939), 766.

A COMMON FAITH. New Haven: Yale University Press; London: Humphrey Milford, Oxford University Press, 1934. 87 pp.

Reissued as a paperback by the Yale University Press, 1960.

The Dwight Harrington Terry Lectures, delivered at Sprague Memorial Hall, Yale University, 17, 18, and 19 January 1934.

Contents. Religion *versus* the Religious—Faith and Its Object—The Human Abode of the Religious Function.

The second chapter was originally published in the *Yale Review*, June 1934, with the title THE LIBERATION OF MODERN RELIGION; see below.

Translations. Italian, with introductory essay, by Guido Calogero (Firenze, 1959); Japanese by Hideo Kishimoto (Tokyo, 1951).

Reviewed in *Boston Transcript*, 1 Sept. 1934 (E. N.); *Catholic World*, Nov. 1934, CXL, 240 (G. A. T.); *Christian Century*, 10 Oct. 1934, LI, 1281 (Winfred Ernest Garrison); *Christian Register*, 27 Dec. 1934, CXIII, 787–789 (Andrew Banning); *Harper's Magazine*, Oct. 1934, CLXIX, front adv. section (Harry Hansen); *Journal of Philosophy*, 11 Oct. 1934, XXXI, 584–585 (Robert Scoon); *London Times Lit-*

erary Supplement, 15 Nov. 1934; *Mind*, July 1935, XLIV, 397–399 (Ferdinand Canning Scott Schiller); *Nation*, 26 Sept. 1934, CXXXIX, 358–359 (Reinhold Niebuhr); *New Masses*, 2 Oct. 1934, XIII, i, 38–39 (Corliss Lamont); *New York Herald Tribune*, 20 Sept. 1934 (Lewis Gannett); *New York Herald Tribune Books*, 4 Nov. 1934 (John Haynes Holmes); *New York Times*, 30 Sept. 1934; *Philosophical Review*, Sept. 1935, XLIV, 496–497 (Max Carl Otto); *Saturday Review of Literature*, 22 Dec. 1934, XI, 389 (A. C. Wyckoff); *Springfield Republican*, 5 Oct. 1934; *Yale Review*, Sept. 1934, XXIV, 166–168 (Henry Hazlitt).

See review by Norbert Guterman in the *New Republic*, 20 Feb. 1935, LXXXII, 53; Dewey's reply, *ib.*, 13 Mar. 1935, LXXXII, 132; rejoinder by Guterman and letter of Irvin Kelley, *ib.*, 20 Mar. 1935, LXXXII, 161.

See Albert Eustace Haydon, MR. DEWEY ON RELIGION AND GOD, *Journal of Religion*, Jan. 1935, XV, 22–25; Max Carl Otto, MR. DEWEY AND RELIGION, *New Humanist*, Apr.-May 1935, VIII, ii, 41–47; Willard Eugene Arnett, CRITIQUE OF DEWEY'S ANTICLERICAL RELIGIOUS PHILOSOPHY, *Journal of Religion*, Oct. 1954, XXXIV, 256–266; and Corliss Lamont, NEW LIGHT ON DEWEY'S *Common Faith*, *Journal of Philosophy*, 5 Jan. 1961, LVIII, 21–28.

See also Henry Nelson Wieman, JOHN DEWEY'S COMMON FAITH, *Christian Century*, 14 Nov. 1934, LI, 1450–1452; and IS JOHN DEWEY A THEIST? *ib.*, 5 Dec. 1934, letter of Edwin Ewart Aubrey, 1550, reply by Wieman, 1550–1551, letter of Dewey, 1551–1552, reply by Wieman, 1552–1553; editorial comment, THE PHILOSOPHERS AND GOD, *ib.*, 12 Dec. 1934, LI, 1582–1584.

EDUCATION FOR A CHANGING SOCIAL ORDER. National Education Association, *Addresses and Proceedings*, 1934, 744–752.

Reprinted in American Association of Teachers Colleges, *Thirteenth Yearbook*, 1934, 60–68, in *Intelligence in the Modern World* (1939), 683–690, with the title THE SCHOOLS IN THE SOCIAL ORDER; and published separately by the League for Industrial Democracy, New York [1934, 1949], 14 pp., with the title EDUCATION AND THE SOCIAL ORDER.

IMPERATIVE NEED: A NEW RADICAL PARTY. *In* Alfred Mitchell Bingham and Selden Rodman, eds., *Challenge to the New Deal* (New York: Falcon Press [ᶜ1934]), 269–273.

Reprinted from *Common Sense*, Sept. 1933, II, iii, 6–7.

The Introduction, v–vii, is also by Dewey.

PHILOSOPHY. *Encyclopaedia of the Social Sciences*, XII (New York: The Macmillan Company, 1934), 118–128.

PRESIDENT'S POLICIES HELP PROPERTY OWNERS CHIEFLY. *People's Lobby Bulletin*, Jan. 1934, III, ix, 1–2.

Open letter to President Roosevelt.

NEW DEAL PROGRAM MUST BE APPRAISED. *People's Lobby Bulletin*, Jan. 1934, III, ix, 5.

Open letter to the members of Congress.

A REAL TEST OF THE ADMINISTRATION. *People's Lobby Bulletin*, Feb. 1934, III, x, 1–2.

In regard to the Revenue Bill.

THE SUPREME INTELLECTUAL OBLIGATION. *Science Education*, Feb. 1934, XVIII, 1–4; *Science*, 16 Mar. 1934, n.s. LXXIX, 240–243.

Reprinted in *Education Today* (1940), 282–287.

Address at a dinner in honor of James McKeen Cattell at the University Club, Boston, 27 Dec. 1933. Condensed in *Bulletin of the American Association of University Professors*, May 1934, XX, 306–309.

ART IN A VACUUM. *Saturday Review of Literature*, 24 Feb. 1934, X, 501–503.

Reprinted as part of Chapter I of *Art as Experience* (1934).

SANTAYANA'S ORTHODOXY. *New Republic*, 28 Feb. 1934, LXXVIII, 79–80.

Review of George Santayana, *Some Turns of Thought in Modern Philosophy: Five Essays*.

TOMORROW MAY BE TOO LATE: SAVE THE SCHOOLS NOW. *Good Housekeeping*, Mar. 1934, XCVIII, iii, 20–21, 222.

Interview with Katherine Glover.

AMERICA'S PUBLIC OWNERSHIP PROGRAM. *People's Lobby Bulletin*, Mar. 1934, III, xi, 1.

Extracts from a speech at a conference of the People's Lobby in Washington.

A GREAT AMERICAN PROPHET. *Common Sense*, Apr. 1934, III, iv, 6–7.

Edward Bellamy and the relevance of his books, *Looking Backward* (1888), and *Equality* (1897).

FACING THE ERA OF REALITIES. *People's Lobby Bulletin*, Apr. 1934, III, xii, 1–2.

INDIVIDUAL PSYCHOLOGY AND EDUCATION. *The Philosopher* (London), Apr. 1934, XII, 56–62.

MEANING, ASSERTION AND PROPOSAL. *Philosophy of Science*, Apr. 1934, I, 237–238.

Comment on Rudolf Carnap, ON THE CHARACTER OF PHILOSOPHIC PROBLEMS, *ib.*, Jan. 1934, 5–19. Reply by Carnap, *ib.*, July 1934, 359–360.

WHY I AM NOT A COMMUNIST. *Modern Monthly*, Apr. 1934, VIII, 135–137.

Reprinted in *The Meaning of Marx, a Symposium*, by Bertrand Russell, John Dewey, Morris Cohen, Sidney Hook, and Sherwood Eddy (New York: Farrar and Rinehart [1934]), 86–90.

See Paul Salter and Jack Librome, DEWEY, RUSSELL AND COHEN: WHY THEY ARE ANTI-COMMUNIST, *New Masses*, 17 and 24 July 1934, XII, ii, 24–27, iii, 22–23.

NEW WORLDS FOR SCIENCE. *Modern Thinker*, Apr. 1934, IV, 323–325.

INTELLIGENCE AND POWER. *New Republic*, 25 Apr. 1934, LXXVIII, 306–307.

ACQUIESCENCE AND ACTIVITY IN COMMUNISM. *The New Humanist*, May-June 1934, VII, iii, 22.

Review of Theodore B. Brameld, *A Philosophic Approach to Communism*.

THE LIBERATION OF MODERN RELIGION. *Yale Review*, June 1934, XXIII, 751–770.

Reprinted in *A Common Faith* (1934) with the title FAITH AND ITS OBJECT.

Reply by Corliss Lamont, JOHN DEWEY CAPITULATES TO "GOD," *New Masses*, 31 July 1934, XII, v, 23–24.

See John Wright Buckham, GOD AND THE IDEAL: PROFESSOR DEWEY REINTERPRETS RELIGION, *Journal of Religion*, Jan. 1935, XV, 1–9; Henry Nelson Wieman, DEWEY AND BUCKHAM ON RELIGION, *ib.*, 10–21, and reply by Buckham, *ib.*, July 1935, 309–315.

CHARACTER TRAINING FOR YOUTH. *Rotarian*, Sept. 1934, XLV, iii, 6–8, 58–59; *Recreation*, June 1935, XXIX, 139–142.

THE NEED FOR A PHILOSOPHY OF EDUCATION. *The New Era in Home and School* (London), Nov. 1934, XV, 211–214.

Reprinted in *Education Today* (1940), 288–299.

CAN EDUCATION SHARE IN SOCIAL RECONSTRUCTION? *Social Frontier*, Oct. 1934, I, i, 11–12.

NO HALF WAY HOUSE FOR AMERICA. *People's Lobby Bulletin*, Nov. 1934, IV, vii, 1.

THE THEORY OF LIBERTY VS. THE FACT OF REGIMENTATION. (American Ideals, I.) *Common Sense*, Dec. 1934, III, xii, 10–11.

RADIO'S INFLUENCE ON THE MIND. *School and Society*, 15 Dec. 1934, XL, 805; *Educational Review* (China), Mar. 1935, XXVII, 178.

Summary of an address delivered from Town Hall, New York City, over the WEVD University of the Air, 8 Dec. 1934.

1935

LIBERALISM AND SOCIAL ACTION. New York: G. P. Putnam's Sons [ᶜ1935]. viii, 93 pp.

Lectures delivered at the University of Virginia upon the Page-Barbour Foundation. "Some passages have been rewritten and the last chapter somewhat enlarged for publication."

Contents. The History of Liberalism—The Crisis in Liberalism—Renascent Liberalism.

Translation. Italian by R. Cresti (Firenze, 1946, 1948).

Reviewed in *Christian Century*, 25 Sept. 1935, LII, 1210 (Edwin Theophil Buehrer); *Current History*, Oct. 1935, XLIII, v (John Chamberlain); *International Journal of Ethics*, Jan. 1936, XLVI, 229–236 (Frank Hyneman Knight); *Nation*, 11 Sept. 1935, CXLI, 303–304 (Reinhold Niebuhr); *New Republic*, 4 Mar. 1936, LXXXVI, 115–116 (Kenneth Burke) also in his *Philosophy of Literary Form* (1941), 388–391; *New York Times*, 20 Aug. 1935 (John Chamberlain), 1 Sept. 1935 (Henry Hazlitt); *People's Lobby Bulletin*, Feb. 1936, V, x, 1–2; *Philosophical Review*, July 1935, XLIV, 388–390 (David Wight Prall); *Saturday Review of Literature*, 14 Dec. 1935, XIII, 7 (Horace Meyer Kallen); *Survey Graphic*, Nov. 1935, XXIV, 555 (Walter Lincoln Whittlesey).

See Corliss Lamont, JOHN DEWEY, MARXISM AND THE UNITED FRONT, *New Masses*, 3 Mar. 1936, XVIII, x, 22–23.

DER PROJEKT-PLAN: GRUNDLEGUNG UND PRAXIS, von John Dewey und William Heard Kilpatrick. [Uebersetzt von Georg Schultz und Ernst Wiesenthal.] (Pädagogik des Auslands herausgegeben im Auftrag des Zentralinstituts für Erziehung und Unterricht von Prof. Dr. Peter Petersen, Jena, VI.) Weimar: Herman Böhlaus Nachfolger, 1935. 213 pp.

Contents. W. H. Kilpatrick: Erziehung für eine sich wandelnde Kultur—John Dewey: Der Ausweg aus dem Pädagogischen Wirrwarr [The Way Out of Educational Confusion, 1931]—John Dewey: Die Quellen einer Wissenschaft von der Erziehung [The Sources of a Science of Education, 1929]—John Dewey: Das Kind und der Lehrplan [The Child and the Curriculum, 1902]—W. H. Kilpatrick: Die Projekt-Methode—Ellsworth Collings: Ein Versuch mit einem Projekt-Lehrplan—W. H. Kilpatrick: Vorwort zur Schrift von Collings—John Dewey: Das Problem der Freiheit in den neuen Schulen [How Much Freedom in New Schools? 1930]—Peter Petersen: Nachwort.

Reviewed in *Società*, Jan.-June 1952, IX, 248 (M. A. M.).

See Mario Mencarelli, *Il metodo dei progetti: G. Dewey e W. H. Kilpatrick* (Firenze: Marzocco-Bemporad, 1952, 50 pp.), and Lamberto Borghi, *Il metodo dei progetti: Un capitolo della storia dell'educazione attiva*, con teste di W. H. Kilpatrick (Firenze: La Nuova Italia [1952], 132 pp.).

AN EMPIRICAL SURVEY OF EMPIRICISMS. In *Studies in the History of Ideas*, edited by the Department of Philosophy of Columbia University, Vol. III (New York: Columbia University Press, 1935), 3–22.

Reprinted in *John Dewey on Experience, Nature, and Freedom* (1960), 70–87.

NEEDED—A NEW POLITICS. *In* Charles Frederick Weller, *World Fellowship* (New York: Liveright Publishing Corporation [ᶜ1935]), 119–125.

Address delivered at the First International Congress of the World Fellowship of Faiths, Chicago, 1933.

FOREWORD. *In* Albert Coombs Barnes and Violette de Mazia, *The Art of Renoir* (New York: Minton, Balch & Co., 1935), vii–x.

FOREWORD. *In* Carl Christian Jensen, *Seventy Times Seven* (Boston: Lothrop, Lee and Shepard Company, 1935), vii–x.

FOREWORD. *In* William Allan Neilson, ed., *Education in the Soviet Union:* An exhibition . . . at the American Museum of Natural History . . . New York, N.Y., January 16 to February 22, 1935 (New York: American Russian Institute, 1935), 3.

INTRODUCTION. *In* Myrtle Byram McGraw, *Growth: A Study of Johnny and Jimmy* (New York: D. Appleton-Century Company [ᶜ1935]), ix–xiii.

SOCIALIZATION OF GROUND RENT. *People's Lobby Bulletin*, Jan. 1935, IV, ix, 1.
Speech at a luncheon of the People's Lobby at the Cosmos Club, Washington, 15 Dec. 1939.

THE TEACHER AND HIS WORLD. *Social Frontier*, Jan. 1935, I, iv, 7.
Reprinted in *Education Today* (1940), 300–302, and in *Problems of Men* (1946), 70–72.

THE FOUNDER OF PRAGMATISM. *New Republic*, 30 Jan. 1935, LXXXI, 338–339.
Review of *Collected Papers of Charles Sanders Peirce*, edited by Charles Hartshorne and Paul Weiss, Vol. V, Pragmatism and Pragmaticism.

THE CRUCIAL ROLE OF INTELLIGENCE. *Social Frontier*, Feb. 1935, I, v, 9–10.
Reprinted in *Problems of Men* (1946), 80–82.

INTERNATIONAL COÖPERATION OR INTERNATIONAL CHAOS. *People's Lobby Bulletin*, Feb. 1935, IV, x, 6–7.

TOWARD ADMINISTRATIVE STATESMANSHIP. *Social Frontier*, Mar. 1935, I, vi, 9–10.
Reprinted in *Problems of Men* (1946), 66–69.

TAXATION AS A STEP TO SOCIALIZATION. *People's Lobby Bulletin*, Mar. 1935, IV, xi, 1–2.

THE TEACHER AND THE PUBLIC. *American Teacher*, Mar.-Apr. 1935, XIX, 34; *Vital Speeches*, 28 Jan. 1935, I, 278–279.
Address delivered over the WEVD University of the Air, 16 Jan. 1935.
Reprinted in *Education Today* (1940), 303–307.

UNITED, WE SHALL STAND. *Social Frontier*, Apr. 1935, I, vii, 11–12; *School and Community*, Apr. 1935, XXI, 143–145.
Reprinted in part in *Problems of Men* (1946), 72–76.

INTIMATIONS OF MORTALITY. *New Republic,* 24 Apr. 1935, LXXXII, 318.

Review of Corliss Lamont, *The Illusion of Immortality.* Reprinted as the Introduction to the second edition of *The Illusion of Immortality* (New York: Philosophical Library, 1950), vii–ix, and the third edition (*ib.,* 1959), ix–xi.

THE FUTURE OF LIBERALISM. *Journal of Philosophy,* 25 Apr. 1935, XXXII, 225–230; *School and Society,* 19 Jan. 1935, XLI, 73–77.

Reprinted in *Problems of Men* (1946), 133–140.

Excerpts in *People's Lobby Bulletin,* Feb. 1935, IV, x, 1–2.

Read at a symposium at the meeting of the Eastern Division of the American Philosophical Association, New York University, 28 Dec. 1934. Dewey was followed by two other speakers on this topic, William Ernest Hocking and William Pepperell Montague, whose papers were printed, respectively, in *Journal of Philosophy,* 25 Apr. 1935, XXXII, 230–247, and *International Journal of Ethics,* Jan. 1935, XLV, 138–169.

Reply by John Herman Randall, Jr., LIBERALISM AS FAITH IN INTELLIGENCE, *Journal of Philosophy,* 9 May 1935, XXXII, 253–264.

MYSTICAL NATURALISM AND RELIGIOUS HUMANISM. *The New Humanist,* Apr.-May 1935, VIII, ii, 74–75.

Comments on an article with the same title by Bernard Meland, in *ib.,* 72–74.

YOUTH IN A CONFUSED WORLD. *Social Frontier,* May 1935, I, viii, 9–10.

Reprinted in *Education Today* (1940), 308–310.

GOVERNMENT AND CHILDREN. *American Teacher,* May-June 1935, XIX, 20.

THE NEED FOR ORIENTATION. *Forum,* June 1935, XCIII, 333–335.

Followed by EDUCATION CANNOT LEAD by Tyler Dennett; the two articles are labeled EDUCATION IN OUR SOCIETY, A DEBATE.

Reprinted in *Problems of Men* (1946), 88–92.

TOWARD A NATIONAL SYSTEM OF EDUCATION. *Social Frontier,* June 1935, I, ix, 9–10.

Reprinted in *Education Today* (1940), 311–315.

EDUCATORS URGED TO JOIN WITH OTHER WORKERS. *School Management,* June 1935, IV, 207.

WHEN AMERICA GOES TO WAR. *Modern Monthly*, June 1935, IX, 200.

Contribution to a symposium; Dewey states what his attitude would be.

BERGSON ON INSTINCT. *New Republic*, 26 June 1935, LXXXIII, 200–201.

Review of Henri Bergson, *The Two Sources of Morality and Religion*, translated by R. Ashley Audra and Cloudesley Brereton.

NATURE AND HUMANITY. *The New Humanist*, Autumn 1935, VIII, 153–157.

Review of Oliver Leslie Reiser, *Philosophy and the Concepts of Modern Science*.

THE MEANING OF ARCHITECTURE. *Architectural Review* (London), Sept. 1935, LXXVIII, 119.

Reprinted from *Art as Experience* (1934).

LIBERTY AND SOCIAL CONTROL. *Social Frontier*, Nov. 1935, II, 41–42.

Reprinted in *Education Today* (1940), 316–319; and in *Problems of Men* (1946), 111–114.

OUR UN-FREE PRESS. *Common Sense*, Nov. 1935, IV, xi, 6–7.

THE MEANING OF LIBERALISM. *Social Frontier*, Dec. 1935, II, 74–75.

Reprinted in *Problems of Men* (1946), 121–125.

PEIRCE'S THEORY OF QUALITY. *Journal of Philosophy*, 19 Dec. 1935, XXXII, 701–708.

Reply to Thomas A. Goudge, THE VIEWS OF CHARLES PEIRCE ON THE GIVEN IN EXPERIENCE, in *ib.*, 26 Sept. 1935, 533–544. Rejoinder by Goudge, FURTHER REFLECTIONS ON PEIRCE'S DOCTRINE OF THE GIVEN, *ib.*, 21 May 1936, XXXIII, 289–295.

Reprinted in *John Dewey on Experience, Nature, and Freedom* (1960), 199–210.

1936

INTRODUCTION. *In* Katherine Camp Mayhew and Anna Camp Edwards, *The Dewey School: The Laboratory School of the University of Chicago 1896–1903* (New York: D. Appleton-Century Company, 1936), xv–xvi.

THE THEORY OF THE CHICAGO EXPERIMENT. Appendix II in *ib.*, 463–477, was also written by Dewey.

INTRODUCTION. *In* Angelo M. Pellegrine and Brents Stirling, *Argumentation and Public Discussion* (Boston: D. C. Heath and Company, 1936).

INTRODUCTION. *In* Richard Ward Greene Welling, *Self Government and Politics in School* (binder's title; bound collection of articles and reprints).

Dewey's introduction, dated 20 July 1936, is reproduced in facsimile. Copy at Boston Public Library.

LIBERALISM AND EQUALITY. *Social Frontier*, Jan. 1936, II, 105–106.

Reprinted in *Problems of Men* (1946), 114–117.

LIBERALISM AND CIVIL LIBERTIES. *Social Frontier*, Feb. 1936, II, 137–138.

Reprinted in *Problems of Men* (1946), 118–121.

THE JAMESES. *New Republic*, 12 Feb. 1936, LXXXVI, 24–25.

Review of Ralph Barton Perry, *The Thought and Character of William James*.

A LIBERAL SPEAKS OUT FOR LIBERALISM. *New York Times Magazine*, 23 Feb. 1936, 3, 24.

Reprinted in *What Is Democracy?* (1939), 3–10, with the title, THE FUTURE OF LIBERALISM, OR THE DEMOCRATIC WAY OF CHANGE.

EDUCATION AND NEW SOCIAL IDEALS. *Vital Speeches*, 24 Feb. 1936, II, 327–328.

Address broadcast from Station WEVD, 14 Jan. 1936.

THE SOCIAL SIGNIFICANCE OF ACADEMIC FREEDOM. *Social Frontier*, Mar. 1936, II, 165–166.

Reprinted in *Education Today* (1940), 320–324; and in *Problems of Men* (1946), 76–80.

HENRY LINVILLE PENSION FUND. *Social Frontier*, Apr. 1936, II, 230.

Letter to the editor.

CLASS STRUGGLE AND THE DEMOCRATIC WAY. *Social Frontier*, May 1936, II, 241–242.

Reprinted in *Intelligence in the Modern World* (1939), 696–702, with the title EDUCATORS AND THE CLASS STRUGGLE; and in *Education Today* (1940), 325–330.

Apropos of Theodore B. Brameld, KARL MARX AND THE AMERICAN TEACHER, *Social Frontier*, Nov. 1935, II, 53–56, and John Lawrence

Childs, CAN TEACHERS STAY OUT OF THE CLASS STRUGGLE? *ib.*, Apr. 1936, II, 219–222. Dewey associates himself with the position of Robert Bruce Raup in SHALL WE USE THE CLASS DYNAMIC? *ib.*, Jan. 1936, II, 106–109.

Replies by Childs, DEMOCRACY, EDUCATION, AND THE CLASS STRUGGLE, *ib.*, June 1936, II, 274–278, and Brameld, AMERICAN EDUCATION AND THE SOCIAL STRUGGLE, *Science and Society*, Fall 1936, I, 1–17.

CHARACTERISTICS AND CHARACTERS: KINDS AND CLASSES. *Journal of Philosophy*, 7 May 1936, XXXIII, 253–261.

WHAT ARE UNIVERSALS? *Ib.*, 21 May 1936, XXXIII, 281–288.

The two articles above are included in *Logic: The Theory of Inquiry* (1938).

SANTAYANA'S NOVEL. *Columbia Review*, Commencement 1936, XVII, iv, 49–51.

Review of George Santayana, *The Last Puritan*.

ONE CURRENT RELIGIOUS PROBLEM. *Journal of Philosophy*, 4 June 1936, XXXIII, 324–326.

In reply to Percy Hughes, CURRENT PHILOSOPHICAL PROBLEMS, *ib.*, 9 Apr. 1936, XXXIII, 212–217.

THE WORK OF GEORGE MEAD. *New Republic*, 22 July 1936, LXXXVII, 329–330.

Review of George Herbert Mead, *Mind, Self and Society*, and *Movements of Thought in the Nineteenth Century*.

ANNIVERSARY ADDRESS. (University of Michigan Official Publication, Vol. 38, No. 8, 25 July 1936.) *Journal of the Michigan Schoolmasters' Club 1936*, pp. [5]–13.

Delivered at the fiftieth anniversary meeting of the club at Ann Arbor in April, 1936.

Abridged in *Education Digest*, Nov. 1936, II, iii, 1–3, with the title THE INTEGRITY OF EDUCATION.

RELIGION, SCIENCE AND PHILOSOPHY. *Southern Review*, Summer 1936, II, 53–62.

Review of Bertrand Russell, *Religion and Science*.

Reprinted in *Problems of Men* (1946), 169–179.

[LETTER TO THE EDITOR.] *New Republic*, 7 Oct. 1936, LXXXVIII, 249.

In response to a request, Dewey states that he intends to vote for Norman Thomas at the coming presidential election.

AUTHORITY AND RESISTANCE TO SOCIAL CHANGE. *School and Society*, 10 Oct. 1936, XLIV, 457–466.

Read at the Harvard Tercentenary Conference of Arts and Sciences, 4 Sept. 1936.

Comment by Alfred Church Lane in *School and Society*, 19 Sept. 1936, XLIV, 376–377.

Reprinted in *Authority and the Individual.* Harvard Tercentenary Publications. (Cambridge: Harvard University Press, 1937), 170–190, with the title AUTHORITY AND SOCIAL CHANGE; in *Intelligence in the Modern World* (1939), 343–363, with the title SCIENCE AND THE FUTURE OF SOCIETY; and in *Problems of Men* (1946), 93–110; abridged in *Survey Graphic*, Nov. 1936, XXV, 603–606.

HORACE MANN TODAY. *Social Frontier*, Nov. 1936, III, 41–42.

Reprinted in *Education Digest*, Jan. 1937, II, v, 12–14.

[STATEMENT IN REGARD TO JEROME DAVIS, *Capitalism and Its Culture.*] *New Republic*, 18 Nov. 1936, LXXXIX, 89.

RATIONALITY IN EDUCATION. *Social Frontier*, Dec. 1936, III, 71–72.

Reprinted in *Education Today* (1940), 331–336.

Apropos of Lancelot Hogben, *The Retreat from Reason*, and Robert Maynard Hutchins, *The Higher Learning in America*.

Comments in Charles Austin Beard and Mary Ritter Beard, *America in Midpassage* (1939), 905–906.

See PRESIDENT HUTCHINS' PROPOSALS TO REMAKE HIGHER EDUCATION, below, and reply by Hutchins, GRAMMAR, RHETORIC, AND MR. DEWEY, *Social Frontier*, Feb. 1937, III, 137–139.

Editorial comment in *ib.*, Feb. 1937, III, 134–135.

See also THE HIGHER LEARNING IN AMERICA, below.

GENERAL PROPOSITIONS: KINDS AND CLASSES. *Journal of Philosophy*, 3 Dec. 1936, XXIII, 673–680.

1937

THE CASE OF LEON TROTSKY. Report of Hearings on the Charges Made against Him in the Moscow Trials, by the Preliminary Commission of Inquiry, John Dewey, Chairman; Carleton Beals (resigned), Otto Ruehle, Benjamin Stolberg, Suzanne

La Follette, Secretary. New York, London: Harper & Brothers, 1937. xix, 617 pp.

Reviewed in *New Republic*, 24 Nov. 1937, LXXXXIII, 79 (Bertram D. Wolfe); editorial comment in *ib.*, 22 Dec. 1937, 181–182.

See report of radio broadcast by Dewey and rejoinder by Corliss Lamont in *New York Times*, 14 Dec. 1937; editorial comment in *ib.*, 15 Dec. 1937; also Sidney Hook, CORLISS LAMONT: "FRIEND OF THE G. P. U." *Modern Monthly*, Mar. 1938, X, xi, 5–8, including telegram from Dewey, 8.

"TRUTH IS ON THE MARCH." Report and Remarks on the Trotsky Hearings in Mexico. New York: American Committee for the Defense of Leon Trotsky [1937]. 15 pp.

Report and speech, delivered at a mass meeting held under the auspices of the American Committee for the Defense of Leon Trotsky at the Mecca Temple in New York City, 9 May 1937.

EDUCATION AND SOCIAL ORGANIZATION. In *Educating for Democracy, a Symposium* (Yellow Springs, Ohio: Antioch Press, 1937), 37–54.

Address delivered at the Horace Mann Conference, Antioch College, in October, 1936.

Abstract in *Journal of the National Education Association*, Dec. 1936, XXV, 274.

FREEDOM. *In* National Education Association, Committee on Social-Economic Goals, *Implications of Social-Economic Goals for Education: A Report* (Washington: The Association, 1937), 99–105.

Reprinted in *Intelligence in the Modern World* (1939), 721–725, with the title, ACADEMIC FREEDOM.

THE TEACHER AND SOCIETY. Written in Collaboration by William Heard Kilpatrick, Editor; John Dewey, George W. Hartmann, Ernest O. Melby, Jesse Homer Newlon, George D. Stoddard, Hilda Taba, Goodwin Watson, Laura Zirbes. (First Yearbook of the John Dewey Society.) New York: D. Appleton-Century Company [c1937]. vi, 360 pp.

Chapter XIII, The Forward View: a Free Teacher in a Free Society, "may be assigned . . . to Professors Dewey and Watson."

Reviewed in *Social Frontier*, Oct. 1937, IV, 28–29 (Alonzo F. Myers).

THE PHILOSOPHY OF WILLIAM JAMES. *Southern Review*, Winter 1937, II, 447–461.

Reprinted in *Problems of Men* (1946), 379–395.

Review of Ralph Barton Perry, *The Thought and Character of William James.*

PRESIDENT HUTCHINS' PROPOSALS TO REMAKE HIGHER EDUCATION. *Social Frontier*, Jan. 1937, III, 103–104.

See RATIONALITY IN EDUCATION, above.

DEMOCRACY IS RADICAL . . . AS AN END, AND THE MEANS CANNOT BE DIVORCED FROM THE END. *Common Sense*, Jan. 1937, VI, i, 10–11.

THE CHALLENGE OF DEMOCRACY TO EDUCATION. *Progressive Education*, Feb. 1937, XIV, 79–85.

Reprinted in *Problems of Men* (1946), 46–56.

Address at a regional conference of the Progressive Education Association in New York City.

CHARLES SANDERS PEIRCE. *New Republic*, 3 Feb. 1937, LXXXIX, 415–416.

Review of *Collected Papers of Charles Sanders Peirce*, edited by Charles Hartshorne and Paul Weiss, Vols. I–VI.

WHITEHEAD'S PHILOSOPHY. *Philosophical Review*, Mar. 1937, XLVI, 170–177.

Read at the symposium on the philosophy of Alfred North Whitehead at the meeting of the Eastern Division of the American Philosophical Association, Cambridge, Massachusetts, 29 Dec. 1936. Professor Whitehead's "Remarks" which followed are published in *ib.*, 178–186.

Reprinted in *Problems of Men* (1946), 410–418.

"THE HIGHER LEARNING IN AMERICA." *Social Frontier*, Mar. 1937, III, 167–169.

Rejoinder to Robert Maynard Hutchins; see above.

PRAVDA ON TROTSKY. *New Republic*, 24 Mar. 1937, LXXXX, 212–213.

Letter to the editor.

RIGHTING AN ACADEMIC WRONG. *New Republic*, 31 Mar. 1937, LXXXX, 242.

Regarding Professor Arthur J. Kraus's breach of contract case against the College of the City of New York

THE EDUCATIONAL FUNCTION OF A MUSEUM OF DECORATIVE ARTS. *Chronicle of the Museum for the Arts of Decoration of Cooper Union* (New York), Apr. 1937, I, 93–99.

DEMOCRACY AND EDUCATIONAL ADMINISTRATION. *School and Society*, 3 Apr. 1937, XLV, 457–462.

Read at the general session of the Department of Superintendence of the National Education Association, New Orleans, 22 Feb. 1935.

Reprinted in American Association of School Administrators, *Official Report*, 1937, 48–55; in *Problems of Men* (1946), 57–66; in *Intelligence in the Modern World* (1939), 400–404 and 716–721, with the titles, THE DEMOCRATIC FORM and DEMOCRACY IN THE SCHOOLS; in *Education Today* (1940), 337–347; and in Hillman Metcalf Bishop and Samuel Hendel, eds., *Basic Issues of American Democracy* (New York: Appleton-Century-Crofts, Inc. [1948]), 20–23.

"EITHER—OR." *Nation*, 10 Apr. 1937, CXLIV, 412–413.

Review of Zalmen Slesinger, *Education and the Class Struggle: A Critical Examination of the Liberal Educator's Program for Social Reconstruction.*

SUBJECT MATTER IN ART. *New Republic*, 21 Apr. 1937, LXXXX, 335.

Review of Walter Abell, *Representation and Form: A Study of Esthetic Values in Representational Art.*

THE FUTURE OF DEMOCRACY. *New Republic*, 28 Apr. 1937, LXXXX, 351.

Statement in a symposium.

EDUCATION AND SOCIAL CHANGE. *Social Frontier*, May 1937, III, 235–238.

Read at the New Orleans meeting of the John Dewey Society, 21 Feb. 1937.

Reprinted in Joshua Lieberman, ed., *New Trends in Group Work* (New York: Association Press, 1938), 15–27, in *Intelligence in the Modern World* (1939), 691–696, and in *Education Today* (1940), 348–358.

Excerpts in *Bulletin of the American Association of University Professors*, Oct. 1937, XXIII, 472–474.

LIBERALISM IN A VACUUM: A CRITIQUE OF WALTER LIPPMANN'S SOCIAL PHILOSOPHY. *Common Sense*, Dec. 1937, VI, xii, 9–11.

Some remarks on Mr. Lippmann's *The Good Society.*

JOHN DEWEY, GREAT AMERICAN LIBERAL, DENOUNCES RUS-
SIAN DICTATORSHIP. *Washington Post*, 19 Dec. 1937.

Interview with Agnes Ernst Meyer (Mrs. Eugene Meyer).

Reprinted with the title THE SIGNIFICANCE OF THE TROTSKY TRIAL,
in *International Conciliation*, Feb. 1938, No. 337, 53–60.

See Dorothy Thompson, THE STATEMENT OF DR. JOHN DEWEY,
New York Herald Tribune, 27 Dec. 1937; Heywood Broun, DR.
DEWEY FINDS COMMUNISTS IN THE C.I.O., *New Republic*, 12 Jan.
1938, LXXXXIII, 280, and reply by Sidney Hook in *ib.*, 16 Feb.
1938, LXXXXIV, 48.

1938

LOGIC: THE THEORY OF INQUIRY. New York: Henry Holt and
Company [ᶜ1938]. viii, 546 pp.

Published also in London by George Allen and Unwin, Ltd., 1939.

"This book is a development of ideas regarding the nature of logical
theory that were first presented, some forty years ago, in *Studies in
Logical Theory;* that were somewhat expanded in *Essays in Experimental Logic* and were briefly summarized with special reference to
education in *How We Think.* While basic ideas remain the same,
there has naturally been considerable modification during the in-
tervening years." PREFACE.

Contents. Part I, Introduction: The Problem of Logical Subject-
Matter—The Existential Matrix of Inquiry: Biological—The Existential Matrix of Inquiry: Cultural—Common Sense and Scientific
Inquiry—The Needed Reform of Logic. Part II, The Structure of
Inquiry and the Construction of Judgments: The Pattern of Inquiry
—The Construction of Judgment—Immediate Knowledge: Understanding and Inference—Judgments of Practice: Evaluation—Affirmation and Negation: Judgment as Requalification—The Function
of Propositions of Quantity in Judgment—Judgment as Spatial-
Temporal Determination: Narration-Description—The Continuum
of Judgment: General Propositions—Generic and Universal Propositions. Part III, Propositions and Terms: General Theory of Propositions—Propositions Ordered in Sets and Series—Formal Functions and Canons—Terms or Meanings. Part IV, The Logic of
Scientific Method: Logic and Natural Science: Form and Matter—
Mathematical Discourse—Scientific Method: Induction and Deduction—Scientific Laws-Causation and Sequences—Scientific Method
and Scientific Subject-Matter—Social Inquiry—The Logic of Inquiry and Philosophies of Knowledge.

Translations. Arabic by Z. Mahmoud; Italian, with Introduction, by Aldo Visalberghi (Torino, 1949); Spanish, with Introduction, by Eugenio Imaz (México–Buenos Aires, 1950).

Reviewed in *Boston Transcript,* 21 Jan. 1939 (Leonard Carmichael); *The Communist,* Feb. 1939, XVIII, 163–169 (Philip Carter); *Ethics,* Oct. 1939, L, 98–102 (W. H. Werkmeister); *Johns Hopkins Alumni Magazine,* Nov. 1938, XXVII, 33 (Albert Lanphier Hammond); *Mind,* Oct. 1939, XLVIII, 527–536 (John Laird); *Nation,* 22 Oct. 1938, CXLVII, 426–427 (William Gruen); *New Republic,* 23 Nov. 1938, LXXXXVII, 79–80 (Paul Weiss); *New York Herald Tribune Books,* 11 Dec. 1938 (Irwin Edman); *New York Times,* 20 Nov. 1938 (Clifford Barrett); *Philosophical Review,* Mar. 1940, XLIX, 259–261 (William Ray Dennes); *Philosophisches Jahrbuch,* LIV (1941), 245–246 (Arnulf Molitor); *Philosophy,* July 1939, XIV, 370–371 (W. Kneale); *Saturday Review of Literature,* 5 Nov. 1938, XIX, ii, 18 (Eliseo Vivas); *Scuola e città,* 1950, I, 95–96 (Aldo Visalberghi); *Sophia,* 1950, iv (Fortunato Brancatisano); *Southern Review,* 1939, V, i, 105–120 (Lyle Hicks Lanier).

See Clarence Edwin Ayres, DEWEY: MASTER OF THE COMMONPLACE, *New Republic,* 18 Jan. 1939, LXXXXVII, 303–306; Robert Bruce Raup, DEWEY'S *Logic* AND SOME PROBLEMS OF PROGRESSIVE EDUCATION, *Progressive Education,* Apr. 1939, XVI, 264–271; Bertrand Russell, DEWEY'S NEW *Logic,* in P. A. Schilpp, ed., *The Philosophy of John Dewey* (1939), 137–156; Jerome Nathanson, DEWEY'S VIVISECTION OF THE LOGICAL PROCESS, *Philosophy of Science,* Jan. 1939, IV, 115–122; the comment by Arthur Fisher Bentley at the end of his article, POSTULATION FOR BEHAVIORAL INQUIRY, *Journal of Philosophy,* 20 July 1939, XXXVI, 405–413; Kenneth Burke, MONADS—ON THE MAKE, in his *Philosophy of Literary Form* (1941), 392–394; Harold Robert Smart, THE UNIT OF DISCOURSE, *Philosophical Review,* May 1941, L, 283–288; William Barrett, ON DEWEY'S LOGIC, *ib.,* 305–315; May Brodbeck, A CRITICAL EXAMINATION OF JOHN DEWEY'S *Logic: The Theory of Inquiry,* Thesis (PH.D.), University of Iowa, 1947; Milton Mayeroff, AN EXAMINATION OF SOME CRITICISM OF JOHN DEWEY'S *Logic: The Theory of Inquiry,* Thesis (A.M.), New York University, 1950; Paul Welsh, JUDGMENT AND PROPOSITIONS IN DEWEY'S *Logic, Methodos,* VII (1955), No. 25–26, 107–114; and Felix Kauffman, JOHN DEWEY'S THEORY OF INQUIRY, *Journal of Philosophy,* 8 Oct. 1959, LVI, 826–836.

The *Journal of Philosophy,* 12 Oct. 1939, Vol. XXXVI, contains A SYMPOSIUM OF REVIEWS OF JOHN DEWEY'S *Logic:* PROFESSOR DEWEY: LOGICIAN-ONTOLOGICIAN, by Evander Bradley McGilvary (561–565); THE NEW LOGIC AND THE OLD, by Gustavus Watts Cunningham (565–572); MEANING AND ACTION, by Clarence Irving Lewis (572–576); SOME LEADING PRINCIPLES OF PROFESSOR DEW-

EY's LOGICAL THEORY, by Ernest Nagel (576–581); and DEWEY's DOCTRINE OF THE SITUATION, by Wendell Marshall Thomas (581–584).

EXPERIENCE AND EDUCATION. New York: The Macmillan Company, 1938. xii, 116 pp.

The Kappa Delta Pi Lecture, delivered before the fraternity at Atlantic City, New Jersey, 1 Mar. 1938.

Contents. Traditional *vs.* Progressive Education—The Need of a Theory of Experience—Criteria of Experience—Social Control—The Nature of Freedom—The Meaning of Purpose—Progressive Organization of Subject-Matter—Experience—The Means and Goal of Education.

Printed in part in *New York Times*, 6 Mar. 1938, and in *Intelligence in the Modern World* (1939), 662–682.

Reviewed in *Philosophy*, Oct. 1939, XIV, 482–483 (F. A. Cavenagh); *Scuola, e città*, 1950, I, 96 (F. De Bartolomeis); *Social Frontier*, May 1938, IV, 269 (George Edward Axtelle).

Translations. Chinese by Li Hsiang-hsü and Juan Ch'un-fang (Kweiyang, 1943) and by Pei-yu Li (Shanghai, 1946); French, *avec présentation de la pedagogie de John Dewey*, by Marie-Anne Carroi (Paris, 1947); Greek by G. Vasdhekis (Athens, 1954); Italian, with Introduction by Ernesto Codignola (Firenze, 1949); Spanish by Lorenzo Luzuriaga (Buenos Aires, 1943, 1954, 1958).

NOT GUILTY. Report of the Commission of Inquiry into the Charges Made against Leon Trotsky in the Moscow Trials. New York, London: Harper and Brothers, 1938. xv, 422 pp.

The commission was headed by Dewey. Miss Suzanne La Follette did the actual writing of the report—"with rare intellectual integrity," J. D. (p. vii).

Reviewed in *New York Herald Tribune*, 24 July 1938 (Sidney Hook).

UNITY OF SCIENCE AS A SOCIAL PROBLEM. In *International Encyclopedia of Unified Science*, Vol. I, No. 1, Encyclopedia and Unified Science [by] Otto Neurath, Niels Bohr, John Dewey, Bertrand Russell, Rudolf Carnap, Charles W. Morris. (Chicago: University of Chicago Press [ᶜ1938]; combined edition [1955]), 29–38.

Contents. The Scientific Attitude—The Social Unity of Science—Education and the Unity of Science.

Reviewed in *Nation*, 17 Sept. 1938, CXLVII, 275–276 (William Gruen); *Philosophical Review*, July 1941, L, 433–434 (Henry Margenau).

Italian translation by Orio Peduzzi (Milano, 1958).

THE DETERMINATION OF ULTIMATE VALUES OR AIMS THROUGH ANTECEDENT OR A PRIORI SPECULATION OR THROUGH PRAGMATIC OR EMPIRICAL INQUIRY. *In* National Society for the Study of Education, *Thirty-seventh Yearbook* (Bloomington, Ill., 1938), Part II, 471–485.

Translation. Spanish in *La ciencia de la educación*, by Lorenzo Luzuriaga (Buenos Aires, 1941, 1948).

TO THOSE WHO ASPIRE TO THE PROFESSION OF TEACHING. *In* Earl Granger Lockhart, comp., *My Vocation . . . or What Eminent Americans Think of Their Calling* (New York: H. W. Wilson Company, 1938), 325–334.

DEMOCRACY AND EDUCATION IN THE WORLD OF TODAY. New York: Society for Ethical Culture, 1938. 15 pp.

Lecture in honor of Dr. Felix Adler, founder of the Society for Ethical Culture, and the sixtieth anniversary of the Ethical Culture Schools, delivered before the society, 24 Oct. 1938.

Reprinted in *Education Today* (1940), 359–370, and in *Problems of Men* (1946), 34–45.

Italian translation in *Scuola e città*, 30 Sept. 1950.

FOREWORD. *In* David Lindsay Watson, *Scientists Are Human* (London: Watts & Co. [1938]), vii–xi.

DOES HUMAN NATURE CHANGE? *Rotarian*, Feb. 1938, LII, ii, 8–11, 58–59.

Reprinted in *Problems of Men* (1946), 184–192, and in Philip Paul Wiener, ed., *Readings in Philosophy of Science: Introduction to the Foundations and Cultural Aspects of the Sciences* (New York: Charles Scribner's Sons [°1953]), 281–287.

THE RELATION OF SCIENCE AND PHILOSOPHY AS THE BASIS OF EDUCATION. *School and Society*, 9 Apr. 1938, XLVII, 470–473.

Reprinted in *Problems of Men* (1946), 164–168.

"TIME AND INDIVIDUALITY" complete text of address . . . April 21, 1938 . . . in the Gould Memorial Library of New York University. . . . Dr. Dewey's address was the seventh annual James Arthur Lecture on "Time and Its Mysteries" . . . [New York, 1938].

At head of title: New York University. Bureau of Public Information.

A preprint. Printed as no. 3 in *Time and Its Mysteries*, Ser. II (1940), *q.v.* Copy in Yale University Library.

WHAT IS SOCIAL STUDY? *Progressive Education*, May 1938, XV, 367–369.

Reprinted in *Problems of Men* (1946), 180–183.

MEANS AND ENDS: Their Interdependence, and Leon Trotsky's Essay on "Their Morals and Ours." *New International*, Aug. 1938, IV, 232–233.

VALUE JUDGMENTS. *Daily Princetonian*, 22 Nov. 1938.

Report of an address to the Philosophy Forum, Princeton University, 21 Nov. 1938.

EDUCATION, DEMOCRACY, AND SOCIALIZED ECONOMY. *Social Frontier*, Dec. 1938, V, 71–72.

1939

INTELLIGENCE IN THE MODERN WORLD: JOHN DEWEY'S PHILOSOPHY. Edited, and with an Introduction by Joseph Ratner. New York: The Modern Library [ᶜ1939]. xv, 1077 pp.

Published also in Toronto by Macmillan in 1939.

A systematic arrangement of selections from Dewey's writings on many topics. Two sections are printed here for the first time, THE ECONOMIC BASIS OF THE NEW SOCIETY (416–433), and THE UNITY OF THE HUMAN BEING (817–835), an address delivered before the College of Physicians in St. Louis, 21 Apr. 1937.

Contents. Introduction to John Dewey's Philosophy, by Joseph Ratner—The Meanings of Philosophy: Philosophy and Culture; Philosophy and the Education of Man; The Critical Function of Philosophy—The Great Philosophic Separation: The Quest for Certainty; The Historic Mission of Philosophy—Philosophy and Science; The Modern Crisis; Ancient and Modern Science Contrasted; Philosophic Implications of Modern Science—Science and the Future of Society—The Modes of Societal Life: The Private and the Public; Government and State; State and Society; Communication and Communal Living; The Democratic Form—The Individual in the New Society: The Individual in the Cultural Crisis; The Economic Basis of the New Society—Intelligence in Social Action: Classes, Groups and Masses; The Class Struggle; The Meaning and Office of Liberalism; Socializing Intelligence—Nationalism and Internationalism: Nationalism and Its Fruits; Ethics and International Relations; Force, Violence and Law—International Law and the Security of Nations: On International Cooperation; On America's Responsibility; Preconditions of the Security of Nations; International Law and the War-

System; Editor's Note; Sanctions and the Security of Nations—Fundamentals of the Educational Process: The Art of Education; Learning and Doing; The Training of Thinking; Individuality and Freedom; The Continuity of the Educational Process—Science and Philosophy of Education: Education as a Science; Sources of a Science of Education; Traditional *vs.* Progressive Education; Philosophy of Experience; The Organization of Study; Means and End of Education—The Schools and the Social Welfare: The Schools in the Social Order; Education and Social Change; Educators and the Class Struggle; The Schools and Religions; Democracy in the Schools; Academic Freedom; Education and American Culture—The Psychology of Conduct: Habits and Will; Impulses and Instincts; Intelligence—Intelligence in Morals: Individual and Social Morality; Reflection in the Moral Situation; Experimentalism in Moral Theory; Endings in Nature and Ends for Man; The Satisfying and the Valuable—Perception, Language and Mind: Theory of Perception; Physical, Psychophysical and Mental; Language and Mind; Mind and Consciousness; The Unity of the Human Being—Thinking and Meaning: The Natural History of Thinking; The Pattern of Reflective Thinking; The Development of Meanings; Systems of Meanings and Symbols—Principles of Logic: The Genesis of Logical Forms; Explanation of *Situation;* Judgment and Proposition; Interpretation of the Syllogism; Induction and Deduction—Knowledge, Science and Truth: Meanings: Valid and Invalid: Knowledge as Instrumental and Hypothetical; Experimental Verification and Truth; Pure and Applied Science; Social Science and Social Control—The Artistic-Esthetic in Experience: The Roots of Esthetic Experience; The Experience of Esthetic Quality; The Work of Art and Esthetic Perception; Substance and Form; Art, Philosophy and Morals—The Religious in Experience—Comprehensive Working Ideas: Continuities in Nature; The Methods of Philosophy; Precarious and Stable Events; Process and Structure; Causes and Effects (Means and Ends); The Social.

Dr. Ratner's Introduction was published in Chinese translation at Taipei, Taiwan (Formosa), in 1953.

Reviewed in *Canadian Forum,* July 1939, XIX, 121–123 (Eric A. Havelock); *Ethics,* 1940, L, 375–376 (William Henry Werkmeister); *Journal of Philosophy,* 12 Oct. 1939, XXXVI, 585–586 (Herbert Wallace Schneider); *Modern Schoolman,* May 1943, XX, 246–247 (G. V. Kennard); *New Republic,* 17 May 1939, XC, 51–52 (Clarence Edwin Ayres); *New York Herald Tribune Books,* 19 Feb. 1939; *New York World-Telegram,* 15 Feb. 1939 (Harry Hansen); *Revue des sciences philosophiques et théologiques,* 1940, No. 1 (H. D. Gardeil); *Survey Graphic,* July 1939, XXVIII, 453 (Joseph Kinmont Hart).

THE UNITY OF THE HUMAN BEING is reprinted in Whit Burnett, ed., *105 Greatest Living Authors Present the World's Best Stories, Humor, Drama, Biography, History, Essays, Poetry* (New York: Dial Press, 1950), 111–123; and in Houston Peterson and James Bayley, eds., *Essays in Philosophy* (Pocket Library, 1959).

FREEDOM AND CULTURE. New York: G. P. Putnam's Sons [ᶜ1939]. 176 pp.

Reprinted in London by Luzac, 1955, 145 pp. Also published in English by Bharatiya Vidya Bhavan, Chaupatty, Bombay, 1952.

Contents. The Problem of Freedom—Culture and Human Nature—The American Background—Totalitarian Economics and Democracy—Democracy and Human Nature—Science and Free Culture—Democracy and America.

Translations. Arabic, with Introduction by Amīn Mursī Qindīl (n.p. 1955); Chinese by Lin I-liang and Lou I-che (Hong Kong, 1954); French by Pierre Messiaen (Paris, 1955); German by J. N. Lorenz (Wien, 1956); Greek by Mar. Oikonomou (Athens, n.d.); Italian by Enzo Enriques Agnoletti (Firenze, 1953); Japanese by Takeo Hosono (Kyoto, 1951); Kannada (Udipi, 1957); Korean by Lee Hae-yong (n.p. 1954); Malayalam by A. N. Nambiar (Kuttipuram, 196—); Marathi by Ambadas S. Agnihotri (Bombay, 1958); Portuguese by Eustáquio Duarte (Rio de Janeiro, 1953); Spanish, with Introduction, by Angela Romera Vera (Rosario, Argentina, 1946); Tamil by K. S. Venkataraman (Bombay [1956]).

Braille edition. Louisville: American Printing House for the Blind, 1940. 2 vols.

Reviewed in *Christian Century*, 7 Feb. 1940, LVII, 178–179 (Edwin Theophil Buehrer); *Journal of Philosophy*, 7 Dec. 1939, XXXVI, 688–690 (Herbert Wallace Schneider); *Nation*, 2 Dec. 1939, CXLIX, 621–622 (William Gruen); *Nature* (London), 28 Dec. 1940, CXLVI, 815–817; *New Republic*, 6 Dec. 1939, CI, 206–207 (Paul Weiss); *New York Herald Tribune Books*, 5 Nov. 1939 (Ernest Sutherland Bates); *New York Times*, 5 Nov. 1939 (Clinton Hartley Grattan); *Philosophical Abstracts*, Spring 1940, I, ii, 7–9 (Albert Hofstadter); *Revue de métaphysique et de morale*, Oct.-Dec. 1955, 448–449 (Gérard Deledalle); *Saturday Review of Literature*, 11 Nov. 1939, XXI, iii, 13 (Robert Bierstedt); *Springfield Republican*, 22 Oct. 1939; *Yale Review*, Winter 1940, XXIX, 388–390 (Homer Edwards Woodbridge).

See comment of James Donald Adams in *New York Times Book Review*, 6 July 1941.

WHAT IS DEMOCRACY? ITS CONFLICTS, ENDS AND MEANS . . . by John Dewey . . . Boyd H. Bode . . . T. V. Smith. (Co-

öperative Books, Ser. I, ii.) Norman, Oklahoma: Coöperative
Books, 1939. 40 pp.

Reprints Dewey's article, A LIBERAL SPEAKS OUT FOR LIBERALISM,
from the *New York Times Magazine*, 23 Feb. 1936, with the title:
THE FUTURE OF LIBERALISM, OR THE DEMOCRATIC WAY OF CHANGE,
3–10.

Reviewed in *Philosophical Review*, May 1940, XLIX, 383 (George
Holland Sabine).

THEORY OF VALUATION. (International Encyclopedia of Unified Science, Vol. II, Foundations of the Unity of Science,
No. 4.) Chicago: University of Chicago Press [ᶜ1939]. 67 pp.

Reviewed in *American Journal of Sociology*, May 1940, XLV, 942–
943 (Frank Hyneman Knight); *Philosophical Review*, July 1941, L,
443–446 (Oscar Bidney); *Philosophy of Science*, Oct. 1939, VI, 490–
491 (William Marias Malisoff); *Revue de métaphysique et de morale*,
1940, XLVII, 250. Abstract in *Philosophical Abstracts*, Spring 1940,
I, ii, 9 (Abraham Edel).

Translations. Italian by Orio Peduzzi (Milano, 1958); another translation by Fortunato Brancatisano, with Introduction by Aldo Visalberghi (Firenze, 1960); Japanese by Tomohiko Isono (Kyoto, 1959);
Spanish by Facultad de Filosofía y Letras de Buenos Aires (1958).

See Herbert Wallace Schneider, A NOTE ON DEWEY'S THEORY OF
VALUATION, *Journal of Philosophy*, 31 Aug. 1939, XXXVI, 490–495;
and Sidney Zink, WARRANTED JUDGMENTS IN DEWEY'S THEORY OF
VALUATION, *Philosphical Review*, Sept. 1942, LI, 502–508.

EXPERIENCE, KNOWLEDGE AND VALUE: A REJOINDER. *In* Paul
Arthur Schilpp, ed., *The Philosophy of John Dewey* (Evanston
and Chicago: Northwestern University, 1939; New York:
Tudor Publishing Co., 1951), 517–608.

INTRODUCTION. (With William Heard Kilpatrick.) *In* William
James, *Talks to Teachers on Psychology*. New edition. (New
York: Henry Holt and Company [ᶜ1939]), [iii]–viii.

INTRODUCTION. *In* Edmund Vincent Cowdry, *Problems of Age-
ing—Biological and Medical Aspects* (Baltimore: Williams and
Wilkins, 1939), xix–xxvii.

[WHAT I BELIEVE.] *In* Clifton Fadiman, ed., *I Believe: The Personal Philosophies of Certain Eminent Men and Women of Our
Time* (New York: Simon and Schuster, 1939), 347–354.

Revision of an article published in *Forum*, Mar. 1930, and in *Living
Philosophies* (1931), *qq.v.*

Translation. Swedish in Alf. Ahlberg, *Min Tro: Ein bok om livraskad-ningar* (Stockholm, 1941), 121–142.

No Matter What Happens—Stay Out! *Common Sense*, Mar. 1939, VII, iii, 11.

Contribution to a symposium, If War Comes, Shall We Participate or Be Neutral?

Education: 1800–1939. *Vermont Alumnus*, May 1939, XVIII, 169–170, 188–189.

Founder's Day address delivered in the Ira Allen Chapel, University of Vermont, Burlington, 1 May 1939.

College Youth Better Mannered. *Vermont Alumnus*, June 1939, XVIII, 196–197.

Interview with Mary Spargo Wardwell.

Review of Charles Austin Beard and Mary Ritter Beard, *America in Midpassage. Atlantic Monthly*, July 1939, CLXIV (*Atlantic Bookshelf*).

A Philosopher's Philosophy. *New York Times*, 15 Oct. 1939.

Interview with Samuel Johnson Woolf.

Higher Learning and the War. *Bulletin of the American Association of University Professors*, Dec. 1939, XXV, 613–614.

The Basis for Hope. *Common Sense*, Dec. 1939, VIII, xii, 9–10.

In answer to the question What Hope for Civilization? asked by the editors of the magazine on the outbreak of World War II.

1940

Education Today. Edited and with a Foreword by Joseph Ratner. New York: G. P. Putnam's Sons [ᶜ1940]. xix, 376 pp.

Abridged English edition published in London by G. Allen & Unwin, 1941. Braille edition, Louisville: American Printing House for the Blind, 1941. 4 vols.

Contents. My Pedagogic Creed—The Primary-Education Fetich—The People and the Schools—The Place of Manual Training in the Elementary Course of Study—Democracy in Education—Religion and Our Schools—Our Educational Ideal in Wartime—Universal Service as Education—The Schools and Social Preparedness—American Education and Culture—Nationalizing Education—Experiment in Education—Learning to Earn—Public Education on Trial—Education and Social Direction—Education as Religion—Education as

Engineering—Education as Politics—Mediocrity and Individuality
—Individuality, Equality and Superiority—Culture and Professionalism in Education—The Prospects of the Liberal College—The
Liberal College and Its Enemies—The Direction of Education—
General Principles of Educational Articulation—How Much Freedom in New Schools?—The Duties and Responsibilities of the Teaching Profession—Monastery, Bargain Counter, or Laboratory in Education?—Political Interference in Higher Education and Research
—Education and Our Present Social Problems—The Economic Situation: A Challenge to Education—Why Have Progressive Schools?—
The Supreme Intellectual Obligation—The Need for a Philosophy of
Education—The Teacher and His World—The Teacher and the
Public—Youth in a Confused World—Toward a National System
of Education—Liberty and Social Control—The Social Significance
of Academic Freedom—Class Struggle and the Democratic Way—
Rationality in Education—Democracy and Educational Administration—Education and Social Change—Democracy and Education
in the World of Today.

Translations. Italian by Lamberto Borghi (Firenze, 1950); Spanish
by Lorenzo Luzuriaga (Buenos Aires, 1951, 1957).

Reviewed in *Scuola e città,* 1950, I, 427–428 (F. De Bartolomeis).

CREATIVE DEMOCRACY—THE TASK BEFORE US. *In* [Sidney
Ratner, ed.], *The Philosophy of the Common Man. Essays in
Honor of John Dewey To Celebrate His Eightieth Birthday* (New
York: G. P. Putnam's Sons [ᶜ1940]), 220–228.

Read (in Dewey's absence by Horace Meyer Kallen) at the dinner
in honor of his eightieth birthday, Hotel Pennsylvania, New York
City, 20 October 1939. See also the accounts of the dinner in the
New York Times and *New York Herald Tribune,* 21 Oct. 1939.

Also printed in *Bulletin of the Association of American Colleges,* May
1940, XXVI, 198–203; Irwin Edman, ed., *John Dewey: His Contribution to the American Tradition* (1955), 308–315; Max Harold Fisch,
ed., *Classical American Philosophers* (1951), 389–394; *Morals in
Politics* (New Leader Publishing Association, New York, 1945), 9–
13; *New Leader,* 18 Mar. 1944, XXVII, xii, 5; Progressive Education
Association, Progressive Education Booklet No. 14, *John Dewey and
the Promise of America* (Columbus, Ohio, 1939), 12–17.

TIME AND INDIVIDUALITY. In *Time and Its Mysteries.* Series II.
Four Lectures given on the James Arthur Foundation, New
York University, by Daniel Webster Hering, William Francis
Gray Swann, John Dewey, Arthur H. Compton (New York:
University Press, 1940), 85–109.

Dewey's lecture was delivered 21 Apr. 1938; see the preprint listed
under 1938.

Reprinted in *John Dewey on Experience, Nature, and Freedom* (1960), 224–243.

Reviewed in *Journal of Philosophy*, 1 Jan. 1942, XXXIX, 22–24 (Ernest Nagel).

THE LIVING THOUGHTS OF THOMAS JEFFERSON presented by John Dewey. (The Living Thoughts Library, edited by Alfred O. Mendel.) New York: Longmans, Green and Co., 1940. 173 pp.

Reprinted at Greenwich [Connecticut] by Fawcett Publications, 1955. 191 pp. (paperback).

Contents. Presenting Thomas Jefferson [by John Dewey], 1–30—Political Philosophy—Economic Philosophy—Morals and Religion—Intellectual Freedom and Progress—Education—American Internal Affairs: I. The Constitution, II. The Judiciary, III. Finance and Debt, IV. Secession, V. Slavery—Foreign Relations, War and Peace—History and the Contemporary World.

THOMAS JEFFERSON AND THE DEMOCRATIC FAITH. *Virginia Quarterly Review*, Jan. 1940, XVI, 1–13.

THE MEANING OF THE TERM: LIBERALISM. *Frontiers of Democracy*, Feb. 1940, VI, 135.

NATURE IN EXPERIENCE. *Philosophical Review*, Mar. 1940, XLIX, 244–258.

In reply to Morris Raphael Cohen, SOME DIFFICULTIES IN DEWEY'S ANTHROPOCENTRIC NATURALISM (*ib.*, 196–228), and William Ernest Hocking, DEWEY'S CONCEPTS OF EXPERIENCE AND NATURE (*ib.*, 228–244).

Read at a symposium on DEWEY'S CONCEPTS OF EXPERIENCE AND NATURE, in honor of his eightieth birthday, at the meeting of the American Philosophical Association, Columbia University, 28 Dec. 1939. See the *New York Times* report, PHILOSOPHERS TILT AT FETE FOR DEWEY, 29 Dec. 1939.

Reprinted in *Problems of Men* (1946), 193–207, and in *John Dewey on Experience, Nature, and Freedom* (1960), 244–260.

REVIEW of Douglas Clyde Macintosh, *Social Religion*. *Review of Religion*, Mar. 1940, IV, 359–361.

[QUOTATION FROM A LETTER TO NELSON PRENTISS MEAD, ACTING PRESIDENT OF CITY COLLEGE, DEFENDING THE APPOINTMENT OF BERTRAND RUSSELL.] *New York Times*, 12 Mar. 1940.

ADDRESS IN HONOR OF AMERICAN ARTISTS WHO CONTRIBUTED TOWARD DECORATIONS IN FEDERAL BUILDINGS. *Congressional*

Record, 76th Congress, 3d Session, 29 Apr. 1940, Appendix, LXXXVI, pt. 15, 2477–2478.

Radio talk given over the N.B.C. network, 25 Apr. 1940.

"CONTRARY TO HUMAN NATURE." *Frontiers of Democracy*, May 1940, VI, 234–235.

INVESTIGATING EDUCATION. *New York Times*, 6 May 1940.

Letter to the editor, opposing the current state and federal searches for "subversive" textbooks.

Reply by Merwin Kimball Hart, DR. DEWEY'S STAND DISPUTED, *ib.*, 9 May 1940, and rejoinder by Dewey, CENSORSHIP NOT WANTED, *ib.*, 14 May 1940.

REVIEW of Max Carl Otto, *The Human Enterprise. An Attempt To Relate Philosophy to Daily Life. Journal of Philosophy*, 23 May 1940, XXXVII, 303–305.

THE CASE FOR BERTRAND RUSSELL. *Nation*, 15 June 1940, CL, 732–733.

THE TECHNIQUES OF RECONSTRUCTION. *Saturday Review of Literature*, 31 Aug. 1940, XXII, xix, 10.

Review of Karl Mannheim, *Men and Society in an Age of Reconstruction*.

[STATEMENT ON ACADEMIC FREEDOM.] *New York Times*, 5 Oct. 1940.

Regarding President Butler's address to the faculty of Columbia University, 3 Oct. 1940, in which he urged the faculty to resign if their convictions brought them into open conflict with the university's pursuit of its ideals in "the war between beasts and human beings."

THE VANISHING SUBJECT IN THE PSYCHOLOGY OF JAMES. *Journal of Philosophy*, 24 Oct. 1940, XXXVII, 589–599.

Reprinted in *Problems of Men* (1946), 396–409.

See Bruce Wallace Brotherston, THE WIDER SETTING OF "FELT TRANSITION," in *Journal of Philosophy*, 12 Feb. 1942, XXXIX, 97–104.

1941

THE BERTRAND RUSSELL CASE. Edited by John Dewey and Horace M. Kallen. New York: The Viking Press, 1941. 227 pp.

Contents. Introduction, by John Dewey (pp. 7–10)—Foreword, by Albert Coombs Barnes—Behind the Bertrand Russell Case, by

Horace Meyer Kallen—Social Realities versus Police Court Fictions, by John Dewey (pp. 55–74)—Trial by Ordeal, New Style, by Walton Hale Hamilton—The Problems of Education in a Democracy, by Richard McKeon—A Scandalous Denial of Justice, by Morris Raphael Cohen—The Attitude of the Episcopal Church, by Guy Emery Shipler—The Case as a School Administrator Sees It, by Carleton Washburne—The College, the Community, and the Bertrand Russell Case, by Yervant Hovhannes Krikorian and others—The General Pattern, by Sidney Hook—Appendixes: I. Decision of Justice John E. McGeehan, II. Statement of the Committee on Cultural Freedom.

Reviewed in *Annals of the American Academy of Political and Social Science*, Jan. 1942, CCXIX, 184 (Edgar Wallace Knight); *Journal of Philosophy*, 9 Oct. 1941, 573–581 (Peter Archibald Carmichael); *Nation*, 6 June 1942, CLIV, 664.

LA CIENCIA DE LA EDUCACIÓN. [Traducción del inglés por Lorenzo Luzuriaga.] (Publicaciones de la Revista de pedagogía. Biblioteca del maestro, 6.) Buenos Aires: Editorial Losada, S.A. [1941]. 110 pp.

Contents. La ciencia de la educación [THE SOURCES OF A SCIENCE OF EDUCATION, 1929]—La filosofía de la educación [THE DETERMINATION OF ULTIMATE VALUES OR AIMS, 1938].

[MY PHILOSOPHY OF LAW.] *In* Northwestern University, Julius Rosenthal Foundation, *My Philosophy of Law: Credos of Sixteen American Scholars* (Boston: Boston Law Book Co. [ᶜ1941]), 73–85.

Reprinted in Clarence Morris, ed., *The Great Legal Philosophers: Selected Readings in Jurisprudence* (Philadelphia: University of Pennsylvania Press [ᶜ1959]), 506–510.

THE PHILOSOPHY OF WHITEHEAD. *In* Paul Arthur Schilpp, ed., *The Philosophy of Alfred North Whitehead* (Evanston and Chicago: Northwestern University, 1941), 643–661.

ADDRESS OF WELCOME. *In* League for Industrial Democracy, *Thirty-five Years of Educational Pioneering* (New York: League for Industrial Democracy [1941]), 3–6.

Presidential address delivered at the thirty-fifth anniversary dinner of the League at the Hotel Edison, New York City, 28 Nov. 1940.

PROPOSITIONS, WARRANTED ASSERTIBILITY, AND TRUTH. *Journal of Philosophy*, 27 Mar. 1941, XXXVIII, 169–186.

Reprinted in *Problems of Men* (1946), 331–353.

Restatement of "some features of the theories I have previously advanced on the topics mentioned" shaped "on the basis of ascriptions and criticisms of my views found in Mr. [Bertrand] Russell's *An Inquiry into Truth and Meaning*." [*Sic*. The reference is to Russell's book, *An Inquiry into Meaning and Truth*, New York: W. W. Norton, 1940, chap. xxiii, WARRANTED ASSERTIBILITY.]

See Horace Standish Thayer, CRITICAL NOTES ON DEWEY'S THEORY OF PROPOSITIONS, *Journal of Philosophy*, 27 Sept. 1951, XLVIII, 607–613, and his TWO THEORIES OF TRUTH, *ib.*, 11 Sept. 1947, XLIV, 516–527.

JAMES MARSH AND AMERICAN PHILOSOPHY. *Journal of the History of Ideas*, Apr. 1941, II, 131–150.

Lecture delivered at the University of Vermont, 26 Nov. 1929, in commemoration of the centenary of the publication of James Marsh's INTRODUCTION to Coleridge's *Aids to Reflection*.

Reprinted in *Problems of Men* (1946), 357–378.

THE BASIC VALUES AND LOYALTIES OF DEMOCRACY. *American Teacher*, May 1941, XXV, ix, 8–9.

FOR A NEW EDUCATION. *The New Era in Home and School* (London), June 1941, XXII, 134–135.

THE OBJECTIVISM-SUBJECTIVISM OF MODERN PHILOSOPHY. *Journal of Philosophy*, 25 Sept. 1941, XXXVIII, 533–542.

Reprinted in *Problems of Men* (1946), 309–321.

Italian translation by Aldo Visalberghi in *Rivista di filosofia*, Jan.-Mar. 1950, XLI, 59–72.

REVIEW of Paul Arthur Schilpp, ed., *The Philosophy of George Santayana* (Evanston and Chicago: Northwestern University, 1940). *Mind*, Oct. 1941, L, 374–385.

[STATEMENT.] *New York Times*. 14 Nov. 1940.

Opposing a resolution of the Board of Education to grant released time for religious instruction to children in the New York City public school system.

1942

GERMAN PHILOSOPHY AND POLITICS. New York: G. P. Putnam's Sons [ᶜ1942]. 149 pp.

The 1915 edition reset; "reprinted without change, save for a few slight verbal corrections," together with a new Introduction: THE ONE WORLD OF HITLER'S NATIONAL SOCIALISM, 13–49.

Translation. German by Hans Hermann Kogge (Meisenheim/Glan, 1954). See Hermann Zeltner, DEUTSCHE PHILOSOPHIE UND DEUTSCHE POLITIK . . . , *Kant-Studien*, 1956–57, XLVIII, 550–558.

WILLIAM JAMES AND THE WORLD TODAY. In *William James, the Man and Thinker. Addresses Delivered at The University of Wisconsin in Celebration of the Centenary of His Birth* (Madison: University of Wisconsin Press, 1942), 91–97.

Read (in Dewey's absence by Carl Boegholt) at the celebration of James's centenary at Madison, [10] Jan. 1942.

WILLIAM JAMES AS EMPIRICIST. In *In Commemoration of William James 1842–1942* (New York: Columbia University Press, 1942), 48–57.

Paper presented at the Conference on Methods in Philosophy and the Sciences, New School for Social Research, New York City, 23 Nov. 1941.

FOREWORD. *In* John E. Stoner, *S. O. Levinson and the Pact of Paris: A Study in the Techniques of Influence* (Chicago: University of Chicago Press, 1942), vii–viii.

See the index for many references to Dewey's association with Mr. Levinson in the movement for the outlawry of war.

[AN OPEN LETTER TO THE CHINESE PEOPLE. Washington: Office of War Information? 1942?] [7 pp.] 14×11½ cm. folded to 7×6 cm.

In Chinese. Includes a biographical statement about Dewey. Apparently a propaganda leaflet distributed by the U.S. Army Air Force; the back page has a reproduction of their insigne, a white star on a blue disc. Copy in Princeton University Library.

INTRODUCTION. *In* Agnes De Lima and the Staff of the Little Red Schoolhouse, *The Little Red Schoolhouse* [New York City] (New York: The Macmillan Company, 1942), ix–x.

RUSSIA'S POSITION: MR. [JOSEPH EDWARD] DAVIES'S BOOK [*Mission to Moscow*] REGARDED AS INCORRECT PICTURE. Letter to the *New York Times*, 11 Jan. 1942.

Reprinted as CAN WE WORK WITH RUSSIA? A LETTER BY JOHN DEWEY TO THE *New York Times*, *Frontiers of Democracy*, 15 Mar. 1942, VIII, 179–180. Comments by John Lawrence Childs, *ib.*, 181–182. Reply by Dewey, DR. DEWEY ON OUR RELATIONS WITH RUSSIA, and rejoinder by Childs, *ib.*, 15 Apr. 1942, [194].

How Is Mind To Be Known? *Journal of Philosophy*, 15 Jan. 1942, XXXIX, 29-35.

Reprinted in *Problems of Men* (1946), 301-308.

Inquiry and Indeterminateness of Situations. *Journal of Philosophy*, 21 May 1942, XXXIX, 290-296.

Reprinted in *Problems of Men* (1946), 322-330.

A reply to Donald Sage Mackay, What Does Mr. Dewey Mean by an "Indeterminate Situation?" in *Journal of Philosophy*, 12 Mar. 1942, XXXIX, 141-148.

The Ambiguity of "Intrinsic Good." *Journal of Philosophy*, 4 June 1942, XXXIX, 328-330.

Reprinted in *Problems of Men* (1946), 282-285.

"This article would not have been written without the stimulus received from Barnett Savery's recent paper on Intrinsic Good, published in this *Journal*, Vol. XXXIX (1942), pp. 234-244."

1943

The Principles. *Psychological Review*, Jan. 1943, L, 121.

William James's *Principles of Psychology*.

Anti-Naturalism in Extremis (The New Failure of Nerve, Part 1). *Partisan Review*, Jan.-Feb. 1943, X, 24-39.

Reprinted in Yervant Hovhannes Krikorian, ed., *Naturalism and the Human Spirit* (New York: Columbia University Press, 1944), *q.v.*, 1-16, and in William Phillips and Philip Rahv, eds., *The Partisan Reader* (New York: Dial Press, 1946), 514-528.

Naturalism and the Human Spirit is reviewed in *Journal of Philosophy*, 19 July 1945, XLII, 400-417 (Arthur Edward Murphy); *Nation*, 30 Dec. 1944, CLIX, 804 (Philip Blair Rice); *New Republic*, 20 Nov. 1944, CXI, 667-668 (Isaac Rosenfeld); *New York Times Book Review*, 3 Sept. 1944 (Irwin Edman).

Several Faults Are Found in "Mission to Moscow" Film. Letter of John Dewey and Suzanne La Follette to the Editor. *New York Times*, 9 May 1943.

Reply by Arthur Upham Pope, *ib.*, 16 May 1943. Response by Dewey and Miss La Follette, *ib.*, 24 May 1943. Second letter by Pope, *ib.*, 12 June 1943. Reply by Dewey and Miss La Follette, *ib.*, 19 June 1943.

VALUATION JUDGMENTS AND IMMEDIATE QUALITY. *Journal of Philosophy*, 10 June 1943, XL, 309–317.

Reprinted in *Problems of Men* (1946), 250–260.

Reply to Philip Blair Rice, "OBJECTIVITY" IN VALUE JUDGMENTS, *Journal of Philosophy*, 7 Jan. 1943, XL, 5–14.

See Rice's paper, QUALITY AND VALUE, *ib.*, 24 June 1943, XL, 337–348, and Dewey's FURTHER AS TO VALUATION AS JUDGMENT, *below*.

Reply by Bruce Wallace Brotherston, SENSUOUS AND NON-SENSUOUS PERCEPTION IN EMPIRICAL PHILOSOPHY, *ib.*, 28 Oct. 1943, XL, 589–597.

FURTHER AS TO VALUATION AS JUDGMENT. *Journal of Philosophy*, 30 Sept. 1943, XL, 543–552.

Reprinted in *Problems of Men* (1946), 261–272.

"The present paper is called out by the article of Professor [Philip Blair] Rice on TYPES OF VALUE JUDGMENT" in *Journal of Philosophy*, 30 Sept. 1943, 533–543.

Reply by Rice, FEELINGS AS EVIDENCE, *ib.*, 30 Sept. 1943, 552–557.

1944

HUMAN NATURE AND CONDUCT. (U.S. War Department Education Manual EM 618.) [Madison, Wis.] Published for the United States Armed Forces Institute by Henry Holt and Company [1944]. vii, 336 pp.

First published in 1922. A paperback reprint from the original plates, "published for use as an aid in instruction in certain educational activities of the armed forces."

Accompanied by . . . INSTRUCTOR'S COURSE OUTLINE, ETHICS. COLLEGE COURSE. . . . (U.S. War Department Education Manual EM 618a.) [Madison, Wis.] United States Armed Forces Institute [1944]. 16 pp.

BY NATURE AND BY ART. *Journal of Philosophy*, 25 May 1944, XLI, 281–292.

Reprinted in *Problems of Men* (1946), 286–300.

THE DEMOCRATIC FAITH AND EDUCATION. *Antioch Review*, June 1944, IV, 274–283.

An attack on the educational theories of Robert Maynard Hutchins. Read (in Dewey's absence by Jerome Nathanson) before the Conference on the Scientific Spirit and Democratic Faith, Ethical Culture School, New York, 27 May 1944; reported in the *New York Times*, 28 May 1944.

Reprinted in *The Authoritarian Attempt To Capture Education*. Papers from the 2d Conference on the Scientific Spirit and Democratic Faith (New York: King's Crown Press, 1945), 1–9; and in *Problems of Men* (1946), 22–23.

The Authoritarian Attempt To Capture Education is reviewed in *America*, 29 July 1945, LXXIII, 340–341; *Christian Century*, 1 Aug. 1945, LXII, 884–885 (Edward Scribner Ames); *Commonweal*, 29 June 1945, XLII, 268 (Leo Camp); *Journal of Philosophy*, 27 Sept. 1945, XLII, 548–550 (Harold Atkins Larrabee); *Nation*, 6 Oct. 1945, CLXI, 341 (Gail Kennedy); *New York Times Book Review*, 12 Aug. 1945 (Benjamin Fine); *Saturday Review of Literature*, 23 June 1945, XXVIII, xxv, 37 (Ordway Tead); *Survey Graphic*, Nov. 1945, XXXIV, 451–452 (Will Carson Ryan).

THE PENNING IN OF NATURAL SCIENCE. *The Humanist*, Summer 1944, IV, 57–59.

Comment on an article in the British *Literary Guide and Rationalist Review* (Mar. 1944) on talks over the B.B.C. by Julian Huxley and Gilbert Murray, and reply by Dr. [Joseph Houldsworth] Oldham, a theologian.

CHALLENGE TO LIBERAL THOUGHT. *Fortune*, Aug. 1944, XXX, ii, 155–157, 180, 182, 184, 186, 188, 190.

Reprinted by Fortune Magazine, 1945 [12] pp.; and in *Problems of Men* (1946), 143–159. Abstracts in *Time*, 21 Aug. 1944, XLIV, viii, 48, 50; and *Educational Digest*, Sept. 1944, X, 1.

Reply by Alexander Meiklejohn, *Fortune*, Jan. 1945, XXXI, i, 207–208, 210, 212, 214, 217, 219; rejoinder by Dewey, *ib.*, Mar. 1945, XXXI, iii, 10, 14. Further reply by Meiklejohn, *ib.*, 14, and letter from Dewey, *ib.*, 14.

See Robert Maynard Hutchins, EDUCATION FOR FREEDOM, *Christian Century*, 15 Nov. 1944, LXI, 1314–1316; and Buell Gordon Gallagher, MR. HUTCHINS AND MR. DEWEY, *ib.*, 24 Jan. 1945, LXII, 106–107.

SOME QUESTIONS ABOUT VALUE. *Journal of Philosophy*, 17 Aug. 1944, XLI, 449–455.

In response to George Raymond Geiger's paper, CAN WE CHOOSE BETWEEN VALUES? *ib.*, 25 May 1944, XLI, 292–298.

Reprinted in *Problems of Men* (1946), 273–281; and in Ray Lepley, ed., *Value: A Cooperative Inquiry* (1949), a book which eventuated from Dewey's article, 4–12.

THE PROBLEM OF THE LIBERAL ARTS COLLEGE. *American Scholar*, Oct. 1944, XIII, 391-393.

Published as part of The American Scholar Forum on The Function of the Liberal Arts College in a Democratic Society.

Reprinted in *Problems of Men* (1946), 83-87; and in Hiram Haydn and Betsy Saunders, eds., *The American Scholar Reader* (New York: Atheneum Publishers, 1960), 120-124.

JOHN DEWEY, AT 85, DEFENDS DOCTRINES. Interview in the *New York Times*, 20 Oct. 1944.

Dewey refutes criticisms of progressive education by Nicholas Murray Butler and Robert Maynard Hutchins.

1945

DEMOCRATIC VERSUS COERCIVE INTERNATIONAL ORGANIZATION: THE REALISM OF JANE ADDAMS. *In* Jane Addams, *Peace and Bread in Time of War*, Anniversary edition, 1915-1945 (New York: King's Crown Press, 1945), ix-xx.

Also published in *Survey Graphic*, Apr. 1945, XXXIV, 117-118, 138-139, with the title PEACE AND BREAD, and in Mercedes Irene Moritz Randall, ed., *Pan, the Logos and John Dewey* . . . (Philadelphia, 1959), 17-25.

Two paragraphs of Dewey's Introduction form the basis of A DISCUSSION OF THE THEORY OF INTERNATIONAL RELATIONS, in *Journal of Philosophy*, 30 Aug. 1945, XL, 477-497, by Lt. Col. Thomas Vernor Smith, Arthur Oncken Lovejoy, Joseph Perkins Chamberlain, William Ernest Hocking, Edwin Arthur Burtt, Glenn Raymond Morrow, Sidney Hook, and Jerome Nathanson.

A SEARCH FOR FIRM NAMES. *Journal of Philosophy*, 4 Jan. 1945, XLII, 5-6.

With Arthur Fisher Bentley.

Reprinted as the Introduction to *Knowing and the Known* (1949).

Reviewed by Alonzo Church in *Journal of Symbolic Logic*, Dec. 1945, X, 132-133.

A TERMINOLOGY FOR KNOWINGS AND KNOWNS. *Journal of Philosophy*, 26 Apr. 1945, XLII, 225-247.

With Arthur Fisher Bentley.

Reprinted in *Knowing and the Known* (1949), 47-78, with the title, THE TERMINOLOGICAL PROBLEM.

Reviewed by Alonzo Church in *Journal of Symbolic Logic*, Dec. 1945, X, 132-133.

THE REVOLT AGAINST SCIENCE. *The Humanist,* Autumn 1945, V, 105–107.

Reprinted in *Problems of Men* (1946), 160–163.

ARE NATURALISTS MATERIALISTS? *Journal of Philosophy,* 13 Sept. 1945, XLII, 515–530.

With Sidney Hook and Ernest Nagel.

Reply to Wilmon Henry Sheldon, CRITIQUE OF NATURALISM, *ib.,* 10 May 1945, XLII, 253–270. Reply by Sheldon, ARE NATURALISTS MATERIALISTS? *ib.,* 11 Apr. 1946, XLIII, 197–209. See also John Herman Randall, Jr., A NOTE ON MR. SHELDON'S MIND, *ib.,* 209–214.

DUALISM AND THE SPLIT ATOM. *New Leader,* 17 Nov. 1945, XXVIII, xlvi, 1, 4.

POSTULATIONS. *Journal of Philosophy,* 22 Nov. 1945, XLII, 645–662.

With Arthur Fisher Bentley.

Reprinted in *Knowing and the Known* (1949), 79–102.

Reviewed by Alonzo Church in *Journal of Symbolic Logic,* Dec. 1945, X, 132–133.

See A DISCUSSION OF DEWEY AND BENTLEY'S "POSTULATIONS," by Charles West Churchman and Thomas Anthony Cowan, *Journal of Philosophy,* 11 Apr. 1946, XLIII, 217–219.

ETHICAL SUBJECT-MATTER AND LANGUAGE. *Journal of Philosophy,* 20 Dec. 1945, XLII, 701–712.

Discussion of a thesis put forward by Charles Leslie Stevenson in his *Ethics and Language* (1944).

Reply by Arthur Pap in *Journal of Philosophy,* 18 July 1946, XLIII, 412–414.

See Dewey's PEIRCE'S THEORY OF LINGUISTIC SIGNS, THOUGHT, AND MEANING (1946), *below.*

1946

PROBLEMS OF MEN. New York: Philosophical Library [ᶜ1946]. 424 pp.

Contents. Introduction: The Problems of Men and the Present State of Philosophy. Part I: Democracy and Education. The Democratic Faith and Education—Democracy and Education in the World of Today—The Challenge of Democracy to Education—Democracy and Educational Administration—The Teacher and His World— The Problem of the Liberal Arts College—The Need for Orientation

—Authority and Resistance to Social Change—Liberty and Social Control—The Future of Liberalism. Part II: Human Nature and Scholarship. Challenge to Liberal Thought—The Revolt against Science—The Relation of Science and Philosophy as the Basis of Education—Religion, Science, and Philosophy—What Is Social Study?—Does Human Nature Change?—Nature in Experience. Part III: Value and Thought. Logical Conditions of a Scientific Treatment of Morality—Valuation Judgments and Immediate Quality—Further as to Valuation as Judgment—Some Questions about Value—The Ambiguity of "Intrinsic Good"—By Nature and By Art—How Is Mind To Be Known?—The Objectivism-Subjectivism of Modern Philosophy—Inquiry and Indeterminateness of Situations—Propositions, Warranted Assertibility, and Truth. Part IV: About Thinkers. James Marsh and American Philosophy—The Philosophy of William James—The Vanishing Subject in the Psychology of James—Whitehead's Philosophy.

Reprinted (through p. 308, How Is MIND To BE KNOWN? plus a revised index, pp. 309–311) as *Philosophy of Education (Problems of Men)* at Ames, Iowa, by Littlefield, Adams & Co., 1956 [°1946]. 311 pp. (Littlefield College Outlines.) A reprint of the abridged Littlefield edition with the title, *Problems of Men*, and the imprint of the Philosophical Library, New York, was marketed with publishers' remainders in 1959.

Translations. Italian by Giulio Preti (Milano, 1950); Spanish by Eduardo Prieto (Buenos Aires, 1952).

Reviewed in *American Sociological Review*, Oct. 1946, XI, 645 (Roy Wood Sellars); *Ethics*, Oct. 1946, LVII, 73–74 (Glenn Negley); *The Humanist*, Winter 1946–47, VI, 147–148 (Edward Fiess); *Journal of Philosophy*, 27 Mar. 1947, XLIV, 189–191 (Max Carl Otto); *Kenyon Review*, Autumn 1946, VIII, 683–685 (Dilman Walter Gotshalk); *Mind*, July 1947, LVI, 257–265 (Karl Britton), *Modern Schoolman*, May 1950, XXVII, 320–322 (James Collins); *Nation*, 19 Oct. 1946, CLXIII, 447–449 (Hannah Arendt); *New Republic*, 28 Oct. 1946, CXV, 562–564 (Jerome Nathanson); *New York Herald Tribune Books*, 1 Sept. 1946 (John Herman Randall, Jr.); *New York Times Book Review*, 9 June 1946 (Alvin Johnson); *Personalist*, Winter 1947, XXVIII, 96–98 (Daniel Sommer Robinson); *Philosophical Review*, Mar. 1947, LVI, 194–202 (Arthur Edward Murphy); *Philosophy and Phenomenological Research*, Sept. 1948, IX, 134–139 (Rubin Gotesky); *San Francisco Chronicle*, 18 Aug. 1946; *Saturday Review of Literature*, 20 July 1946, XXIX, xxix, 14–15 (Ordway Tead); *School Review*, Oct. 1946, LIV, 493 (C. D. Champlin); *Scuola e città*, 1951, II, i, 39 (F. De Bartolomeis); *Social Studies*, Nov. 1946, XXXVII, 327 (Charles Peters); *Springfield Republican*, 30 June 1946 (E.A.F.); *Survey Graphic*, May 1946, XXXV, 166

(Harry Hansen); *Time*, 24 June 1946, XLVII, xxv, 45–47; *Western Review*, Winter 1947, XI, 59–71 (Eliseo Vivas); *Yale Review*, Autumn 1946, N.S. XXXVI, 156–159 (Raphael Demos).

THE PUBLIC AND ITS PROBLEMS. An Essay in Political Inquiry. Chicago: Gateway Books, 1946. xii, 224 pp. (paperback).

First published in 1927.

New Introduction (iii–xii) dated Hubbards, Nova Scotia, 22 July 1946; the text is reprinted from the original plates.

Reviewed in *The Humanist*, Autumn 1947, VII, 96–97 (Alfred Stiernotte).

PEIRCE'S THEORY OF LINGUISTIC SIGNS, THOUGHT AND MEANING. *Journal of Philosophy*, 14 Feb. 1946, XLIII, 85–95.

See letter of Charles William Morris in *ib.*, 28 Mar. 1946, 146; reply by Dewey, *ib.*, 9 May 1946, 280; and rejoinder by Morris, *ib.*, 20 June 1946, 363–364.

THE CRISIS IN HUMAN HISTORY: THE DANGER OF THE RETREAT TO INDIVIDUALISM. (The Crisis of the Individual, IV.) *Commentary*, Mar. 1946, I, v, 1–9.

TRAGEDY OF A PEOPLE: RACIALISM IN CZECHO-SLOVAKIA. With an Appeal by John Dewey, Roger N. Baldwin, Christopher Emmet, Oswald Garrison Villard, Robert J. Watt, and others. Published by American Friends of Democratic Sudetens. New York, June 1946. 32 pp.

Dewey signed the appeal, HITLER'S SPIRIT STILL LIVES: INTRODUCTION, 3–6.

INTERACTION AND TRANSACTION. *Journal of Philosophy*, 12 Sept. 1946, XLIII, 505–517.

With Arthur Fisher Bentley.

Reprinted in *Knowing and the Known* (1949), 103–118.

TRANSACTIONS AS KNOWN AND NAMED. *Journal of Philosophy*, 26 Sept. 1946, XLIII, 533–551.

With Arthur Fisher Bentley.

Reprinted in *Knowing and the Known* (1949), 119–143.

SPECIFICATION. *Journal of Philosophy*, 21 Nov. 1946, XLIII, 645–663.

With Arthur Fisher Bentley.

Reprinted in *Knowing and the Known* (1949), 144–169.

1947

ART AND EDUCATION. [By] John Dewey, Albert C. Barnes, Laurence Buermeyer, Mary Mullen, Violette de Mazia. Second edition, revised and enlarged. Merion, Pa.: Barnes Foundation Press [ᶜ1947]. viii, 315 pp.

First published in 1929, *q.v.*

Reviewed in *Journal of Philosophy*, 25 Sept. 1947, XLIV, 558–559 (Helmut Kohn).

A third edition, revised and enlarged, was published in 1954, xiii, 316 pp.

FOREWORD. *In* Earl C. Kelley, *Education for What Is Real* (New York: Harper & Brothers [ᶜ1947]), v–vi.

INTRODUCTION. *In* Alexander Dorner, *The Way Beyond "Art"— The Work of Herbert Bayer* (New York: Winterborn, Schultz, Inc., 1947), 9–11.

A revised edition was published in 1958.

S.2499: ITS ANTIDEMOCRATIC IMPLICATIONS. *Nation's Schools*, Mar. 1947, XXXIX, 20–21.

Reprinted in *Progressive Education*, Apr. 1947, XXIV, 206–207.

Discussion of the Educational Development Act of 1947 sponsored by Senators James Edward Murray, Wayne Morse, and Claude Pepper.

"DEFINITION." *Journal of Philosophy*, 22 May 1947, XLIV, 281–305.

With Arthur Fisher Bentley.

Reprinted in *Knowing and the Known* (1949), 170–204, with the title, THE CASE OF DEFINITION.

Reviewed by Arthur Francis Smullyan in *Journal of Symbolic Logic*, Sept. 1947, XII, 99.

CONCERNING A VOCABULARY FOR INQUIRY INTO KNOWLEDGE. *Journal of Philosophy*, 31 July 1947, XLIV, 421–434.

With Arthur Fisher Bentley.

Reprinted in *Knowing and the Known* (1949), 287–306, with the title, A TRIAL GROUP OF NAMES.

LIBERATING THE SOCIAL SCIENTIST: A PLEA TO UNSHACKLE THE STUDY OF MAN. *Commentary*, Oct. 1947, IV, 378–385.

Article in a series on THE STUDY OF MAN.

MAN AND MATHEMATICS. *The Humanist,* Winter 1947, VII, 121.

Comment on a review (in *ib.,* Autumn 1947, VII, 101) of an article by Sir Edmund Whittaker, F.R.S., MATHEMATICS, MATTER, AND THE MIND OF THE UNIVERSE, in *Current Religious Thought,* June 1947.

1948

RECONSTRUCTION IN PHILOSOPHY. Enlarged edition, with a new Introduction by the Author. Boston: The Beacon Press [ᶜ1948]. xlvii, 224 pp.

Originally published in New York by Henry Holt and Company, 1920. The text of this edition is printed from the same plates. Dewey's added INTRODUCTION: RECONSTRUCTION AS SEEN TWENTY-FIVE YEARS LATER occupies pages v–xli. First published as a Beacon Paperback, and in Toronto by S. J. R. Saunders, 1957. Published in London by Mayflower, 1958.

This book was reset and published as a Mentor Book (paperback) by the New American Library, New York, 1950, 168 pp., with an Editor's Note by Eduard Christian Lindeman.

Dewey's new preface was used as a radio talk in Italy by the Voice of America, and is printed as RICOSTRUZIONE DELLA FILOSOFIA in *Il pensiero moderno in America* (Università internazionale G. Marconi, Pubblicazioni 1; Torino: Edizioni Radio Italiana, 1955); reviewed in *Rivista di filosofia,* Oct. 1955, XLVI, 473–474 (Nicola Abbagnano).

Reviews of 1948 edition: *The Humanist,* Spring 1949, IX, 46 (Edwin H. Wilson); *New Republic,* 27 June 1949, CXX, xxvi, 15–16 (Yervant Hovhannes Krikorian).

Chap. I, Changing Conceptions of Philosophy, was translated into German as VOM URSPRUNG DES PHILOSOPHIERENS: PHILOSOPHIE IM WANDEL DER AUFFASSUNGEN, in *Der Monat,* Oct. 1949, II, 25–35.

FOREWORD. *In* Henry Schaefer-Simmern, *The Unfolding of Artistic Activity* (Berkeley: University of California Press, 1948), ix–x.

BOYD H. BODE: AN APPRECIATION. *Teachers College Record,* Jan. 1948, XLIX, 266–267.

WILLIAM JAMES'S MORALS AND JULIAN BENDA'S: IT IS NOT PRAGMATISM THAT IS OPPORTUNIST. *Commentary,* Jan. 1948, V, 46–50.

Reply to Benda's criticism of pragmatism, THE ATTACK ON WESTERN MORALITY, *ib.,* Nov. 1947, IV, 416–422.

A COMMENT ON THE FOREGOING CRITICISMS. *Journal of Aesthetics and Art Criticism*, Mar. 1948, VI, 207–209.

Reply to Benedetto Croce, ON THE AESTHETICS OF DEWEY, *ib.*, 203–207.

COMMON SENSE AND SCIENCE: THEIR RESPECTIVE FRAMES OF REFERENCE. *Journal of Philosophy*, 8 Apr. 1948, XLV, 197–208.

Reprinted in *Knowing and the Known* (1949), 270–286.

AMERICAN YOUTH, BEWARE OF WALLACE BEARING GIFTS. *The Liberal* (Organ of the New York State Liberal Party), Oct. 1948, II, viii, 3–4.

Reprinted as WALLACE VS. A NEW PARTY (with minor editing) in *New Leader*, 30 Oct. 1948, XXXI, xliv, 1, 14.

HOW TO ANCHOR LIBERALISM. *Labor and Nation*, Nov.-Dec. 1948, IV, vi, 14–15.

Part of a symposium: CRISIS IN LIBERALISM.

1949

KNOWING AND THE KNOWN. [By] John Dewey and Arthur F. Bentley. Boston: The Beacon Press, 1949. xiii, 334 pp.

Contents. Introduction: A Search for Firm Names (J. D. and A. F. B.) —Vagueness in Logic (A. F. B.)—The Terminological Problem (J. D. and A. F. B.)—Postulations (J. D. and A. F. B.)—Interaction and Transaction (J. D. and A. F. B.)—Transactions as Known and Named (J. D. and A. F. B.)—Specification (J. D. and A. F. B.)— The Case of Definition (J. D. and A. F. B.)—Logic in an Age of Science (A. F. B.)—A Confused "Semiotic" (A. F. B.)—Common Sense and Science (J. D.)—A Trial Group of Names (J. D. and A. F. B.)—Summary of Progress Made (J. D. and A. F. B.)—Appendix: A Letter from John Dewey [to Albert G. A. Balz].

Reviewed in *American Journal of Sociology*, Sept. 1951, LVII, 200 (Anselm Strauss); *Annals of the American Academy of Political and Social Science*, Mar. 1950, CCLXVIII, 224 (Charles William Morris); *The Humanist*, Jan.-Feb. 1950, X, 30 (Harold Atkins Larrabee); *Journal of Symbolic Logic*, June 1950, XV, 156 (Paul Ziff); *Modern Schoolman*, May 1950, XXVII, 322–326 (James Collins); *New Yorker*, 29 Oct. 1949, XXV, xxxvi, 115; *Philosophical Review*, Apr. 1950, LIX, 269–270 (Max Black); *Saturday Review of Literature*, 22 Oct. 1949, XXXII, xliii, 15, 44 (Harold Atkins Larrabee); *Scientific Monthly*, Feb. 1951, LXXII, 135–136 (Solomon Weinstock); *Social Research*, June 1950, XVII, 248–250 (Sidney Ratner).

See Aldo Visalberghi, "INTERAZIONE" E "TRANSAZIONE" NELLA RI-
CERCA LOGICA E SCIENTIFICA, *Rivista di filosofia*, Oct. 1955, XLVI,
415-431, Jan. 1956, XLVII, 57-71.

THE WIT AND WISDOM OF JOHN DEWEY. Edited, with an Introduction [pp. 3-41], by A[llison] H[eartz] Johnson. Boston: The
Beacon Press, 1949. 111 pp.

> "This book is an attempt to provide a sample of John Dewey's wit
> and aphoristic wisdom. It takes the form of a series of quotations
> arranged under major topic headings . . . ," *viz.* Philosophy and
> Philosophers, Thinking, Science, Facts and Values, Morality, Art,
> Religion, Social Philosophy, Education.

> Reviewed in *The Humanist*, Jan.-Feb. 1950, X, 30 (Harold Atkins
> Larrabee); *Christian Century*, 4 Jan. 1950, LXVII, 18; *Saturday
> Review of Literature*, 22 Oct. 1949, XXXII, xliii, 15, 44 (Harold
> Atkins Larrabee).

THE FIELD OF "VALUE." *In* Ray Lepley, ed., *Value: A Cooperative Inquiry* (New York: Columbia University Press, 1949),
64-77.

HAS PHILOSOPHY A FUTURE? *Proceedings of the Tenth International Congress of Philosophy (Amsterdam, August 11-18
1948)* (Amsterdam: North-Holland Publishing Company,
1949), 108-116.

> Read at the Congress in Dewey's absence by Professor Sidney Hook.
> Revised and expanded as PHILOSOPHY'S FUTURE IN OUR SCIENTIFIC
> AGE: NEVER WAS ITS ROLE MORE CRUCIAL, *Commentary*, Oct.
> 1949, VIII, 388-394.

EDUCATION AND THE SOCIAL ORDER. New York: League for Industrial Democracy, 1949. 14 pp. (Pamphlet series.)

> Reprinted in *New Leader*, as EDUCATION: SERVANT OF THE COM-
> MUNITY, 16 Apr. 1949, XXXII, xvi, 5, and EDUCATION: SERVANT OF
> SOCIETY, 23 Apr. 1949, xvii, 8-9.

> Originally published as EDUCATION FOR A CHANGING SOCIAL ORDER
> (1934), *q.v.*

FOREWORD. *In* Philip Paul Wiener, *Evolution and the Founders
of Pragmatism* (Cambridge: Harvard University Press, 1949),
xiii-xiv.

[LETTER TO ALBERT GEORGE ADAM BALZ.] *Journal of Philosophy*,
26 May 1949, XLVI, 329-342.

> Reply to Balz, A LETTER TO MR. DEWEY CONCERNING JOHN
> DEWEY'S DOCTRINE OF POSSIBILITY, *ib.*, 313-329.

Reprinted in *Knowing and the Known* (1949), 313–329; and in *John Dewey on Experience, Nature, and Freedom* (1960), 133–149, with the title, IN DEFENSE OF THE THEORY OF INQUIRY.

EXPERIENCE AND EXISTENCE: A COMMENT. *Philosophy and Phenomenological Research*, June 1949, IX, 709–713.

The comment is upon Sholom J. Kahn's article, EXPERIENCE AND EXISTENCE IN DEWEY'S NATURALISTIC METAPHYSICS, *ib.*, Dec. 1948, IX, 316–321. Reply by Kahn, THE STATUS OF THE POTENTIAL: A REPLY TO PROFESSOR DEWEY, *ib.*, 714–716.

COMMUNISTS AS TEACHERS. *New York Times*, 21 June 1949.

Letter to the editor expressing his doubts on the view that "no one who is known to be a member of the Communist party should be permitted to teach in any higher institution of learning."

Reprinted in *Journal of Philosophy*, 7 June 1956, LIII, 375–376.

[MESSAGE TO THE AMERICAN FEDERATION OF TEACHERS.] *American Teacher*, Oct. 1949, XXXIV, i, 16.

Read at the convention dinner in Milwaukee, 24 Aug. 1949.

JOHN DEWEY, AT 90, FINDS TENSION OF WORLD MAY RESULT IN GOOD. *New York Herald Tribune*, 15 Oct. 1949.

Interview with Lester Grant.

JOHN DEWEY, AT 90, REITERATES HIS BELIEF THAT GOOD SCHOOLS ARE ESSENTIAL IN A DEMOCRACY. *New York Times*, 16 Oct. 1949.

Interview with Benjamin Fine.

"RELIGION HAS LOST ITSELF." John Dewey's Religious Insights Set Forth in Compilation from Writings. Edited by A[llison] H[eartz] Johnson. *Christian Register*, Nov. 1949, CXXVIII, 16–18, 39.

1950

GREETINGS TO THE URBANA CONFERENCE. *In* Kenneth Dean Benne and William Oliver Stanley, eds., *Essays for John Dewey's Ninetieth Birthday* [Urbana, Illinois: 1950], 3–4.

Read for Dewey at a conference on education and philosophy at the University of Illinois, 20 Oct. 1949.

JOHN DEWEY RESPONDS. *In* Harry Wellington Laidler, ed., *John Dewey at Ninety* (New York: League for Industrial Democracy [ᶜ1950]), 32–35.

Remarks at the dinner given to Dewey on his ninetieth birthday, Hotel Commodore, New York, 20 Oct. 1949.

RELIGION AND THE INTELLECTUALS. *Partisan Review*, Feb. 1950, XVII, 129–133.

Reprinted in *Religion and the Intellectuals. A Symposium* . . . [New York: Partisan Review, 1950], 53–57.

AESTHETIC EXPERIENCE AS A PRIMARY PHASE AND AS AN ARTISTIC DEVELOPMENT. *Journal of Aesthetics and Art Criticism*, Sept. 1950, IX, 56–58.

Reply to Patrick Romanell, A COMMENT ON CROCE'S AND DEWEY'S AESTHETICS, *ib.*, Dec. 1949, VIII, 125–128.

MR. ACHESON'S CRITICS: THEIR ATTACKS FEARED DAMAGING TO OUR WORLD PRESTIGE. *New York Times*, 19 Nov. 1950.

Letter to the editor regarding the Republican attacks on the Secretary of State.

1951

DAVID DUBINSKY: A PICTORIAL BIOGRAPHY. Text by John Dewey. New York: Inter-Allied Publications [ᶜ1951]. 95 pp.

DAVID DUBINSKY, MODERN LABOR LEADER (pp. 13–19), and DAVID DUBINSKY, MASTER CRAFTSMAN OF LABOR (pp. 21–28), are by Dewey.

[CONTRIBUTION TO A SYMPOSIUM.] *In* Richard McKeon and Stein Rokkan, eds., *Democracy in a World of Tensions: A Symposium prepared by UNESCO* (Chicago: University of Chicago Press [ᶜ1951]), 62–68.

INTRODUCTION. *In* Samuel Tenenbaum, *William Heard Kilpatrick: Trail Blazer in Education* (New York: Harper & Brothers [ᶜ1951]), vii–x.

ON PHILOSOPHICAL SYNTHESIS. *Philosophy East and West*, Apr. 1951, I, i, 3.

SCIENZE E FILOSOFIA. *Minerva: Rivista delle riviste* (Roma), July 1951, LXI, 219–222.

"Conferenza di John Dewey de la 'Voce dell'America' di Roma, 27 aprile 1951."

1952

MODERN PHILOSOPHY. *In* Frederick Burkhardt, ed., *The Cleavage in Our Culture: Studies in Scientific Humanism in Honor of Max Otto* (Boston: The Beacon Press [ᶜ1952]), 15-29.

INTRODUCTION. *In* Elsie Ripley Clapp, *The Use of Resources in Education* (New York: Harper & Brothers [ᶜ1952]), vii-xi.
Reprinted in *Dewey on Education* (1959), 127-134.

1953

INTRODUCTION. *In* Claude McKay, *Selected Poems* (New York: Bookman Associates, 1953), 7-9.

[LETTER TO GERTRUDE STEIN.] *In* Donald Gallup, ed., *The Flowers of Friendship: Letters Written to Gertrude Stein* (New York: Alfred A. Knopf, 1953), 254.
Dewey writes from New York, 19 Feb. 1932, to acknowledge a copy of Miss Stein's book, *Lucy Church Amiably*.

1954

IL MIO CREDO PEDAGOGICO: ANTOLOGIA DEI SCRITTI SULL'EDUCAZIONE. [Scelta, introduzione e annotazione a cura di Lamberto Borghi.] (Educatori antichi e moderni, 136.) Firenze: La Nuova Italia Editrice [1954, 1959]. liii, 268 pp.
Anthology of Dewey's pedagogical writings selected from the Italian translations of his works.
Contents. Introduzione: La concezione pedagogica di John Dewey (L. Borghi)—Notizia bio-bibliografica—Il mio credo pedagogico—La scuola e il processo sociale—La scuola e la vita del fanciullo—Psicologia dell'istruzione elementare—Interesse e disciplina—Esperienza e pensiero—Il pensare nell'educazione—I criteri dell'esperienza—Controllo sociale—La natura della libertà—Organizzazione progressiva della materia di studio—L'esperienza mezzo e fine dell'educazione—Democrazia e amministrazione scolastica.

1955

JOHN DEWEY: HIS CONTRIBUTION TO THE AMERICAN TRADITION. [Edited by] Irwin Edman. (Makers of the American Tradi-

tion Series.) Indianapolis: The Bobbs-Merrill Company, Inc.
[ᶜ1955]. 322 pp.

Contents. Introduction [by Irwin Edman]—Reconstruction in Philosophy [from *ib.*]—Philosophy as Education [from *Democracy and Education*]—Human Nature and Conduct [from *ib.*]—Intelligence and Inquiry [from *Logic*]—The Human Uses of Freedom [from *Freedom and Culture*]—The Religion of Shared Experience [from *A Common Faith*]—Democracy as a Moral Ideal [CREATIVE DEMOCRACY—THE TASK BEFORE US].

Reviewed in *Nation*, 10 Dec. 1955, CLXXXI, 518 (Abraham Edel); *New York Herald Tribune Books*, 25 Sept. 1955; *New York Times Book Review*, 24 July 1955 (Sidney Hook); *New Yorker*, 27 Aug. 1955, XXXI, xxviii, 104; *San Francisco Chronicle*, 1 Aug. 1955 (G. E. Arnstein); *Saturday Review*, 13 Aug. 1955, XXXVIII, xxxiii, 9 (Brand Blanshard).

1956

PHILOSOPHY OF EDUCATION (PROBLEMS OF MEN). (Littlefield College Outlines.) Ames, Iowa: Littlefield, Adams & Co., 1956. 311 pp.

A partial reprint of *Problems of Men* (1946), *q.v.*

Translation. Hindi by Surendrapala Simha (Allahabad, 1957).

1959

JOHN DEWEY: DICTIONARY OF EDUCATION. Edited by Ralph B[ubrich] Winn. With a Foreword by John Herman Randall, Jr. New York: Philosophical Library [ᶜ1959]. x, 150 pp.

A compilation of the "basic as well as casual theories and statements of the late philosopher on the subject of education and pedagogy," arranged by topic, *e.g.*, Abstraction, Authority, Belief, Civilization, Democracy, Experimental Method, etc.

REFLECTIONS OF JOHN DEWEY: EXCERPTS FROM UNPUBLISHED CORRESPONDENCE. (Vol. LXXXVIII, no. 3 of the Proceedings of the American Academy of Arts and Sciences.) *Dædalus*, Summer 1959, 549-559.

Nine letters written to Corinne Chisholm Frost (Mrs. Frank G. Frost) between 1930 and 1949. The Dewey-Frost correspondence, consisting of some one hundred and fifty letters from Dewey, was presented to the Columbia University Library, 20 Oct. 1959.

DEWEY ON EDUCATION. Selections with an Introduction and Notes by Martin S. Dworkin. (Classics in Education, 3.) New York: Bureau of Publications, Teachers College, Columbia University [ᶜ1959]. 134 pp.

Contents. John Dewey: A Centennial Review, by Martin S. Dworkin —My Pedagogic Creed—The School and Society—The Child and the Curriculum—Progressive Education and the Science of Education—Introduction by John Dewey to *The Use of Resources in Education* by Elsie Ripley Clapp.

LETTERS OF JOHN DEWEY TO ROBERT V[INCENT] DANIELS, 1946– 1950. *Journal of the History of Ideas*, Oct.-Dec. 1959, XX, 569– 576.

Eight letters written to a graduate student at Harvard.

1960

JOHN DEWEY ON EXPERIENCE, NATURE, AND FREEDOM: REPRESENTATIVE SELECTIONS. Edited, with an Introduction, by Richard J[acob] Bernstein. (The Library of Liberal Arts, No. 41.) New York: Liberal Arts Press [ᶜ1960]. xlix, 293 pp.

Contents. Introduction—From Absolutism to Experimentalism— The Need for a Recovery of Philosophy—An Empirical Study of Empiricisms—Context and Thought—The Pattern of Inquiry—In Defense of the Theory of Inquiry—Having an Experience—Qualitative Thought—Peirce's Theory of Quality—The Subject Matter of Metaphysical Inquiry—Time and Individuality—Nature in Experience—Philosophies of Freedom.

THEORY OF THE MORAL LIFE. With an Introduction by Arnold Isenberg. New York: Holt, Rinehart and Winston [1960]. 179 pp.

Part II of Dewey and Tufts, *Ethics*, from the revised edition of 1932, *q.v.*

CORRESPONDENCE WITH JOHN DEWEY. In *The Morning Notes of Adelbert Ames, Jr.*, including a Correspondence with John Dewey. Edited and with a preface by Hadley Cantril (New Brunswick: Rutgers University Press [ᶜ1960]), 171–231.

Forty-eight letters which passed between Ames and Dewey from Dec. 1946 to Nov. 1950.

Writings about John Dewey

ABBAGNANO, NICOLA. Dewey. In his *Storia della filosofia* (Torino: U.T.E.T., 1950), II, ii, 650–670.

Third edition (Torino, 1958), Dewey, II, ii, 540–552. Spanish translation (Barcelona, 1956), Dewey, III, 375–385.

———. Dewey: Esperienza e possibilità. *Rivista critica di storia della filosofia*, Oct.-Dec. 1951, VI, 257–268.

Reprinted as ESPERIENZA E POSSIBILITÀ IN DEWEY in his *Possibilità e libertà* (Torino: Taylor, 1956), 198–214.

———. *Storia del pensiero scientifico*. 3d ed. (1st ed. 1951). Torino: Paravia, 1961.

Dewey, 219–229, 307–315.

———. Verso il nuovo illuminismo: John Dewey. *Rivista di filosofia*, Oct.-Dec. 1948, XXXIX, 313–325.

Reprinted in his translation of *Experience and Nature* (Torino, 1948).

ABEL, REUBEN. *The Pragmatic Humanism of F. C. S. Schiller.* New York: King's Crown Press, 1955. 207 pp.

Dewey, *passim*.

ACKLEY, SHELDON CARNER. John Dewey's Conception of Shared Experience as Religious.

Thesis (PH.D.), Boston University, 1948.

ADDAMS, JANE. Toast to John Dewey. *Survey*, 15 Nov. 1929, LXIII, 203–204.

ADLER, MORTIMER JEROME. The Chicago School. *Harper's Magazine*, Sept. 1941, CLXXXIII, 377–388.

———. *The Idea of Freedom: A Dialectical Examination of the Conceptions of Freedom*, by Mortimer J. Adler for The Institute for Philosophical Research. Garden City, N.Y.: Doubleday & Company, 1958. xxvii, 689 pp.

Dewey, *passim*.

AGAZZI, ALDO. *Panorama della pedagogia d'oggi.* 2d ed. Brescia: La scuola, 1950.

Dewey, 82–87.

AHERN, ALVIN A. The Significance of the Views of John Dewey and William Ernest Hocking for Moral Education.

Thesis (A.M.), New York University, 1939.

AIKEN, HENRY DAVID. A Pluralistic Analysis of the Ethical "Ought." *Journal of Philosophy,* 2 Aug. 1951, XLVIII, 497–505.

———. Reflections on Dewey's Questions about Value. *In* Ray Lepley, ed., *Value: A Cooperative Inquiry* (New York: Columbia University Press, 1949), 15–42.

ALAMSHAH, WILLIAM H. John Dewey's Ethical Theory.

Thesis (PH.D.), University of Southern California, 1955.

ALBERTY, HAROLD BERNARD. Appraisal of Dewey's Aphorism: Education Is Life. National Education Association, Department of Superintendence, *Official Report* 1930, p. 152.

———. Direction of Learning on the Elementary School Level· *Educational Outlook,* Nov. 1933, VIII, 10–20.

ALDRICH, VIRGIL CHARLES. John Dewey's Use of Language. *Journal of Philosophy,* 11 May 1944, XLI, 261–271.

ALEXANDROV, GEORGI F. [The Philosophizing Armor-Bearers of American Reaction.] *Bolshevik,* 15 July 1947, II, 23–51.

In Russian. The Harvard College Library has a copy of this title separately printed (38 pp., Moscow, 1947); stenographic report of a lecture.

ALGER, GEORGE WILLIAM. Recollections of John Dewey. Letter in *Saturday Review,* 19 Dec. 1959, XLII, li, 21.

ALILUNAS, LEO J. John Dewey's Pragmatic Ideas about School History and Their Early Applications. *Social Studies,* Mar. 1950, XLI, 111–114.

A LIOTTA, ANTONIO. *The Idealistic Reaction against Science* Translated by Agnes McCaskill. London: Macmillan and Co. Ltd., 1914. xxii, 483 pp.

Translation and revision of the author's *La reazione idealistica contro la scienza* (Palermo, 1912); DEWEY'S INSTRUMENTAL LOGIC, 174–179.

————. *Le origini dell'irrazionalismo contemporaneo.* Napoli: Libreria Scientifica Editrice, 1950.

Dewey, 297–303 *et passim*.

ALLEN, DEVERE. Education in Action. In his *Adventurous Americans* (New York: Farrar and Rinehart [ᶜ1932]), 130–140.

ALLEN, HAROLD. Dewey's Criticism of the British Empiricists. Thesis (A.M.), Columbia University, 1951.

ALLPORT, GORDON WILLARD. Psychology and the Fourth R. *New Republic*, 17 Oct. 1949, CXXI, xvi, 23–26.

AMERICA. John Dewey Meets the Absolute. *America*, 14 June 1952, LXXXVII, 281.

AMES, VAN METER. John Dewey as Aesthetician. *Journal of Aesthetics and Art Criticism*, Dec. 1953, XII, 145–168.

————. Esthétique: Les principes de la critique. *Les Études philosophiques*, July-Dec. 1949, N.S. IV, 430–438.

ANDERBERG, CLIFFORD W. The Impact of Evolution on Dewey's Theory of Knowledge and the Critics of Dewey. Thesis (PH.D.), University of Wisconsin, 1953.

ANDERSON, HAROLD A. John Dewey. *School Review*, Sept. 1952, LX, 320–322.

AÑO ANIVERSARIO 1859–1959: JOHN DEWEY. [Buenos Aires: Servicio Informativo de los Estados Unidos de América, 1959.] 23 pp.

Contents. John Dewey, algunas reflexiones, por Jerome Nathanson—La filosofia de la democracia en el pensamiento de John Dewey, por Gustavo F. J. Cirigliano—John Dewey: Una inteligencia siempre joven, por Gordon Hullfish—Bibliografia de John Dewey, compilada por el Dr. Gustavo F. J. Cirigliano, presidente de la Sociedad de John Dewey, Buenos Aires—I. En inglés, II. En espanol.

ANTON, JOHN PETER. John Dewey and the Ancient Philosophies. *Journal of Philosophy*, 19 Nov. 1959, LVI, 963–965.

Abstract of a paper read at the meeting of the American Philosophical Association, Columbia University, 30 Dec. 1959.

ANTORCHA, LA. Por que contra Dewey. *La Antorcha: Revista Hispanoamericana* (Paris), July 1931, I, iv, 18–24.

APPELL, MORRIS LIONEL. John Dewey—Pattern for Adventuring.

Master's thesis, Ohio State University, 1941.

ARDURA, ERNESTO. John Dewey: Filósofo de la libertad. *Boletín del comisión nacional cubana de la UNESCO*, Aug. 1952, I, 4–7.

ARMENTROUT, WINFIELD DOCKERY. The Optimism in Dewey's Philosophy of Education. *Journal of Educational Method*, Feb. 1927, VI, 236–239.

ARNDT, RUTH SPENCE. *John Dewey's Philosophy of Education*. Pretoria: J. L. van Schaik, 1929. 105 pp.

ARNETT, WILLARD EUGENE. Critique of Dewey's Anticlerical Religious Philosophy. *Journal of Religion*, Oct. 1954, XXXIV, 256–266.

ARONOWITZ, ALFRED. The Foundations of John Dewey's Political Theory.
Submitted for Bennett Prize, Harvard University, 1950.

ARSCOTT, JOHN ROBERT. Moral Freedom and the Educative Process: A Study in the Educational Philosophy of William Torrey Harris.
Doctoral thesis, New York University, 1949.

———. Two Philosophies of Freedom. *School and Society*, 3 Nov. 1951, LXXIV, 276–279.
William Torrey Harris's Hegelianism and John Dewey's instrumentalism.

ASCHENER, MARY JANE. A Study of John Dewey's Conception of the Improvement of Thinking.
Thesis (A.M.), University of Illinois, 1953.

AULETTA, GENNARO. Dewey educatore senza schemi. *La fiera letteraria*, 17 Sept. 1950.

AUSTIN, AVEL. Symbol and Existence in Locke and Dewey.
Thesis (A.M.), Columbia University, 1953.

AUT AUT (Milano). John Dewey. *Aut Aut* 9, May 1952, 175–192.

AXTELLE, GEORGE EDWARD. Philosophy in American Education. *Harvard Educational Review*, Spring 1956, XXVI, ii, 184–189.

———. William Heard Kilpatrick: An Interpretation. *Progressive Education*, Mar. 1957, XXXIV, 35–37.

AYRES, CLARENCE EDWIN. Dewey: Master of the Commonplace. *New Republic*, 18 Jan. 1939, LXXXXVII, 303–306.
Reprinted in Malcolm Cowley and Bernard Smith, eds., *Books That*

Changed Our Minds (New York, 1939), 111–126, with the title
DEWEY AND HIS STUDIES IN LOGICAL THEORY.

———. Instrumental Economics. *New Republic*, 17 Oct 1949,
CXXI, xvi, 18–20.

BAEGE, F. P. Zwei ausländische Beeinflusser der deutschen
Schulreform. *Neue Bahnen*, Sept. 1912, XXIII, 548–554.

BAGLEY, WILLIAM CHANDLER. John Dewey, Vigorous at Age 85,
Defends Progressive Education. *School and Society*, 4 Nov.
1944, LX, 292.

BAIN, A. E. *John Dewey and the Peculiar Traits of American
Thought*. 1948. (Contemporary Issues, No. 1, 2.)
Copy in British Museum.

BAKER, MELVIN CHARLES. *Foundations of John Dewey's Educational Theory*. New York: King's Crown Press, Columbia
University, 1955. ix, 214 pp.
Reviewed in *Les Études philosophiques*, Apr.-June 1956, 316–317
(Gérard Deledalle).

BALDAUF, VIOLET MIRIAM. The Religious Implications of the
Philosophy of John Dewey.
Thesis (A.M.), New York University, 1938.

BALDWIN, JAMES MARK. The Limits of Pragmatism. *Psychological Review*, Jan. 1904, XI, 30–60.

BALLINGER, STANLEY E. John Dewey: Man Ahead of His Times.
Educational Digest, Nov. 1959, XXV, 9–11.

BALZ, ALBERT GEORGE ADAM. A Letter to Mr. Dewey concerning John Dewey's Doctrine of Possibility. *Journal of Philosophy*, 26 May 1949, XLVI, 313–329.
Reply by Dewey in *ib.*, 329–342.

BANFI, ANTONIO. Ripensando a Dewey. *Rivista critica di storia
della filosofia*, Oct.-Dec. 1951, VI, 269–274.

———. *L'uomo copernicano*. Milano: Mondadori, 1950.
Dewey, 84–87 *et passim*.

BARCEWICZ, REGINA. Thomas Edward Shields and John Dewey:
A Comparative Study.
Master's thesis, University of Detroit, 1955.

BARIE, G. E. *L'io transcendentale*. Messina: Principato, 1948.
Dewey, 312–313, 318–322.

BARNES, ALBERT COOMBS. Art as Experience. *In* Progressive Education Association, Progressive Education Booklet No. 13, *The Educational Frontier* (Columbus, Ohio, 1939), 13–25. Delivered at the celebration of Dewey's eightieth birthday in New York, Oct. 1939.

———. Dewey and Art. *New Leader*, 22 Oct. 1949.

———. The Educational Philosophy of John Dewey. *The Humanist*, Winter 1946, V, 160–162. Adapted from the author's pamphlet, *The Case of Bertrand Russell versus Democracy and Education* (Merion, Pennsylvania, n.d.). Spanish translation in *Ultra* (Cuba). Apr. 1946.

BARONI, A. L'esperienza di John Dewey. *Studium*, 1950, XLVI, 401–405.

BARR, HELEN A. The Ethics of John Dewey. Thesis (A.M.), University of Wisconsin, 1932.

BARRON, JOSEPH T. Professor Dewey and Truth. *Catholic World*, Nov. 1922, CXVI, 212–221.

BARROWS, ALICE. Some Results of Dewey's Philosophy. *Platoon School*, Dec. 1929, III, 150–151.

BARRY, ROBERT M., and JOHN D. FEARON. John Dewey and American Thomism. *American Benedictine Review*, Dec. 1959, Dec. 1960, X, 219–228, XI, 268–280.

BARTON, GEORGE ESTES, JR. John Dewey: Too Soon a Period Piece? *School Review*, Summer 1959, LXVII, 128–138.

BATES, ERNEST SUTHERLAND. John Dewey, America's Philosophic Engineer. *Modern Monthly*, Aug. 1933, VII, 387–396, 404.

BATTLE, JOHN J. The Metaphysical Presuppositions of the Philosophy of John Dewey. Fribourg, 1951. iv, 128 pp. Thesis (DR.PHIL.), Fribourg.

BAUM, MAURICE JAMES. A Comparative Study of the Philosophies of William James and John Dewey. Thesis (PH.D.), University of Chicago, 1928.

BAUMGARTEN, EDUARD. Amerikanische Philosophie. In *Amerikakunde: Zwölf Beiträge von Eduard Baumgarten [et al.].* (Handbücher der Auslandskunde, hrsg. von Paul Hartig und

Wilhelm Schellberg.) 2d ed. (Frankfurt am Main: Moritz Diesterweg, 1952), 162–199.

Dewey, 182–196, 199.

————. John Dewey. I. Die Idee der Demokratie. *Internationale Zeitschrift für Erziehung*, 1936, V, ii, 81–97; II. Die Auseinandersetzung mit dem deutschen Idealismus. *Ib.*, 1936, V, vi, 407–430; III. Theorie der Menschlichen Natur. *Ib.*, 1937, VI, iii, 177–200.

————. Die pragmatische und instrumentale Philosophie John Deweys. *Neue Jahrbücher für Wissenschaft und Jugendbildung* (Berlin), 1934, X, 236–248.

————. *Der Pragmatismus: R. W. Emerson, W. James, J. Dewey.* (Die geistigen Grundlagen des amerikanischen Gemeinwesens, Bd. II.) Frankfurt am Main: Vittorio Klostermann [1938]. xvi, 483 pp.

Dewey, 212–332, 435–450.

Reviewed in *Blätter für deutsche Philosophie* (Berlin), 1939, XIII, 226–229 (Rudolf Metz); *Deutsche Literaturzeitung*, 1939, LX, 581–583 (F. Rippe); *Internationale Zeitschrift für Erziehung* (Berlin), 1938, VIII, 65–67 (Gerhard Lehmann); *Die Tatwelt* (Berlin), 1940, XVI, 27–30 (Helmut Schelsky).

————. Schulreformer der Neuzeit: John Dewey. *Zeitgeist* (Stuttgart), 7, 4, 156.

Title from *Bibliographie der deutschen Zeitschriftenliteratur*, Ergänzungsband X (1914–1915), 39.

BAUSOLA, ADRIANO. L'antimetafisicismo di John Dewey. *Rivista di filosofia neo-scolastica* (Milano), Jan.-Feb. 1955, XLVII, 41–67.

————. *L'etica di John Dewey.* (Pubblicazioni dell'Università Cattolica del Sacro Cuore. Serie terza. Scienze filosofiche, II.) Milano: Società Editrice Vita e Pensiero, 1960. 224 pp.

————. Fide e ricerca in Dewey. *Rivista di filosofia neo-scolastica*, 1960, LII, 465–471.

BAWDEN, HENRY HEATH. *The Principles of Pragmatism: A Philosophical Interpretation of Experience.* Boston: Houghton Mifflin Company, 1910. x, 364 pp.

Dewey, *passim.*

BAWDEN, HENRY HEATH (*continued*). What Is Pragmatism? *Journal of Philosophy*, 4 Aug. 1904, I, 421–427.

BAY, JAMES CAMPBELL. Our Public Schools: Are They Failing? *Nation*, 26 June 1954, CLXXVIII, 539–541.

Reply by Paul Woodring, A PRAGMATIC POINT, *ib.*, 31 July 1954, CLXXIX, 99.

BAYLES, ERNEST E. Deweyism and Doctor [Frederick Stephen] Breed's New Realism. *Educational Administration and Supervision*, Nov. 1939, XXV, 561–568.

———. A Relativistic Religion. *Phi Delta Kappan*, Oct. 1958, XL, 33–36.

The religion of John Dewey.

BEACH, JOSEPH WARREN. Incoherence in the Philosopher: Mr. John Dewey. In his *The Outlook for American Prose* (Chicago: University of Chicago Press [ᶜ1926]), 41–52.

BEARD, CHARLES AUSTIN. America in Midpassage. *In* Progressive Education Association, Progressive Education Booklet No. 14, *John Dewey and the Promise of America* (Columbus, Ohio, 1939), 18–25.

Delivered at the celebration of Dewey's eightieth birthday in New York, Oct. 1939.

BEATH, PAUL ROBERT. John Dewey: Pragmatist. *The Daily Illini* (University of Illinois), 26 Feb. 1928.

BECCHI, EGLE. Aspetti del criterio transazionale e del concetto di "Gestalt" nella logica di Dewey. *Rivista di filosofia*, July 1960, LI, 247–253.

BECK, ROBERT HOLMES. American Progressive Education, 1875–1930.

Thesis (PH.D.), Yale University, 1942. Abstract in *Curriculum Journal*, Mar. 1943, XIV, 115–118.

———. Progressive Education and American Progressivism: Caroline Pratt. *Teachers College Record*, Nov., Dec., 1958, Jan. 1959, LX, 77–89, 129–137, 198–208.

BELTH, MARC. The Concept of Democracy in Dewey's Theory of Education.

Thesis (PH.D.), Columbia University, 1956.

———. Concerning Dewey's Contribution to a Philosophy of

Education. *In* Frederick Charles Gruber, ed., *Education in Transition* (Philadelphia, 1960), 260–264.

BEN-HORIN, MEIR. John Dewey and Jewish Education. *Religious Education*, May 1960, LV, 201–202.

BENNE, KENNETH DEAN. *Essays for John Dewey's Ninetieth Birthday*. Kenneth Dean Benne and William Oliver Stanley, eds. [Urbana: Bureau of Research and Service, College of Education, University of Illinois, 1950]. 92 pp.
Report of a conference on education and philosophy at the University of Illinois, 20 Oct. 1949.
Contents. Introduction: Greetings to the Urbana Conference, by John Dewey—On Celebrating John Dewey's Birthday, by Kenneth Dean Benne—Dewey's Place in the Classic Period of American Philosophy, by Max Harold Fisch—Dewey's Theory of Language with Some Implications for Educational Theory, by Alfred S. Clayton—The Problems of Verification in Formal School Learning, by Foster McMurry—Educational Foundations of Social Planning, by Horace Snyder Fries—John Dewey and Adult Education, by Kenneth Dean Benne—Dewey's Philosophy as a Program of Action, by Sing-Nan Fen—Closing Remarks, by Leo A. Molinaro.

———. The Human Individual: John Dewey. *The University* [of Kansas City] *Review*, Oct. 1940, VII, 48–56.

———. John Dewey and Adult Education. *Adult Education Bulletin*, Oct. 1949, XIV, vii, 7–12; reprinted in *Essays for John Dewey's Ninetieth Birthday, above.*

———. On Celebrating John Dewey's Birthday. *Progressive Education*, Oct. 1949, XXVII, i, 25–26; *see above.*

BENNETT, CHARLES ALPHEUS. John Dewey and Industrial Education. *Industrial Education Monthly*, Nov. 1930, XXXII, 146–147.

BENTLEY, ARTHUR FISHER. *Behavior, Knowledge, Fact*. Bloomington, Ind.: The Principia Press, Inc., 1935. xii, 391 pp.

———. Decrassifying Dewey. *Philosophy of Science*, Apr. 1941, VIII, 147–156.

———. *Inquiry into Inquiries: Essays in Social Theory*. Edited and with an Introduction by Sidney Ratner. Boston: Beacon Press [ᶜ1954]. xvi, 365 pp.
Many references to Dewey; see index.

Reviewed in *Rivista di filosofia*, Oct. 1955, XLVI, 470–471 (Nicola Abbagnano).

BERGER, GASTON. La philosophie de John Dewey. *Les Études philosophiques*, Jan.-June 1952, N.S. VII, 5–15.

BERGER, MORRIS ISAIAH. John Dewey and Progressive Education Today. *School and Society*, 28 Mar. 1959, LXXXVII, 140–142.

Reprinted in William Wolfgang Brickman and Stanley Lehrer, eds., *John Dewey: Master Educator* (New York, 1959), 83–88.

BERINGAUSE, ARTHUR F. The Double Martyrdom of Randolph Bourne. *Journal of the History of Ideas*, Oct. 1957, XVIII, 594–603.

Dewey, *passim*.

BERKSON, ISAAC BAER. *The Ideal and the Community: A Philosophy of Education*. New York: Harper & Brothers [ᶜ1958]. xii, 302 pp.

Critique of Dewey and educational experimentalism.

———. Science, Ethics, and Education in the Deweyan Experimentalist Philosophy. *School and Society*, 10 Oct. 1959, LXXXVII, 387–391.

Reprinted in William Wolfgang Brickman and Stanley Lehrer, eds., *John Dewey: Master Educator* (New York, 1959), 58–71.

BERLEANT, ARNOLD. Dewey's Methodological Approach to Social Philosophy.

Thesis (PH.D.), University of Buffalo, 1962.

BERNSHTEIN, M. S. [The Reactionary Conceptions of American Pedagogical Philosophy.] *Sovyetskaya Pedagogika*, 1949, xiv.

BERNSTEIN, RICHARD JACOB. Dewey's Naturalism. *Review of Metaphysics*, Dec. 1959, XIII, 340–353.

Reply to John Edwin Smith, JOHN DEWEY: PHILOSOPHER OF EXPERIENCE, *ib.*, Sept. 1959, XIII, 60–78.

———. John Dewey's Metaphysics of Experience.

Thesis (PH.D.), Yale University, 1958.

———. John Dewey's Metaphysics of Experience. *Journal of Philosophy*, 5 Jan. 1961, LVIII, 5–14; abstract in *ib.*, 19 Nov. 1959, LVI, 961–962.

Read at the meeting of the American Philosophical Association, Columbia University, 29 Dec. 1959.

See Gail Kennedy, COMMENT ON PROFESSOR BERNSTEIN'S PAPER, *ib.*, 5 Jan. 1961, LVIII, 14–21.

BERTINI, E. M. Afirmaciones y negaciones en el Credo pedagógico de Dewey. *Revista de educación* (La Plata), 1950, iii, 9–26.

BESTOR, ARTHUR EUGENE, JR. John Dewey and American Liberalism. *New Republic*, 29 Aug. 1955, CXXXIII, ix, 18–19.
Reply by Vernon F. Haubricht, PRAGMATISM AND LIBERALISM, *ib.*, 19 Sept. 1955, CXXXIII, xii, 23.

BETTA, BRUNO. *Dewey*. Brescia: "Vita Scolastica," 1950. 62 pp.

BILSTAD, INGEBORG WARNE. Aspects of Dewey's *The Public and Its Problems* as Reflected in Selected Secondary Textbooks. Master's thesis, University of Wisconsin, 1946.

BISHOP, WILLIAM WARNER. College Days [University of Michigan]: 1889–1893. Fragments of Autobiography. *Michigan Alumnus, Quarterly Review*, Summer 1948, LIV, 340–352. Dewey, 348.

BIXLER, JULIUS SEELYE. The Patriot and the Pragmatist. *Journal of Religion*, July 1934, XIV, 253–264.

———. *Religion for Free Minds*. New York and London: Harper & Brothers, 1939. xii, 247 pp.
DEWEY AND THE SOCIAL GOOD, chap. ix, 117–127.

BLACKHURST, JAMES HERBERT. Does the World-View of John Dewey Support Creative Education? *Educational Theory*, Oct. 1955, Jan., Apr. 1956, V, 193–202, 248; VI, 1–9, 34, 65–73.

BLANSHARD, BRAND. Can the Philosopher Influence Social Change? *Journal of Philosophy*, 25 Nov. 1954, LI, 741–753.
Reply by John Lawrence Childs, *ib.*, 753–763.

BLAU, JOSEPH LEON. Darwin, Dewey and Beyond. *Christian Register*, Nov. 1949, CXXVIII, x, 19–21, 39.

———. Experimental Naturalism: John Dewey. In his *Men and Movements in American Philosophy* (New York: Prentice-Hall, Inc., 1952), 343–355.
Italian translation by Alberto Pasquinelli (Firenze, 1957).

———. John Dewey and American Social Thought. *Teachers College Record*, Dec. 1959, LXI, 121–127; condensed in *Education Digest*, Mar. 1960, XXV, vii, 28–31.

BLAU, JOSEPH LEON (*continued*). John Dewey's Theory of History. *Journal of Philosophy*, 4 Feb. 1960, LVII, 89–100.

BLEWETT, JOHN, ed. *John Dewey: His Thought and Influence.* Edited by John Blewett, s.j. With a foreword by John Seiler Brubacher. (Orestes Brownson Series on Contemporary Thought and Affairs, 2.) New York: Fordham University Press [ᶜ1960]. xiv, 242 pp.

Contents. The Genesis of Dewey's Naturalism, by James Collins— Democracy as Religion: Unity in Human Relations, by John Blewett, s.j.—Dewey's Theory of Knowledge, by Beatrice Hope Zedler—John Dewey and Progressive Education, by Sister Joseph Mary Raby, s.s.j.—Dewey and the Problem of Technology, by John W. Donohue, s.j.—Dewey's Ambivalent Attitude toward History, by Thomas P. Neill—Process and Experience, by Robert Channon Pollock—Dewey's Influence in China, by Thomas Berry, c.p.— A Chronological and Bibliographical Note.

———. John Dewey, Salvationist. *Social Order*, Dec. 1959, IX, 422–451.

———. John Dewey's Case against Religion. *Catholic World*, Apr. 1959, CLXXXIX, 16–21.

BLIVEN, BRUCE. Farewell to John Dewey. *New Republic*, 16 June 1952, CXXVI, xxiv, 9.

BLUMENFIELD, SAMUEL M. John Dewey and Jewish Education. *Chicago Jewish Forum*, Spring 1950, VIII, iii, 169–176.

Hebrew versions: Mishnat Dyui veha-ḥinukh ha-'ivri [The Doctrine of Dewey and Hebrew Education], in *Safer Hashanah* [New York, 1940] and John Dewey Ultrumato Lahinuch Hayhudi [John Dewey and His Contribution to Hebrew Education], *Sheviley Hachinuch*, XX, ii [New York, 1960?].

BOARDMAN, WILLIAM GILES. A Study in Dewey's Theory of Knowledge.

Thesis (A.M.), Columbia University, 1936.

BOAS, GEORGE. Communication in Dewey's Aesthetics. *Journal of Aesthetics and Art Criticism*, Dec. 1953, XII, 177–183.

———. The Literature of Diversity. *New Republic*, 17 Oct. 1949, CXXI, xvi, 26–29.

BODE, BOYD HENRY. Dewey's Doctrine of the Learning Process. *In* Progressive Education Association, Progressive Education

Booklet No. 12, *Freedom and Education* (Columbus, Ohio, 1939), 16–23.

Delivered at the celebration of Dewey's eightieth birthday in New York, Oct. 1939.

——. John Dewey. *Educational Research Bulletin*, 23 Oct. 1929, VIII, 342–343.

——. John Dewey, Philosopher of Science and Democracy. *Progressive Education*, Oct. 1952, XXX, i, 2–5; condensed in *Education Digest*, Dec. 1952, XVIII, iv, 13–15.

——. Pragmatism in Education. *New Republic*, 17 Oct. 1949, CXXI, xvi, 15–18.

BOER, TJITZE J. DE. *Amerikaansche Denkers*. (Volksuniversiteits-bibliotheek, 61.) Haarlem: Erven F. Bohn, 1934. 225 pp.

HET INSTRUMENTALISME VAN JOHN DEWEY, 177–215.

——. De naturalistiche Wijsbegeerte van John Dewey: *Tijdschrift voor Wijsbegeerte*, 1927, XXI, 151–157, 208.

——. Pragmatisme. *Ib.*, 1913, VII, 325–364, 412–436.

——. *School en Maatschappij* door John Dewey. Vertaald en Ingeleid door Dr. Tj. de Boer. Groningen: J. B. Wolter, 1929, 218 pp.

Contents. Het Leven van John Dewey—Dewey als Wijsgeer—Dewey als Opvoedkundige—Bibliographie—School en Maatschappij.

BÖGHOLT, CARL M. John Dewey's Views on Philosophic Method in His Early Writings, 1882–1903.

Thesis (PH.D.), University of Wisconsin, 1933.

BOGGS, LUCINDA PEARL. *Über John Deweys Theorie des Interesses und seine Anwendung in der Pädagogik*. Halle a. S.: C. A. Kaemmerer & Co., 1901, 73 pp.

Thesis (DR.PHIL.), University of Halle-Wittenberg.

BOGNETTI, GIOVANNI. State e diritto nel pensiero di Dewey. *Rivista di filosofia*, July 1960, LI, 254–261.

BOGOSLOVSKY, BORIS BASIL. *The Technique of Controversy: Principles of Dynamic Logic*. (International Library of Psychology, Philosophy and Scientific Method.) New York: Harcourt, Brace & Co., 1928. viii, 266 pp.

Thesis (PH.D.), Columbia University.

Numerous references to Dewey.

BOOR, JOHN G. A Validation of Brubacher's Interpretation of Progressive Education Based on the Writings of John Dewey. Master's thesis, St. Louis University, 1957.

BORGHI, LAMBERTO. La categoria della socialità nel pensiero pedagogico di John Dewey. *In* Ferruccio Rossi-Landi, ed., *Il pensiero americano contemporaneo* (Milano: Edizioni di Comunità, 1958), I, 25–52.

————. La critica degli educatori e dei filosofi al Dewey. *Scuola a città*, Apr. and 30 June 1951.

————. L'educazione sociale nel marxismo e nel pragmatismo. *Scuola e città*, 1957, 1–8.

————. I fondamenti della concezione pedagogica di John Dewey. *Rivista critica di storia della filosofia*, Oct.-Dec. 1951, VI, 342–359.

————. *L'ideale educativo di John Dewey.* (Educatori antichi e moderni, 147.) Firenze: La Nuova Italia [1955]. 123 pp.

————. John Dewey e altri aspetti del rapporto tra scuole e città. *Scuola e città*, Feb. 1951.

————. *John Dewey e il pensiero pedagogico contemporaneo negli Stati Uniti.* (Educatori antichi e moderni, 79.) Firenze: La Nuova Italia Editrice [1951]. viii, 269 pp.
Reviewed in *Aut Aut* 5, Sept. 1951, 466 (Enzo Paci); *Salesianum*, Apr.-Sept. 1952, XIV, 418–419 (Renzo Titone); *Scuola e città*, 1951, 342–343 (Francesco de Bartolomeis). See Andrea Daziano, NOTA SUL PROBLEMA DEI VALORI IN J. DEWEY, *Rivista di filosofia*, Apr. 1953, XLIV, 198–200.

————. John Dewey e la prima guerra mondiale. *Scuola e città*, Mar. 1951.

————. La motivazione storica dello sperimentalismo del Dewey. *Scuola e città*, Mar. 1957, 81–88.

————. Pensiero e socialità nella concezione pedagogica di John Dewey. *Scuola e città*, 1955, 217–226.

————. Personalità, attività immaginativa ed esperienza religiosa in John Dewey. *Rivista di filosofia*, July 1960, LI, 262–278.

————. La scuola di Dewey nei suoi ultimi sviluppi. *Scuola e città*, 31 July 1951.

BOSCHENSTEIN, HERMANN. John Dewey und die amerikanische Erziehung. *Neue schweizer Rundschau* (Zurich), Jan. 1931, XXIV, 5–22.

BOURNE, RANDOLPH SILLIMAN. John Dewey's Philosophy. *New Republic*, 13 Mar. 1915, II, 154–156.

―――. Twilight of Idols. *Seven Arts Magazine*, Oct. 1917, II, 688–702.

Reprinted in his *Untimely Papers*, edited by James Oppenheim (New York: B. W. Huebsch, 1919), 114–139; and in his *The History of a Literary Radical and Other Papers* (New York: S. A. Russell, 1956), 241–259.

BOWERS, DAVID FREDERICK. Hegel, Darwin, and the American Tradition. In his *Foreign Influences in American Life* (Princeton: Princeton University Press, 1944), 146–171 (Dewey 164–171).

BOYER, MINOR WALLER. An Expedition of Dewey's Groundwork for a General Theory of Value. *Journal of Aesthetics and Art Criticism*, Sept. 1956, XV, 100–105.

BOYLE, W. E. The Philosophical Background of John Dewey, Educator. *Catholic Educational Review*, June 1939, XXXVII, 385–392.

BRADLEY, RITAMARY, SISTER. Analysis of a Symposium for John Dewey. *Catholic Educator*, Apr. 1953, XXIII, 383–385.

BRADY, MARY L. John Dewey: Philosophy as a Methodology.

Thesis (PH.D.), Fordham University, 1945.

BRANCATISANO, FORTUNATO. La concezione pedagogica di J. Dewey. *Rassegna di pedagogia*, 1950, VIII, 125–127, 214–233; reprinted, Padova: Liviana, 1950, 51 pp.

Reviewed in *Scuola e città*, 1951, II, iv, 158 (Aldo Visalberghi).

―――. Dall'arte alla filosofia. *Calabria letteraria*, Mar. 1950.

―――. Dewey e Marx. *Historica: Rivista bimestrale di cultura* (Reggio Calabria), 1950, III, iii, 93–97; 1951, IV, i, 25–28, ii, 61–64.

Copy at Harvard College Library.

―――. La forma mentis della borghesia al lume della filosofia del Dewey. *L'Airone*, 1951, II, i–ii, 3–10.

BRANCATISANO, FORTUNATO (*continued*). John Dewey nella filosofia contemporanea. *Nuova rivista pedagogica* (Roma), Sept. 1952.

————. John Dewey nella filosofia moderna. *Scuola e città*, 1952, 62–66, 96–100, 135–143.

————. John Dewey e lo storicismo. *Richerche filosofiche*, Dec. 1950.

————. La metafisica della libertà in Dewey. *I problemi della pedagogia*, Mar. 1955, 161–181.

————. La posizione di Dewey nella filosofia moderna. *Il Saggiatore* (Torino), July-Dec. 1952, II, 286–337; reprinted, Torino: Editore Gheroni, 1953, 52 pp.

————. A proposito della pedagogia di John Dewey. *Nuova rivista pedagogica* (Roma), 1951, I, iv.

————. Sulla formazione di John Dewey. *Rivista critica di storia della filosofia*, Oct.-Dec. 1951, VI, 409–426.

BRANDENBURG, KARL HEINZ. Kunst als Qualität der Handlung: John Deweys Grundlegung der Aesthetik.
Thesis (DR.PHIL.), Königsberg, 1942.

BRATTON, FRED GLADSTONE. *The Legacy of the Liberal Spirit: Men and Movements in the Making of Modern Thought.* New York: Charles Scribner's Sons, 1943. xi, 319 pp.
Dewey, 257–274.

BRAUN, JOHN T. John Dewey: Systematic Theologian.
Master's thesis, Reed College, 1954.

BRECHT, ARNOLD. *Political Theory: The Foundations of Twentieth-Century Political Thought.* Princeton: Princeton University Press, 1959. xviii, 603 pp.
Dewey, *passim.*

BREED, FREDERICK S. "Progressive Education." *School and Society*, 29 Apr. 1933, XXXVII, 544–548.
Reply by William F. Bruce, COMMENT UPON BREED'S CRITICISM OF DEWEY, *ib.*, 24 June 1933, 812–814.

BREISACH, ERNEST. Benedetto Croce, John Dewey, and the Traditional Concept of Liberty. *In* Michigan Academy of Science, Arts and Letters, *Papers* (Ann Arbor, 1959), XLIV, 335–344.

BRETT, GEORGE SIDNEY. *A History of Psychology*. London: George Allen & Unwin, Ltd., New York: The Macmillan Co., 1912–1921. 3 vols.

Dewey, III, 242–272.

BRICKMAN, WILLIAM WOLFGANG, and STANLEY LEHRER, eds. *John Dewey: Master Educator*. New York: Society for the Advancement of Education, 1959. 123 pp. paperback.

The John Dewey Centennial special issue of *School and Society*, 10 Oct. 1959, reprinted in book form, with additions.

Contents. John Dewey's Life and Work in Outline, by William Wolfgang Brickman—Reminiscences of Dewey and His Influence, by William Heard Kilpatrick—John Dewey in History, by Junius Lathrop Meriam—Dewey and American Education, 1894–1920, by Maxine Greene—John Dewey as Teacher, by Harold Atkins Larrabee—Science, Ethics, and Education in Dewey's Philosophy, by Isaac Baer Berkson—Dewey's Culture Theory and Pedagogy, by Robert Emmett Mason—John Dewey and Progressive Education Today, by Morris Isaiah Berger—John Dewey: Educator of Nations, by William Wolfgang Brickman—Dewey and Russia, by William Wolfgang Brickman—Dewey's Letters, 1894–1904: A Preliminary Listing, by Robert Lawrence McCaul.

Second edition (New York, 1961, 172 pp.) adds CHICAGO IN THE 1890's, by Franklin Parker, 25–30; and Robert L. McCaul, DEWEY, HARPER, AND THE UNIVERSITY OF CHICAGO, JULY 1894 . . . -JUNE 1904, 31–74.

———. John Dewey's Foreign Reputation as an Educator. *School and Society*, 22 Oct. 1949, LXX, 257–265.

Revised version, JOHN DEWEY: EDUCATOR OF NATIONS, in *John Dewey: Master Educator*, above.

See also Isaac Leon Kandel, THE INFLUENCE OF EDUCATIONAL THEORISTS, *School and Society*, 10 Dec. 1949, LXX, 379.

BRINKLEY, S. G. John Dewey's Universal. *Educational Theory*, Aug. 1951, I, 131–133.

BRODBECK, MAY. A Critical Examination of John Dewey's *Logic: The Theory of Inquiry*.

Thesis (PH.D.), University of Iowa, 1947.

———. The Emergence of American Philosophy. *American Quarterly*, Spring 1950, II, 39–52.

———. La filosofia di John Dewey. *Rivista di filosofia*, Oct. 1959, L, 391–422.

BRODBECK, MAY (*continued*). John Dewey. *In* May Brodbeck, James Gray, and Walter Metzger, *American Non-Fiction 1900–1950* (Chicago: Henry Regnery Company, 1953), 40–57.

———. The New Rationalism: Dewey's Theory of Induction. *Journal of Philosophy*, 24 Nov. 1949, XLVI, 780–791.

Reply by Milton Mayeroff, THE NATURE OF PROPOSITIONS IN JOHN DEWEY'S "LOGIC," *ib.*, 8 June 1950, XLVII, 353–358.

BROTHERSTON, BRUCE WALLACE. The Genius of Pragmatic Empiricism. *Journal of Philosophy*, 7 and 21 Jan. 1943, XL, 14–21, 29–39.

BROUDY, HARRY SAMUEL. Realism and the Philosophy of Education. *In* John Daniel Wild, ed., *The Return to Realism: Essays in Realistic Philosophy* (Chicago: Henry Regnery Company, 1953), 293–312.

BROWN, GEORGE P. Dr. John Dewey's Educational Experiment. *Public School Journal*, June 1897, XVI, 533–537.

———. The University [of Chicago] Elementary School. *School and Home Education*, Oct. 1899, XVIII, 98–99.

BROWN, JAMES GOOD. The Evolutionary Concept in John Dewey's Philosophy and Its Implications for Religious Education.

Thesis (PH.D.), Yale University, 1936.

BROWN, JAMES NISBET. *Educational Implications of Four Conceptions of Human Nature: A Comparative Study.* Washington: Catholic University of America, 1940. xiii, 139 pp.

John Dewey, William Chandler Bagby, Herman Harrell Horne, The Catholic Viewpoint.

Thesis (PH.D.), Catholic University of America.

BROWN, MARCUS. Concerning the Abandonment of a Certain "Deweyan" Conception of Metaphysics. *Educational Theory*, Jan. 1957, VII, 19–27, 75.

———. The Questions of Ontology in Dewey's Philosophy.

Thesis (A.M.), New York University, 1954.

BROWNING, ROBERT W. Reason in Ethics and Morals, with Special Reference to the Contribution of Hume and Dewey.

Thesis (PH.D.), University of California, 1947.

BRUCE, LEE. John Dewey's Theory of Experience.

Thesis (A.M.), University of Chicago, 1932.

BRUCE, WILLIAM F. The Relation of Experimentalism to Democracy. *Educational Administration and Superintendence*, Apr. 1932, XVIII, 241–249.

BRUNER, JEROME SEYMOUR. After John Dewey, What? *Saturday Review*, 17 June 1961, XLIV, xxiv, 58–59, 76–78.

BUCHANAN, SCOTT. John Dewey. *Nation*, 23 Oct. 1929, CXXIX, 458–459.

Reprinted in part in *Teachers College Record*, Dec. 1929, XXXI, 222.

BUCHCIK, ANTHONY ALFRED. The Concept of Morals in the Philosophies of St. Augustine and John Dewey.

Thesis (PH.D.), University of Chicago, 1955.

BUCHHOLZ, HEINRICH EWALD. Dewey Mocked by the N.E.A. *Educational Administration and Supervision*, Sept. 1932, XVIII, 413–421.

BURKHARDT, FREDERICK, ed. *The Cleavage in Our Culture: Studies in Scientific Humanism in Honor of Max Otto*. Boston: Beacon Press [ᶜ1952]. ix, 201 pp.

Dewey, *passim*.

BURNS, EDWARD McNALL. *Ideas in Conflict: The Political Theories of the Contemporary World*. New York: W. W. Norton & Company, Inc. [ᶜ1960]. xiv, 587 pp.

Dewey, 93–97 *et passim*.

BURNS, ROBERT W. John Dewey y la teoría del conocimiento. *Nueva educación* (Lima, Peru), Dec. 1959, XXIV, cxxvi, 6–13.

BURR, JOHN ROY. Three Dimensions of Philosophic Intelligence: Private, Public, and Visional, in the Philosophies of Warner Fite, John Dewey, and George Santayana.

Thesis (PH.D.), Columbia University, 1959.

BURTT, EDWIN ARTHUR. The Core of Dewey's Way of Thinking. *Journal of Philosophy*, 23 June 1960, LVII, 401–419.

Read at the meeting of the American Philosophical Association, Columbia University, 28 Dec. 1959.

Comments by Gail Kennedy and John Allan Irving, *ib.*, 436–450.

———. *Principles and Problems of Right Thinking: A Textbook for Logic, Reflective Thinking, and Orientation Courses*. New York: Harper & Brothers, 1928. xii, 590 pp.

"Part II . . . constitutes a revision of traditional logic achieved by organizing the material around the five steps in a complete act of thought as set forth in Dewey's *How We Think*." Daniel Sommer Robinson in *Journal of Philosophy*, XXVI, 159.

BURTT, EDWIN ARTHUR (*continued*). *Types of Religious Philosophy*. New York: Harper & Brothers [ᶜ1939]. 512 pp.
Discussion of Dewey's pragmatic humanism, 403 ff.

BUSWELL, JAMES OLIVER, JR. *The Philosophies of F[rederick] R[obert] Tennant and John Dewey*. New York: Philosophical Library [ᶜ1950]. xvii, 516 pp.
Thesis (PH.D.), New York University.
Letter of Dewey to the author, 8 Dec. 1946, p. 464.

BUTTS, ROBERT FREEMAN. Centenary of John Dewey. *Teachers College Record*, Dec. 1959, LXI, 117–120.

BYRNS, RUTH KATHERINE. John Dewey on Russia: A Leading American Philosopher Has Been Cool to the Soviets. *Commonweal*, 18 Sept. 1942, XXXVI, 511–513.

—— and WILLIAM O'MEARA. Concerning Mr. Hutchins: Three Philosophies of Education—Dewey, Hutchins, and a Catholic View. *Commonweal*, 31 May 1940, XXXII, 114–116.

CAFARO, FRANCESCO. John Dewey e il pensiero italiano. *Italia che scrive* (Roma), July 1950, 101–102.

——. John Dewey e la critica italiana. *Rivista critica di storia della filosofia*, Oct.-Dec. 1951, VI, 427–441.

CAHAN, RUTH. The Implementation of the John Dewey Philosophy in the University Elementary School, U.C.L.A.
Master's thesis, University of California at Los Angeles, 1958.

CAHILL, HOLGER. American Resources in the Arts. *In* Progressive Education Association, Progressive Education Booklet No. 15, *Resources for Building America* (Columbus, Ohio, 1939), 41–57.
Delivered at the celebration of Dewey's eightieth birthday in New York, Oct. 1939.

CALANDRA, G. La cultura come esperienza associata nel pensiero di John Dewey. *Rassegna di pedagogia*, 1955, XIII, 222–237.

CALDWELL, WILLIAM. *Pragmatism and Idealism*. London: Adam and Charles Black, 1913. ix, 268 pp.
Dewey, 16–17 *et passim*.

CAMPANALE, DOMENICO. Significato e aporie della logica naturalistica nel pensiero di J. Dewey. *Rassegna di scienze filosofiche* (Roma), 1955, VIII, 18–45, 277–306.

CAMPBELL, PAUL E. Fundamental Fallacies in Education. *Homiletic and Pastoral Review*, Sept. 1932, XXXII, 1287–1295.

CANTONI, REMO. John Dewey e l'estetica. *Il pensiero critico*, Mar. 1952, II, 1–14.

CARCANO, PAOLO FILIASI. Il pensiero americano contemporaneo. *Giornale critico della filosofia italiana*, 1960, XXXIX.
Dewey, 288–289.

CARLOYE, JACK CLOYD. Bradley and Dewey: On Objective Knowledge.
Thesis (A.M.), University of Chicago, 1953.

CARROI, MARIE-ANNE. L'Oeuvre psychopédagogique de John Dewey. *L'Information pédagogique* (Paris), 1940, IV, i.

CARY, C. P. John Dewey's Educational Ideas. *Wisconsin Journal of Education*, Mar.-Apr. 1932, LXIV, 333, 390–391.

CASAGRANDE, MARIO. Scuola, società e democrazia. *Società*, Dec. 1919, V, 662–673.
Discussion of Italian translations of *School and Society* (Firenze, 1949) and *Democracy and Education* (Firenze, 1949).

CASE, MATTHEW H. The Ethics of John Dewey Compared with the Moral Teachings of Jesus.
Master's thesis, Eastern Washington College of Education (Cheney), 1955.

CASSIRER, ERNST. *Substance and Function and Einstein's Theory of Relativity*. Authorized translation by William Curtis Swabey and Marie Collins Swabey. Chicago and London: Open Court Publishing Company, 1923. 465 pp.
Dewey, pp. 318 ff.

CASTRO, MARTHA DE. *Estudio crítico de las ideas pedagógicas de John Dewey*. Habana: Imprenta Ninon, 1939. 133, iii, pp.
Thesis (PED.D.), University of Havana.

CASWELL, HOLLIS LELAND. Influence of John Dewey on the Curriculum of American Schools. *Teachers College Record*, Dec. 1949, LI, 144–146.

CHADBOURNE, RICHARD McCLAIN. Two Organizers of Divinity, Ernest Renan and John Dewey. *Thought: Fordham University Quarterly*, Sept. 1949. XXIV, 430–448.

CHAMPLIN, NATHANIEL LEWIS. Controls in Qualitative Thought. Report (ED.D.), Teachers College, 1952.

———. John Dewey: Beyond the Centennial. *Educational Leadership*, Oct. 1960, XVIII, i, 33–35, 38–42.

CHANG, CHIEH-MIN. The Utilitarian Theory of Jeremy Bentham Defended from Certain Criticism of John Stuart Mill and John Dewey.
Thesis (A.M.), Columbia University, 1925.

CHANG, YIN-LIN. A Comparative Study of the Ethical Theories of G. E. Moore and John Dewey.
Thesis (A.M.), Leland Stanford, Jr., University, 1932.

CHAO, CHEN. An Account of John Dewey's Conception of the Three Logical "Laws of Thought."
Thesis (A.M.), Columbia University, 1950.

CHASSELL, LAURA MERRILL, and CLARA FRANCES CHASSELL A Restatement of Important Educational Conceptions of Dewey in the Terminology of Thorndike. *Journal of Educational Method*, Mar. 1924, III, 286–298.

CHELEDEN, ALGERDAS NICODEMUS. Some Misconceptions concerning the Pragmatism of John Dewey.
Thesis (A.M.), University of California at Los Angeles, 1945.

CHERUBINI, GIOVANNI. Strumentalismo e materialismo dialettico. *Società*, Mar. 1952, VIII, 63–79.
Reply by Franco Fergnani, Fulvio Papi, and Vittorio Strada, DEWEY E IL MARXISMO, *ib.*, June 1952, VIII, 314–321, and rejoinder by Cherubini, *ib.*, 321–324.
Reply by Andrea Vasa, STRUMENTALISMO E MATERIALISMO DIALETTICO, *Revista critica di storia della filosofia*, May-June 1952, VII, 201–206.
Review by Aldo Visalberghi in *Rivista di filosofia*, July 1952, XLIII, 333–337.

CHIANG, J. M. TSE-YU. The Philosophy of Social Education According to John Henry Newman and John Dewey.
Master's thesis, Manhattanville College of the Sacred Heart, 1955.

CHILD, ARTHUR HENRY. *Making and Knowing in Hobbes, Vico, and Dewey.* Berkeley and Los Angeles: University of California Press, 1953 (University of California Publications in Philosophy, XVI, xiii, 271–310).

CHILDS, JOHN LAWRENCE. *American Pragmatism and Education: An Interpretation and Criticism.* New York: Henry Holt and Company [ᶜ1956]. x, 373 pp.
Dewey, *passim.*

———. Cultural Factors in Dewey's Philosophy of Education. *Teachers College Record,* Dec. 1949, LI, 130–132.

———. *Education and the Philosophy of Experimentalism.* (Century Studies in Education.) New York: The Century Company [1931]. xix, 264 pp.
A critical examination of the ideas of Peirce, James and Dewey.
Thesis (PH.D.), Columbia University.

———. John Dewey. *Educational Theory,* July 1954, IV, 183–186.

———. John Dewey and American Education. *Teachers College Record,* Dec. 1959, LXI, 128–133.

———. John Dewey and the Educational Frontier. *In* Progressive Education Association, Progressive Education Booklet No. 13, *The Educational Frontier* (Columbus, Ohio, 1939), 5–12.
Delivered at the celebration of Dewey's eightieth birthday in New York, Oct. 1939.

———. *John Dewey as Educator.* Two Essays: THE EDUCATIONAL PHILOSOPHY OF JOHN DEWEY, by John L. Childs; DEWEY'S INFLUENCE ON EDUCATION, by William H. Kilpatrick, with a separate preface by Professors Childs and Kilpatrick, and the complete table of contents of *The Philosophy of John Dewey* . . . [New York: Progressive Education Association, 1940]. 3 p.l., 419–473, xi–xii pp.
Reprinted from Paul Arthur Schilpp, ed., *The Philosophy of John Dewey, q.v.*

———. Laboratory for "Personhood." *Saturday Review of Literature,* 22 Oct. 1949, XXXII, xliii, 11–12, 36–38.

CHOY JYAN (Tshwei Tsai-yang). *Étude comparative sur les doc-*

trines pédagogiques de Durkheim et de Dewey. Lyon: Bosc Frères & Riou, 1926. 243 pp.
"Thèse de doctorat . . . Université de Lyon."
"Ecrits de Dewey," 237–240.

CHRISTIAENS, F. De John Dewey à Ernst Krieck. *Revue des sciences pédagogiques* (Bruxelles), 1945, VII, 63–68, 144–145.

CHRISTIAN CENTURY. John Dewey [Editorial]. *Christian Century*, 18 June 1952, LXIX, 717–719.
See the letters from readers in *ib.*, 9 July 1952, 805–806, and communication from Charles Clayton Morrison, *ib.*, 23 July 1952, 854.

CIMMARUTA, MATILDE. La pedagogia de Giovanni Dewey. *L'educazione nazionale* (Roma), July 1927, IX, 446–457.

CLAPARÈDE, EDOUARD. John Dewey. *Svobodno Vaspitanie* [Sofia, Bulgaria]. May-June 1924, II, 257–266.

———. *La Pedagogía de John Dewey.* México: Sociedad de edicion y libreria franco-americana, s. a., 1926. 45 pp.

CLARK, GORDON HADDON. *Dewey by Clark.* (International Library of Philosophy and Theology: Modern Thinkers Series.) Philadelphia: Presbyterian and Reformed Publishing Co., 1960. 69 pp.

———. *Thales to Dewey: A History of Philosophy.* Boston: Houghton Mifflin Company [ᶜ1957]. xii, 548 pp.
Dewey, 517–533.

CLAYTON, ALFRED STAFFORD, ed. *John Dewey in Perspective: Three Papers in Honor of John Dewey.* (Indiana University School of Education Bulletin, 36.) Bloomington: Indiana University Division of Research and Field Services [1960]. 44 pp.
Papers presented at Indiana University's celebration of the centennial of John Dewey's birth.
Contents. Dewey and His Contemporaries, by Harold Rugg— Dewey's Analysis of the Act of Thought, by Harry Samuel Broudy— Ten Misunderstandings of Dewey's Educational Philosophy, by John Seiler Brubacher.

———. Philosophy of Education: Interpretations of Dewey's Educational Thought. *Review of Educational Research*, Feb. 1961, XXXI, 32.

CLAYTON, FRANK L. Variant Philosophies and their Significance to Education.
Doctoral thesis, New York University, 1936.

CLIFT, VIRGIL A. Does the Dewey Philosophy Have Implications for Desegregating the Schools? *Journal of Negro Education,* Spring 1960, XXIX, ii, 145–154.

CODIGNOLA, ERNESTO. *Maestri e problemi dell'educazione moderna.* Firenze: La Nuova Italia, 1951.

Dewey, 164–184.

———. *Il problema educativo.* 3 vols. Firenze: La Nuova Italia, 1946.

Dewey, III, 280–285.

———. *Le "scuole nuove" e i loro problemi.* Firenze: La Nuova Italia, 1946 (4th ed., 1952, 114 pp.).

Dewey, 24–53 in 1946 edition.

Reviewed in *Società,* Jan.-June 1953, IX, 246–247 (M.C.).

COHEN, MORRIS RAPHAEL. *American Thought: A Critical Sketch.* Glencoe, Illinois: The Free Press [ᶜ1954]. 360 pp.

JOHN DEWEY AND HIS SCHOOL, 290–303, and other references, *passim.*

Reviewed in *Philosophical Review,* Apr. 1956, LXV, 254–260 (Marcus George Singer).

———. The Intellectual Love of God. *Menorah Journal,* Aug. 1925, XI, 332–341.

THE SPINOZISTIC IDEAL IN CONTEMPORARY THINKERS . . . DEWEY, 340.

———. John Dewey's Philosophy. *New Republic,* 2 Sept. 1916, VIII, 118–119.

Review of *Essays in Experimental Logic* (1916); reprinted in his *A Preface to Logic* (New York, 1944), 196–202 (Italian translation, Milano, 1948).

———. Later Philosophy. In *The Cambridge History of American Literature,* edited by William Peterfield Trent, John Erskine, Stuart Pratt Sherman, and Carl Van Doren (New York: G. P. Putnam's Sons, 1921), III, 226–265.

Dewey, III, 254–257 *et passim;* bibliography, IV, 756.

———. Our American Philosophy III: John Dewey and the Chicago School. *New Republic,* 17 Mar. 1920, XXII, 82–86.

———. Some Difficulties in Dewey's Anthropocentric Naturalism. *Philosophical Review,* Mar. 1940, XLIX, 196–228.

Reprinted in his *Studies in Philosophy and Science* (New York, 1949), 139–175.

See Dewey's reply, NATURE IN EXPERIENCE, *Philosophical Review*, Mar. 1940, XLIX, 244–258.

COIT, JOHN KNOX. A Criticism of Moritz Schlick's Ethics in the Light of Dewey's Naturalism.

Thesis (A.M.), Columbia University, 1945.

COLLINS, JAMES. Metaphysics in an Empirical Climate. *Giornale di metafisica*, 1947, II, iv–v, 338–351.

COLLINS, RUSSELL J. The Metaphysical Foundations of John Dewey's Theory of Knowledge.

Master's thesis, Catholic University of America, 1945.

COLUMBIA ALUMNI NEWS. Prof. John Dewey Will Retire from Columbia Faculty in June. *Columbia Alumni News*, 28 Mar. 1930, XXI, xxiv, 5.

COMEL, CLAUDIO. Sul significato della religiosità in Dewey. *Rivista di filosofia neo-scolastica*, 1959, LI, 535–541.

COMFORT, EUNICE NICHOLAS. The Bearing of John Dewey's Philosophy upon Christianity.

Thesis (S.T.M.), Union Theological Seminary, 1923.

CONDON, EDWARD UHLER. Contemporary Science. *New Republic*, 13 Feb. 1950, CXXII, vii, 11–15.

Remarks on Dewey's understanding of science and the scientific method, 15.

CONTRI, S. A proposito di J. Dewey. *Criterion*, 1938, i–ii.

COONS, JOHN WARREN. *The Idea of Control in John Dewey's Philosophy*. [Rochester, N.H.: The Record Press, Inc., ᶜ1936.] 96 pp.

Thesis (PH.D.), University of Iowa, 1933.

CORALLO, GINO. L'esigenza della libertà etica nella pedagogia di John Dewey. *Notizie bibliografiche della Società Editrice Internazionale*, 1952.

———. *John Dewey*. (Pedagogisti ed educatori, 4.) Brescia: La Scuola, 1957. 196 pp.

———. La logica dello strumentalismo di John Dewey. *Rivista di filosofia neo-scolastica*, Jan.-Feb. 1950, XLII, 159–169.

———. *La pedagogia di Giovanni Dewey*. Torino: Società Editrice Internazionale, 1950. xlix, 557 pp.

Reviewed in *Aut Aut* 5, Sept. 1951, 467–468 (Enzo Paci); *Filosofia*,

Oct. 1952, III, 636–638 (Maria Teresa Viretta Gillio Tos); *Giornale di metafisica*, May-June 1951, VI, 342–343 (Franco Amerio); *Rivista di filosofia*, July 1952, XLIII, 333–337 (Aldo Visalberghi); *Rivista di filosofia neo-scolastica*, July-Aug. 1950, 375–377 (N. Conca); *Salesianum*, Apr.-June 1950, XII, 289–290 (Pietro Braido).

―――. A proposito di una "filosofia dell'educazione." *Rivista di filosofia neo-scolastica*, Apr.-June 1949, 260–270.

CORCORAN, TIMOTHY. Child Labor within School Years from Dewey back to Pestalozzi. *Thought: Fordham University Quarterly*, June 1931, VI, 88–107.

CORK, JIM. John Dewey, Karl Marx, and Democratic Socialism. *Antioch Review*, Dec. 1949, IX, 435–452.

Reprinted in Sidney Hook, ed., *John Dewey: Philosopher of Science and Freedom* (New York, 1950), 331–350; and in Paul Bixler, ed., *Antioch Review Anthology* (Cleveland, 1953), 137–152.

CORYA, FLORENCE. Bust of Professor Dewey. *School and Society*, 1 Dec. 1928, XXVIII, 684–685.

The Jacob Epstein bust in the library of Teachers College. See *New York Times*, 10 Nov. 1928.

COSTA, ANGIOLA MASSUCCO. Breve nota sulla psicologia americana. *Scuola e città*, 1955, 227–231.

Dewey's pedagogy and Freud's psychoanalysis.

COSTELLO, HARRY TODD. Logic in 1914 and Now. *Journal of Philosophy*, 25 Apr. 1957, LIV, 245–264.

COUNTS, GEORGE SYLVESTER, AND NUCIA LODGE. *The Country of the Blind: The Soviet System of Mind Control*. Boston: Houghton Mifflin Company, 1949. xvii, 378 pp.

Dewey, 271, 277–278.

COWAN, THOMAS ANTHONY, ed. *The American Jurisprudence Reader*. New York: Oceana Publications, 1956. 254 pp.

Dewey, *passim*.

COWLEY, MALCOLM. Dewey in an Age of Unreason. *New Republic*, 16 June 1952, CXXVI, xxiv, 8.

CRARY, RYLAND W. John Dewey and American Social Thought. *Teachers College Record*, Dec. 1949, LI, 133–135.

CRAWFORD, CLAUDE C. Functional Education in the Light of Dewey's Philosophy. *School and Society*, 24 Sept. 1938, XLVIII, 381–385.

CREMIN, LAWRENCE A. John Dewey and the Progressive Education Movement, 1915–1952. *School Review*, Summer 1959, LXVII, 160–173.

————. The Origins of Progressive Education. *Educational Forum*, Jan. 1960, XXIV, 133–140.
Paper read before the American Historical Association, Washington, 28 Dec. 1958.

————. The Progressive Movement in American Education: A Perspective. *Harvard Educational Review*, Fall 1957, XXVII, 251–270.

————. *The Transformation of the School: Progressivism in American Education 1876–1957*. New York: Alfred A. Knopf, 1961. xi, 387, xxiv pp.
Dewey, *passim*.

————. What Happened to Progressive Education? *Teachers College Record*, Oct. 1959, LXI, 23–29; condensed in *Education Digest*, Jan. 1960, XXV, v, 4–7.

CRISSMAN, PAUL. A Companion and Critique of Dewey's and Perry's Theories of Value. *University of Wyoming Publications*, 15 July 1951, XVI, iii, 55–73.

————. Dewey's Theory of the Moral Good. *Monist*, Oct. 1928, XXXVIII, 592–619.

————. The Psychology of John Dewey. *Psychological Review*, Sept. 1942, XLIX, 441–462.
Abstract by A. G. Bills in *Psychological Abstracts*, Jan. 1943, XVII, 46.

CROCE, BENEDETTO. Filosofia americana e filosofia europea. *Quaderni della critica*, Sept. 1951, xix–xx, 20–22.
Discussion by Valentino Gerratana in *Società*, Sept. 1951, VII, 478–487.

————. Intorno all'estetica del Dewey. *La critica*, 20 Nov. 1940, XXXVIII, 348–353; reprinted as L'ESTETICA DI JOHN DEWEY, in his *Discorsi di varia filosofia* (Bari: Giuseppe Laterza e Figli, 1945), II, 112–119.
Review of *Art as Experience* (1934). Translation by Katharine Everett Gilbert, ON THE AESTHETICS OF JOHN DEWEY, *Journal of Aesthetics and Art Criticism*, Mar. 1948, VI, 203–207; reply by Dewey, A COMMENT ON THE FOREGOING CRITICISMS, *ib.*, 207–209.

————. Intorno all'estetica e alla teoria del conoscere del Dewey. *Quaderni della critica*, Mar. 1950, xvi, 60–68.

Translated by Frederic S. Simoni as DEWEY'S AESTHETICS AND THEORY OF KNOWLEDGE, *Journal of Aesthetics and Art Criticism*, Sept. 1952, XI, 1–6. See also Simoni, BENEDETTO CROCE: A CASE OF INTERNATIONAL MISUNDERSTANDING, *ib.*, 7–14; letter from Croce, *ib.*, 285; and Amalia de Maria, CROCE E DEWEY, *Filosofia*, Apr. 1958, IX, 302–336, also published separately as *Studi di estetica 2* (Torino: Edizioni di filosofia [1957]), 39 pp.

————. Nota. In his *Filosofia e storiografia* (Bari, 1949), 6.

CROSSER, PAUL K. *The Nihilism of John Dewey*. New York: Philosophical Library [ᶜ1955]. xi, 238 pp.

Reviewed in *The Humanist*, Mar.-Apr. 1956, XVI, 98 (Sidney Ratner); *Philosophical Review*, Apr. 1956, LXV, 274–277 (George Dykhuisen).

CROWELL, NELSON JOHN. *John Dewey et l'education nouvelle.* Lausanne: Pache-Varidel & Bron, 1928. 78 pp.

"Thèse de doctorat . . . Université de Lausanne."

CRUCHAGA, ALBERTO HURTADO. Examen du système pédagogique de John Dewey du point de vue des exigences de la doctrine catholique.

Doctoral dissertation, University of Louvain, 1935.

CUA, ANTONIO SO. A Study of Dewey's Conception of Problematic Situation.

Thesis (A.M. IN ED.), University of California, 1954.

CUBBERLEY, ELLWOOD PATTERSON. *Public Education in the United States*. Boston: Houghton Mifflin Company [ᶜ1919]. xxv, 517 pp.

Dewey, 359 ff., 445.

CURRENT BIOGRAPHY. John Dewey. *Current Biography*, 1944, 156–161.

CURTI, MERLE. *The Growth of American Thought*. New York: Harper & Brothers [ᶜ1943]. xx, 848 pp.

Dewey, 560–566 *et passim*.

————. John Dewey. In his *Social Ideas of American Educators*. Report of the Commission on the Social Studies, American Historical Association, Part X (New York: Charles Scribner's Sons, 1935), 499–541.

CUSHING, HELEN ISABEL. Dewey's Theory of Sense Perception. Thesis (A.M.), University of Illinois, 1914.

D'ALLESANDRO, VITTORIO. *L'Educazione attiva nei suoi principi psicologici*. Palermo: S. F. Flaccovio Editore, 1954. 168 pp.
Chapters on James and Dewey.

DAL PRA, MARIO. Anti-metafisica e metafisica nella logica di Dewey. *Rivista critica di storia della filosofia*, Oct.-Dec. 1951, VI, 275–285.

————. Dewey e il pensiero del giovane Marx. *Rivista di filosofia*, July 1960, LI, 279–292.

————. Hume e Dewey. *Revue internationale de philosophie* (Bruxelles), 1952, VI, ii, 236–249.

————, ed. *Il pensiero di John Dewey*. Saggi di N. Abbagnano [*et al*.] con contributi bibliografici; a cura di Mario dal Pra. (Rivista critica di storia della filosofia. Pubblicazioni, I.) Milano: Fratelli Bocca [1952]. 202 pp.
Reprinted from *Rivista critica di storia della filosofia*, Oct.-Dec. 1951, anno VI, fasc. iv. Essays by Nicola Abbagnano, Antonio Banfi, Mario dal Pra, Giulio Preti, Andrea Vasa, Ludovico Geymonat, Ferdinando Vegas, Lamberto Borghi, Dino Formaggio, Aldo Visalberghi, Maria Elena Reina, Salvatore Onufrio; reviews by Fortunato Brancatisano and Francesco Cafaro (*qq.v.*), and Contributi bibliografici, a supplement to our 1939 *Bibliography of John Dewey*: OPERE DI DEWEY (1939–1951) and STUDI STRANIERI SU DEWEY (1939–1951) by Milton Mayeroff; TRADUZIONI ITALIANE DI SCRITTI DI DEWEY, and STUDI ITALIANI SU DEWEY (1921–1951) by Francesco Cafaro; with assistance from A. Leroy, V. Strada and Maria Elena Reina.

D'AMOUR, O'NEIL C. The Concept of the Universal and Its Relation to the Experimental Trend in Modern Educational Philosophy.
Master's thesis, Catholic University of America, 1950.

D'ANDREA, A. Introduzione al pragmatismo. *La nuove Italia*, 19 Oct. 1940.

DANILOWICZ, RICHARD D. Absolutes in the Philosophy of John Dewey.
Master's thesis, Catholic University of America, 1951.

DANIN, ELIZABETH. The Social Philosophy of John Dewey. Thesis (A.M.), New York University, 1942.

DANNEKER, CARL J. The Concept of Religion as Held by Recent Non-Catholic Educational Writers.

Master's thesis, Catholic University of America, 1950.

DASGUPTA, DEBENDRA CHANDRA. The Rise of the Theory of Sense-Training from John Locke to John Dewey.

Thesis (A.M. IN ED.), University of California, 1928.

DAVENPORT, FRANCES LITTLEFIELD. The Education of John Dewey.

Thesis (ED.D.), University of California at Los Angeles, 1946.

DAVIDSON, ROBERT FRANKLIN. Naturalistic Humanism: John Dewey. In his *Philosophies Men Live By* (New York: The Dial Press, 1952), 251–293.

DAVIS, SYDNEY CHARLES. Theories of Education for the Development of Freedom and Responsibility.

Report (ED.D.), Teachers College, 1953.

DE ANDREA, JOSEPH. Philosophy of Man According to Karl Marx and John Dewey: A Comparative Study.

Master's thesis, Catholic University of America, 1957.

Abstract in *Catholic Educational Review*, Feb. 1959, LVII, 124.

DEARBORN, NED HARLAND. Democracy and Education. *In* Progressive Education Association, Progressive Education Booklet No. 13, *The Educational Frontier* (Columbus, Ohio, 1939), 58–63.

Delivered at the celebration of Dewey's eightieth birthday in New York, Oct. 1939.

DE BARTOLOMEIS, FRANCESCO. *La pedagogia come scienza*. Firenze: La Nuova Italia Editrice (2d ed.), 1961. xli, 416 pp.

Dewey is discussed in Part II, chap. 3: JOHN DEWEY E LA NASCITA DELLA SCUOLA ATTIVA, 131–179.

DE CAMARGO, CANDIDO PROCOPIO FERRERA. Social Relativism and the Philosophy of John Dewey.

Thesis (A.M.), Columbia University, 1956.

DE HOVRE, FRANZ. *Essai de philosophie pédagogique*. Bruxelles: A. Dewitt, 1927.

Dewey, 87–99.

———. Some Radical-Social Educators: John Dewey. In his

Philosophy and Education (New York: Benziger Bros., 1931), 101–116.

Translated from the French edition of G. Siméons by Rev. Edward Benedict Jordan.

DEININGER, WHITAKER THOMPSON. John Dewey's Theory of Valuation Appraised.

Thesis (A.M.), Columbia University, 1948.

DELEDALLE, GÉRARD. Durkheim et Dewey, un double centenaire. *Les Études philosophiques*, Oct.-Dec. 1959, XIV, 493–498.

———. *L'Existentiel: Philosophies et littératures de l'existence.* Paris: Editions Renée Lacoste, 1949. 292 pp.

Dewey, 211–220.

———. *Histoire de la philosophie américaine de la guerre de sécession à la second guerre mondiale.* . . . Paris: Presses Universitaires de France, 1954. xvi, 206 pp.

On Dewey: L'INSTRUMENTALISME DE DEWEY, 32–37; LE NATURALISME TRANSACTIONNEL DE DEWEY, 67–71; LES GRANDES PHILOSOPHIES . . . JOHN DEWEY, 144–167; BIBLIOGRAPHIE DES TRADUCTIONS FRANÇAISES DES OUVRAGES DE DEWEY, 191; *et passim.*

———. John Dewey et le problème de la vérité.

Thesis (Diplôme d'Études Supérieures de Philosophie), Sorbonne, 1951.

———. La pédagogie de John Dewey. I. Pédagogie de la continuité. *Pédagogie* (Paris), Oct. 1950, 478–482; II. La pédagogie: science de l'éducation. *Ib.*, Nov. 1950, 548–552; III. L'intérêt et l'effort. *Ib.*, Jan. 1951, 38–45; IV. L'initiation à la vie démocratique. *Ib.*, Feb. 1951, 103–113; V. Influence et valeur. *Ib.*, Mar. 1951, 174–180.

———. La philosophie américaine classique (1865–1940). *Critique* (Paris), June 1954, 549–559.

———. La psychologie expérimentale americaine. *In* Paul Foulquié and Gérard Deledalle, *La psychologie contemporaine* (Paris: Presses Universitaires de France, 1951), 48–95.

Dewey, 57–59 *et passim.*

DELLA VOLPE, GALVANO. John Dewey. *Enciclopedia Italiana*, XII (1931), 713.

De Ruggiero, Guido. Note sulla più recente filosofia europea e americana: John Dewey. *La Critica*, 20 Sept. 1931, XXIX, 341–357.

A critical exposition of Dewey's philosophy.

Also published as the introduction to the Italian translation of *Reconstruction in Philosophy* (1931), and in *Filosofia del novecento* (Bari: Laterza, 3d ed. 1946), 63–87.

De Smet, H. John Dewey als wijsgeer, paedagoog en taalkundige. In *Handelingen van het Twintigste Vlaamse Filologencongres, Antwerpen, 7–9 Apr. 1953* (Leuven: Vlammse Filologencongres, J. L. Pauwels, 1953), 35–39.

D'Espalliez, Victor. John Dewey. In *Katholicke Encyclopaedie voor opvoedung en onderwijs* I (Antwerpen, 't Groeit, 's Gravenhage: N. V. Uitgeversmaatschappij Pax, 1951), 458–461.

Destler, Chester McArthur. Some Observations on Contemporary Historical Theory. *American Historical Review*, Apr. 1950, LV, 503–529.

See communication in *ib.*, Jan. 1951, LVI, 450–452, from Merle Curti, Bert James Loewenberg, John Herman Randall, Jr., and Harold Taylor regarding the "basic misinterpretations of a number of contemporary historians and philosophers, among them ... John Dewey" in the above article.

Dewey, Adelbert M., and Louis Marinus Dewey. *Life of George Dewey, Rear Admiral, U.S.N., and Dewey Family History*. Westfield, Mass.: Dewey Publishing Co., 1898. 1117 pp.

Genealogy of John Dewey, 910, 961 *et passim*.

Dewey and Creative Education. *Saturday Review*, 21 Nov. 1959, XLII, xlvii, 19–25.

Manifesto signed by Joe Burnett, Robert W. Burns, Nathaniel L. Champlin, Otto Krash, Frederick C. Neff, and Francis T. Villemain. *Contents.* 1. Education in Society—2. Creative Intelligence—3. Creative Experience—4. Creative Inquiry—5. Creative Individuality—6. Creative Ethics.

De Witt, Dale, and William Heard Kilpatrick. John Dewey: Humanist and Educator. *The Humanist*, July-Aug. 1952, XII, 161–165; *Michigan Educational Journal*, May 1953, XXX, 522–523.

Radio interview presented by the American Humanist Association over N.B.C. stations, 28 June 1952.

DHAMI, SADHU SINGH. The Philosophy of John Dewey: Its Bearing on India.
Thesis (PH.D.), University of Toronto, 1937.

DICKEY, THOMAS WILSON. The Genesis of Dewey's Ethical Method.
Thesis (A.M.), Columbia University, 1933.

DICKINSON, MARY COOPE. The Implications of Dewey's Philosophy Found in Current Theories regarding the Teaching of Literature.
Thesis (A.M.), Ohio State University, 1931.

DIGGINS, JOHN P. Freedom and Authority in Education.
Master's thesis, Catholic University of America, 1936.

DI LAGHI, GIUSEPPINA. Il pensiero pedagogico di Giovanni Dewey. Introduction (pp. 7–21) to her *Una scuola elementare di New York: Documenti didattici della scuola Horace Mann.* (Firenze: "La Voce," 1924.)

DILLICK, SIDNEY. The Political Philosophy of John Dewey.
Thesis (PH.D.), University of Toronto, 1942.

DOESCHER, WALDEMAR OSWALD. Dewey's Educational Philosophy and Its Implications for Christian Education. *Christian Education*, June 1939, XXII, 377–389.

DOMMEYER, FREDERICK CHARLES. Four Pragmatic Theories of Meaning [Dewey, Peirce, James, C. I. Lewis].
Thesis (PH.D.), Brown University, 1937.

DONOHUE, JOHN W., S.J. Dewey's Theory of Work in Education. In his *Work and Education: The Role of Technical Culture in Some Distinctive Theories of Humanism* (Chicago: Loyola University Press, 1960), 57–94.

———. John Dewey: The Centennial of an Educator. *Catholic Educational Review*, Jan. 1960, LVIII, 16–27.

DONOSO, ANTON. John Dewey's Philosophy of Law. *University of Detroit Law Journal*, June 1959, XXXVI, 579–606.

———. The Relation between Commonsense and Science According to John Dewey.
Thesis (PH.D.), University of Toronto, 1960.

DORFMAN, JOSEPH. Philosophers and Social Reforms: John Dewey. In his *The Economic Mind in American Civilization* (New York: The Viking Press), IV (1959), 125–126.

DOWNES, CHAUNCEY B. Some Problems concerning Dewey's View of Reason. *Journal of Philosophy*, 2 Mar. 1961, LVIII, 121–137.

DUCASSE, CURT JOHN. The Instrumentalist Theory of Art. In his *The Philosophy of Art* (New York: Lincoln MacVeagh, The Dial Press [ᶜ1929]), 84–94.

DUFRAIN, VIOLA MAUDE. Implications for Religion in John Dewey's Philosophy.
Thesis (A.M.), University of Chicago, 1933.

DUNKEL, HAROLD BAKER. Dewey and the Fine Arts. *School Review*, Summer 1959, LXVII, 229–245.

——. Sniper's Nest: Dewey in 2059. *Ib.*, Autumn 1959, LXVII, 368–369.

DUPRAT, ÉMILE. Les Rapports de la connaissance et de l'action d'après John Dewey. *Revue de métaphysique et de morale*, Oct.-Dec. 1930 and Jan.-Mar. 1931, XXXVII, 534–553, XXXVIII, 107–123.

DURANT, WILLIAM JAMES. . . . *Contemporary American Philosophers; Santayana, James, and Dewey.* (Little Blue Book No. 813.) Girard, Kansas: Haldeman-Julius Company [ᶜ1925].

——. John Dewey. *Encyclopaedia Britannica* (14th ed. Chicago, ᶜ1936), VII, 297–298.

——. *The Story of Philosophy: The Lives and Opinions of the Greater Philosophers.* New York: Simon and Schuster, 1926. xiii, 586 pp.
Dewey, 565–575.

DWORKIN, MARTIN S. John Dewey: A Centennial Review. In his *Dewey on Education. Selections* . . .(New York: Bureau of Publications, Teachers College, Columbia University [ᶜ1959]), 1–18.
Abridged version in *School Executive*, Oct. 1959, LXXIX, 52–55.

DYKHUISEN, GEORGE. Dewey's Philosophy and Theory of Education. *Vermont Alumni Weekly,* 20 Mar. 1935, XIV, 247–248, 254–255.

———. An Early Chapter in the Life of John Dewey. *Journal of the History of Ideas,* Oct. 1952, XIII, 563–572.

———. John Dewey: American Philosopher and Educator. *Educational Theory,* Oct. 1957, VII, 263–268.

———. John Dewey: The Vermont Years. *Journal of the History of Ideas,* Oct.-Dec. 1959, XX, 515–544.

Read at the annual meeting of the American Philosophical Association, University of Vermont, 27 Dec. 1958. Abstract in *Journal of Philosophy,* 9 Oct. 1958, LV, 881–882.

———. John Dewey, Vermonter. *Vermont Life,* Winter 1950–51, V, ii, 11–15.

———. John Dewey at Johns Hopkins (1882–1884). *Journal of the History of Ideas,* Jan.-Mar. 1961, XXII, 103–116.

DYNNIK, M. Contemporary Bourgeois Philosophy in the U.S. *Modern Review,* Nov. 1947, I, 653–660.

Abridged translation by Mirra Ginsburg from the Russian original in *Bolshevik,* Mar. 1947. Foreword by Sidney Hook, THE U.S.S.R. VIEWS AMERICAN PHILOSOPHY, *Modern Review,* I, 649–653.

Comments by Ralph Barton Perry, George Boas, Frederick Burkhardt, Curt John Ducasse, Edgar Sheffield Brightman, Filmer Stuart Cuckow Northrop, Horace Meyer Kallen, and Glenn Raymond Morrow in *ib.,* Feb. 1948, II, 157–160.

EAMES, ELIZABETH R. Quality and Relation as Metaphysical Assumptions in the Philosophy of John Dewey. *Journal of Philosophy,* 13 Feb. 1958, LV, 166–169.

A reply to Paul Welsh, SOME METAPHYSICAL ASSUMPTIONS IN DEWEY'S PHILOSOPHY, *ib.,* 23 Dec. 1954, LI, 861–867.

EAMES, SAMUEL MORRIS. The Cognitive and Non-Cognitive in Dewey's Theory of Valuation. *Journal of Philosophy,* 30 Mar. 1961, LVIII, 179–195.

———. Dewey's Views of Truth, Beauty, and Goodness. *Educational Theory,* July 1961, XI, 174–185.

———. Some Methodological Problems in John Dewey's Theory of Valuation.

Thesis (PH.D.), University of Chicago, 1958.

EASTMAN, MAX. America's Philosopher. *Saturday Review of Literature*, 17 Jan. 1953, XXXVI, iii, 23–24, 38.

Abridged, with the title OUR CHILDREN'S DEBT TO JOHN DEWEY, in *Readers' Digest*, Feb. 1953, LXII, ii, 104–108.

———. John Dewey. *Atlantic Monthly*, Dec. 1941, CLXVIII, 671–685.

Reprinted with revisions and additions as THE HERO AS TEACHER: THE LIFE STORY OF JOHN DEWEY in his *Heroes I Have Known* (New York: Simon and Schuster, 1942), 275–321, and as JOHN DEWEY: MY TEACHER AND FRIEND in his *Great Companions* (New York: Farrar, Straus and Cudahy [°1959]), 249–298.

EASTON, LOYD DAVID. Empiricism and Ethics in Dietzgen. *Journal of the History of Ideas*, Jan. 1958, XIX, 77–90.

The author traces certain kinship of views of Dewey and Joseph Dietzgen (1828–1888).

ECHEVARRÍA RIVERA, LUIS. John Dewey. *Bordon* (Madrid), 1952, IV, 271–273.

EDDY, LYLE KRENZIEN. The Challenge of Dewey's Philosophy to Its Critics.

Thesis (A.M.), University of Chicago, 1948.

EDEL, ABRAHAM. *Ethical Judgment: The Use of Science in Ethics.* Glencoe, Illinois: The Free Press, 1955. 348 pp.

Dewey, *passim.*

———. *Science and the Structure of Ethics.* (Foundations of the Unity of Science, II, 3.) Chicago: University of Chicago Press [°1961]. 101 pp.

Dewey, *passim.*

EDMAN, IRWIN. America's Philosopher Attains an Alert 90. *New York Times Magazine*, 16 Oct. 1949.

———. [Former Teachers: John Dewey.] In his *Philosopher's Holiday* (New York: The Viking Press, 1938), 138–143.

Reprinted as COLUMBIA GALAXY: JOHN DEWEY AND OTHERS, in Houston Peterson, ed., *Great Teachers Portrayed by Those Who Studied under Them* (New Brunswick: Rutgers University Press, 1946), 195–199.

———. The New Puritanism. *Columbia University Quarterly*, Jan. 1919, XXI, 38–50.

EDMAN, IRWIN (*continued*). Our Foremost Philosopher at Seventy. *New York Times Magazine*, 13 Oct. 1929.

Reprinted in part in *Teachers College Record*, Dec. 1929, XXXI, 214–215.

————. The Resources of Art in American Life. *In* Progressive Education Association, Progressive Education Booklet No. 15, *Resources for Building America* (Columbus, Ohio, 1939), 33–40.

Delivered at the celebration of Dewey's eightieth birthday in New York, Oct. 1939.

————. The Victories of the Imagination. *New Republic*, 17 Oct. 1949, CXXI, xvi, 36–39.

EGBERT, DONALD DREW, ed. *Socialism in American Life*. Editors, Donald Drew Egbert and Stow Persons. Bibliographer: Thomas Day Seymour Bassett. 2 vols. Princeton: Princeton University Press, 1952.

Dewey, *passim*.

EHRENREICH, ISAAC. The Idea of God in Dewey and Whitehead.

Thesis (A.M.), Columbia University, 1942.

EISLER, RUDOLF. *Philosophen Lexicon; Leben, Werke und Lehren der Denker*. Berlin: E. S. Mittler und Sohn, 1912. v, 889 pp.

Dewey, 127, 869–870.

ELLIOTT, JOHN LOVEJOY. Personality in Education. *In* Progressive Education Association, Progressive Education Booklet No. 12, *Freedom and Education* (Columbus, Ohio, 1939), 24–32.

Delivered at the celebration of Dewey's eightieth birthday in New York, Oct. 1939.

ELLIOTT, WILLIAM YANDELL. *The Pragmatic Revolt in Politics: Syndicalism, Fascism, and the Constitutional State*. New York: The Macmillan Co., 1928. xvii, 540 pp.

ELLIS, FREDERICK EUGENE. Dewey's Concept of Education for Growth. *Educational Theory*, Jan. 1955, V, 12–15.

ENSLEY, FRANCIS G. The Naturalistic Interpretation of Religion by John Dewey.

Thesis (PH.D.), Brown University, 1938.

ERNST, FREDERIC. How Dangerous Is John Dewey? *Atlantic Monthly*, May 1953, CXCI, v, 59–62.

Reply to Albert Lynd, WHO WANTS PROGRESSIVE EDUCATION? *ib.*, Apr. 1953, CXCI, iv, 29–34.

ESBENSEN, THORWALD. John Dewey: Whipping Boy for Critics. *Wisconsin Journal of Education*, Apr. 1959, XCI, 7–10.

ESSAYS IN HONOR OF JOHN DEWEY, ON THE OCCASION OF HIS SEVENTIETH BIRTHDAY, OCTOBER 20, 1929. New York: Henry Holt and Company [ᶜ1929]. xi, 425 pp.

Contents. Personality: How To Develop It in the Family, the School, and Society, by Felix Adler—Religious Values and Philosophical Criticism, by Edward Scribner Ames—Evolution and Time, by Albert George Adam Balz—Art, Action, and Affective States, by Harold Chapman Brown—Two Basic Issues in the Problem of Meaning and of Truth, by Edwin Arthur Burtt—Kant, Aquinas, and the Problem of Reality, by Cornelius Clifford—A Pragmatic Approach to Being, by William Forbes Cooley—Consolation and Control. A Note on the Interpretation of Philosophy, by John Jacob Coss—A Philosophy of Experience as a Philosophy of Art, by Irwin Edman—Dimensions of Universality in Religion, by Horace Leland Friess—A Criticism of Two of Kant's Criteria of the Aesthetic, by Kate Gordon—A Pragmatic Critique of the Historico-Genetic Method, by Sidney Hook—Certain Conflicting Tendencies within the Present-Day Study of Education, by William Heard Kilpatrick—Casuality, by Sterling Power Lamprecht—Externalism in American Life, by Matthew Thompson McClure—The Empiricist and Experimentalist Temper in the Middle Ages. A Prolegomenon to the Study of Mediaeval Science, by Richard McKeon—The Nature of the Past, by George Herbert Mead—A Functional View of Morals, by Simon Fraser MacLennan—A Materialistic Theory of Emergent Evolution, by William Pepperell Montague—What Is Meant by Social Activity? by Ernest Carroll Moore—The Cult of Chronology, by Helen Huss Parkhurst—Dualism in Metaphysics and Practical Philosophy, by John Herman Randall, Jr.—Prolegomena to a Political Ethics, by Arthur Kenyon Rogers—Radical Empiricism and Religion, by Herbert Wallace Schneider—The Rôle of the Philosopher, by Thomas Vernor Smith—A Methodology of Thought, by John Storck—Individualism and American Life, by James Hayden Tufts—Looking to Philosophy, by Matilde Castro Tufts—Some Implications of Locke's Procedure, by Frederick James Eugene Woodbridge.

Reviewed in *Mind*, Oct. 1930, XXXIX, 484–488 (F. C. S. Schiller); *Nation*, 22 Jan. 1930, CXXX, 100–101 (Henry Hazlitt); *New York Herald Tribune Books*, 13 July 1930; *New York Times*, 30 Mar. 1930 (Axton Clark).

EWING, RAYMOND. Dewey's Conception of Philosophy.
Thesis (A.M.), Columbia University, 1951.

EZORSKY, GERTRUDE. Inquiry as Appraisal: The Singularity of
John Dewey's Theory of Valuation. *Journal of Philosophy*, 30
Jan. 1958, LV, 118–124.

FAIN, HASKELL. A Comparison of the Theories of Logic of John
Dewey and Charles Sanders Peirce.
Thesis (A.M.), University of Illinois, 1949.

FANIZZA, FRANCO. Dewey, filosofo dell'esistenza e filosofo della
scienza. *Rivista di filosofia*, July 1950, LI, 293–302.

FARBER, MARVIN, ed. *Philosophic Thought in France and the
United States: Essays Representing Major Trends in Contemporary French and American Philosophy*. (University of Buffalo Publications in Philosophy.) Buffalo: University of Buffalo, 1950. 775 pp.
See the article of Sidney Hook, 483–503, *et passim*.
French version: *L'Activité philosophique contemporaine en France et
aux États-Unis*. 2 vols. (Paris: Presses Universitaires de France,
1950.)

FARRAND, HARRIET A. Dr. Dewey's University Elementary
School: An Experiment in Education. *Journal of Education*,
15 Sept. 1898, XLVIII, 172.

FARRELL, JAMES THOMAS. Dewey in Mexico. In his *Reflections
at Fifty and Other Essays* (New York: The Vanguard Press
[ᶜ1954]), 97–123.
First printed in Sidney Hook, ed., *John Dewey: Philosopher of Science and Freedom* (New York, 1950), 351–377.

FAY, JAY WHARTON. *American Psychology before William James.*
New Brunswick, N.J.: Rutgers University Press, 1939. 232
pp.

FEIBLEMAN, JAMES KERN. An Estimate of Dewey. In his *Re-
vival of Realism: Critical Studies in Contemporary Philosophy*
(Chapel Hill: University of North Carolina Press, 1946),
84–98.

———. The Influence of Peirce on Dewey's Logic. *Education*
(Boston), Sept. 1945, LXVI, 18–24; abstract in *Journal of
Philosophy*, 7 Dec. 1939, XXXVI, 682.

FELDMAN, WILLIAM TAFT. *The Philosophy of John Dewey: A Critical Analysis.* Baltimore: The Johns Hopkins Press, 1934. vii, 127 pp.
Thesis (PH.D.), Johns Hopkins University.
Reviewed in *Boston Transcript*, 28 July 1934 (E. N.), *Journal of Philosophy*, 11 Oct. 1934, XXXI, 583–584 (Arthur E. Murphy).

FEN, SING-NAN. Dewey's Philosophy as a Program of Action. *Progressive Education*, Oct. 1949, XXVII, i, 27–30; reprinted in Kenneth Dean Benne and William Oliver Stanley, eds., *Essays for John Dewey's Ninetieth Birthday* [Urbana, Illinois, 1950], 82–87.

FÊNG, YU-LAN. *A Short History of Chinese Philosophy.* New York: The Macmillan Company, 1948. 368 pp.
See INTRODUCTION OF WESTERN PHILOSOPHY, 329.

FENNER, MILDRED SANDISON. Tribute to John Dewey, Honorary President of the N.E.A. *Journal of the National Education Association*, Oct. 1949, XXXVIII, 528–529.

FERRIÈRE, ADOLPH. La démocratie et l'éducation selon Dewey. *L'Education*, Feb. 1927, N.S. XVIII, 274–280.

———. *L'École active.* (4th ed.), Geneva: Editions Forum, 1930. Dewey, *passim*.
Italian translation by E. Mazzoni (Firenze, 1948).

FEUER, LEWIS SAMUEL. Ethical Theories and Historical Materialism. *Science and Society*, Summer 1942, VI, 242–272. Dewey, 264–268.

———. H[enry] A[ugustus] P[earson] Torrey and John Dewey: Teacher and Pupil. *American Quarterly*, Spring 1958, X, 34–54.

———. John Dewey and the Back-to-the-People Movement in American Thought. *Journal of the History of Ideas*, Oct.-Dec. 1959, XX, 545–568; abstract, THE SOCIAL SOURCES OF DEWEY'S THOUGHT, in *Journal of Philosophy*, 9 Oct. 1958, LV, 882–884.
Read at the American Philosophical Association meeting at the University of Vermont, 27 Dec. 1958.

———. John Dewey's Reading at College. *Journal of the History of Ideas*, June 1958, XIX, 415–421.

———. The Standpoints of Dewey and Freud: A Contrast and

Analysis. *Journal of Individual Psychology*, Nov. 1960, XVI, 121–136.

FIESS, EDWARD. Dewey's View of Art. *The Humanist*, Winter 1944–45, IV, 161–165.

FILLER, LOUIS. *Randolph Bourne*. Washington: American Council on Public Affairs [ᶜ1950]. 158 pp.
Dewey, *passim*.

FILOGRASSO, N. Socialità e educazione in J. Dewey. *Nuova rivista pedagogica*, June 1959.

FINGARETTE, HERBERT. How Normativeness Can Be Cognitive But Not Descriptive in Dewey's Theory of Valuation. *Journal of Philosophy*, 11 Oct. 1951, XLVIII, 625–635.
See Lester Meckler, NORMATIVE AND DESCRIPTIVE EXPRESSIONS, *ib.*, 10 Sept. 1953, L, 577–583.

FINNEGAN, J. F. Remarks concerning Certain Phases of the Moral Philosophy of John Dewey. *American Catholic Philosophical Association Proceedings*, 1930, 125–134.

FIORE, MARIO. *Pedagogisti contemporanei valutati da Sergio Hessen, saggi critici su G. Gentile, G. Lombardo Radice, Maria Montessori, G. Kerschensteiner e J. Dewey*. Molfetta: Tip. dell'Ist. prov. Apicella, 1958. 44 pp.

FISCH, MAX HAROLD, ed. *Classic American Philosophers: Peirce, James, Royce, Santayana, Dewey, Whitehead*. New York: Appleton-Century-Crofts, Inc. [ᶜ1951]. x, 493 pp.
John Dewey: Introduction, by Gail Kennedy, 327–335; The Influence of Darwinism on Philosophy (1910), 336–344; The Supremacy of Method (from *The Quest for Certainty*, 1929), 344–360; The Construction of Good (from *ib.*), 360–381; Science and Society (from *Philosophy and Civilization*, 1931), 381–389; Creative Democracy—The Task Before Us (1940); 389–394; Suggestions for further reading: Dewey, 475–477.

———. Justice Holmes, the Prediction Theory of Law, and Pragmatism. *Journal of Philosophy*, 12 Feb. 1942, XXXIX, 85–97.

FISHER, DOROTHY (CANFIELD). John Dewey. In *American Portraits*. Pictures by Enit Kaufman, Text by Dorothy Canfield Fisher (New York: Henry Holt and Company [ᶜ1946]), 37–39.

———. John Dewey. In her *Vermont Tradition: The Biography of an Outlook on Life* (Boston: Little, Brown and Company [ᶜ1953]), 366–383.

FITCH, ROBERT ELLIOT. Character Education à la Mode. *Religion in Life*, Autumn 1954, XXIII, 528–536.

———. John Dewey—the "Last Protestant." *Pacific Spectator*, Spring 1953, VII, 224–230.

———. John Dewey and Jahweh: An Imaginary Dialogue. *Journal of Religion*, Jan. 1943, XXII, 12–22.

FITE, WARNER. *Moral Philosophy: The Critical View of Life.* New York: Lincoln MacVeagh, The Dial Press, 1926. ix, 320 pp.

Dewey, 103–118.

FLECKENSTEIN, NORBERT J. *A Critique of John Dewey's Theory of the Nature and Knowledge of Reality in the Light of the Principles of Thomism.* Washington: Catholic University of America Press, 1954. vii, 193 pp.

Thesis (PH.D.), Catholic University of America.

FLORES, HORACIO. Reflexiones críticas en torno a algunas aspectos del pensamiento pedagógico de John Dewey. *Anales del Instituto de Investigaciónes Pedagógicas* (San Luis, Argentina), 1952–53, II, 149–173.

FOERSTER, NORMAN. Education Leads the Way. *American Review*, Sept. 1933, I, 385–408.

FORCEY, CHARLES. *The Crossroads of Liberalism: Croly, Weyl, Lippmann, and the Progressive Era, 1900–1925.* New York: Oxford University Press, 1961. xxix, 358 pp.

Dewey, *passim.*

FOREST, ILSE. The Meaning of Faith: The Scholastics vs. the Non-Scholastics. *Thomist*, July 1943, VI, 231–238.

FORMAGGIO, DINO. L'estetica di John Dewey. *Rivista critica di storia della filosofia*, Oct.-Dec. 1951, VI, 360–372.

FOX, MARVIN. On the Diversity of Methods in Dewey's Ethical Theory. *Philosophy and Phenomenological Research*, Sept. 1951, XII, 123–129.

FRANCISCO, FELIX JUNIOR. The Concepts of Instinct, Habit and Mind in the Educational Philosophies of William James and John Dewey.

Thesis, University of Missouri, 1957.

FRANK, JEROME. Modern and Ancient Legal Pragmatism—John Dewey & Co. vs. Aristotle. *Notre Dame Lawyer*, Winter and Spring 1950, XXV, 207–257, 460–504.

Includes discussions of "some notable legal Deweyites": Walter Wheeler Cook, Karl Nickerson Llewellyn, Edwin Wilhite Patterson, and Benjamin Nathan Cardozo.

———. Some Tame Reflections on Some Wild Facts. *In* Sidney Ratner, ed., *Vision & Action: Essays in Honor of Horace M. Kallen on His 70th Birthday* (New Brunswick: Rutgers University Press, 1953), 56–82.

FRANK, WALDO. Our Leaders: John Dewey. *New Republic*, 20 June 1928, LV, 114–116.

Reprinted in his *The Rediscovery of America* (1929), 168–177.

Reply by Philip M. Glick, *New Republic*, 1 Aug. 1928, LV, 281–282, and short rejoinder by Frank, 282.

———. The Man Who Made Us What We Are [by "Searchlight"]. *New Yorker*, 22 May 1926, II, xiv, 15–16.

Reprinted in *Time Exposures*, by "Searchlight" (1926), 121–127.

FRANKEL, CHARLES. *The Golden Age of American Philosophy*. New York: George Braziller, Inc., 1960. viii, 534 pp.

Dewey, 381–449, with reprints of FROM ABSOLUTISM TO EXPERIMENTALISM (1930); CHANGING CONCEPTIONS OF PHILOSOPHY from *Reconstruction in Philosophy* (1920); THE ART OF ACCEPTANCE AND THE ART OF CONTROL and THE NATURALIZATION OF INTELLIGENCE from *The Quest for Certainty* (1929); EDUCATION AS GROWTH and THE DEMOCRATIC CONCEPTION IN EDUCATION from *Democracy and Education* (1916); and DEMOCRACY AND AMERICA from *Freedom and Culture* (1939).

———. John Dewey's Legacy. *American Scholar*, Summer 1960, XXIX, 313–331.

Derived from an address presented at Johns Hopkins University at a centennial celebration of Dewey's birth; a slightly abridged version appears in *The Johns Hopkins Magazine*, Dec. 1959, XI, iii, 7, 19–23, with the title JOHN DEWEY: WHERE HE STANDS.

FRANKFURTER, FELIX. *Of Law and Men: Papers and Addresses of Felix Frankfurter 1939–1956.* Edited by Philip Elman. New York: Harcourt, Brace and Company [ᶜ1956]. xiii, 364 pp.
Remarks on Dewey at the 90th birthday celebration at the Hotel Commodore, New York, 20 Oct. 1949, 284–287.

FRANQUIZ VENTURA, JOSÉ ANTONIO. La lógica y la epistemología de John Dewey. *Luminar: Revista de orientación dinámica* (México, D.F.), 1941, V, 205–221; reprinted as *Lógica y epistemología de John Dewey*, México [Casa Unida de publicaciónes], 1941, 24 pp.

———. Orientaciónes y critica. Principios fundamentales de las filosofías educativas de Dewey y Kilpatrick. *Revista de la asociación de maestros* (San Juan, P.R.), Feb. 1943, II, i, 7–14; reprinted, 1943, 24 pp.

FRANSSON, EVALD. John Dewey om democrati och uppfostran. *Folklig Kultur* (Sweden), 1948, X, 245–257.

FRIES, HORACE SNYDER. The Development of John Dewey's Utilitarianism.
Thesis (PH.D), University of Wisconsin, 1934.

———. Dewey's Theory of Method. *The New Leader*, 22 Oct. 1949.

———. The Method of Proving Ethical Realism. *Philosophical Review*, Sept. 1937, XLVI, 485–502.

———. Social Planning. *In* Frederick Burkhardt, ed., *The Cleavage in Our Culture: Studies in Scientific Humanism in Honor of Max Otto* (Boston: Beacon Press [ᶜ1952]), 81–104.
Dewey, *passim*.

FROSINI, VITTORIO. John Dewey (1859–1952). *Rivista internazionale di filosofia del diritto* (Milano), 1952, XXIX, 322–325.

FUCHS, HENRY CHARLES. *Die Pädagogik Herbarts und Deweys in vergleichender Betrachtung.* Friedberg-Augsburg: K. Baur, 1935. iv, 67 pp.
Thesis (DR.PHIL.), München.

GALANDRA, G. La cultura come esperienza associata nel pensiero di John Dewey. *Rassegna di pedagogia*, 1955, XIII, 222–237.

GALE, RICHARD M. Russell's Drill Sergeant and Bricklayer and Dewey's Logic. *Journal of Philosophy*, 23 Apr. 1959, LVI, 401–406.

GANS, ROMA. John Dewey and the Understanding of Children. *Teachers College Record*, Dec. 1949, LI, 136–138.

GARCIA, JOAQUIN. Deweyism and Democracy. *The Tablet* (Brooklyn, N.Y.), 25 Aug. 1945; condensed in *Catholic Digest*, Oct. 1945, IX, xii, 78–80.

See Dewey's comment in *The Humanist*, Jan.-Feb. 1960, XX, 6.

GARNETT, ARTHUR CAMPBELL. *Religion and the Moral Life.* New York: The Ronald Press Company [ᶜ1955]. viii, 223 pp. Dewey, 43–59.

GEHRING, RALPH B., s.j. John Dewey's Substitute for Religion. *Philippine Studies* (Cebu City, P.I.), Mar. 1956, IV, 41–56.

———. The Origins of Religion, According to John Dewey. *Ib.*, Sept. 1955, III, 275–287.

GEIGER, GEORGE RAYMOND. Dewey's Challenge to Irrational Man: Human Possibilities. *Unitarian Register*, Mid-Summer 1959, CXXXVIII, vii, 3–5.

———. Dewey and the Experimental Attitude in American Culture: An Essay in Memory of John Dewey, 1859–1952. *American Journal of Economics and Sociology*, Jan. 1953, XII, 111–121.

———. *John Dewey in Perspective.* New York: Oxford University Press, 1958. 248 pp.

Contents. The Affirmation of Experience—Experience as Art—The Nature of Value—Inquiry, Knowing, and Truth—Thinking, Logic, and Scientific Method—Values and Inquiry—Nature, Communication, and Mind—Intelligence and Liberalism—Some Outcomes for Education—Scientific Humanism.

Reviewed in *Antioch Review*, Fall 1959, XIX, 412–416 (Glenn Negley); *Les Études philosophiques*, Oct.-Dec. 1958, 562 (Gérard Deledalle); *The Humanist*, Jan.-Feb. 1959, XIX, 54–55 (Sidney Ratner); *Saturday Review*, 14 Feb. 1959, XLII, 56; *Social Education*, Mar. 1959, XXIII, 136–138 (H. H. Giles).

See Ralph William Sleeper, DEWEY'S METAPHYSICAL PERSPECTIVE: A NOTE ON WHITE, GEIGER, AND THE PROBLEM OF OBLIGATION, *Journal of Philosophy*, 4 Feb. 1960, LVII, 100–115.

————. John Dewey in Perspective. *Antioch Review*, Fall 1959, XIX, 293–298.

Introduction to a special issue of the magazine devoted to Dewey, with articles by Horace Meyer Kallen, Sidney Ratner, Morton Gabriel White, Francis Trowbridge Villemain, and Nathaniel L. Champlin, *qq.v.*

————. John Dewey's Social Philosophy. *In* Frederick Charles Gruber, ed., *Education in Transition* (Philadelphia: University of Pennsylvania Press [°1960]), 243–255.

Read at Schoolmen's Week, University of Pennsylvania, in Oct. 1959; followed by COMMENTS ON PROFESSOR GEIGER'S PAPER, by Israel Scheffler, *ib.*, 256–259.

————. Preface to a Consistent Philosophy of Education. *Saturday Review*, 21 Nov. 1959, XLII, xlvii, 17–18.

————. The Scientific Quest for Values. *The Humanist*, Sept.-Oct. 1959, XIX, 259–261.

Read at the Dewey centennial observance of the American Humanist Association, New York City, 28 Feb. 1959.

GERRATANA, VALENTINO. Filosofia americana e filosofia europea. *Società*, Sept. 1951, VII, 478–487.

Apropos of Benedetto Croce's note in *Quaderni della critica*, Sept. 1951, xix–xx, 20–22.

Review by Aldo Visalberghi in *Rivista di filosofia*, July 1952, XLIII, 333–337.

GETMAN, ARTHUR KENDAL. Influence of John Dewey in Education. *Agricultural Education*, Dec. 1932, V, 83–84.

GEYER, DENTON LORING. *The Pragmatic Theory of Truth as Developed by Peirce, James, and Dewey.* [Urbana, Ill.?], 1914. 55 pp.

Thesis (PH.D.), University of Illinois.

THE PRAGMATIC DOCTRINE AS SET FORTH BY DEWEY, 35–40.

THE WORKS OF JOHN DEWEY, 45–47.

————. Three Types of Education for Freedom. *School and Society*, 29 Nov. 1947, LXVI, 406–409.

Hegelian, Classical, and Deweyan.

GEYMONAT, LUDOVICO. La logica di Dewey e il nuovo razionalismo. *Rivista critica di storia della filosofia*, Oct.-Dec. 1951, VI, 319–327.

GILLIO-TOS, MARIA TERESA VIRETTO. *Il pensiero di Giovanni Dewey*. Napoli: Luigi Loffredo [1938]. xxi, 350 pp.

Reviewed in *Archivio della cultura italiana*, 1941 (Gaetano Pottino); *Criterion*, Jan.-Aug. 1938, VI, 97–105; *Logos* (Napoli-Roma), 1939, XXII, 341–342 (Michele Federico Sciacca); *Philosophy* (London), 1939, XIV, 469–470; *Philosophical Review*, July 1940, XLIX, 482–483 (George Gaines Leckie); *Revue des sciences philosophiques et théologiques*, 1940, XXIX, 129–130 (H.-D. Gardeil).

GINGER, RAY. *Altgeld's America. The Lincoln Ideal versus Changing Realities*. New York: Funk & Wagnalls Company [ᶜ1958]. 376 pp.

Dewey, *passim*.

———. The Idea of Process in American Social Thought. *American Quarterly*, Fall 1952, IV, 253–265.

GIRDLER, JOHN. What's Wrong with Our Teachers: Reply to John Dewey. *Rotarian*, Jan. 1935, XLVI, 36–37.

GIULETTI, GIOVANNI. I fondamenti dell'operativismo logico di John Dewey. *Giornale di metafisica* (Torino), 15 Jan.-15 Feb. 1956, XI, 13–33.

GLICKSBERG, CHARLES IRVING. *American Literary Criticism 1900–1950*. New York: Hendricks House, Inc. [ᶜ1951]. x, 574 pp.

Dewey, 349–377, with reprint of CRITICISM AND PERCEPTION, chap. xiii of *Art as Experience*.

GOEHEGAN, GRACE. The Educational Theories of Rousseau and Dewey.

Master's thesis, Birmingham-Southern College, 1933.

GOLDMAN, CARL ALLEN. Notes on the Political Philosophy of John Dewey; Experimentalism as a Method of Politics.

Honors thesis, Harvard College, 1955.

GOLDMAN, ERIC FREDERICK. *Rendezvous with Destiny*. New York: Alfred A. Knopf, 1952, xi, 503, xxxvii pp.

Dewey, 155–159 *et passim*.

GOMENSORO, ARNALDO. *John Dewey y la filosofía del lenguaje*. Montevideo: Departamento de Lingüística, Universidad de la República, 1956. 66 pp.

GORAN, MORRIS HERBERT. The Nature of Science for Dewey and Einstein and Certain Educational Implications of These Views.

Thesis (PH.D.), University of Chicago, 1957.

GOWIN, D. BOB. Is Dewey's Experimentalism Compatible with Gestalt Theory? *School Review*, Summer 1959, LXVII, 195–212.

GRAHAM, EDNA JEANNE. John Dewey's Philosophy of Religion.

Thesis (A.M.), University of Nebraska, 1938.

GRANA, GIANNI. *John Dewey e la metodologia americana*. (Nuova collana pedagogica.) Roma: Libreria Editrice Ricerche, 1955. 248 pp.

Reviewed in *Rivista critica di storia della filosofia*, May-Aug. 1955, X, 303–304 (Aldo Visalberghi).

GRAY, JESSE GLEN. Is Progressive Education a Failure? Some of the Current Criticisms Examined. *Commentary*, Aug. 1952, XIV, 107–116.

GREENE, MAXINE. Dewey and American Education, 1894–1920. *School and Society*, 10 Oct. 1959, LXXXVII, 381–386.

Reprinted in William Wolfgang Brickman and Stanley Lehrer, eds., *John Dewey: Master Educator* (New York, 1959), 32–49.

GREENLEAF, MRS. LILLIAN SNOW. A Philosophy of Democracy as Worked Out by John Dewey.

Thesis (A.M.), University of Chicago, 1919.

GRETZINGER, MARGUERITE. Commonsense in the Classroom. *Michigan Education Journal*, Apr. 1950, XXVII, 425–427.

GRIFFITH, FRANCIS. John Dewey: Theory and Practice. *Commonweal*, 24 Sept. 1954, LX, 603–606.

Reply by Brother Adelbert James, *ib.*, 15 Oct. 1954, LXI, 38–39.

GRIFFITHS, NELLIE LUCY. A History of the Organization of the Laboratory School of the University of Chicago.

Thesis (A.M.), University of Chicago, 1927.

GROSS, MASON WELCH. [Announcement of the Dewey Archive at Rutgers University.] *Saturday Review*, 21 Nov. 1959, XLII, xlvii, 26.

GUCCIONE MONROY, ANTONIO. Logica della mente e logica della responsibilità in J. Dewey. *Scuola e città*, 1957, 343–351, 402–411.

———. Una prospettiva empirica del filosofare: categorie di inter-relazione nella filosofia di John Dewey. *Studi Urbinati* (Urbino), 1955, XXIX, 72–84.

GUIDUCCI, ROBERTO. Influenze e contra influenze nella filosofia contemporanea: Marx e Dewey. *Nuovi argomenti*, 1954, ix, 174–184.

GURLITT, L. Ein neuer Kampfgenosse (John Dewey). *Blatter für deutsche Erziehung*, 1903, V, 150–151.

GUSTAFSON, G. J. John Dewey. *Catholic Mind*, Sept. 1952, L, 513–519.

GUTH, HANS PAUL. Threat as the Basis of Beauty: Pragmatist Elements in the Aesthetics of [Ivor Armstrong] Richards, Dewey, and [Kenneth] Burke.
Thesis (PH.D.), University of Michigan, 1957.

GUTZKE, MANFORD GEORGE. *John Dewey's Thought and Its Implications for Christian Education*. New York: King's Crown Press, 1956 [ᶜ1955], xv, 270 pp.

HAAVIO, MARTTI H. Kaski pedagogista elämäntyötä: John Dewey and Maria Montessori. *Kasavatus ja koulu* (Finland), 1953, i, 1–13.

HAGEDORN, HERMANN. John Dewey. In his *Americans: A Book of Lives* (New York: The John Day Company [ᶜ1946]), 181–204.

HALBACH, ARTHUR ANTHONY. *A Definition of Meaning for American Education*. Washington: Catholic University Press, 1948. x, 160 pp.
Thesis, Catholic University of America.

HALL, CLIFTON L. "Exegit monumentum aere perennius. . . . " *Peabody Journal of Education*, July 1952, XXX, 2–7.

HALL, GRANVILLE STANLEY. *Life and Confessions of a Psychologist*. New York: D. Appleton and Company, 1923. ix, 622 pp.
Criticism of Dewey, 499–500.

HALL, ROYAL G. The Significance of John Dewey for Religious Interpretation. *Open Court*, June 1928, XLII, 331–340.

HAMADA, IKUJIRO. Ethical Implication of Two Contrasted Philosophies of Life, Illustrated in John Dewey and Bertrand Russell.

Thesis (A.M.), Columbia University, 1919.

HAMILTON, JAMES T. The Philosophy of John Dewey in Relation to American Education.

Master's thesis, University of Oregon, 1933.

HAMILTON, WALTON HALE. Our Man-Made Natural Resources. *In* Progressive Education Association, Progressive Education Booklet No. 15, *Resources for Building America* (Columbus, Ohio, 1939), 58–63.

Delivered at the celebration of Dewey's eightieth birthday in New York, Oct. 1939.

HAMM, WILLIAM CONRAD. Applications of Dewey's Philosophy of Education to College Education.

Thesis (A.M.), Yale University, 1932.

HAN LIH WU. Professor Dewey's Second Visit to China. *China Weekly Review*, 4 Apr. 1931, LVI, 176–177.

HANDLIN, OSCAR. American Secondary Education at the Dewey Centennial. *In* Syracuse University, School of Education, *Frontiers of Secondary Education*, 1959, IV, 1–7.

———. *John Dewey's Challenge to Education: Historical Perspectives on the Cultural Context.* Foreword by Arthur G. Wirth. (The John Dewey Society Lectureship Series, 2.) New York: Harper & Brothers [ᶜ1959]. 59 pp.

Reviewed in *Annals of the American Academy of Political and Social Science*, May 1960, CCCXXIX, 195 (Theodore Brameld); *Commonweal*, 5 Feb. 1960, LXXI, 527–528 (John J. McDermott); *Saturday Review*, 21 Nov. 1959, XLII, xlvii, 56 (David W. Adams).

———. Rejoinder to Critics of John Dewey. *New York Times Magazine*, 15 June 1958.

Condensed in *Education Digest*, Nov. 1958, XXIV, iii, 1–4.

"If Johnny can't read . . . the fault lies not in 'progressive education,' but in distorting the true spirit of Dewey's teachings."

HANDSCHY, HARRIET WILD. Educational Theories of Cardinal Newman and John Dewey. *Education*, Nov. 1928, XLIX, 129–137.

HARADA, MICHAEL. A Comparative Study of the Pragmatism of Sir Francis Bacon and John Dewey.

Master's thesis, Occidental College, 1957.

HARDIE, CHARLES DUNN. *Truth and Fallacy in Educational Theory*. Cambridge [England]: The University Press, 1942. x, 151 pp.

HARDON, JOHN A., S.J. John Dewey antesignano del naturalismo americano. *Civiltà Cattolica*, 9 Feb. 1952, CIII, i, 417–428.

English translation: John Dewey, Prophet of American Naturalism, *Catholic Educational Review*, Sept. 1952, L, 433–445.

———. John Dewey, educatore sociale radicale. *Civiltà Cattolica*, 29 Mar. 1952, CIII, ii, 40–52.

English translation: John Dewey—Radical School Educator, *Catholic Educational Review*, Oct. 1952, L, 505–517.

———. La leggenda di John Dewey nel campo dell'educazione americana. *Civiltà Cattolica*, 26 Apr. 1952, CIII, ii, 272–283.

English translation: The Dewey Legend in American Education, *Catholic Educational Review*, Nov. 1952, L, 577–588.

HARLOW, REX FRANCIS. The Educational Implications of the Theories of Value of Nicolai Hartmann and John Dewey.

Master's thesis, University of Texas, 1935.

HARMON, FRANCES BOLLES. The Social Philosophy of the St. Louis Hegelians.

Thesis (PH.D.), Columbia University, 1943.

Dewey, *passim.*

HARRIS, P. E. John Dewey as Pioneer in the Newer Discipline of the Child. *Understanding the Child*, June 1933, III, 23–24.

HARRIS, PATRICIA. A Comparison of the Linguistic Formulations of Alfred K. Korzybski and the Pragmatism of John Dewey.

Master's thesis, Arizona State College (Tempe), 1954.

HART, JOSEPH KINMONT. Edmund Wilson and the American Mind. *New Republic*, 11 May 1932, LXX, 354–355.

———. *Inside Experience: A Naturalistic Philosophy of Life and the Modern World*. New York: Longmans, Green and Co., 1927. xxvi, 287 pp.

Reviewed in *Journal of Philosophical Studies*, Jan. 1928, III, 116–118 (Joseph John Findlay); *Journal of Philosophy*, 18 July 1929, XXVI, 409–411 (Mary Shaw Kuypers); *New Scholasticism*, Apr. 1928, II, 179–180 (Virgil Michel).

———. Judging Our Progressive Schools. *New Republic*, 11 June 1930, LXIII, 93–96.

———. Principles of Character Development in the Philosophy of John Dewey. *Religious Education*, Feb. 1929, XXIV, 113–116.

HARTMAN, DONALD GEORGE. The Application of a Personal Philosophy of Education in the Field of the Social Studies. Thesis (A.M.), Ohio State University, 1936.

HATINGUAIS, EDMÉE. *L'Oeuvre de John Dewey*, par Mme. Hatinguais. . . . (Allocution de Mme. Suzanne Herbinière-Lebert et de M. Aristide Beslais.) (Comité français pour l'education préscolaire, Journée internationale, Paris, 8 mars 1954.) Pantin, Seine: Secrétariat du C.F.E.P. [1955]. 20 pp. Copy in Bibliothèque Nationale.

HAWORTH, LAWRENCE LINDLEY. The Experimental Society: Dewey and Jordan. *Ethics*, Oct. 1960, LXXI, 27–40.

———. The Practical Philosophies of John Dewey and Elijah Jordan. Thesis (PH.D.), University of Illinois, 1952.

HAYDON, ALBERT EUSTACE. Mr. Dewey on Religion and God. *Journal of Religion*, Jan. 1935, XV, 22–25.

HENDEL, CHARLES WILLIAM, ed. *John Dewey and the Experimental Spirit in Philosophy*. Four Lectures Delivered at Yale University Commemorating the 100th Anniversary of the Birth of John Dewey. New York: The Liberal Arts Press [ᶜ1959]. 119 pp.

Contents. The New Empiricism and the Philosophical Tradition, by Charles William Hendel—Education as Social Process, by Nathaniel Morris Lawrence—Knowledge, Value, and Freedom, by Richard Jacob Bernstein—John Dewey: Philosopher of Experience, by John Edwin Smith.

———. John Dewey and the Philosophical Tradition: A Study

of Some Significant Affiliations. *Journal of Philosophy*, 9 Oct. 1958, LV, 884–886.

Abstract of a paper read before the American Philosophical Association at the University of Vermont, 27 Dec. 1958.

HENLE, ROBERT J., S.J. Hutchins and Dewey Again. *Modern Schoolman*, Jan. and Mar. 1938, XV, 30–33, 56–59.

HENNIG, PAUL. *Die weltanschaulichen Grundlagen von John Deweys Erziehungstheorie*. Leipzig, 1928 (Bielefeld: G. Mülot & Co.). 49 pp.

Thesis (DR.PHIL.), University of Leipzig.

Includes bibliography.

HERZSTEIN, ROBERT ERWIN. Pascal and Dewey: The Quest for Certainty and the Naturalistic Imperative.

Honors thesis, Harvard College, 1952.

HESSEN, SERGIO. *Fondamenti della pedagogia come filosofia applicata*, trad. Vera Dolghin. (2ª ed.) Firenze: Sandron, 1942.

Dewey, 174–183.

———. John Deweys Erziehungslehre. *Die Erziehung*, Sept. 1930, V, 657–684.

———. *La pedagogia di Giovanni Dewey*; trad. A. Manari; ridotta da G. Fano. *In* Istituto di pedagogia della facoltà di magisterio dell'Università di Roma, *Consigli, bibliografie, ricerche*. Roma, 1937. 37 pp. (Also Roma, Avio, 1958.)

Translation of the preceding work?

HILKER, FRANZ. Pädagogische Amerikafahrt. *Pädagogisches Zentralblatt*, 1928, VIII, ix, 529 ff.

Title from Hennig dissertation.

HILL, KNOX CALVIN. Philosophic Method and Theory of Art in Croce and Dewey.

Thesis (PH.D.), University of Chicago, 1954.

HILL, WALKER H. The Founder of Pragmatism. In *In Commemoration of William James 1842–1942* (New York: Columbia University Press, 1942), 223–234.

Dewey, *passim*.

———. Peirce and Dewey and the Spectator Theory of Knowledge.

Thesis (PH.D.), University of Wisconsin, 1938.

Abstract, PEIRCE AND PRAGMATISM, in *Journal of Philosophy*, 7 Dec. 1939, XXXVI, 682.

[HINDLE, WILFRID HOPE.] John Dewey (Representative Men, VI.) *English Review*, June 1936, LXII, 644–646.

HOCKING, WILLIAM ERNEST. Action and Certainty. *Journal of Philosophy*, 24 Apr. 1930, XXVII, 225–238.

Read before the session on the Philosophy of John Dewey at the meeting of the American Philosophical Association, Columbia University, 30 Dec. 1929.

See Dewey's reply in *ib.*, 8 May 1930, 271–277.

———. Dewey's Concepts of Experience and Nature. *Philosophical Review*, Mar. 1940, XLIX, 228–244.

See Dewey's reply, NATURE AND EXPERIENCE, *ib.*, 244–248.

HODGES, DONALD CLARK. Dewey's Theory of Political Conflict. Thesis (A.M.), Columbia University, 1949.

HOFSTADTER, RICHARD. The Current of Pragmatism. In his *Social Darwinism in American Thought 1860–1915* (Philadelphia: University of Pennsylvania Press, 1945), 103–120.

HOLDEN, DAVID. John Dewey and His Aims of Education. *Educational Forum*, Nov. 1953, XVIII, 72–81.

Reprinted in Mortimer Brewster Smith, ed., *Public Schools in Crisis: Some Critical Essays* (Chicago: Henry Regnery Co., 1956), 15–29.

HOLMES, OLIVER WENDELL (1841–1935). *Holmes-Laski Letters: The Correspondence of Mr. Justice Holmes and Harold J. Laski 1916–1935*. Edited by Mark DeWolfe Howe with a foreword by Felix Frankfurter. 2 vols. Cambridge, Massachusetts: Harvard University Press, 1953.

Many references to Dewey.

———. *Holmes-Pollock Letters: The Correspondence of Mr. Justice Holmes and Sir Frederick Pollock 1874–1932*. Edited by Mark DeWolfe Howe . . . with an Introduction by John Gorham Palfrey. 2 vols. Cambridge, Massachusetts: Harvard University Press, 1941.

Comments on Dewey: II, 242, 272, 287.

HOMBERGER, CONRAD PAUL. An Introduction to John Dewey. *Educational Theory*, Apr. 1955, V, 98–109.

HOOK, SIDNEY. *American Philosophers at Work: The Philosophic Scene in the United States.* New York: Criterion Books, 1956. 512 pp.
Dewey, *passim.*

———. *Education for Modern Man.* New York: The Dial Press, 1946. xiv, 237 pp.
Dewey, *passim.*

———. The Ends and Content of Education. *Daedalus,* Winter 1959, LXXXVIII, 7–24.

———. The Ethical Theory of John Dewey. In his *The Quest for Being* (New York: St. Martin's Press, 1961), 49–70.

———. Experimental Naturalism. *In* Horace Meyer Kallen and Sidney Hook, eds., *American Philosophy Today and Tomorrow* (New York: Lee Furman, Inc. [ᶜ1935]), 205–225.

———. *John Dewey: An Intellectual Portrait.* New York: The John Day Company [ᶜ1939]. ix, 242 pp.
Contents. The Man—Philosophy and Culture—The Nature of Ideas —Truth—Logic and Action—Body, Mind, and Behavior—Standards, Ends, and Means—The Good Society—The Frontiers of Education—Art as Experience—Nature and Man—The Philosopher of American Democracy.
Reviewed in *Journal of Philosophy,* 7 Dec. 1939, XXXVI, 695 (Herbert Wallace Schneider); *Nation,* 6 Jan. 1940, CL, 22–23 (Eliseo Vivas); *Philosophical Review,* Jan. 1941, L, 86–87 (Everett Wesley Hall); *Saturday Review of Literature,* 11 Nov. 1939, XXI, iii, 13 (Robert Bierstedt).

———. *John Dewey: His Philosophy of Education and Its Critics.* (A Tamiment Institute Public Service Pamphlet.) New York: 1959. 23 pp. Issued as Sec. 2 of *The New Leader,* 2 Nov. 1959, XLII, xl. (Correction in *ib.,* 9 Nov. 1959, xli, 30.)
Elaboration of an address delivered by Professor Hook at the League for Industrial Democracy's April 1959 conference to commemorate the centenary of Dewey's birth.

———. John Dewey—Philosopher of Growth. *Journal of Philosophy,* 17 Dec. 1959, LVI, 1010–1018.
Talk delivered at the John Dewey Centenary in the Rotunda of Low Memorial Library, Columbia University, 20 Oct. 1959. On this occasion Mrs. Corinne Chisholm Frost presented to the Columbia University Library some 150 letters written to her by Dewey.

————, ed. *John Dewey: Philosopher of Science and Freedom. A Symposium*. New York: The Dial Press, 1950. viii, 383 pp.

Contents. John Dewey and the Spirit of Pragmatism, by Horace Meyer Kallen—Dewey and Art, by Irwin Edman—Instrumentalism and the History of Philosophy, by George Boas—Culture and Personality, by Lawrence K. Frank—Social Inquiry and Social Doctrine, by Horace Leland Friess—Dewey's Theories of Legal Reasoning and Valuation, by Edwin Wilhite Patterson—Dewey's Contribution to Historical Theory, by Sidney Ratner—John Dewey and Education, by John Lawrence Childs—Dewey's Revision of Jefferson, by Milton Ridvas Konvitz—Laity and Prelacy in American Democracy, by Herbert Wallace Schneider—Organized Labor and the Dewey Philosophy, by Mark Starr—The Desirable and Emotive in Dewey's Ethics, by Sidney Hook—John Dewey's Theory of Inquiry, by Felix Kaufmann—Dewey's Theory of Natural Science, by Ernest Nagel—Concerning a Certain Deweyan Conception of Metaphysics, by Albert Hofstadter—Dewey's Theory of Language and Meaning, by Paul De Velin Wienpahl—Language, Rules and Behavior, by Wilfrid Sellars—The Analytic and the Synthetic: an Untenable Dualism, by Morton Gabriel White—John Dewey and Karl Marx, by Jim Cork—Dewey in Mexico, by James Thomas Farrell.

Reviewed in *Ethics*, Oct. 1950, LXI, 89 (Alan Gewirth); *The Humanist*, Sept.-Oct. 1950, X, 223; *Journal of Philosophy*, 15 Mar. 1951, XLVIII, 192–195 (Harold Atkins Larrabee); *New York Times Book Review*, 23 Apr. 1950 (Thomas Vernor Smith); *Saturday Review of Literature*, 19 Aug. 1950, XXXIII, xxxiv, 35 (Robert Bierstedt).

————. John Dewey and His Critics. *New Republic*, 3 June 1931, LXVII, 73–74.

Reprinted in Gail Kennedy, ed., *Pragmatism and American Culture* (Boston, 1950), 92–94.

————. John Dewey at Ninety: The Man and His Philosophy. *New Leader*, 22 Oct. 1949.

————. John Dewey 1859–1952. *In* Raymond Klibansky, ed., *Philosophy in the Mid-Century*, IV (Milano, 1959), 210–214.

————. *The Metaphysics of Pragmatism*. Chicago: Open Court Publishing Co., 1927. v, 144 pp.

Thesis (PH.D.), Columbia University.

————. The Place of John Dewey in Modern Thought. *In* Marvin Farber, ed., *Philosophic Thought in France and the United States* (Buffalo: University of Buffalo, 1950), 483–503.

French translation, Paris, 1950.

HOOK, SIDNEY (*continued*). Portrait . . . John Dewey. *American Scholar*, Winter 1947–48, XVII, 105–110.

German translation, JOHN DEWEY: EIN PORTRÄT DES ALTMEISTERS DES AMERIKANISCHEN GEISTLEBENS, in *Der Monat*, Mar. 1949, I, vi, 40–46.

————. The Quest for "Being." *Journal of Philosophy*, 19 Nov. 1953, L, 709–731.

Reprinted in Richard Wirth Taylor, ed., *Life, Language, Law: Essays in Honor of Arthur F. Bentley* (Yellow Springs, Ohio: Antioch Press [ᶜ1957]), 132–154.

————. *Reason, Social Myths, and Democracy*. New York: The John Day Company [ᶜ1940]. xii, 302 pp.

Dewey, *passim*.

————. Some Memories of John Dewey. *Commentary*, Sept. 1952, XIV, 245–253.

See *ib*., Nov. 1952, 503–504, for letter of Joseph Waldman on John Dewey and Dr. Albert Coombs Barnes, and reply by Hook.

————. The U.S.S.R. Views American Philosophy. *Modern Review*, Nov. 1947, I, 649–653.

Foreword to the translation of an article by M. Dynnik, *q.v.*

HORNE, HERMAN HARRELL. *The Democratic Philosophy of Education; Companion to Dewey's Democracy and Education; Exposition and Comment*. New York: The Macmillan Company, 1932. xxiii, 547 pp.

————. *John Dewey's Philosophy*, especially *The Quest for Certainty*. Boston: Boston University School of Religious Education and Social Service [1931]. 27 pp.

————. *The Philosophy of Education; Being the Foundations of Education in the Related Natural and Mental Sciences*. Revised Edition with Special Reference to the Educational Philosophy of Dr. John Dewey. New York: The Macmillan Company, 1927. xvii, 329 pp.

HORRIDGE, FREDERICK. A Comparison of Dewey's *Democracy and Education*, [Ernest Carroll] Moore's *What Is Education?* and [James] Welton's *What Do You Mean by Education?*

Thesis (A.M. IN ED.), University of California, 1917.

HORVATH, WALTER JULIUS. The Inadequacy of Representative Government as Reviewed by Mill, Lippmann and Dewey.
Thesis (A.M.), Columbia University, 1932.

HORWITZ, ROBERT HENRY. The Political Philosophy of Civic Education.
Thesis (PH.D.), University of Chicago, 1954.

HOWARD, DELTON THOMAS. *John Dewey's Logical Theory*. New York: Longmans, Green & Co., 1918. 135 pp.
Thesis (PH.D.), Cornell University, 1916.
Reviewed in *Philosophical Review*, July 1919, XXVIII, 424–426 (Evander Bradley McGilvary).

HUDDLESTON, NANCY. Dewey's Logic in Relation to His Theory of Religious Quality.
Thesis (A.M.), University of Chicago, 1947.

HUEBSCH, ARTHUR. Jean-Jacques Rousseau and John Dewey: A Comparative Study and a Critical Estimate of Their Philosophies and Their Educational and Related Theories and Practices.
Thesis (PH.D.), New York University, 1930.

HUGHES, ERNEST RICHARD. *The Invasion of China by the Western World*. London: Adam and Charles Black, 1937. xvi, 324 pp. (Also published in New York by Macmillan, 1938.)
Dewey's visit to China, 183–185, *et passim*.

HUIZINGA, J. *Amerika Levend en Denkend*. Losse Opmerkingen. Haarlem: H. D. Tjeenk Willink & Zoon [1926]. 190 pp.
Dewey, *passim*.

HULLFISH, HENRY GORDON. Educational Confusion. *Educational Research Bulletin*, 17 Feb. and 2 Mar. 1932, XI, 85–90, 113–119.

———. John Dewey. In *Toward a Democratic Education* (Columbus: The College of Education, Ohio State University, 1960), 76–90.

IRELAND, ALLEYNE. John Dewey on Making People Citizens. *New York World*, 21 Apr. 1915.

IRIARTE, JOAQUÍN. Una filosofía con sede en los rascacielos: Dewey, Russell, [Will] Durant, [Ch.] Smith. *Razon y fé* (Madrid), 1957, LV, 549–560.

IRVING, JOHN ALLAN. Comments [on Edwin Arthur Burtt, THE CORE OF DEWEY'S WAY OF THINKING; and Arthur Edward Murphy, JOHN DEWEY AND AMERICAN LIBERALISM]. *Journal of Philosophy*, 23 June 1960, LVII, 442–450.

JABLONOWER, JOSEPH. John Dewey Memorial Address. *American Teacher*, Nov. 1952, XXXVII, ii, 12–16.
Delivered at the 35th annual American Federation of Teachers convention at Syracuse, N.Y.

JACOBSON, NOLAN PLINY. The Faith of John Dewey. *Journal of Religion*, July 1960, XL, 191–197.
From the context of *Is There a God? A Conversation*, by Henry Nelson Wieman, Douglas Clyde Macintosh, and Max Carl Otto (Chicago: Willett, Clark & Co., 1932); paper read before the American Philosophical Association, Earl Hall, Columbia University, 28 Dec. 1959.

JACOBSSON, MALTE. *Pragmatiska Uppfostringsprinciper . . .* jämte Barnet och Skolkursen av John Dewey, Auktoriserad översättning av Agnes Jacobsson-Undén. Lund: C. W. K. Gleerup, 1912. 170 pp.

JAEGER, GERTRUDE OTTILIE. John Dewey's Theory of Valuation: A Critical Statement.
Thesis (A.M.), University of Chicago, 1947.

JAMES, WILLIAM. *Pragmatism, a New Name for Some Old Ways of Thinking*. New York: Longmans, Green & Co., 1907. xiii, 309 pp.

JAMISON, HOWARD LOUIS. The Methodology of Scientific Social Practice: J. S. Mill and John Dewey.
Thesis (PH.D.), Harvard University, 1950.

JASCALEVICH, ALEJANDRO A. Tendencias Filosóficas en los Estados Unidos. *Verbum* (Buenos Aires), Oct.-Dec. 1920, XIV, 389–409.

JOHN DEWEY, THE MAN AND HIS PHILOSOPHY; ADDRESSES DELIVERED IN NEW YORK IN CELEBRATION OF HIS SEVENTIETH BIRTHDAY. Cambridge: Harvard University Press, 1930. vii, 181 pp.
Contents. Foreword, by Henry Wyman Holmes—Inaugurating the Plan, by Henry Richardson Linville—Introduction, by William Heard Kilpatrick—John Dewey's Contribution to Educational The-

ory, by Ernest Carroll Moore—John Dewey's Influence in the Schools, by Jesse Homer Newlon—John Dewey's Influence on Education in Foreign Lands, by Isaac Leon Kandel—The Philosophies of Royce, James and Dewey in Their American Setting, by George Herbert Mead—The Prospect for Empirical Philosophy, by Herbert Wallace Schneider—The Toastmaster's Words, by James Rowland Angell—John Dewey and Social Welfare, by Jane Addams—John Dewey and Liberal Thought, by James Harvey Robinson—In Response, by John Dewey.

Reviewed in *The New Scholasticism*, Jan. 1932, 76–77 (Virgil Michel).

JOHN DEWEY SOCIETY OF JAPAN. *Bulletin*, 1960–. Tokyo: Shunjusha, Inc.

In Japanese.

Contents of No. 1, Nov. 1960. Preface, by Yoshio Nagano—John Dewey's Attitude in Setting an Educational End-in-View, by T. Oura—The Relation between Science of Education and Philosophy of Education, referring mainly to Dewey's *The Sources of a Science of Education*, by H. Sasaki—A Study on the View of Reality and Truth in "Pragmatism," by T. Doi—Rhythm and Balance, The Situation Theory in Art and Education, by M. Meguri—Dewey's Theory of History, by Merle Curti—John Dewey in the American Tradition, by Adrienne Koch—Review of Nagano's *The Social Philosophy of John Dewey*, by R. Hiroike—Notes and News.

———, ed. [*John Dewey: The Individual and His Thoughts*.] Tokyo: Oct. 1959. 78 pp.

In Japanese. Commemorating Dewey's Centennial. Contains a chronology of Dewey and articles by Sidney Hook, Henry Gordon Hullfish, Yoshio Nagano, and Risaburo Hiroike.

THE JOHNS HOPKINS MAGAZINE. Profile of a Visionary: John Dewey 1859–1952. *The Johns Hopkins Magazine*, Dec. 1959, XI, iii, 3–6, illus.

JOHNSON, ALLISON HEARTZ. John Dewey: 1859–1952. *Nation*, 25 Oct. 1952, CLXXV, 381–382.

JOHNSON, ALVIN SAUNDERS. Dewey, the Greek. *New Republic*, 31 Oct. 1949, CXXI, xviii, 9.

JOHNSON, FRANK WAGNER. An Analysis of Bertrand Russell's, Brand Blanshard's, and John Dewey's Views on Causality. Thesis (A.M.), Columbia University, 1947.

JONES, FRANK PIERCE. The Work of F. M. Alexander as an Introduction to Dewey's Philosophy of Education. *School and Society*, 2 Jan. 1943, LVII, 1–4.

JONES, MARC EDMUND. *George Sylvester Morris: His Philosophical Career and Theistic Idealism.* Philadelphia: David McKay Company, 1948. 430 pp.
Thesis (PH.D.), Columbia University, 1948.
Dewey, *passim.*

JONES, WILLIAM THOMAS. *A History of Western Philosophy.* New York: Harcourt, Brace and Company [ᶜ1952]. xviii, 1036 pp.
Dewey, 949–965.

JORDAN, ELIJAH. *Forms of Individuality: An Inquiry into the Grounds of Order in Human Relations.* Indianapolis: Charles W. Laut and Company, 1927. 469 pp.
Dewey, 66–74.

JORDAN, JAMES A., JR. Interest, Choice, and Desirability. *School Review,* Summer 1959, LXVII, 174–185.

———. John Dewey's Theory of Knowing and the Christian Teacher.
Master's thesis, Emory University, 1956.

JORNADAS PEDAGÓGICAS, APATA, PERU. Jornadas Pedagógicas de Apata, incluye un mensaje del filósofo John Dewey a los maestros del Peru. Caratula de Hernán Ponce Sánchez. (Biblioteca "Seminario pedagógico Hermilio Valdizán"). Lima, 1944. 32 pp.
Copy at New York Public Library.

JOURNAL OF THE NATIONAL EDUCATION ASSOCIATION. Influence of John Dewey. *Journal of the National Education Association,* Dec. 1929, XVIII, 282.
JOHN DEWEY, THE HUMANIST, *ib.,* 286.

KAHAN, SALOMON. [*Dzhon Diui.*] [México, D.F.], 1952. 47 pp.
In Hebrew; above title transliterated.

KAHN, SHOLOM J. Experience and Existence in Dewey's Naturalistic Metaphysics. *Philosophy and Phenomenological Research,* Dec. 1948, IX, 316–321.
See Dewey's comment, EXPERIENCE AND EXISTENCE, *ib.,* 709–713, and Kahn's reply, THE STATUS OF THE POTENTIAL, *ib.,* 714–716.

———. Transaction vs. Interaction. *Journal of Philosophy,* 20 Nov. 1947, XLIV, 660–663.
Reply by Benjamin Wolstein, A TRANSACTION WITH MR. KAHN, *ib.,* 663–666.

KALLEN, HORACE MEYER. *American Philosophy Today and To-morrow* (ed., with Sidney Hook). New York: Lee Furman, Inc. [ᶜ1935]. viii, 518 pp.

Dewey, *passim.*

―――. *Art and Freedom: A Historical and Biographical Inter-pretation of the Relations between the Ideas of Beauty, Use and Freedom in Western Civilization from the Greeks to the Present Day.* 2 vols. New York: Duell, Sloane and Pearce [ᶜ1942].

JOHN DEWEY ON THE POWER AND FUNCTION OF ART IN FREE SO-CIETY, 906–916, *et passim.*

―――. Creative Intelligence. *The Humanist,* Sept.-Oct. 1959, XIX, 262–265.

Address at the Dewey centennial observance of the American Hu-manist Association, New York City, 28 Feb. 1959.

―――. Freedom and Education. *In* Progressive Education As-sociation, Progressive Education Booklet No. 12, *Freedom and Education* (Columbus, Ohio, 1939), 5–15.

Reprinted in Sidney Ratner, ed., *The Philosopher of the Common Man* (New York, 1940), 15–32.

Delivered at the celebration of Dewey's eightieth birthday in New York, Oct. 1939.

―――. Human Rights and the Religion of John Dewey. *Ethics,* Apr. 1950, LX, 169–177.

―――. *Individualism; an American Way of Life.* New York: Liveright, 1933. x, 241 pp.

"Grew out of discussions with John Dewey more than a year ago" (Lorine Pruette in *New York Herald Tribune Books,* 2 Apr. 1933.)

―――. Individuality, Individualism, and John Dewey. *Antioch Review,* Fall 1959, XIX, 299–314.

―――. John Dewey, America's Foremost Thinker. *Forward* (English section), 20 Oct. 1929.

―――. Of Truth. *In* Frederick Burkhardt, ed., *The Cleavage in Our Culture: Studies in Scientific Humanism in Honor of Max Carl Otto* (Boston: Beacon Press [ᶜ1952]), 30–50.

Dewey, *passim.*

―――. Pragmatism. *Encyclopaedia of the Social Sciences,* XII (1934), 307–311.

KAMINSKY, JACK. Dewey's Concept of *An* Experience. *Philosophy and Phenomenological Research*, Mar. 1957, XVII, 216–330.

———. Dewey's Defense of the Humanities. *Journal of General Education*, Jan. 1956, IX, 66–72.

KANDEL, ISAAC LEON. A Controversy Ended. *Educational Forum*, Jan. 1958, XXII, 175–181; condensed in *Education Digest*, Apr. 1958, XXIII, viii, 16–19.
On Dewey and progressive education.

———. The Influence of Dewey Abroad. *School and Society*, 23 Nov. 1929, XXX, 700–704; *Teachers College Record*, Dec. 1929, XXXI, 239–244.
Address delivered at the Dewey Seventieth Birthday Celebration, Horace Mann Auditorium, Teachers College, 18 Oct. 1929.

———. John Dewey, 1859–1952. *School and Society*, 7 June 1952, LXXV, 363.

———. John Dewey's Ninetieth Birthday. *School and Society*, 15 Oct. 1949, LXX, 250.

———. *Twenty-five Years of American Education: Collected Essays*. New York: The Macmillan Company, 1924. xvi, 469 pp.
Dewey, *passim*.

KANE, WILLIAM J. A Critique of the Concept of Nature in the Philosophy of John Dewey According to Thomistic Principles of Being.
Master's thesis, Catholic University of America, 1950.

KANTOROVICH, HAIM. A Revolutionary Interpretation of Philosophy. *Modern Quarterly*, Summer 1924, II, 22–31.

KAO CHIEN. Progressive Education Undermined China. *The Freeman*, Dec. 1954, 216–218.
"How China's new educational policy, adopted in 1922 through the influence of Western-trained intellectuals [especially Dewey], helped the Communists take over."

KAPLAN, SIDNEY. Social Engineers as Saviors: Effects of World War I on Some American Liberals. *Journal of the History of Ideas*, June 1956, XVII, 347–369.
Analysis of certain features of the political philosophies of four major figures of American liberalism: John Dewey, Randolph Bourne, Walter Lippmann, and Herbert Croly.

KAUFFMANN, FELIX. John Dewey's Theory of Inquiry. *Journal of Philosophy*, 8 Oct. 1959, LVI, 826–836.

Written in August 1949 in connection with the observance of Dewey's ninetieth birthday. First published in Sidney Hook, ed., *John Dewey: Philosopher of Science and Freedom* (New York, 1950), 217–230.

KAZIN, ALFRED. *On Native Grounds*. New York: Reynal & Hitchcock [ᶜ1942]. xiii, 541 pp.

For Dewey, see Chap. 5, PROGRESSIVISM: SOME INSURGENT SCHOLARS, 127–164.

KEENAN, KEVIN BRENDAN. Toward Philosophic Reconstruction: Comments on the Philosophy of John Dewey.

Thesis (A.M.), Columbia University, 1946.

KELLEY, TRUMAN LEE. The Passing of the P[rogressive] E[ducation] A[ssociation]. *School and Society*, 23 Dec. 1944, LX, 401–402.

KEMPSKI, JÜRGEN VON. *Charles Sanders Peirce und der Pragmatismus*. (Archiv für Philosophie. Buchreihe I.) Stuttgart und Köln: W. Kohlhammer Verlag, 1952. 115 pp.

Dewey, *passim*.

Reviewed in *Journal of Philosophy*, 13 Aug. 1953, L, 535–538 (Philip Paul Wiener).

KENNEDY, GAIL. Comment on Professor Bernstein's Paper, "John Dewey's Metaphysics of Experience" [pp. 5–14]. *Journal of Philosophy*, 5 Jan. 1961, LVIII, 14–21.

———. Comments [on Edwin Arthur Burtt, THE CORE OF DEWEY'S WAY OF THINKING; and Arthur Edward Murphy, JOHN DEWEY AND AMERICAN LIBERALISM, 401–436]. *Journal of Philosophy*, 23 June 1960, LVII, 436–442.

———. Dewey's Concept of Experience: Determinate, Indeterminate, and Problematic. *Journal of Philosophy*, 8 Oct. 1959, LVI, 801–804.

Read at a meeting of the Conference on Methods in Philosophy and the Sciences held at the New School for Social Research, 24 May 1959. The paper is related to the following articles by the author: SCIENCE AND THE TRANSFORMATION OF COMMON SENSE: THE BASIC PROBLEM OF DEWEY'S PHILOSOPHY; THE HIDDEN LINK IN DEWEY'S THEORY OF EVALUATION; PRAGMATISM, PRAGMATICISM, AND THE WILL TO BELIEVE—A RECONSIDERATION; and THE PROCESS OF EVALUATION IN A DEMOCRATIC COMMUNITY, *qq.v.*

KENNEDY, GAIL (*continued*). The Hidden Link in Dewey's
Theory of Evaluation. *Journal of Philosophy*, 17 Feb. 1955,
LII, 85–94; *Teachers College Record*, May 1955, LVI, 421–428.
Read as part of a symposium sponsored by the John Dewey Society
on Systems of Value, held at Teachers College, Columbia University,
20 Oct. 1954, in commemoration of John Dewey.

———. Pragmatism, Pragmaticism, and the Will To Believe—A
Reconsideration. *Journal of Philosophy*, 3 July 1958, LV, 578–
588.

———, ed. *Pragmatism and American Culture*. (Problems in
American Civilization.) Boston: D. C. Heath and Company
[ᶜ1950]. 114 pp.
Contents. What Pragmatism Means, by William James—What I Believe, by John Dewey—What I Believe, Revised, by John Dewey—
The Pragmatic Acquiescence, by Lewis Mumford—The Pragmatic
Acquiescence, by John Dewey—The Pragmatic Acquiescence: A Reply, by Lewis Mumford—Pragmatic America, by John Dewey—
Moral Man and Immoral Society, by Reinhold Niebuhr—God and
the Professors, by Mortimer Jerome Adler—The New Medievalism,
by Sidney Hook—Science and Ethics, by Howard Selsam—John
Dewey and His Critics, by Sidney Hook—Liberalism and Social Action, by John Dewey.

———. The Process of Evaluation in a Democratic Community.
Journal of Philosophy, 12 Mar. 1959, LVI, 253–263.
This paper is a sequel to two earlier ones by the author: SCIENCE AND
THE TRANSFORMATION OF COMMON SENSE: THE BASIC PROBLEM OF
DEWEY'S PHILOSOPHY and THE HIDDEN LINK IN DEWEY'S THEORY
OF EVALUATION, *qq.v.*

———. Science and the Transformation of Common Sense: The
Basic Problem of Dewey's Philosophy. *Journal of Philosophy*,
27 May 1954, LI, 313–325.

KENNEDY, WILLIAM F. John Dewey and the Platoon School.
Platoon School, Dec. 1929, III, 150.

KENNICK, WILLIAM ELMER. A Methodological Approach to
Metaphysics, with Special Reference to the Philosophies of
Aristotle, Hume, Dewey, and Whitehead.
Thesis (PH.D.), Cornell University, 1952.

KENT, WILLIAM PHELPS. John Dewey's Philosophical Principles
and Their Political Significance. *Western Political Quarterly*
(Salt Lake City), Sept. 1953, VI, 446–457.

————. The Political Philosophy of John Dewey.

Thesis (PH.D.), University of Chicago, 1950.

KERBY-MILLER, SINCLAIR [*formerly* Kerby Sinclair Miller]. The Early Development of Dewey's Logical Theory.

Thesis (A.M.), Columbia University, 1921.

KERLINGER, FRED N. The Origin of the Doctrine of Permissiveness in American Education. *Progressive Education*, Nov. 1956, XXXIII, 161–165.

The contributions of Dewey and Freud.

KETONEN, OIVA. John Dewey 1859–1952. In *Ajatus filosofisen yhdistyksen vuosikirja* (Helsinki: Akateemínen kirjakauppa, 1954), XVIII, 85–98.

KILBRIDGE, JOHN THOMAS. The Concept of Habit in the Philosophy of John Dewey.

Thesis (PH.D.), University of Chicago, 1949.

KILLEEN, MARY VINCENT, SISTER. *Man in the New Humanism*. Washington: Catholic University of America, 1934. v, 100 pp.

Thesis (PH.D.), Catholic University of America.

KILPATRICK, FRANKLIN PIERCE, ed. *Explorations in Transactional Psychology*. New York: New York University Press, 1961. xiv, 405 pp.

Dewey, *passim*.

KILPATRICK, WILLIAM HEARD. Apprentice Citizens. *Saturday Review of Literature*, 22 Oct. 1949, XXXII, xliii, 12.

————. The Child and the Curriculum. *In* Progressive Education Association, Progressive Education Booklet No. 12, *Freedom and Education* (Columbus, Ohio, 1939), 33–36.

Delivered at the celebration of Dewey's eightieth birthday in New York, Oct. 1939.

————. Dewey's Philosophy of Education. *Educational Forum*, Jan. 1953, XVII, 143–154.

————. Education by Interest and Effort. *The Humanist*, Sept.-Oct. 1959, XIX, 265–266.

Remarks at the Dewey centennial observance of the American Humanist Association, New York City, 28 Feb. 1959.

KILPATRICK, WILLIAM HEARD (*continued*). *John Dewey and His Contributions to American Education.* (Henry Barnard Lectures, I.) [New Britain, Conn., 1949.] 18 pp.
Address at the Teachers College of Connecticut, New Britain, 17 Oct. 1949.

———. John Dewey and His Educational Theory. *Educational Theory*, Oct. 1952, II, 217–221; *Progressive Education*, Oct. 1952, XXX, i, 5–8.

———. John Dewey in American Life. *In* Progressive Education Association, Progressive Education Booklet No. 14, *John Dewey and the Promise of America* (Columbus, Ohio, 1939), 5–11.
Delivered at the celebration of Dewey's eightieth birthday in New York, Oct. 1939.

———. John Dewey's Ninetieth Birthday. *Journal of the National Education Association*, Oct. 1949, XXXVIII, 529.

———. Personal Reminiscences of Dewey and My Judgment of His Present Influence. *School and Society*, 10 Oct. 1959, LXXXVII, 374–375.
Reprinted in William Wolfgang Brickman and Stanley Lehrer, eds., *John Dewey: Master Educator* (New York, 1959), 20–23.

———. Remarks at the Unveiling of Dr. Dewey's Bust. *School and Society*, 22 Dec. 1928, XXVIII, 778–780.

———. What Has John Dewey Meant to Childhood Education? *Childhood Education*, Apr. 1950, XXVI, 380–381.
Italian translation in *Puer*, June–Sept. 1952.

KIMPTON, LAWRENCE ALPHEUS. The University and the High School: Past and Future. *School and Society*, 1 Mar. 1958, LXXXVI, 100–102.
Reprinted in Francis S. Chase and Harold A. Anderson, eds., *The High School in a New Era* (Chicago: University of Chicago Press 1958), 31–37, and in part in *School Review*, Summer 1958, LXVII, 125–127, with the title DEWEY AND PROGRESSIVE EDUCATION.

KITTRELL, JEAN MCCARTY. Objectivity in John Dewey's Moral Theory.
Thesis (A.M.), University of Chicago, 1952.

KLING, CARLOS. On the Instrumental Analysis of Thought. *Journal of Philosophy*, 12 May 1932, XXIX, 259–265.
Apropos of Laurence Buermeyer, PROFESSOR DEWEY'S ANALYSIS

OF THOUGHT (*ib.*, XVII, 673–681) and John Dewey, AN ANALYSIS OF REFLECTIVE THOUGHT (*ib.*, XIX, 29–38).

KLUBERTANZ, GEORGE PETER, S.J. The Man Whom Dewey Would Educate. *Modern Schoolman*, Mar. 1939, XVI, iii, 60–64.

KLYCE, SCUDDER. *Dewey's Suppressed Psychology . . . Being Correspondence between John Dewey . . . and Scudder Klyce.* . . . Winchester, Mass: S. Klyce, 1928. 294 pp. Mimeographed.
See index, *s.v.* Dewey.

KOCH, ADRIENNE. John Dewey. *Washington Post*, 8 June 1952.

KOLKO, GABRIEL. Morris R. Cohen: The Scholar and/or Society. *American Quarterly*, Fall 1957, IX, 325–336.

KOMAROVSKY, BORIS BORISOVICH. Filosofiia vospitaniia Dzhona D'iui v sviazi s istorei amerikanskoi pedagogiki. *Sovremennye pedagogicheskie techeniia*, I. (Azerbaidzhan University. Faculty of Pedagogy. Izvestia. XV.) Baku, 1930.
Copy in British Museum.

KONVITZ, MILTON RIDVAS. *The American Pragmatists*. Selected Writings edited by Milton R. Konvitz and Gail Kennedy. (An Original Meridian Book.) New York: Meridian Books, Inc. [ᶜ1960]. 413 pp.
Dewey, 173–256.

———. Dewey, Society, and Religion. *New Leader*, 22 Oct. 1949.

KOPP, JOYCE GOFORTH. Dewey's Criticism of the Platonic "Absolute."
Thesis (A.M.), University of Chicago, 1948.

KREMER, RENÉ. *Le néo-realisme américain*. Louvain: Institut de Philosophie, 1920. 310 pp.
Dewey, *passim*.

KRIKORIAN, YERVANT HOVHANNES. The Ethics of Naturalism. *New Republic*, 17 Oct. 1949, CXXI, xvi, 32–36.

———, ed. *Naturalism and the Human Spirit*. (Columbia Studies in Philosophy, 8.) New York: Columbia University Press, 1944. 397 pp.
Contents. Antinaturalism in Extremis, by John Dewey (pp. 1–16)—Naturalism and Religion, by Sterling Power Lamprecht—Naturalism and Democracy, by Sidney Hook—Naturalism and Ethical Theory, by Abraham Edel—A Natural History of the Aesthetic Transaction,

by Eliseo Vivas—The Unnatural, by Herbert Wallace Schneider—
The History of Philosophy, by George Boas—The Materials of
Historical Knowledge, by Edward William Strong—Naturalism and
the Sociological Analysis of Knowledge, by Thelma Z. Lavine—Logic
without Ontology, by Ernest Nagel—A Naturalistic View of Mind,
by Yervant Hovhannes Krikorian—The Categories of Naturalism,
by William Ray Dennes—The Naturalism of Frederick Woodbridge,
by Harry Todd Costello—Naturalism in America, by Harold Atkins
Larrabee—Epilogue: The Nature of Naturalism, by John Herman
Randall, Jr.

Reviewed in *Canadian Forum*, Dec. 1944, XXIV, 217–218 (J.M.);
Journal of Philosophy, 19 July 1945, XLII, 400–417 (Arthur Edward
Murphy); *Nation*, 30 Dec. 1944, CLIX, 804 (Philip Blair Rice);
New Republic, 20 Nov. 1944, CXI, 667–668 (Isaac Rosenfeld);
New York Times, 3 Sept. 1944 (Irwin Edman).

See Wilmon Henry Sheldon, Critique of Naturalism, *Journal of
Philosophy*, 10 May 1945, XLII, 253–270, and reply by Dewey,
Sidney Hook, and Ernest Nagel, Are Naturalists Materialists?
ib., 13 Sept. 1945, 515–530.

Kursanov, G. A. [The Reactionary Gnoseology and the "Theories" of the Concept of Neopositivism.] *Izvestia* (Serija istorii
i filosofii), Akademia nauk S.S.S.R. 1948, V, 422–436.

In Russian.

Ladd, John. "Desirability" and "Normativeness" in White's
Article on Dewey. *Philosophical Review*, Jan. 1951, LX, 91–98.

Reply to Morton Gabriel White, Value and Obligation in Dewey
and Lewis, *ib.*, July 1949, LVIII, 321–329.

Lafferty, Theodore Thomas. Empiricism and Objective Realism in Value Theory. *Journal of Philosophy*, 17 Mar. 1949,
XLVI, 141–155.

———. Inter-Communication in Philosophy. *Ib.*, 15 Aug. 1946,
XLIII, 449–466.

Laguna, Grace Andrus de. The Practical Character of Reality.
Philosophical Review, July 1909, XVIII, 396–415.

Laidler, Harry Wellington, ed. *John Dewey at Ninety*.
Addresses and Greetings on the Occasion of Dr. Dewey's
Ninetieth Birthday Dinner October 20, 1949 at the Hotel
Commodore, New York. New York: League for Industrial
Democracy [1950]. 37 pp. illus.

Contents. Message from President Truman—Introductory Remarks,
by Harry Wellington Laidler—Columbia Greets Dewey, by Frank

Diehl Fackenthal—The Meaning of Dewey to Us All, by Felix Frankfurter—Dewey, a Leader in Public Affairs, by John Haynes Holmes—Dewey and the World of Labor, by David Dubinsky and Walter Reuther—Dewey as Philosopher, by Ralph Barton Perry—Dewey's Contribution to Art, by Irwin Edman—Dewey and Education for Democracy, by William Heard Kilpatrick—Teachers and Students Pay Tribute, by Joy Elmer Morgan, Rebecca Simonson, and Alice Hoffman—Salute from the Orient, by Hu Shih and Jawaharlal Nehru—Citation from the Committee, Presented by William Pepperell Montague—John Dewey Responds—A Few of Hundreds of Messages, from Alvin Johnson, Clement Attlee, Henri Bonnet, Stephen Duggan, Lady Allen of Hurtwood, Channing Heggie Tobias, Bryn Jacob Hovde, Horace Meyer Kallen, and Felix Kaufmann.

LAMANNA, EUSTACHIO PAOLO. *Il prammatismo anglo-americano* (*James, Schiller, Dewey*): Corso di storia della filosofia di E. P. Lamanna, anno academico 1951–52 [Università di Firenze]. Firenze: Ed. Universitaria, 1952. 294 pp. Mimeographed.

LAMONT, CORLISS. *Dialogue on John Dewey.* [Participants:] James Thomas Farrell, James Gutmann, Alvin Johnson, Horace Meyer Kallen, Harry Wellington Laidler, Corliss Lamont, Ernest Nagel, John Herman Randall, Jr., Herbert Wallace Schneider, Harold Taylor, Milton Halsey Thomas. Edited by Corliss Lamont, with the assistance of Mary Redmer. New York: Horizon Press, 1959. 155 pp.

Transcription of an informal evening of reminiscences and personal impressions at Mr. Lamont's New York home, 13 Dec. 1958.

Translation: Japanese by Yoshio Nagano and others (Tokyo, 1960).

Reviewed in *Rivista di filosofia*, July 1960, LI, 367–368 (Aldo Visalberghi).

———. John Dewey and the American Humanist Association. *The Humanist*, Jan.-Feb. 1960, XX, 3–10.

———. [John Dewey:] Philosopher and Educator. *The Humanist*, June 1959, XIX, 133–134.

Remarks as chairman at the Dewey centennial observance of the American Humanist Association, New York City, 28 Feb. 1959.

———. John Dewey in Theory and Practice. *Science and Society*, Winter 1941, V, 61–64.

Comment on Vivian Jerauld McGill, PRAGMATISM RECONSIDERED: AN ASPECT OF JOHN DEWEY'S PHILOSOPHY, *ib.*, Summer 1939, III,

289–322. Reply by McGill. FURTHER CONSIDERATIONS, *ib.*, Winter, 1941, V, 65–71.

LAMONT, CORLISS (*continued*). Materialism and John Dewey— A Discussion (with Howard Selsam). *New Masses*, 25 Feb. 1947, LXII, 17–23.

————. New Light on Dewey's *Common Faith. Journal of Philosophy*, 5 Jan. 1961, LVIII, 21–28.

This article is drawn from a lecture given at Burlington 19 Nov. 1959 in the University of Vermont John Dewey Centennial Series.

————. "Philosophy in Revolution": A Discussion. *Science and Society*, Winter 1958, XXII, 56–62.

Discussion of Howard Selsam, *Philosophy in Revolution* (1957), especially his treatment of Dewey; reply by Selsam, *Science and Society*, Winter 1958, XXII, 62–68.

————. The Pragmatism of John Dewey. *Marxist Quarterly*, Apr.-June 1937, I, 298–300.

Apropos of Theodore B. Brameld's review of August Thalheimer, *Introduction to Dialectical Materialism, the Marxist World-View* ... translated by George Simpson and George Weltner; and discussion by Simpson, *Modern Quarterly*, Jan.-Mar. 1937, I, 144–150.

LAMONT, MRS. MARGARET HAYES (IRISH). Dewey's Conception of Intelligence and the International Mind.

Thesis (A.M.), Columbia University, 1928.

LAMPRECHT, STERLING POWER. *Empiricism and Natural Knowledge*. (University of California Publications in Philosophy, XVI, iv, 71–94.) Berkeley and Los Angeles: University of California Press, 1940.

————. An Idealist Source of Instrumentalist Logic. *Mind*, Oct. 1924, N.S. XXXIII, 415–427.

————. *Our Philosophical Traditions: A Brief History of Philosophy in Western Civilization*. New York: Appleton-Century-Crofts [ᶜ1955]. xi, 523 pp.

Dewey, 497–512.

————. The Philosophy of John Dewey. *New World Monthly*, Jan. 1930, I, 1–16.

LANCASTER, LANE W. John Dewey. In his *Masters of Political Thought*, III. Hegel to Dewey (Boston: Houghton Mifflin Company, 1960), 332–369.

LARKIN, RICHARD ANDERSON. The Influence of John Dewey on Physical Education.

Thesis (A.M.), Ohio State University, 1936.

LARRABEE, HAROLD ATKINS. John Dewey as Teacher. *School and Society*, 10 Oct. 1959, LXXXVI, 378–381.

Reprinted in William Wolfgang Brickman and Stanley Lehrer, eds., *John Dewey: Master Educator* (New York, 1959), 50–57; condensed in *Education Digest*, Jan. 1960, XXV, v, 20–23.

———. *Reliable Knowledge*. Boston: Houghton Mifflin Company [ᶜ1945]. vii, 685 pp.

Dewey, *passim*.

———. The Twenty-ninth Meeting of the American Philosophical Association [at Columbia University, 30–31 Dec. 1929]. *Journal of Philosophy*, 30 Jan. 1930, XXVII, 70–79.

Includes summaries and comment on the papers on John Dewey read by Messrs. Woodbridge, Hocking, Lewis, Ratner, Horne and Ward, *qq.v.*

LAWSON, DAVID. Changing Modes of Thought in Moral Education.

Report (ED.D.), Teachers College, 1959.

LEANDER, FOLKE. *Estetik och kunskapsteori: Croce, Cassirer, Dewey*. Göteborg: Elanders Boktryckeri, Wettergren & Kerber, 1950. 253 pp.

———. John Dewey and the Classical Tradition. *American Review*, Oct. 1937, IX, 504–527.

———. *John Deweys pedagogik och dess etiska förutsättningar: En kritik*. (Pedagogiska skrifter, 175.) Stockholm: Svensk Läraretidningsforlag, 1942. 88 pp.

———. *The Philosophy of John Dewey. A Critical Study*. (Göteborgs Kunglinga vetenskaps—och vitterhets—samhället. Handlingar. Följden 5, ser. A, band 7, no. 2.) Göteborg: Elanders Boktryckeri Aktiebolag, 1939. 154 pp.

Reviewed in *Journal of Philosophy*, 12 Oct. 1939, XXXVI, 586–587 (Herbert Wallace Schneider), rejoinder by Leander, *ib.*, XXXVII, 407–408; *Philosophical Abstracts*, Winter 1940, I, i, 21–22 (Sidney Hook); *Philosophical Review*, Mar. 1940, XLIX, 262–264 (Max Carl Otto); *Philosophy*, Oct. 1939, XIV, 481–482 (John Laird); *Revue des sciences philosophiques et théologiques*, 1940, XXIX, 130 (H. D. Gardeil).

LeBoutillier, Mrs. Cornelia Throop (Geer). *Religious Values in the Philosophy of Emergent Evolution.* New York, 1936. 104 pp.

Thesis (ph.d.), Columbia University.

Includes a chapter on The Religious Philosophy of John Dewey.

Lee, Grace Chin. *George Herbert Mead: Philosopher of the Social Individual.* New York: King's Crown Press, 1945. vii, 100 pp.

Thesis (ph.d.), Bryn Mawr College.

Dewey, *passim.*

Lee, Otis. Instrumentalism and Action. *Journal of Philosophy,* 1 Feb. 1940, XXXVII, 57–75.

Lepley, Ray, ed. *The Language of Value.* New York: Columbia University Press, 1957. viii, 428 pp.

Dewey, *passim.*

———, ed. *Value: A Cooperative Inquiry.* New York: Columbia University Press, 1949. ix, 487 pp.

"The present volume is the product of a cooperative study of some of the underlying issues regarding value. The immediate stimulus to the study was an article by John Dewey that appeared in the *Journal of Philosophy* in 1944 [17 Aug., XLI, 449–455]." (Introduction, p. 3). The text is reprinted in this volume, 4–12, together with a new article by Dewey, The Field of "Value", 64–77. See the index for other references to Dewey.

Contents. Part I: Essays. Reflections on Dewey's Questions about Value, by Henry David Aiken—The Value Economy, by Clarence Edwin Ayres—The Field of "Value", by John Dewey—Intrinsic Good: Its Definition and Referent, by Arthur Campbell Garnett—Values and Inquiry, by George Raymond Geiger—A Contextualist Looks at Value, by Lewis Edwin Hahn—On Value, by Bertram Emil Jessup—Methodology of Value Theory, by Harold Newton Lee—Sequel on Value, by Ray Lepley—Values, Valuing, and Evaluation, by Edwin Thomas Mitchell—Axiology as the Science of Preferential Behavior, by Charles William Morris—Discussion of John Dewey's "Some Questions about Value," by DeWitt Henry Parker—Observations on Value from an Analysis of a Simple Appetition, by Stephen Coburn Pepper—Science, Humanism, and the Good, by Philip Blair Rice. Part II. Criticisms and Rejoinders.

Reviewed in *Journal of Philosophy,* 25 Oct. 1951, XLVIII, 705–706.

———. *Verifiability of Value.* (Columbia Studies in Philosophy, 7.) New York: Columbia University Press, 1944. 267 pp.

Dewey, *passim.*

LERNER, MAX. Randolph Bourne and Two Generations. *Twice a Year* 5–6, Fall-Winter 1940/Spring-Summer 1941, 54–78. Dewey, *passim.*

LEROUX, EMMANUEL. *Le Pragmatisme américain et anglais: étude historique et critique, suivie d'un bibliographie méthodique.* Paris: Felix Alcan, 1913, 429 pp.

LA LOGIQUE INSTRUMENTALE DE M. DEWEY ET L'ÉCOLE DE CHICAGO, 140–159.

ÉCRITS DE JOHN DEWEY, 346–355.

ÉCRITS DE L'ÉCOLE DE DEWEY, 356–363.

LEVI, ALBERT WILLIAM. *Philosophy and the Modern World.* Bloomington: Indiana University Press [ᶜ1959]. xiv, 591 pp.

REASON IN SOCIETY: JOHN DEWEY, 283–330, *et passim.*

LEVINSON, JOSEPH DAVID. The Problem of Freedom in the Political Philosophy of John Dewey.

Master's thesis, Ohio State University, 1954.

LEVIT, MARTIN. The Context of a Contextualist Philosophy. *School Review*, Summer 1959, LXVII, 246–257.

LEVITT, MORTON. *Freud and Dewey on the Nature of Man.* New York: Philosophical Library, 1960. 180 pp.

Revision of his PH.D. thesis, FREUD AND DEWEY: A COMPARISON OF THEIR PSYCHOLOGICAL SYSTEMS, University of Michigan, 1956.

LEWIS, CLARENCE IRVING. Pragmatism and Current Thought. *Journal of Philosophy*, 24 Apr. 1930, XXVII, 238–246.

Read before the session on the Philosophy of John Dewey at the meeting of the American Philosophical Association, Columbia University, 30 Dec. 1929.

See Dewey's reply in *ib.*, 8 May 1930, 271–277.

LEYS, WAYNE ALBERT RISSER. Dewey's Instrumental Thinking. In his *Ethics for Policy Decisions* (New York: Prentice-Hall, Inc., 1952), 150–175.

LIBRARIES. Celebration of John Dewey's Seventieth Birthday. *Libraries*, July 1930, XXXV, 310.

LIEURANCE, WILLIAM BERRY. Certain Implications of John Dewey's Theory of Habit for Social Studies Teachers.

Master's thesis, Ohio State University, 1950.

LIFE. *Life* Congratulates John Dewey. *Life*, 31 Oct. 1949, XXVII, xviii, 43.

LILGE, FREDERIC. John Dewey, 1859–1959: Reflections on His Educational and Social Thought. *Educational Forum*, Mar. 1960, XXIV, 351–356.

———. John Dewey in Retrospect: An American Reconsideration. *British Journal of Educational Studies*, May 1960, VIII, 99–111.

———. The Vain Quest for Unity: John Dewey's Social and Educational Thought. Philosophy of Education Society, *Proceedings of 15th Annual Meeting*, 1959.

LIND, LEVI ROBERT. Dewey Pictured as Prophet and Reconstructionist. *The Daily Illini* (University of Illinois), 26 Feb. 1928.

LINDEL, BERTHA NEOLA. A Study of the Poems of Robert Browning with the Object of Finding Ideas Contributory to the Educational Theory of John Dewey.
Thesis (A.M. IN ED.), University of Southern California, 1933.

LINDEMAN, EDUARD CHRISTIAN. John Dewey and Social Action. *In* Progressive Education Association, Progressive Education Booklet No. 13, *The Educational Frontier* (Columbus, Ohio, 1939), 42–57.
Reprinted in *School and Society*, 13 Jan. 1940, LI, 33–37, with the title JOHN DEWEY AS EDUCATOR.
Delivered at Cooper Union in Oct. 1939 as part of a symposium on the philosophy of John Dewey and in commemoration of his eightieth birthday.

LINVILLE, HENRY RICHARDSON. John Dewey at Seventy. *New Republic*, 16 Oct. 1929, LX, 245.
Letter to the editor regarding the plans for the celebration of Dewey's seventieth birthday.

LINZMEYER, ROBERT A. An Appraisal of the Five-Step Thought Method of John Dewey in the Light of Some Thomistic Principles.
Master's thesis, Catholic University of America, 1956.
Abstract in *Catholic Educational Review*, Apr. 1958, LVI, 263.

LIPPS, H. Pragmatisme et philosophie de l'existence. *Recherches philosophiques* (Paris), 1936–37, V, 333–345.

LISSNER, WILL. In Memoriam: John Dewey (1859–1952). *American Journal of Economics and Sociology*, Jan. 1953, XII, 122.

LIST, DAVIDA NORMA. A Comparative Study of John Dewey's Concept of Learning and Its Conditions with Those of Some Modern Secondary Schools.
Thesis (A.M.), New York University, 1955.

LIU, KWOH C. John Dewey's Logical Theory.
Thesis (A.M.), University of Wisconsin, 1932.

LOMBARDO RADICE, GIUSEPPE. L'impostazione del problema pedagogico in John Dewey. *L'educatore della Svizzera Italiana*, Mar. 1927; reprinted in *L'educazione nazionale*, June-July 1930, XII, 281–287.

LOMBARDO RADICE, LUCIO. Scuole e città (O della provincia pedagogica). *Società*, 1950, 706–707.

LONG, MARCUS. The Relation between the Logical Theories of Lotze, Bosanquet, and Dewey: A Study in the Morphology of Knowledge.
Thesis (PH.D.), University of Toronto, 1940.

LONG, WILBUR. Mr. Dewey's Faith without Religion. *Personalist*, Summer and Autumn 1937, XVIII, 239–253, 369–388.

LOVECCHIO, A. La logica del Dewey. *Ricerche filosofiche*, July-Dec. 1953.

LOVETT, ROBERT MORSS. John Dewey at Seventy. *New Republic*, 23 Oct. 1929, LX, 262–264.

LUDWIG, FR. Moderne Schulreformer: John Dewey. *Monistische Jahrhundert*, 1915, p. 97.

LUZURIAGA, LORENZO. La Pedagogía de Dewey: la educación por la acción. *El Sol* [Madrid?], 22 Apr. 1918.

LYNCH, JARMON ALVIS. Concerning the Emphasis on Methods. *Journal of Philosophy*, 9 May 1940, XXXVII, 269–273.

———. A Criticism of Dewey's Theory of the Stimulus. *Philosophical Review*, May 1940, XLIX, 356–360.

———. Two Ways of Misconstruing the Doctrine of Interest. *Texas Outlook*, Aug. 1931, XV, 18–19.

LYND, ALBERT. *Quackery in the Public Schools*. Boston: Little, Brown and Company [°1953]. 282 pp.

Chap. viii, The Influence of John Dewey (pp. 183–211), *et passim*.

———. Who Wants Progressive Education? The Influence of John Dewey on the Public Schools. *Atlantic Monthly*, Apr. 1953, CXCI, iv, 29–34.

Reply by Frederic Ernst, How DANGEROUS IS JOHN DEWEY? *ib.*, May 1953, CXCI, v, 59–62.

McCADDEN, HELEN M. John Dewey and Education. *Commonweal*, 27 Nov. 1929, XI, 113.

McCARTHY, HAROLD E. Dewey, Suzuki, and the Elimination of Dichotomies. *Philosophy East and West* (Honolulu), Apr. 1956, VI, 35–48.

McCAUL, ROBERT LAWRENCE. Dewey and the University of Chicago. I. July, 1894–March, 1902 (*School and Society*, 25 Mar. 1961, LXXXIX, 152–157); II. April, 1902–May, 1903 (*ib.*, 8 Apr. 1961, 179–183); III. September, 1903–June, 1904 (*ib.*, 22 Apr. 1961, 202–206).

Reprinted in William Wolfgang Brickman and Stanley Lehrer, eds., *John Dewey: Master Educator* (2d ed., 1961), 31–74, with the title, DEWEY, HARPER, AND THE UNIVERSITY OF CHICAGO. . . .

———. Dewey's Chicago. *School Review*, Summer 1959, LXVII, 258–280.

———. Educational Biography: Dewey and [Samuel Gridley] Howe. *Elementary School Journal*, Oct. 1957, LVIII, 1–7.

———. A Preliminary Listing of Dewey Letters, 1894–1904. *School and Society*, 10 Oct. 1959, LXXXVII, 395–399.

Letter of James Hayden Tufts to President William Rainey Harper, proposing Dewey for the position of Head-Professor of Philosophy at the University of Chicago, 399.

Reprinted in William Wolfgang Brickman and Stanley Lehrer, eds., *John Dewey: Master Educator* (New York, 1959), 105–119, and 2d ed. (1961).

MACCIA, GEORGE S. A Comparison of the Educational Aims of Charles Peirce and John Dewey. *Educational Theory*, Oct. 1954, IV, 289–296.

McClellan, James E. Dewey and the Concept of Method: Quest for the Philosopher's Stone in Education. *School Review*, Summer 1959, LXVII, 213–228.

McCluskey, Neil Gerard, s.j. John Dewey and Progressivism. *America*, 4 Apr. 1959, CI, i, 16–22.

————. *Public Schools and Moral Education: The Influence of Horace Mann, William Torrey Harris, and John Dewey.* New York: Columbia University Press, 1958. 315 pp.

Thesis (ph.d.), Columbia University.

Includes several quotations from unpublished letters of Dewey to William Torrey Harris in the School of Philosophy Library, University of Southern California.

McCormack, Eric David. Frederick Matthias Alexander and John Dewey: A Neglected Influence.

Thesis (ph.d.), University of Toronto, 1959.

McCreary, John Kenneth. The Matrix of Dewey's Theory of Education. *Education* (Boston), Mar. 1948, LXVIII, 439–448.

McDermott, John J. Experience Is Pedagogical: The Genesis and Essence of the American Nineteenth Century Notion of Experience.

Thesis (ph.d.), Fordham University, 1959.

McDonald, Gerald Edmund. Coöperation in Education between the Thomist and the Experimentalist. *Educational Administration and Supervision*, Jan. 1959, XLV, 13–25.

McElroy, Howard Clifford. *Modern Philosophers: Western Thought since Kant.* New York: Russell F. Moore Company [ᶜ1950]. xii, 268 pp.

Dewey, 101–122.

McGill, Vivian Jerauld. Pragmatism Reconsidered: An Aspect of John Dewey's Philosophy. *Science and Society*, Summer 1939, III, 289–322.

See Corliss Lamont, John Dewey in Theory and Practice, *ib.*, Winter 1941, V, 61–64, and reply by McGill, Further Considerations, *ib.*, 65–71.

McGrane, Joan. Leslie Stephen and John Dewey: The Relation of Scientific Method to the Problems of Men.

Thesis (ph.d.), Columbia University, 1950.

MACK, ROBERT DONALD. *The Appeal to Immediate Experience. Philosophic Method in Bradley, Whitehead and Dewey.* New York: King's Crown Press, 1945. vii, 86, i pp.
Thesis (PH.D.), Columbia University.

MACKAY, DONALD SAGE. What Does Mr. Dewey Mean by an "Indeterminate Situation"? *Journal of Philosophy*, 12 Mar. 1942, XXXIX, 141–148.
Replies by Dewey, INQUIRY AND INDETERMINATENESS OF SITUATIONS, *ib.*, 21 May 1942, XXXIX, 290–296, and Arthur Fisher Bentley, AS THROUGH A GLASS DARKLY, *ib.*, 30 July 1942, XXXIX, 432–439. Comment by Mackay, OUTCOME OF INQRY, AS "END-RESULT" OR AS "END-IN-VIEW"? *ib.*, 24 Sept. 1942, XXXIX, 547–550.

McKENNEY, JOHN L. Dewey and Russell: Fraternal Twins in Philosophy. *Educational Theory*, Jan. 1959, IX, 24–30.

———. The Problem of a Science of Ethics in the Philosophies of John Dewey and Bertrand Russell.
Thesis (PH.D.), Ohio State University, 1952.

McMAHON, EDWIN M. A Study of John Dewey and Experimentalism in Relation to the Contemporary Problem of Re-evaluation of Education in Our Democracy.
Master's thesis, Gonzaga University, 1958.

McMANIS, JOHN T. *Ella Flagg Young and a Half Century of the the Chicago Public Schools.* Chicago: A. C. McClurg & Co., 1916. 238 pp.
Dewey, 101–122.

McMULLEN, ROBERT JOHNSTON. A Comparative Study of the Ethics of Confucius and John Dewey. [New York], 1936.
Typewritten manuscript in the library of Union Theological Seminary.

McMURRAY, FOSTER. The Present Status of Pragmatism in Education. *School and Society*, 17 Jan. 1959, LXXXVII, 14–17.

McNITT, HAROLD AUSTIN. John Dewey's Democratic Liberalism: Its Philosophical Foundations.
Thesis (PH.D.), University of Michigan, 1957.

McNUTT, WALTER SCOTT. Instrumentalism at Its Best. *Education*, Nov. 1925, XLVI, 149–153.

MacPartland, John. Aristotle and the Spectator Theory of Knowledge. *Journal of Philosophy*, 24 May 1945, XLII, 291–293.

McWilliams, James Aloysius, s.j. Dewey's Esthetic Experience as a Substitute for Religion. *Modern Schoolman*, Nov. 1937, XV, 9–13.

———. Education for Progress. *Modern Schoolman*, Jan. 1942, XIX, 27–29.

———. John Dewey, Nonagenarian. *America*, 15 Oct. 1949, LXXXII, 39–40.

———. John Dewey's Educational Philosophy. *Modern Schoolman*, Mar. 1945, XXII, 144–154.

Mañach, Jorge. *Dewey y el pensamiento americano.* Madrid: Taurus Ediciones, S.A., 1959. 52 pp.

———. *El pensamiento de Dewey y su sentido americano.* (Cuadernos de Divulgación Cultural, Comisión Nacional Cubana de la UNESCO, No. 9.) La Habana, 1953. 31 pp.

Manasse, Ernst Moritz. Moral Principles and Alternatives in Max Weber and John Dewey. *Journal of Philosophy*, 20 Jan. and 3 Feb. 1944, XLI, 29–48, 57–68.

Manferdini, Tina. *Ontologismo critico e filosofia dell'esperienza.* Reggio Calabria: Ed. Historica, 1954. 26 pp.
Partly on Dewey and Whitehead.

———. Storicismo, sociologismo e naturalismo nel pensiero di Dewey. *In* Felice Battaglia, Nicola Abbagnano [*e.a.*], *Filosofia e sociologia* [Atti del convegno tenuto a Bologna dal 23 al 25 aprile 1954] (Bologna: Ed. Il Mulino, 1954).

Mannison, Donald Sherwood. The Function of Impulse in Dewey's Theory.
Thesis (a.m.), University of Illinois, 1957.

Manny, Frank Addison. John Dewey. *Seven Arts Magazine*, June 1917, II, 214–228.

Marie Theresa, Sister. Two Moderns and Aquinas. *Catholic Educational Review*, Mar. 1945, XLIII, 159–169.

Marotta, Sante. *Giovanni Dewey.* Siracusa: Ed. Ciranna, 1958. 72 pp.

MARSDEN, MALCOLM M. General Education: Compromise between Transcendentalism and Pragmatism. *Journal of General Education*, July 1953, VIII, 228–239.

MARTIN, CLYDE V. The Metaphysical Development of John Dewey. *Educational Theory*, Jan. 1958, VIII, 55–58.
Replies by Dorothy June Newbury, A NOTE ON "THE METAPHYSICAL DEVELOPMENT OF JOHN DEWEY" (*ib.*, July 1958, VIII, 186–187) and Marcus Brown, ANOTHER NOTE ON "THE METAPHYSICAL DEVELOPMENT OF JOHN DEWEY" (*ib.*, Oct. 1958, VIII, 284–285).

MARVIN, FRANCIS SYDNEY. Science and Society. *Nature*, 5 Mar. 1932, CXXIX, 329–331.

MASON, ROBERT EMMETT. Implications of Dewey's Culture Theory for Pedagogy. *School and Society*, 10 Oct. 1959, LXXXVII, 391–395.
Reprinted in William Wolfgang Brickman and Stanely Lehrer, eds., *John Dewey: Master Educator* (New York, 1959), 72–82.

MASSA, C. *La filosofia di John Dewey: esposizione critica.* Lecce: R. tip. ed. Salentina, 1940. 189 pp.

MATHUR, DINESH CHANDRA. The Significance of "Qualitative Thought" in Dewey's Philosophy of Art.
Thesis (PH.D.), Columbia University, 1955.

MAYER, FREDERICK. *A History of American Thought: An Introduction.* Dubuque, Iowa: Wm. C. Brown Company [ᶜ1951]. 399 pp.
Dewey, 303–309 *et passim.*

MAYEROFF, MILTON. An Examination of Some Criticisms of John Dewey's *Logic: The Theory of Inquiry.*
Thesis (A.M.), New York University, 1950.

———. The Nature of Propositions in John Dewey's "Logic." *Journal of Philosophy*, 8 June 1950, XLVII, 353–358.
Reply to May Brodbeck, THE NEW RATIONALISM: DEWEY'S THEORY OF INDUCTION, *ib.*, 24 Nov. 1949, XLVI, 780–791.

MAYHEW, KATHERINE CAMP, and ANNA CAMP EDWARDS. *The Dewey School: The Laboratory School of the University of Chicago 1896–1903.* New York: D. Appleton-Century Company, 1936. 489 pp.
Includes THE THEORY OF THE CHICAGO EXPERIMENT by Dewey, 463–477.

MD. Democracy's Schoolmaster. *MD*, Oct. 1959, III, x, 170–174.

MEAD, GEORGE HERBERT. *Movements of Thought in the Nineteenth Century*. Edited by Merritt Hadden Moore. Chicago: University of Chicago Press [ᶜ1936]. xxxix, 519 pp.
Dewey, *passim*.

————. The Philosophies of Royce, James and Dewey in Their American Setting. *International Journal of Ethics*, Jan. 1930, XL, 211–231; *John Dewey, The Man and His Philosophy* (Cambridge, 1930), 75–105; Walter George Muelder and Laurence Sears, eds. *The Development of American Philosophy: A Book of Readings* (Boston, 1940), 319–329.
Read at the Dewey Seventieth Birthday celebration in New York, 18 Oct. 1929.

————. The Philosophy of John Dewey. *International Journal of Ethics*, Oct. 1935, XLVI, 64–81.

————. *The Social Psychology of George Herbert Mead*. Edited and with an Introduction by Anselm Strauss. Chicago: University of Chicago Press, Phoenix Books [ᶜ1956]. xvi, 298 pp.
See Introduction for Dewey.

MECKLER, LESTER. Normative and Descriptive Expressions. *Journal of Philosophy*, 10 Sept. 1953, L, 577–583.
Apropos of Herbert Fingarette's article, How NORMATIVENESS CAN BE COGNITIVE BUT NOT DESCRIPTIVE IN DEWEY'S THEORY OF VALUATIONS, *ib.*, 11 Oct. 1951, XLVIII, 625–635.

MEDINA ECHAVARRÍA, JOSÉ. John Dewey y la libertad. *Trimestre economico* (México, D.F.), 1940, VI, 613–624.

MEEHAN, FRANCIS X. Absolute and Relative in the Moral Order. American Catholic Philosophical Association, *Proceedings*, 1947, XXII, 53–80.
Attack on Dewey's theory of morals.

MEENAN, DANIEL F. X. John Dewey's Theory of Valuation. *Modern Schoolman*, Mar. 1953, XXX, 187–201.

MEIKLEJOHN, ALEXANDER. *Education between Two Worlds*. New York and London: Harper and Brothers [ᶜ1942]. x, 304 pp.
Book III (123–195), THE PRAGMATIC EPISODE—A STUDY OF JOHN DEWEY, is a detailed criticism of Dewey's pragmatism.

Reviewed by Ernest Nagel in *The Humanist*, Summer 1943, III, 81–83; reply by Meiklejohn, *ib.*, Autumn 1943, 120–121, and rejoinder by Nagel, 122–123.

MEIKLEJOHN, DONALD [WALDRON]. The Relation between Ethical and Intellectual Judgments in the Philosophy of John Dewey.

Thesis (PH.D.), Harvard University, 1936.

MELVIL, J. K. [Pragmatism, Philosophy of Imperialistic Reaction.] *Voprosy Filosofii* (U.S.S.R.), 1950, II, 306–330.

In Russian; critical study of pragmatism, including Dewey.

MENCARELLI, MARIO. J. Dewey: naturalista umanistico. *Puer*, Feb.-Mar. 1952.

———. J. Dewey e la scuola attiva. *Puer*, Oct.-Nov. 1951.

———. *Il metodo dei progetti: G. Dewey e W. H. Kilpatrick.* Firenze: Marzocco-Bemporad, 1952. 50 pp.

MENDOZA DE MONTERO, ANGÉLICA. *Lineas fundamentales de la filosofía de John Dewey.* (Publicaciones del Instituto Cultural Argentino-Norte Americano.) Buenos Aires: [J. Perrotti], 1940. 19 pp.

MERIAM, JUNIUS LATHROP. John Dewey in History. *School and Society*, 10 Oct. 1959, LXXXVII, 376–378.

Reprinted in William Wolfgang Brickman and Stanley Lehrer, eds., *John Dewey: Master Educator* (New York, 1959), 24–31.

MESTHENE, EMMANUEL G. The Role of Language in the Philosophy of John Dewey. *Philosophy and Phenomenological Research*, June 1959, XIX, 511–517.

METELLI DI LALLO, CARMELA. *La dinamica dell'esperienza nel pensiero di Dewey.* (Università di Padova. Quaderni dell'Istituto di padagogia.) Padova: Liviana Editrice, 1958. 112 pp.

———. Il significato del termine esperienza nelle opere di J. Dewey. *Rivista di filosofia*, July 1960, LI, 303–321.

MEYER, ADOLPH ERICH. *John Dewey and Modern Education, and Other Essays.* New City, Rockland Co., N.Y.: The Avon Press, 1931. 154 pp.

The title essay covers pp. 3–17.

MEYER, AGNES (ERNST). *The Quest of the Good.* (John Dewey Memorial Lecture, 1954.) Bennington, Vermont: Bennington College [1954]. 20 pp.

MICHAEL, FRANZ HENRY, and GEORGE EDWARD TAYLOR. *The Far East in the Modern World.* New York: Henry Holt and Company [ᶜ1956]. x, 724 pp.

Dewey's visit to China, 229–235 *passim.*

MICHEL, VIRGIL. Some Thoughts on Professor Dewey. *New Scholasticism,* Oct. 1928, II, 327–341.

MILA, MASSIMO (*pseud.* LECTOR). Scuola e società. *Minerva: Rivista delle riviste,* Oct. 1949, LXIX, 356–358.

MILMED, BELLA KUSSY. Dewey's Treatment of Causality. *Journal of Philosophy,* 3 Jan. 1957, LIV, 5–19.

MISNER, PAUL JAMES. What Did Dewey Do for Education? *National Parent-Teacher,* Dec. 1959, LIV, iv, 9.

MITCHELL, EDWIN THOMAS. Dewey's Theory of Valuation. *Ethics,* July 1945, LV, 287–297.

MITCHELL, LUCY (SPRAGUE). *Two Lives: The Story of Wesley Clair Mitchell and Myself.* New York: Simon and Schuster, 1953. 575 pp.

John and Alice Dewey, *passim.*

MOHR, ROBERT L. The Relation of John Dewey's Educational Theory to His Metaphysics.

Master's thesis, Lehigh University, 1928.

MONTAGUE, WILLIAM PEPPERELL. *The Ways of Knowing, or the Methods of Philosophy.* London: George Allen & Unwin, Ltd. [1925]. 427 pp.

Dewey, *passim.*

MONTENEGRO, ERNESTO. John Dewey's Ideas. *Américas,* Sept. 1952, IV, ix, 32–33.

Translated from *El Mercurio* (Santiago, Chile).

MONTES UGARTE, RAUL. Los fines de la educación segua Dewey: exposición y crítica. *Estudios* (Buenos Aires), 1938, XV, 419–430.

MONTGOMERY, LEROY JEREMIAH. Comparison of the Theism of the American Personalists with the Naturalism of John Dewey.

Thesis (S.T.M.), Union Theological Seminary, 1930.

MONTGOMERY, RAY. John Dewey and Continuity of Growth. *Phi Delta Kappan*, Mar. 1953, XXXIV, 215–218.

———. John Dewey and the Blunted Instrument. *Ib.*, Feb. 1955, XXXVI, 177–180.

———. John Dewey and the Broken Circuit. *Ib.*, Feb. 1953, XXXIV, 201–203.

———. John Dewey and the Death Valley Daze. *Ib.*, Apr. 1953, XXXIV, 273–278.

———. John Dewey and the Double-Edged Danger. *Ib.*, Jan. 1953, XXXIV, 114–118.

———. John Dewey and the Egg-in-the-Bottle. *Ib.*, Dec. 1952, XXXIV, 95–97.

———. John Dewey and the Oyster's Pain. *Ib.*, May 1953, XXXIV, 311–315.

———. John Dewey and the Seven-Eyed Teacher. *Ib.*, June 1953, XXXIV, 424–430.

MOORE, ADDISON WEBSTER. *Pragmatism and Its Critics*. Chicago: University of Chicago Press [°1910]. xi, 283 pp.

MOORE, CHARLES ALEXANDER, ed. *Essays in East-West Philosophy: An Attempt at World Philosophical Synthesis* [Papers presented at the second East-West Philosophers' Conference, University of Hawaii, June-July 1949]. Honolulu: University of Hawaii Press, 1951. 467 pp.

Dewey, *passim*.

MOORE, EDWARD CARTER. *American Pragmatism: Peirce, James, and Dewey*. New York: Columbia University Press, 1961. 285 pp.

MOORE, ERNEST CARROLL. John Dewey's Contribution to Educational Theory. *School and Society*, 11 Jan. 1930, XXXI, 37–47.

Reprinted in *California Quarterly of Secondary Education*, Jan. 1930, V, 113–126, and in *John Dewey, the Man and His Philosophy* (Cambridge, 1930), pp. 7–36.

Read at the Dewey Seventieth Birthday celebration in New York, 18 Oct. 1929.

MORE, PAUL ELMER. Religion and Social Discontent. In his *On Being Human* (Princeton: Princeton University Press, 1936), 117–143.

A defense of religion against the philosophy of John Dewey; address delivered at the inauguration of the president of Lake Forest College in 1921, and originally published in *Christianity and Problems of To-Day* (New York: Charles Scribner's Sons, 1922), 75–106.

MORENO, RAFAEL. J. Dewey: La Experiencia y la naturaleza. *Filosofía y letras* (México. Universidad nacional. Facultad de filosofía y letras), Oct.-Dec. 1948, XVI, 311–318.

MORGAN, JOY ELMER. John Dewey's Worldwide Influence. *Journal of the National Education Association*, Dec. 1949, XXXVIII, 647.

———. Presentation of Life Membership [in the National Education Association to Dewey]. *Ib.*, Dec. 1929, XVIII, 281.

MORISON, ELTING ELMORE, ed. *The American Style: Essays in Value and Performance*. A Report on the Dedham Conference of May 23–27, 1957. (American Project Series, Center for International Studies, Massachusetts Institute of Technology.) New York: Harper & Brothers [ᶜ1958]. 426 pp.

Dewey, *passim*.

MORPURGO-TAGLIABUE, GUIDO. J. Dewey e la metafisica. *Rivista di filosofia*, July 1960, LI, 322–334.

———. Metafisica e gnoseologia nel pensiero di J. Dewey. *Pensiero*, 1960, V, 176–206.

———. Su la problematica del naturalismo contemporaneo. *Giornale critico della filosofia italiana*, Apr.-June 1958, 3d ser., XII, 165–200.

MORRIS, CHARLES WILLIAM. General Education and the Unity of Science Movement. *In* Progressive Education Association, Progressive Education Booklet No. 14, *John Dewey and the Promise of America* (Columbus, Ohio, 1939), 26–40.

Delivered at the celebration of Dewey's eightieth birthday in New York, Oct. 1939.

———. Peirce, Mead, and Pragmatism. *Philosophical Review*, Mar. 1938, XLVII, 109–127.

MORRIS, CHARLES WILLIAM (*continued*). *Pragmatism and the Crisis of Democracy*. (Public Policy Pamphlet, 12.) Chicago: University of Chicago Press [ᶜ1934]. 25 pp.

————. *Signs, Language and Behavior*. New York: Prentice-Hall, Inc., 1946. 365 pp.

Dewey, *passim*.

————. *Six Theories of Mind*. Chicago: University of Chicago Press [ᶜ1932]. xi, 337 pp.

Dewey, 290–330 *et passim;* see also the author's PRAGMATISM AND METAPHYSICS, *Philosophical Review*, Nov. 1934, XLIII, 549–564.

MORRIS, CLARENCE, ed. *The Great Legal Philosophers: Selected Readings in Jurisprudence*. Philadelphia: University of Pennsylvania Press [ᶜ1959]. 571 pp.

Dewey, 495–510, including excerpts from *Human Nature and Conduct*, and the full text of MY PHILOSOPHY OF LAW (1941).

————. The Political Philosophy of Jacques Maritain. *Daedalus*, Fall 1959, LXXXVIII, 700–711.

Dewey, *passim*.

MORRIS, LEONARD C. A Comparison of the Value Theories of DeWitt Parker and John Dewey.

Master's thesis, University of Utah, 1957.

MORRIS, LLOYD. A Pragmatist Looks at Tomorrow. In his *Postscript to Yesterday. America: The Last Fifty Years* (New York: Random House [ᶜ1947]), 368–378.

MORRISON, CHARLES CLAYTON. The New Modernism. *Christian Century*, 4 Mar. 1936, LIII, 352–353.

————. The Past Foreshadows the Future. *Ib.*, 5 Mar. 1958, LXXV, 271–274.

MOSIER, RICHARD DAVID. *The American Temper: Patterns of Our Intellectual Heritage*. Berkeley and Los Angeles: University of California Press, 1952. 306 pp.

Dewey, 253, 280–281.

————. Education as Experience. *Progressive Education*, Apr. 1952, XXIX, 200–203.

MUELDER, WALTER GEORGE, and LAURENCE SEARS, eds. *The Development of American Philosophy: A Book of Readings*. Boston: Houghton Mifflin Company [ᶜ1940]. 533 pp.

Dewey, 315–316 *et passim*, extracts from THE NEED FOR A RECOVERY OF PHILOSOPHY, *Human Nature and Conduct*, and *Experience and Nature*, 376–403.

MÜLLER, GUSTAV EMIL. *Amerikanische Philosophie*. Stuttgart: Fr. Frommanns Verlag, 1936. 303 pp.

Dewey, 209–217 *et passim;* second edition, revised and enlarged, 1950: Dewey, 222–228 *et passim*.

———. John Deweys Aesthetik. *Neue Schweitzer Rundschau*, Jan. 1952, IX, 542–549.

MULLER, HERBERT JOSEPH. *Science and Criticism: The Humanistic Tradition in Contemporary Thought*. New Haven: Yale University Press, 1943. xiv, 303 pp.

Dewey, *passim*.

MUNK, ARTHUR W. John Dewey in Retrospect. *Christian Century*, 30 Sept. 1959, LXXVI, 1113–1114.

MURPHY, ARTHUR EDWARD. John Dewey and American Liberalism. *Journal of Philosophy*, 23 June 1960, LVII, 420–436.

Read at the meeting of the American Philosophical Association, Columbia University, 28 Dec. 1959; comments by Gail Kennedy and John Allan Irving, *ib.*, 436–450.

———. John Dewey's Philosophy of Religion. *In* Progressive Education Association, Progressive Education Booklet No. 13, *The Educational Frontier* (Columbus, Ohio, 1939), 26–41.

Delivered at the celebration of Dewey's eightieth birthday in New York, Oct. 1939.

———. Objective Relativism in Dewey and Whitehead. *Philosophical Review*, Mar. 1927, XXXVI, 121–144.

———. *The Uses of Reason*. New York: The Macmillan Company, 1943. 346 pp.

Remarks on Dewey and the pragmatic theory of truth, 86–92.

MURPHY, JAY WESLEY. John Dewey—A Philosophy of Law for Democracy. *Vanderbilt Law Review*, Dec. 1960, XIV, 291–316.

MYERS, CAROLINE E. Should Teachers' Organizations Affiliate with the American Federation of Labor? *School and Society*, 22 Nov. 1919, X, 594–597.

Discussion of an address by Dewey.

MYERS, FRANCIS M. *The Warfare of Democratic Ideals.* [Yellow Springs, Ohio]: The Antioch Press [ᶜ1956]. 261 pp.

NAGANO, YOSHIO. [*The Social Philosophy of John Dewey.*] Tokyo: Shunjusha, Inc., 1960.

In Japanese.

———. [*A Systematic Study in John Dewey's Educational Theory.*] Tokyo, 1919. v.p.

In Japanese.

NAGEL, ERNEST. Pure Science and Gross Experience. *New Republic,* 17 Oct. 1949, CXXI, xvi, 20–23.

———. *Sovereign Reason and Other Studies in the Philosophy of Science.* Glencoe, Illinois: The Free Press [ᶜ1954]. 315 pp.

Includes DEWEY'S THEORY OF NATURAL SCIENCE (101–117) from *John Dewey: Philosopher of Science and Freedom* (1950); DEWEY'S RECONSTRUCTION OF LOGICAL THEORY (118–140) from *The Philosophy of the Common Man* (1940); REFLECTIONS ON SOME LOGICAL AND METAPHYSICAL THEMES IN DEWEY'S PHILOSOPHY (141–149); and reviews from the *Journal of Philosophy.*

NAJARIAN, PERGROUHI HAROUTUN. The Education Frontier in Lebanon; and John Dewey's Philosophy of Education.

Thesis (M.S.), Cornell University, 1950.

NASH, J. V. The Ethics of John Dewey. *Open Court,* Sept. 1924, XXXVIII, 527–538.

NASLUND, ROBERT A. The Impact of the Power Age on the Community-School Concept. National Society for the Study of Education, *Yearbook 52,* part 2 (1953), 251–264.

Dewey's contribution, 257–259.

NASSIF, RICARDO. John Dewey (1859–1952). *Humanitas* (Tucumán), 1953, I, i, 417–419.

———. *En el Centenario de John Dewey* (with Gustavo F. J. Cirigliano). [Buenos Aires:] Departamento de Ciencias de la Educación, Instituto de Pedagogía; Facultad de Humanidades y Ciencias de la Educación, Universidad Nacional de La Plata, 1961. 63 pp.

Contents. Ricardo Nassif, El humanismo pedagógico de John Dewey —Gustavo F. J. Cirigliano, Actualidad del pensamiento pedagógico de John Dewey—Bibliografía de John Dewey por Susana Beatriz Molina Carlotti y Martha Campayo de Galaburrí.

NATANSON, MAURICE. *The Social Dynamics of George H. Mead.* Introduction by Horace M. Kallen. Washington: Public Affairs Press [1956]. 102 pp.

Dewey, *passim.*

NATHANSON, JEROME. John Dewey: American Radical. *Nation,* 22 Oct. 1949, CLXIX, 392–394.

———. John Dewey: Democracy as Reconstruction. In his *Forerunners of Freedom: The Reconstruction of the American Spirit* (Washington: American Council on Public Affairs [ᶜ1941]), 116–154.

Reviewed in *Journal of Philosophy,* 14 Aug. 1941, XXXVIII, 474–475 (Herbert Wallace Schneider).

———. *John Dewey: The Reconstruction of the Democratic Life.* New York: Charles Scribner's Sons, 1951. ix, 127 pp. (Twentieth Century Library.)

Reviewed in *The Humanist,* May-June 1952, XII, 138 (Edward William Strong); *Journal of Philosophy,* 3 July 1952, XLIX, 478–479 (George Dykhuizen); *New York Herald Tribune Books,* 11 Nov. 1951 (Joseph Leon Blau); *Saturday Review of Literature,* 5 Jan. 1952, XXXV, i, 16 (Brand Blanshard).

NAUMBURG, MARGARET. A Challenge to John Dewey. *Survey,* 15 Sept. 1928, LX, 598–600.

"She challenges both the philosophy and the practice of the project method as they have been worked out by American educators under John Dewey's leadership."

———. The Crux of Progressive Education. *New Republic,* 25 June 1930, LXIII, 145–147.

NEFF, FREDERICK C. John Dewey and the Luce Ends of Education. *Phi Delta Kappan,* Dec. 1958, XL, 130–131.

Reply to THE DEEPER PROBLEMS IN EDUCATION, editorial in *Life,* 31 Mar. 1958, XLIV, iii, 32.

———. Our Debt to John Dewey. *California Journal of Secondary Education,* Dec. 1949, XXIV, 466–471.

———. The Status of John Dewey in American Educational Thought: A Current Appraisal. University of Leeds, Institute of Education, *Researches and Studies,* xvii, Jan. 1958, 16–23; also in Philosophy of Education Society, *Proceedings of 14th Annual Meeting,* 1958.

NEILL, THOMAS P. Democracy's Intellectual Fifth Column, *Catholic World*, May 1942, CLV, 151–155.

NEUMANN, HENRY. *Education for Moral Growth*. New York: D. Appleton and Company, 1924.

Dewey, *passim*.

NEW INTERNATIONAL ENCYCLOPEDIA. 2d ed. New York: Dodd, Mead & Co., 1914 ff.

Dewey, VI, 749–750. See also "Empiricism," VII, 710; "Instrumentalism," XII, 232–233; "Pragmatism," XIX, 151–152.

NEW LEADER. Salute to John Dewey. Special Section Commemorating John Dewey's Ninetieth Birthday. *New Leader*, 22 Oct. 1949, Vol. XXXII, 8 pp.

Contains editorial comments, highlights of Dewey's life, articles by Sidney Hook, Albert Coombs Barnes, Max Carl Otto, Milton Ridvas Konvitz and Horace Snyder Fries (*qq.v.*), a selected bibliography, and greetings from President Truman, Vice-Premier Giuseppe Saragat of Italy, Cyril Edwin Mitchinson Joad, Lady Allen of Hurtwood, British Ambassador Oliver Franks, Arnold Toynbee, James Bryant Conant, Director Chih Meng of the China Institute of America, President Omer Celal Sarc of the University of Istanbul, Jawaharlal Nehru, and the Senate of the University of Leiden.

NEW REPUBLIC. John Dewey: An Appraisal of His Contributions to Philosophy, Education, and the Affairs of Men. Presented on the Occasion of His Ninetieth Birthday. *New Republic*, 17 Oct. 1949, CXXI, xvi, 10–39.

Papers by Gordon Willard Allport, Clarence Edwin Ayres, George Boas, Boyd Henry Bode, Irwin Edman, Y. H. Krikorian, Ernest Nagel, Ralph Barton Perry, and Wilmon Henry Sheldon, *qq.v.*

Statements by Jan Christiaan Smuts, Charles Seymour, Alexander Meiklejohn, Luther Harris Evans, Joseph Wood Krutch, William Heard Kilpatrick, Frederick Burkhardt, Lucy Sprague Mitchell, Harold Taylor, and Robert Hillyer.

Reviewed in *Modern Schoolman*, May 1950, XXVII, 319–320 (James Collins).

NEW SCHOLASTICISM. John Dewey 1859–1952. Editorial in *The New Scholasticism*, 1952, XXVI, 391–392.

NEW YORK TIMES. John Dewey: American [Editorial]. *New York Times*, 20 Oct. 1949.

———. John Dewey and His Creed [Editorial]. *Ib.*, 3 June 1952.

———. John Dewey at 85 [Editorial]. *Ib.*, 20 Oct. 1944.

——. Philosopher of Americanism [Editorial]. *Ib.*, 20 Oct. 1939.

NEW YORK WORLD. John Dewey and Our Time [Editorial]. New York *World*, 20 Oct. 1929.

Reprinted in *Teachers College Record*, Dec. 1929, XXXI, 211–212.

NEWBURY, DOROTHY JUNE. The Idea of Freedom in Dewey and Some Consequences of the Idea for Educational Practice.

Thesis (A.M.), University of Chicago, 1949.

——. A Search for the Meaning of Discipline in John Dewey's Theory of Growth. *Educational Theory*, Oct. 1956, VI, 236–245.

——. A Theory of Discipline Derived from Dewey's Theory of Inquiry. *Ib.*, Apr. 1957, VII, 102–111.

——. A Theory of Discipline Developed from Dewey's Theory of Growth in Explicit Relationship to His Theory of Inquiry.

Thesis (PH.D.), University of Chicago, 1953.

NEWLON, JESSE HOMER. John Dewey's Influence in the Schools. *School and Society*, 23 Nov. 1929, XXX, 691–700.

Address delivered at the Dewey Seventieth Birthday Celebration, Horace Mann Auditorium, Teachers College, 18 Oct. 1929. Reprinted in *Teachers College Record*, Dec. 1929, XXXI, 224–238, *Journal of the National Education Association*, Dec. 1929, XVIII, 283–285, and in *John Dewey, the Man and His Philosophy* (Cambridge, 1930), 37–63.

——. John Dewey, Dean of Educational Theorists. (With Lester Hancil Dix.) *School Executives Magazine*, Dec. 1933, LIII, 99–101, 119.

NEWSWEEK. Death of Dewey. *Newsweek*, 9 June 1952, XXXIX, xxiii, 58.

——. John Dewey at 90. *Ib.*, 24 Oct. 1949, XXXIV, xvii, 80.

——. Married. *Ib.*, 23 Dec. 1946, XXVIII, xxvi, 52.

——. Philosopher at 80 Objects to Another Canonization. *Ib.*, 23 Oct. 1939, XIV, xvii, 33–34.

NOONAN, JOSEPH FRANCIS. The Practical Significance of Dewey's Educational Ideals.

Thesis (A.M.), New York University, 1925.

NØRSTEBØ, SIGURD. *John Deweys oppsedingsteori: opphav og ut-vikling.* (Skrifter utg. av Noregs lærarhøgskule, 1.) [Trond-heim, 1953.] 317 pp.

NORTHROP, FILMER STUART CUCKOW. The Comparative Philos-ophy of Comparative Law. *Cornell Law Quarterly,* Summer 1960, XLV, 617–658.
Dewey, *passim.*

———. The Initiation of Inquiry. In his *The Logic of the Sciences and the Humanities* (New York: The Macmillan Company, 1947), 1–18.

———. The Mediational Approval Theory of Law in American Legal Realism. *Virginia Law Review,* Apr. 1958, XLIV, 347–363.
Dewey, *passim.*

NÜCHTER, FRIEDRICH. Von der individualistischen zur sozialen Demokratie—ein Problem der amerikanischen Pädogogik: John Deweys soziale Pädagogik. *Jahrbuch des Vereins für wissenschaftliche Pädagogik,* XLVII (1915), 15–74.
Title from *Bibliographie der deutschen Zeitschriftenliteratur,* XXXVI, 83.

OCCHIO, GIUSEPPE. *Umanesimo americano anti-deweyano. Uno studio su Irving Babbit* [sic] *con un'appendice su R. M. Hutch-ins e W. Lippmann.* (Pontificum Athenæum Salesianum. Fa-cultas Philosophica. Theses ad lauream, n. 22.) Torino: P. A. S., 1955. xxix, 243 pp.
Dewey, xv–xvi.

O'CONNELL, GEOFFREY. *Naturalism in American Education.* Washington: Catholic University of America, 1936. xi, 2 10 pp.
Thesis (PH.D.), Catholic University of America, 1936.
Dewey, 104–138.

O'CONNOR, JOHN JOSEPH. Dewey's Logical Theory: Some Clari-fications and Criticisms.
Thesis (PH.D.), Columbia University, 1952.

———. Indeterminate Situation and Problem in Dewey's Logi-cal Theory. *Journal of Philosophy,* 3 Dec. 1953, L, 753–770.

OESTERREICH, TRAUGOTT KONSTANTIN. *Die Philosophie des*

Auslandes vom Beginn des 19. Jahrhunderts bis auf die Gegenwart. (Ueberwegs Grundriss der Geschichte der Philosophie, Bd. 5.) Berlin: E. S. Mittler & Sohn, 1928.
DER REALISTISCHE PRAGMATISMUS: JOHN DEWEY, pp. 401–403.

O'FARRELL, JOHN J. A Thomistic Evaluation of the Epistemological and Ontological Bases of John Dewey's Instrumentalist Philosophy.
Thesis (PH.D.), Fordham University, 1951.

O'GRADY, FRANCIS THOMAS. The Theory of Good in the Philosophy of John Dewey.
Thesis (PH.D.), University of Ottawa, 1950.

O'HARA, JAMES HENRY. *The Limitations of the Educational Theory of John Dewey.* Washington, 1929. vii, 113 pp.
Thesis (PH.D.), Catholic University of America.

OKADA, GOSAKU. The Significance of Dr. John Dewey's Philosophy for Religion.
Thesis (A.M.), New York University, 1931.

OKUN, SID. *John Dewey: A Marxian Critique.* [Chicago]: Revolutionary Workers League, U.S. [1942]. 25 pp.

OLSEN, STANLEY L. The Educational Philosophy of Dr. John Dewey: Exposition and Evaluation.
Thesis (A.M.), New York University, 1933.

O'MEARA, WILLIAM. John Dewey and Modern Thomism: Introductory Notes. *Thomist,* Jan. 1943, V, 308–318.

OMOHUNDRO, ARTHUR T. "Habit" in Peirce, Dewey, and Mead. *Philosophy: A Student Journal at the University of Chicago,* Winter 1961, I, iii, 55–61.

ONUFRIO, SALVATORE. John Dewey e la storia come esperienza e come indagine. *Rivista critica di storia della filosofia,* Oct.-Dec. 1951, VI, 402–408.

O'REILLY, FRANCIS JOSEPH. A Presentation and Criticism of John Dewey's Moral Reconstruction.
Master's thesis, St. Louis University, 1933.

O'ROURKE, EDWARD W. John Dewey, Champion of Democracy or Decadence? *Homiletic and Pastoral Review,* Sept. 1951, LI, 1080–1086.

ORTINEZ, JAMES. A Comparison between St. Joseph Calasanctius and John Dewey.
Master's thesis, Immaculate Heart College (Los Angeles), 1958.

OTTERNESS, OMAR GORDON. Human Nature as Interpreted by John Dewey and Reinhold Niebuhr.
Thesis (A.M.), University of Illinois, 1944.

OTTO, MAX CARL. Contemporary Thought around the World: John Dewey. *Christian Register*, 11 Jan. 1934, CXIII, 19–21.

———. Dewey and "Experience." *New Leader*, 22 Oct. 1949.

———. Instrumentalism. *In* Edward Leroy Schaub, ed., *Philosophy Today* (Chicago: The Open Court Publishing Company, 1928), 37–53.

———. Mr. Dewey and Religion. *New Humanist*, Apr. 1935, VIII, 41–47.

———. Philosopher of a New Age. *Social Frontier*, May 1937, III, 230–233; John Dewey's Philosophy, *ib.*, June 1937, 264–267.
Read at the New Orleans meeting of the John Dewey Society, 21 Feb. 1937.

———. The Social Philosophy of John Dewey. *Journal of Social Philosophy*, Oct. 1939, V, 43–60.

OU TSUIN-CHEN. *La doctrine pédagogique de John Dewey*. Paris: Les presses modernes, 1931. 280 pp.
Thesis (DR. DE L'UNIVERSITÉ), Paris.
Includes French translation of *My Pedagogic Creed*, 255–272.
Second edition with Introduction by Luther Harris Evans. (Bibliothèque d'histoire de la philosophie.) Paris: Vrin, 1958. 280 pp.
Translation. Spanish by A. Jover Peralta (*Enciclopedia de educación*, Montevideo, Uruguay, July-Dec. 1932).

———. A Re-evaluation of the Educational Theory and Practice of John Dewey. *Educational Forum*, Mar. 1961, xxv, 277–300.

OUTLOOK. Dr. Dewey's Third Party. *Outlook*, 7 Jan. 1931, CLVII, 10.

OUYANG, TZE-HSIANG. John Dewey's Concept of Experience in Its Relation to Education.
Thesis (PH.D.), University of Toronto, 1942.

PACI, ENZO. Giovanni Dewey. In his *Il pensiero scientifico contemporaneo* (Firenze: Sanoni, 1950), 195–210.

———. Moby Dick e la filosofia americana. *Aut Aut* 2, Mar. 1951, 97–120.

———. *Il nulla e il problema dell'uomo*. Torino: Taylor, 1950. Dewey, 145–146.

———. Il problematicismo positivo di John Dewey. *Il pensiero critico*, Oct. 1950, 66–73.

———. Sull'estetica di Dewey. *Aut Aut* 10, July 1952, 317–330.

PADELLARO, NAZARENO. John Dewey. In *Il lavoro produttivo nella carta della scuola* (Messina: G. D'Anna, 1940), 119–133.

PADOVER, SAUL KUSSIEL. The American Pragmatist: John Dewey. In his *The Genius of America* (New York: McGraw-Hill Book Company, 1960), 271–285.

PAELIAN, GARABED H. Nicholas Roerich's Contribution to Modern Life and Education.
Doctoral thesis, New York University, 1936.
Compares Roerich's philosophy of education with Dewey's.

PALA, ALBERTO. La logica di J. Dewey. Cagliari, Italy, Università. Facoltà di lettere e filosofia e di magistero. *Annali*, 1957. 182 pp.

———. Metafisica e a priori in John Dewey. *Ib.*, 1952, XIX, i, 107–126.

PALMER, DAVID JAMES. An Analysis of John Dewey's Conception of Democracy.
Thesis (A.M.), University of Illinois, 1953.

PALMER, LEWIS C. A Study of John Dewey's Application of Scientific Method to Social Problems.
Thesis (PH.M.), University of Wisconsin, 1934.

PAN AMERICAN UNION. DIVISION OF PHILOSOPHY, LETTERS, AND SCIENCES. *John Dewey en sus noventa años*. (La filosofia en America, 1.) Washington: Unión Panamericana [1949]. 45 pp.
Contents. John Dewey, por Aníbal Sánchez Reulet—Autobiografía filosófica, por John Dewey [Spanish translation of FROM ABSOLUTISM TO EXPERIMENTALISM (1930)]—Bibliografía—John Dewey en sus noventa años [abstracts in Spanish of essays and articles published in commemoration of Dewey's ninetieth birthday].

Reviewed in *The Humanist*, Nov.-Dec. 1950, X, 278 (Van Meter Ames).

PAP, ARTHUR. On the Meaning of Universality. *Journal of Philosophy*, 16 Sept. 1943, XL, 505–514.

PAPE, LESLIE MANOCK. The Naturalistic Ethics of John Dewey. Thesis (PH.D.), University of Chicago, 1930.

PARDINAS, FELIPÉ, S.J. A Bogotá Jesuit Philosopher Discusses Basic Controversy in North American Pedagogy. Excerpts in *Catholic Educational Review*, Oct. 1945, XLIII, 490–492.

PARK, JOE. Experience in Contemporary Education. I. The Development of the Conception of Experience in Philosophy and Education (*Educational Theory*, July 1957, VII, 207–215). II. Dewey's Concept of Experience (*ib.*, Oct. 1957, VII, 269–275, 280). III. The Modification of Dewey's Viewpoint (*ib.*, Jan. 1958, VIII, 8–16).

————. Three Views of the Problem of Instruction. *Social Studies*, Feb. 1961, LII, 54–58.

PARKER, DeWITT HENRY. Discussions of John Dewey's SOME QUESTIONS OF VALUE. *In* Ray Lepley, ed., *Value: A Cooperative Inquiry* (New York: Columbia University Press, 1949), 223–244.

PARKES, HENRY BAMFORD. John Dewey. *Southern Review*, Autumn 1936, II, 260–278.

Reprinted in his *The Pragmatic Test: Essays on the History of Ideas* (San Francisco: The Colt Press [°1941]), 95–119.

PARKINS, IVAN WORTH. John Dewey: Freedom as Intellectual Participation.

Thesis (PH.D.), University of Chicago, 1955.

PARSONS, HOWARD LEE. Dewey's Religious Thought: The Challenge of Evolution. *Journal of Philosophy*, 2 Mar. 1961, LVIII, 113–121.

————. The Meaning and Significance of Dewey's Religious Thought. *Journal of Religion*, July 1960, XL, 170–190.

PASCH, ALAN. Dewey and the Analytical Philosophers. *Journal of Philosophy*, 8 Oct. 1959, LVI, 814–826.

A slightly revised version of a paper read before the Dewey Centennial meeting of the Conference on Methods in Philosophy and the Sciences, New School for Social Research, 24 May 1959.

PASCUAL, RICARDO R. The Pragmatism of John Dewey. *Philippine Social Science Review*, June 1937, IX, 142–156.

PASSMORE, JOHN. *A Hundred Years of Philosophy*. London: Gerald Duckworth & Co. Ltd. [1957]. 523 pp.

Dewey, 117–121, 172–174, *et passim*.

PATTERSON, EDWIN WILHITE. John Dewey and the Law: Theories of Legal Reasoning and Valuation. *American Bar Association Journal*, Aug. 1950, XXXVI, 619–622, 699–701.

Reprinted in Sidney Hook, ed., *John Dewey, Philosopher of Science and Freedom* (1950), 118–133.

———. *Jurisprudence: Men and Ideas of the Law*. Brooklyn: Foundation Press, 1953. 649 pp.

See JOHN DEWEY: INSTRUMENTAL REASONING (486–494), JOHN DEWEY: SCIENTIFIC ETHICS (494–500) *et passim*.

PAUL, GEORGE CASE. A Comparison of the Educational Philosophies of Plato and John Dewey.

Master's thesis, Temple University, 1929.

PEEL, JAMES CLAUDIUS. A Comparative Study of the Educational Theories of Lester F. Ward and John Dewey.

Thesis (PH.D.), New York University, 1944.

——— et al. *Some Interpretations of John Dewey's Educational Philosophy*. (F. S. C. Bulletin, LXVII, 1.) Lakeland, Fla.: Florida Southern College [1951]. 31 pp.

Contents. Many of Dewey's Educational Reforms Have Become Accepted Procedure, by James Claudius Peel—Thinking with John Dewey, by Robert A. Chapman—The Religious, by Grace de Casterline—John Dewey as a Moral Philosopher, by Robert MacGowan—What John Dewey Means by Habit, by Ludd Myrl Spivey.

PEGIS, ANTON CHARLES. Man and the Challenge of Irrationalism. *In* J. M. Corrigan and G. B. O'Toole, eds., *Social Aspects of the Race Problem, A Symposium* (New York: Barnes & Noble, Inc., 1944), 67–93.

"In the pages that follow Professor Pegis explores the meaning and implications of Dewey's *anti-intellectualist* philosophy of education." EDITOR'S NOTE, p. 69.

PEIRCE, CHARLES SANTIAGO SANDERS. To John Dewey, on the Nature of Logic. In his *Collected Papers* VIII (Cambridge: Harvard University Press, 1958), 180–184.

Letters written to Dewey in 1904 and 1905.

PELL, ORLIE ANNA HAGGERTY. Value-Theory and Criticism. New York, 1930. 81 pp.

Thesis (PH.D.), Columbia University.

Discussion of the value-theories of David Wight Prall, Ralph Barton Perry and John Dewey.

PEPPER, STEPHEN COBURN. The Concept of Fusion in Dewey's Aesthetic Theory. *Journal of Aesthetics and Art Criticism*, Dec. 1953, XII, 169–176.

Reprinted in his *The Work of Art* (Bloomington: Indiana University Press, 1955).

———. *The Sources of Value*. Berkeley and Los Angeles: University of California Press, 1958. xiv, 732 pp.

Dewey, *passim*.

PERLMUTTER, OSCAR WILLIAM. Some Aspects of the Political Philosophy of John Dewey.

Thesis (A.M.), University of Chicago, 1949.

PERRY, RALPH BARTON. *Characteristically American*. New York: Alfred A. Knopf, 1949. x, 162, v. pp.

Five lectures delivered on the William Wilson Cook Foundation at the University of Michigan, Nov.-Dec. 1948.

Dewey, *passim*.

———. The Influence of a First-Hand Mind. *New Republic*, 17 Oct. 1949, CXXI, xvi, 11–14.

German translation with the title JOHN DEWEY, *Die Amerikanische Rundschau*, Dec. 1949–Jan. 1950, VI, xxviii, 43–49.

———. James and Dewey. In his *The Thought and Character of William James* (Boston: Little, Brown, and Company, 1935), II, 514–533.

Includes ten letters written by Dewey to James between 1891 and 1909.

———. *Philosophy of the Recent Past; an Outline of European and American Philosophy since 1860*. New York: Charles Scribner's Sons [°1926]. viii, 230 pp.

Dewey, 194–195.

———. *Present Philosophical Tendencies; a Critical Survey of Naturalism, Idealism, Pragmatism, and Realism, together with a Synopsis of the Philosophy of William James.* New York: Longmans, Green and Co. [°1912]. xv, 383 pp.
Dewey, *passim.*

PERSONS, STOW SPAULDING. *American Minds: A History of Ideas.* New York: Henry Holt and Company [°1958]. 467 pp.
Dewey, 394–408.

———. *Evolutionary Thought in America.* New Haven: Yale University Press, 1950. 462 pp.
Dewey, *passim.*

PESCE, DOMENICO. *Il concetto dell'arte in Dewey e in Berenson: saggi sull'estetica americana contemporanea.* (Pensatori antichi e moderni, 50.) Firenze: La Nuova Italia [1956]. xvii, 110 pp.

PETRUZZELIS, NICOLA. L'arte come esperienza nella concezione del Dewey [Abstract]. In *Estetica. Atti del VII convegno di studi filosofici cristiani tra professori universitari. Gallarate 1951.* (Padova: Editoria Liviana, 1952), 254–255.

———. Il concetto di ricerca e la struttura del giudizio secondo Dewey. *Rassegna di scienze filosofiche,* 1950, III, ii, 75–91.

———. Filosofia dell'arte. In Appendix of *L'arte come esperienza nella concezione del Dewey* (2d ed. Roma: Mazara, Soc. Ed. Siciliana, 1952, 452 pp.).

———. I valori educativi nel pensiero del Dewey. *Rassegna di scienze filosofiche,* Apr.-June 1952.

PFEUTZE, PAUL EUGENE. *The Social Self.* New York: Bookman Associates [°1954]. 392 pp.
On George Herbert Mead and Martin Buber; Dewey, *passim.*

PHENIX, PHILIP HENRY. John Dewey's War on Dualism: Its Bearing on Today's Educational Problems. *Phi Delta Kappan,* Oct. 1959, XLI, 5–9.

PHILOSOPHY IN AMERICAN EDUCATION. Brand Blanshard, Curt J. Ducasse, Charles W. Hendel, Arthur E. Murphy, Max C. Otto. New York: Harper & Brothers [1945]. 306 pp.
Dewey, *passim.*

PIATT, DONALD AYRES. Immediate Experience. *Journal of Philosophy,* 30 Aug. 1928, XXV, 477–492.

Picco, Iclea. Note sul Dewey in Italia. *Problemi della pedagogia*, 1955, I, 509–515.

Pillsbury, Walter Bowers. John Dewey 1859–1952. National Academy of Sciences of the United States of America, *Biographical Memoirs*, Vol. XXX (New York: Columbia University Press, 1957), 105–124.

Pingel, Martha Mary. The Relation of Morality and Politics to Art as Discussed by Taine, Guyau, Tolstoi, Santayana, and John Dewey.
Thesis (a.m.), Columbia University, 1945.

Pironti, C. La scuola e la società di John Dewey. *Rivista pedagogica*, No. 2, 1911.

Polakov, Walter N. Our Productive Potentialities. *In* Progressive Education Association, Progressive Education Booklet No. 15, *Resources for Building America* (Columbus, Ohio, 1939), 20–32.
Delivered at the celebration of Dewey's eightieth birthday in New York, Oct. 1939.

Pollock, Robert Channon. Process and Experience: Dewey and American Philosophy. *Cross Currents*, Fall 1959, IX, 341–366.
Reprinted with revisions in John Blewett, ed., *John Dewey: His Thought and Influence* (1960), 161–197.

Pottino, Gaetano. *L'analisi sociologica ed il problema della persona nella filosofia di John Dewey*. Palermo: Flaccovio, 1941. 142 pp.

———. *La psicologia della pratica nel pensiero di John Dewey*. Palermo: Flaccovio, 1941.

Prantl, Rudolf. Dewey als Pädagog. *Vierteljahrsschrift für wissenschaftliche Pädagogik*, Hefte 2, 3, 4, 1925.
Bibliography at the end.

Pratt, James Bisset. Truth and Ideas. *Journal of Philosophy*, 27 Feb. 1908, V, 122–131.

———. *What Is Pragmatism?* New York: The Macmillan Company, 1909, xiii, 256 pp.
Dewey, *passim*.

PRETI, GIULIO. Dewey e la filosofia della scienza. *Rivista critica di storia della filosofia*, Oct.-Dec. 1951, VI, 286–303.

———. Dewey e la crisi del mondo americano. Introduction to his translation of Dewey's *Problems of Men* (Milano, 1950).

———. La ricostruzione filosofica della società nel pensiero di J. Dewey. *Studi filosofici*, Jan.-Apr. 1949, X, i, 36–74.

PRICE, KINGSLEY BLAKE. American Thinking: Some Doctrines of John Dewey. *1957 Year Book of Education* (London and Cleveland), 52–64; *Cross Currents*, Fall 1958, VIII, 334–344.

RABY, JOSEPH MARY, SISTER. *A Critical Study of the New Education*. Washington: Catholic University of America, 1932. xi, 123 pp.

Thesis (PH.D.), Catholic University of America

RADER, MELVIN MILLER. The Way of the Pragmatist: John Dewey. In his *The Enduring Questions: Main Problems of Philosophy* (New York: Henry Holt and Company [ᶜ1956]), 134–156.

Text of Dewey's essay, THE INFLUENCE OF DARWINISM ON PHILOSO-PHY, with commentary and criticism.

———. Morality Based on Experimental Logic. *Ib.*, 421–435.

Text of Dewey's chapter, RECONSTRUCTION IN MORAL CONCEP-TIONS, from *Reconstruction in Philosophy*, with commentary and criticism; reprinted in Edward Harry Madden, ed., *The Structure of Scientific Thought: An Introduction to the Philosophy of Science* (Boston: Houghton Mifflin Company [ᶜ1960]), 358–362, with the title COMMENT ON DEWEY'S ETHICAL VIEWS.

RADLOW, SYDNEY S. Contrasting Conceptions of the Social Function of the Public Schools in the Period between the Two World Wars.

Report (ED.D.), Teachers College, 1948.

RAGGIUNTI, RENZO. Criterio transazionale e criterio trascendentale. *Giornale critica della filosofia italiana*, 1960, XXXIX, 391–407.

———. Due possibili criteri di interpretazione del linguaggio filosofico di J. Dewey. *Rivista di filosofia*, July 1960, LI, 335–342.

———. Esperienza artistica e esperienza scientifica nel pensiero di John Dewey. *Filosofia*, 1960, XI, 69–92.

RAGUSA, THOMAS JOSEPH. *The Substance Theory of Mind and Contemporary Functionalism.* Washington: Catholic University of America, 1937. viii, 101 pp.

Thesis (PH.D.), Catholic University of America.

"A critical estimate of the theory of mind in the philosophy of Thomas Aquinas in its relation to the theories of mind in Aristotle and in the functionalism of John Dewey."

RAMOS, SAMUEL. La estética de John Dewey. *Cuadernos Americanos* (México, D.F.), Sept.-Oct. 1949, VIII, v, 113–130.

RAMSEY, KATHERINE HOLBROOK. A Comparative Study of the Educational Theories of Rousseau and John Dewey.

Master's thesis, Texas Technological College, 1931.

RANDALL, JOHN HERMAN, JR. The Department of Philosophy. *In* Jacques Barzun, ed., *A History of the Faculty of Philosophy, Columbia University* (New York: Columbia University Press, 1957), 102–145.

Dewey, *passim.*

———. Dewey's Contribution to Scientific Humanism. *The Humanist,* June 1959, XIX, 134–138.

Read at the Dewey centennial observance of the American Humanist Association, New York City, 28 Feb. 1959.

———. The Future of John Dewey's Philosophy. *Journal of Philosophy,* 17 Dec. 1961, LVI, 1005–1010.

Informal talk given at the John Dewey Centenary Dinner, Faculty House, Columbia University, 20 Oct. 1959.

———. John Dewey 1859–1952. *Journal of Philosophy,* 1 Jan. 1953, L, 5–13.

———. *Nature and Historical Experience: Essays in Naturalism and in the Theory of History.* New York: Columbia University Press, 1958. viii, 326 pp.

Dewey, *passim.*

———. Salute to John Dewey—"Going on 91." *Survey,* Oct. 1949, LXXXV, 508–510.

RANDALL, MERCEDES IRENE (MORITZ), ed. *Pan, the Logos and John Dewey: A Legend of the Green Mountains,* by Herbert Wallace Schneider; *The Realism of Jane Addams,* by John

Dewey. Philadelphia: Women's International League for Peace and Freedom, 1959. 25 pp.

Reprinted for the John Dewey–Jane Addams Centennial 1959–1960, with an Introduction, JOHN DEWEY AND JANE ADDAMS, by Mrs. Randall.

RAPTON, AVRA. A Naturalistic Esthetics: A Study in the Esthetics of Leo Tolstoy, I. A. Richards and John Dewey.

Thesis (A.M.), New York University, 1953.

RASMUSSEN, CARL C. Some Reactions to Dewey's Philosophy. *Personalist*, July 1922, III, 171–182.

RATNER, JOSEPH. Introduction to John Dewey's Philosophy. In *Intelligence in the Modern World: John Dewey's Philosophy*, edited, and with an Introduction by Joseph Ratner (New York: The Modern Library [°1939]), pp. 3–241.

Chinese translation (Taipeh, Taiwan, 1953).

———. Editor's Note. *Ib.*, pp. 525–566.

A discussion of the Plan to Outlaw War as an application of Deweyan method.

———. John Dewey's Theory of Judgment. *Journal of Philosophy*, 8 May 1930, XXVII, 253–264.

Read before the session on the Philosophy of John Dewey at the meeting of the American Philosophical Association at Columbia University, 30 Dec. 1929.

RATNER, SIDNEY. A. F. Bentley's Inquiries into the Behavioral Sciences and the Theory of Scientific Inquiry. *In* Richard Wirth Taylor, ed., *Life, Language, Law: Essays in Honor of Arthur F. Bentley* (Yellow Springs, Ohio: Antioch Press [°1957]), 26–57.

———. The Development of Dewey's Evolutionary Naturalism. *Social Research*, Summer 1953, XX, 127–154.

Statement of Dewey on William James's *Principles of Psychology* and of James's influence on him, dated 27 June 1946, p. 134 *note*.

———. The Ethics of Democracy: Of John Dewey, Liberalism, and Ends and Means. *The Humanist*, Jan.-Feb. 1955, XV, 15–17.

———. Evolution and the Rise of the Scientific Spirit in America. *Philosophy of Science*, Jan. 1936, III, 104–122.

RATNER, SIDNEY (*continued*). The Evolutionary Naturalism of John Dewey. *Social Research*, Dec. 1951, XVIII, 435–448.

————. Facts and Values in History. *Teachers College Record*, May 1955, LVI, 429–434.

Read at the John Dewey Memorial Program at Teachers College, 20 Oct. 1954.

————. History as Experiment. *Antioch Review*, Fall 1959, XIX, 315–327.

————. The Naturalistic Humanism of John Dewey and Arthur F. Bentley. *The Humanist*, Mar.-Apr. 1954, XIV, 81–87.

Address before the American Humanist Association at Toledo, Ohio, 30 Jan. 1954.

[————, ed.] *The Philosopher of the Common Man. Essays in Honor of John Dewey To Celebrate His Eightieth Birthday.* New York: G. P. Putnam's Sons [°1940]. 228 pp.

Contents. Foreword, by Sidney Ratner—Freedom and Education, by Horace Meyer Kallen—Dewey's Theory of the Nature and Function of Philosophy, by Arthur Edward Murphy—Dewey's Reconstruction of Logical Theory, by Ernest Nagel—Methods in Aesthetics, by Albert Coombs Barnes—The Religion of Shared Experience, by John Herman Randall, Jr.—A Deweyesque Mosaic, by Walton Hale Hamilton—Pragmatism as a Philosophy of Law, by Edwin Wilhite Patterson—The Political Philosophy of Experimentalism, by Hu Shih—Creative Democracy–The Task before Us, by John Dewey.

Papers read before the Conference on Methods in Philosophy and the Sciences, New School for Social Research, New York City, 22 Oct. 1939, together with Dewey's message to his eightieth anniversary dinner, 20 Oct. 1939.

Reviewed in *Journal of Philosophy*, 6 June 1940, XXXVII, 332–334 (James Hayden Tufts).

————. Pragmatism in America. *In* Donald Henry Sheehan and Harold Coffin Syrett, eds., *Essays in American Historiography: Papers Presented in Honor of Allan Nevins* (New York: Columbia University Press, 1960), 193–216.

————. A Salute around the Globe. *Saturday Review*, 21 Nov. 1959, XLII, xlvii, 18, 53.

The John Dewey centennial observances of 1959.

RAVENHILL, ALICE. *Teaching of Domestic Science in the U.S.A.* *In* England. Board of Education. *Special Reports on Educational Subjects*, Vol. XV, part 1.
DEWEY'S VIEWS ON EDUCATION, 7–8.
DEWEY'S VIEWS ON THE TRAINING OF CHILDREN, 143–148.
Quotations in *School Journal*, 30 Sept. 1905, LXXI, 322.

RAYMONT, THOMAS. John Dewey, Educationist and Philosopher. *Journal of Education* (London), Mar. 1950, LXXXII, 144.

READ, WALDEMAR PICKETT. John Dewey's Conception of Intelligent Social Action.
Thesis (PH.D.), University of Chicago, 1947.

RECK, ANDREW JOSEPH. Comments on Dewey, Randall, and Parker concerning Experience and Substance. *Journal of Philosophy*, 16 Mar. 1961, LVIII, 162–166.

REEDER, EDWIN HEWETT. John Dewey and the Activist Movement. National Council for the Social Studies, *Fifth Yearbook*, 1935, pp. 38–49.

REESE, HOBART LAWRENCE. A Methodological Examination of the Ethical Writings of John Stuart Mill and John Dewey.
Master's thesis, Ohio State University, 1949.

REHAGE, KENNETH JOSEPH. John Dewey's Ninetieth Birthday. *Elementary School Journal*, Nov. 1949, L, 127–128.

REID, JOHN R. The Apotheosis of Intelligence. *Journal of Philosophy*, 4 July 1935, XXXII, 375–385.
Reply by Robert Rothman, VALUE AND INTELLIGENCE, *ib.*, 26 Mar. 1936, XXXIII, 176–186.

REINA, MARIA ELENA. Il "circolo" di esperienza e "natura" in Dewey. *Rivista critica di storia della filosofia*, Oct.-Dec. 1951, VI, 398–401.

REINERT, PAUL CLARE, S.J. Deweyism: The Modern Philosophy of Education and the Catholic Student in a Secular University. *Catholic School Journal*, Jan. 1952, LII, 13–16.

RIAN, EDWIN HAROLD. *Christianity and American Education.* San Antonio: The Naylor Co. [ᶜ1949]. 272 pp.
Dewey, *passim*.

RICE, CHARLES A. Our Debt to John Dewey. *Platoon School*, Dec. 1929, III, 149–150.

RICH, JOHN MARTIN. Aspects of the Social Philosophies of John Dewey and Reinhold Niebuhr as They Relate to Education. Thesis, Ohio State University, 1958.

RICHEY, HOMER GILMER. *Die Ueberwindung der Subjektivität in der empirischen Philosophie Diltheys und Deweys.* Göttingen, 1935. 53 pp.
Thesis (DR.PHIL.), Göttingen.

RILEY, WOODBRIDGE. *American Thought, from Puritanism to Pragmatism and Beyond.* New York: Henry Holt and Company, 1923. x, 438 pp.
Dewey, *passim.*

RIMAUD, JEAN. Maria Montessori et John Dewey sont morts. *Études* (Paris), July-Aug. 1952, CCLXXIV, 115.

RIPLEY, EDWARD FRANKLIN. John Dewey's Philosophy of Religion.
Thesis (A.M.), Columbia University, 1953.

RIPPA, SOL ALEXANDER. Epilogue to the John Dewey Centenary. *Education*, Mar. 1960, LXXX, 428–429.

RIPPE, FRITZ. *Die Pädagogik John Deweys unter besonderer Berücksichtigung ihrer erfahrungswissenschaftlichen Grundlage.* Breslau: Druck von Anton Schreiber, 1934. 47 pp.
Thesis (DR.PHIL.), Breslau.

RIVISTA DI FILOSOFIA. John Dewey. *Rivista di filosofia*, July 1952, XLIII, 362–363.

———. Studi su Dewey. *Ib.*, July 1960, LI, iii.
Papers read at a symposium in commemoration of the centenary of Dewey's birth, held at Hotel Regina Elena, Santa Margherita Ligure, Italy, 26 and 27 May 1960. (See NOTIZIE E COMMENTI, pp. 374–377.) Contributions by Egle Becchi, Giovanni Bognetti, Lamberto Borghi, Mario Dal Pra, Franco Fanizza, Carmela Metelli di Lallo, Guido Morpurgo-Tagliabue, Renzo Raggiunti, and Giuseppe Semerari, *qq.v.*

ROBACK, ABRAHAM AARON. *History of American Psychology.* New York: Library Publishers [°1952]. xv, 426 pp.
Dewey, *passim.*

————. *William James: His Marginalia, Personality, and Contribution.* Cambridge, Massachusetts: Sci-Art Publishers [1942]. 336 pp.
Dewey, *passim.*

ROBERTSON, ROBERT E. John Dewey and the Given. *Educational Theory,* July 1958, VIII, 182–185.

ROBET, HENRI. L'École de Chicago et l'instrumentalisme. *Revue de métaphysique et de morale,* July 1913, XXI, 537–575.

ROBINSON, EDGAR STERN. John Dewey's Political Thought.
Thesis (PH.D.), Columbia University, 1953.

ROBINSON, GERTRUDE JOCH. The Relationship between the Theories of Truth and Verification in the Philosophies of Russell and Dewey.
Thesis (A.M.), University of Chicago, 1952.

ROBINSON, JAMES HARVEY. John Dewey and His World. *Harvard Teachers Record,* Feb. 1932, II, 9–16.

ROBINSON, JOSEPH A. A Comparison of the Educational Philosophy of John Dewey with That of Scholasticism.
Doctoral thesis, Boston University, 1944.

ROBISCHON, THOMAS GREGORY. The Historical Development of John Dewey's Ethical Theory.
Thesis (A.M.), Columbia University, 1952.

————. What Is Objective Relativism? *Journal of Philosophy,* 18 Dec. 1958, LV, 1117–1132.

RODOLFI, EUGENIA. A proposito della teoria del valore di Dewey. *Rivista di filosofia neo-scolastica* (Milano), 1957, XLIX, 368–370.

ROE, CHUNGIL YHAN. *The True Function of Education in Social Adjustment; a Comparative Estimate and Criticism of the Educational Teachings of Confucius and the Philosophy of John Dewey, with a View to Evolving a Project for a System of National Education Which Will Meet the Needs of Korea.* Lincoln, Neb., 1927. 60 pp.
Thesis (PH.D.), University of Nebraska.

ROGERS, ARTHUR KENYON. *English and American Philosophy since 1800, a Critical Survey.* New York: The Macmillan Company, 1922. xiv, 468 pp.

Dewey, pp. 388–406.

ROGERS, CAROLYN GRACE AIKEN. John Dewey's Educational Philosophy.

Master's thesis, Leland Stanford, Jr., University, 1956.

ROGERS, DONALD. Pragmatism: The Philosophy of America. *Educational Theory*, Oct. 1959, IX, 207–216, 222.

ROMANELL, PATRICK. A Comment on Croce's and Dewey's Aesthetics. *Journal of Aesthetics and Art Criticism.* Dec. 1949, VIII, 125–128.

Reply by Dewey, AESTHETIC EXPERIENCE AS A PRIMARY PHASE AND AS AN ARTISTIC DEVELOPMENT, *ib.*, Sept. 1950, IX, 56–58.

———. Some Difficulties in John Dewey's Case for a Scientific Ethics. *Actes du XIᵉ Congrès International de Philosophie* (Amsterdam: North-Holland Publishing Co.; Louvain: Editions E. Nauwelaerts, 1952), XIII, 194–199.

Italian translation in *Atti del congresso di studi metodologici promosso dal Centro di studi metodologici, Torino, 17–20 dicembre 1952* (Torino: Edizioni Ramella, 1954).

———. *Toward a Critical Naturalism: Reflections on Contemporary American Philosophy.* New York: The Macmillan Company [°1958]. 88 pp.

See JOHN DEWEY AND THE NATURALISTIC APPROACH TO ETHICS, 39–47, *et passim*.

Previously published (in part) in Italian (Torino, 1953) and in Spanish (1956).

Reviewed in *Les Études philosophiques*, Oct.-Dec. 1958, 562 (Gérard Deledalle).

ROMANINI, L. John Dewey, oggi. *L'indice d'oro*, July-Aug. 1952.

ROODKOWSKY, NIKITA DMITRIEVITCH. Marxism's Appeal for American Intellectuals. *Catholic World*, Oct. 1960, CXCII, 35–39.

ROSENFELD, ISAAC LOUIS. The Conception of Animal Nature in the Philosophy of John Dewey.

Thesis (A.M.), University of Chicago, 1941.

ROSENSTOCK-HUESSY, EUGEN. John Dewey. In his *The Christian Future or The Modern Mind Outrun* (New York: Charles Scribner's Sons, 1946), 43–53.

ROSSI, PIETRO. Storicità e mondo umano in John Dewey. *Rivista di filosofia*, Oct. 1952, XLIII, 399–419.

ROSSI LONGHI, M. L. La pedagogia di Giovanni Dewey. *L'educazione nazionale* (Roma), Oct. 1927, IX, 582–589.

ROTHMAN, ROBERT. Philosopher Dewey at 91. *American Teacher*, Apr. 1951, XXXV, vii, 5–6.
From an article in *The Detroit Teacher*.

———. *The Place of Knowledge in Valuation; a Comparative Study of John Dewey's Philosophy of Value.* [Ann Arbor?], 1936. v, 338 pp.
Thesis (PH.D.), University of Michigan.

RUGG, HAROLD and ANN SHUMAKER. *The Child-Centered School, an Appraisal of the New Education.* Yonkers, N.Y.: World Book Company [°1928]. xiv, 359 pp.
Dewey, *passim*.

RUHLEN, RALPH L. The Relationship of the Economic Order to the Moral Ideal in the Thought of Maritain, Brunner, Dewey, and Temple.
Thesis (PH.D.), Boston University, 1959.

RUNYON, LAURA LOUISA. A Day with the New Education. *Chautauquan*, Mar. 1900, N.S. XXI, 589–592.
At the University of Chicago Elementary School.

RUSPANTINI, NOEMI. *Direttive e tendenze della pedagogia contemporanea (John Dewey e Giorgio Kerschensteiner).* Esercitazioni per il corso di pedagogia, anno academico 1952–1953. Firenze: Soc. Editrice Universitaria [1953?]. 43 pp.

RUSSELL, BERTRAND. John Dewey. In his *A History of Western Philosophy and Its Connection with Political and Social Circumstances from the Earliest Times to the Present Day* (New York: Simon and Schuster [°1945]), 819–828.

———. *My Philosophical Development.* London: George Allen & Unwin Ltd. [1959]. 277 pp.
Dewey, *passim*.

RUSSELL, BERTRAND (*continued*). Pragmatism. *Edinburgh Review*, Apr. 1909, CCIX, 363–388.

Review of William James, *The Will To Believe* and *Pragmatism;* Ferdinand Canning Scott Schiller, *Humanism: Philosophical Essays* and *Studies in Humanism;* John Dewey *et al., Studies in Logical Theory;* and *Essays, Philosophical and Psychological, in Honor of William James.* Reprinted in Russell's *Philosophical Essays* (London, 1910), 87–126.

RUSSELL, JOHN DALE, and CHARLES HUBBARD JUDD. *The American Educational System.* Boston: Houghton Mifflin Company, 1940. xviii, 554 pp.

Dewey, *passim.*

RUSSELL, WILLIAM FLETCHER. Introductory Remarks [written for the celebration of Dewey's ninetieth birthday, Teachers College, 20 Oct. 1949]. *Teachers College Record*, Dec. 1949, LI, 127–128.

SALZMAN, SAMUEL. A Comparison of the Educational Theories of John Dewey and Bertrand Russell.

Thesis (A.M.), New York University, 1930.

SANDERS, WILLIAM JOSEPH. The Hegelian Dialectic in the Educational Philosophy of John Dewey.

Thesis (PH.D.), Yale University, 1935.

Published in part as THE LOGICAL UNITY OF JOHN DEWEY'S EDUCATIONAL PHILOSOPHY, *Ethics*, July 1940, L, 424–440.

SANTAYANA, GEORGE. Three American Philosophers. *American Scholar*, Summer 1953, XXII, 281–284.

Dewey, James, and himself. Apropos of an article, SPIRITO E ORIENTAMENTO DELLA FILOSOFIA IN AMERICA in *Humana* (Milano).

SANTEE, JOSEPH FREDERICK, and WILLARD EARL GIVENS. John Dewey, Educational Philosopher. *Phi Delta Kappan*, Oct. 1952, XXXIV, 9–10.

SARKAR, BENOY KUMAR. *The Political Philosophies since 1905.* Madras: B. G. Paul & Co., 1928. xxvii, 377 pp.

Dewey, 303–304.

SAVAGE, WILLINDA HORTENSE. The Evolution of John Dewey's Philosophy of Experimentalism as Developed at the University of Michigan.

Thesis (ED.D.), University of Michigan, 1950.

———. John Dewey and "Thought News." *In* Claude Eggertson, ed., *Studies in the History of Higher Education in Michigan* (Ann Arbor, 1950), 12–17.

SAVAN, DAVID. John Dewey's Conception of Nature. *University of Toronto Quarterly*, Oct. 1947, XVII, 18–28.

SCHACK, WILLIAM. *Art and Argyrol: The Life and Career of Dr. Albert C. Barnes*. New York: Thomas Yoseloff [°1960]. 412 pp. Dewey, *passim*.

SCHEFFLER, ISRAEL. Educational Liberalism and Dewey's Philosophy. *Harvard Educational Review*, 1956, XXVI, 190–198.

———. Is the Dewey-like Notion of Desirability Absurd? *Journal of Philosophy*, 30 Sept. 1954, LI, 577–582.

SCHILPP, PAUL ARTHUR. John Dewey, America's Typical Voice at the Philosophical Round-Table. In his *Commemorative Essays* (Stockton, Cal. [°1930]), pp. 41–47.

———, ed. *The Philosophy of John Dewey*. (The Library of Living Philosophers, Vol. I.) Evanston and Chicago: Northwestern University, 1939. xv, 708 pp.

A facsimile reprint, with the bibliography extended to 1950 by Muriel Murray, was published by the Tudor Publishing Company, New York, 1951. 733 pp.

Contents. Biography of John Dewey, edited by Jane Mary Dewey. Descriptive and Critical Essays on the Philosophy of John Dewey: Dewey's Conception of Philosophy, by Joseph Ratner; Dewey's Interpretation of the History of Philosophy, by John Herman Randall, Jr.; Dewey's Logical Theory, by Donald Ayres Piatt; Dewey's New *Logic*, by Bertrand Russell; Dewey's Theory of Science, by Hans Reichenbach; Dewey's Epistemology and Metaphysics, by Arthur Edward Murphy; Knowledge and Action in Dewey's Philosophy, by Dominique Parodi; Dewey's Naturalistic Metaphysics, by George Santayana; Dewey's Individual and Social Psychology, by Gordon Willard Allport; Dewey's Ethical Theory, by Henry Waldgrave Stuart; Dewey's Social and Political Philosophy, by George Raymond Geiger; Some Questions on Dewey's Esthetics, by Stephen Coburn Pepper; Dewey's Interpretation of Religion, by Edward Leroy Schaub; The Educational Philosophy of John Dewey, by John Lawrence Childs; Dewey's Influence on Education, by William Heard Kilpatrick; John Dewey and His Influence, by Alfred North Whitehead; The Significance of Dewey's Philosophy, by William Savery. The Philosopher Replies: Experience, Knowledge and Value: A Rejoinder, by John Dewey. Bibliography of the Writings of John Dewey to October 1939.

Reviewed in *Archivio di filosofia*, 1939, ix, 288–289 (R. Miceli); *Boston Transcript*, 30 Dec. 1939; *Ethics*, Apr. 1940, L, 353–359 (William Henry Werkmeister); *Frontiers of Democracy*, 15 Apr. 1940, VI, 221–222 (John R. Reid); *Journal of Philosophy*, 7 Dec. 1939, XXXVI, 691–695 (Sterling Power Lamprecht); *New Republic*, 6 Dec. 1939, CI, 206 (Paul Weiss); *New York Herald Tribune Books*, 5 Nov. 1939 (Ernest Sutherland Bates); *Philosophical Review*, Jan. 1940, XLIX, 69–74 (Gustavus Watts Cunningham); *Philosophy*, Apr. 1940, XV, 207–208 (John Laird); *Religious Education*, Jan. 1940, XXXV, 45–50 (George Albert Coe); *Saturday Review of Literature*, 11 Nov. 1939, XXI, iii, 12–13 (Robert Bierstedt); *Science and Society*, Winter 1940, IV, 120–125 (Howard Selsam); *Studi filosofici*, Jan.-Mar. 1941, II, 93–95 (Antonio Banfi).

The essays by Professors Childs and Kilpatrick were separately printed with a preface and the title, *John Dewey as Educator* [New York, 1939]. 419–473 pp.

SCHINZ, ALBERT. *Anti-pragmatisme: Examen des droits respectifs de l'artistocratie intellectuelle et la démocratie sociale.* Paris: Felix Alcan, 1909. 309 pp.

LE CAS DEWEY, 72–93.

English translation, Boston: Small, Maynard & Co. [ᶜ1909], THE DEWEY CASE, 88–109.

Discussion of *Anti-pragmatisme*, *Journal of Philosophy*, 27 May 1909, VI, 291–295, by Addison Webster Moore; and reply by Schinz, *ib.*, 5 Aug. 1909, VI, 434–438. See Dewey's review of *Anti-pragmatisme* in *Philosophical Review*, July 1909, XVIII, 446–449.

————. Professor Dewey's Pragmatism. *Journal of Philosophy*, 5 Nov. 1908, V, 617–628.

Published in his *Anti-pragmatisme* as LE CAS DEWEY, *see above*.

SCHIPPER, GERRIT. The Empirical Naturalism of John Dewey.

Thesis (PH.D.), Harvard University, 1942.

SCHNEIDER, HERBERT WALLACE. Biographical Memoir: John Dewey (1859–1952). American Philosophical Society, *Year Book 1952* (Philadelphia, 1953), 311–315.

————. Dewey's Eighth Decade. *In* Milton Halsey Thomas, *A Bibliography of John Dewey 1882–1939* (New York : Columbia University Press, 1939), ix–xviii.

———. He Modernized Our Schools. *New York Herald Tribune*, 13 Oct. 1929.

Dewey's influence on American life, particularly on education.

———. *A History of American Philosophy*. New York: Columbia University Press, 1946. xiv, 646 pp.

Dewey, 513–539 *et passim*.

Translations. French by Cl. Simmonet (Paris, 1955); German by Peter Krausser (Hamburg, 1957).

———. John Dewey and His Influence. *New Era* (London), Jan. 1921, II, 136–140.

Translated into Bulgarian and published in *Svobodno Vaspitanie* [Sofia], May-June 1924, II, 266–273.

———. John Dewey's Empiricism. *In* Milton Halsey Thomas and Herbert Wallace Schneider, *A Bibliography of John Dewey*. (New York: Columbia University Press, 1929), ix–xxi.

———. Moral Obligation. *Ethics*, Oct. 1939, L, 45–56.

Dewey, 55 *n*.

———. Pan, the Logos and John Dewey: A Legend of the Green Mountains. *In* Mercedes Irene Moritz Randall, ed., *Pan, the Logos and John Dewey* [etc.] (Philadelphia: Women's International League for Peace and Freedom, 1959), 7–15.

Reprinted from his article, THE PROSPECT FOR EMPIRICAL PHILOSOPHY, in *John Dewey, the Man and His Philosophy* (Cambridge, 1930), 122–134.

SCHNITTKIND, HENRY THOMAS, and DANA ARNOLD SCHNITTKIND. John Dewey—The Architect of a Better World. In their *Living Adventures in Philosophy* (Garden City: Hanover House, 1954), 301–312.

SCHOENCHEN, GUSTAVE G. *The Activity School: A Basic Philosophy for Teachers*. New York: Longmans, Green and Co., 1940. 359 pp.

———. Eduard Burger and John Dewey: A Comparative Study of Burger's Arbeitsschule and Contemporary American Activity Schools as Representative of Dewey's Educational Philosophy.

Doctor's thesis. New York University, 1939.

Abstract in *Journal of Experimental Education*, Sept. 1939, VIII, 51–54.

SCHOOL EXECUTIVES MAGAZINE. Doctor John Dewey, Educator, Philosopher, and Exponent of Social Progress. *School Executives Magazine*, Dec. 1929, XLIX, 172–174.

SCHRADER, GEORGE. Der Pragmatismus von James und Dewey. *Kant-studien*, 1956–57, XLVIII, 425–436.

SCHRICKEL, KLAUS. Ueber den pragmatischen Freiheitsbegriff bei William James, Ralph Barton Perry, John Dewey und Sidney Hook. *Deutsche Zeitschrift für Philosophie* (Berlin), 1957, V, 144–186.

SCHUMACHER, PATRICIA ANNE. The Principle of Continuity in John Dewey's Ethics. Thesis (A.M.), Columbia University, 1947.

SCHWAB, JOSEPH JACKSON. The "Impossible" Role of the Teacher in Progressive Education. *School Review*, Summer 1959, LXVII, 139–159.

———. John Dewey: The Creature as Creative. *Journal of General Education*, Jan. 1953, VII, 109–121.

SCIACCA, MICHELE FEDERICO. *La filosofia oggi*. Milano: Mondadori, 1954. Dewey, 50–53.

SCOTT, FRED NEWTON. John Dewey. *The Castalian*, Published by the Independents of the Senior Class, University of Michigan, 1891, 25–28.

SEARLES, HERBERT LEON. John Dewey and the New Liberalism. *Personalist*, Spring 1947, XXVIII, 161–172.

SEARS, LAURENCE. *Responsibility: Its Development through Punishment and Reward*. New York: Columbia University Press, 1932. ix, 198 pp. Dewey, 59–67.

SEASHOLES, HENRY CRAIG. Dewey or Marx? *Ohio Schools*, Oct. 1948, XXVI, 309.

SEEGERS, ARTHUR JOHN. A Comparative Study of the Views of John Dewey and Martin Luther on Moral Education. Thesis (A.M.), University of Nebraska, 1930.

SELLARS, ROY WOOD. Dewey on Materialism. *Philosophy and Phenomenological Research*, June 1943, III, 381–392. Abstract in *Journal of Philosophy*, 4 Dec. 1941, XXXVIII, 684–685.

————. *Philosophy for the Future: The Quest of Modern Material-ism.* Edited by Roy Wood Sellars, V. J. McGill and Marvin Farber. New York: The Macmillan Company, 1949. 657 pp.

See George Perrigo Conger, PRAGMATISM AND THE PHYSICAL WORLD, 522–543, and Marvin Farber, DEWEY ON IMMEDIATE KNOWLEDGE AND THE NATURE OF THE "GIVEN," 604–609.

————. The Status of Epistemology. *Journal of Philosophy*, 6 Dec. 1917, XIV, 673–680.

Chiefly about Dewey.

SELSAM, HOWARD. *Philosophy in Revolution.* New York: International Publishers, 1957. 160 pp.

Dewey, *passim.*

See Corliss Lamont, "PHILOSOPHY IN REVOLUTION": A DISCUSSION, *above.*

SEMERARI, GIUSEPPE. Il criticismo religioso di Dewey. *Rivista di filosofia*, July 1960, LI, 343–362.

SEN, KRISHNA. A Comparative Study of the Concept of Faith of [Walter Terence] Stace, Dewey, [Søren] Kierkegaard, and St. Thomas Aquinas. *Philosophical Quarterly* (Amalner, India), 1956–57, XXIX, 69–74.

SHAW, WILFRED BYRON, ed. *The University of Michigan: An Encyclopedic Survey.* Ann Arbor: University of Michigan Press, 1941 f.

See DeWitt Henry Parker and Charles B. Vibbert, THE DEPARTMENT OF PHILOSOPHY, iv, 668–679; Walter Bowers Pillsbury, THE DEPARTMENT OF PSYCHOLOGY, iv, 708–714; and Robert Cooley Angell, THE DEPARTMENT OF SOCIOLOGY, iv, 725–730 (1944).

SHEARER, EDNA ASTON. Dewey's Esthetic Theory. *Journal of Philosophy*, 7 and 21 Nov. 1935, XXXII, 617–627, 650–664.

SHEERIN, JOHN B. John Dewey and Christmas, 1950. *Catholic World*, Dec. 1950, CLXXII, 161–165.

SHELDON, WILMON HENRY. *America's Progressive Philosophy.* New Haven: Yale University Press, 1942. 232 pp.

Dewey, *passim.*

————. The Conquest of Dualism. *New Republic*, 17 Oct. 1949, CXXI, xvi, 29–32.

SHEPPARD, DAVID IRVING. A Study of the Resemblances between the Educational Ideas of John Dewey and those of Rousseau, Herbart, and Froebel.

Master's thesis, University of California at Los Angeles, 1942.

SHEVKIN, V. S. [The Pedagogy of J. Dewey in the Service of Contemporary American Reaction.] *Sovyetskaya Pedagogika*, No. 12, 1947.

In Russian. A portion of this book was translated into German as *Die Pädagogik J. Deweys* (Berlin, East Germany: Volk und Wissen Verlag, 1955. 83 pp. Informationsmaterial aus der pädagogischen Literatur der Sowjetunion der Länder der Volksdemokratie, Heft 13).

SHISHKIN, A. F. [Dewey's Theory of Middle-Class Amorality.] *Voprosyi filosofiii*, 1947, ii.

In Russian. Title from Aldo Visalberghi, *John Dewey* (1951, 1961), 8*n*, 114*n*.

SHOEN, HARRIET H., ed. Conference To Celebrate John Dewey's Eightieth Birthday. *School and Society*, 11 Nov. 1939, L, 633–635.

Excerpts from papers read at the conference of the Progressive Education Association, New York City, 20 and 21 Oct. 1939.

SHOUSE, JAMES BLAINE. The Educational Philosophy of John Dewey. *Educational Forum*, May 1947, XI, 429–436.

SIBLEY, WILLIAM MAURICE. An Examination of Dewey's Theory of Knowledge.

Thesis (PH.D.), Brown University, 1943.

SIMEC, SOPHIE, SISTER. Human Nature According to John Dewey. American Catholic Philosophical Association, *Proceedings*, 1955, XXIX, 225–234.

SIMONSON, REBECCA M. The Making of Free, Responsible Citizens. I. Without Lock-Step. *Saturday Review of Literature*, 22 Oct. 1949, XXXII, xliii, 13.

SINGER, IRVING. John Dewey's Theory of Value: A Critical Analysis.

Honors thesis, Harvard College, 1948.

———. The Role of Valuation in John Dewey's Theory of Value: A Critical Analysis.

Francis Bowen Prize Essay, Harvard University, 1951.

SINGER, MARCUS GEORGE. Formal Logic and Dewey's *Logic*. *Philosophical Review*, July 1951, LX, 375–385.

SKEELES, ARTHUR G. The Parent and the Pedagogue on Dewey. *Ohio Schools*, Nov. 1947, XXV, 360–361.

SKOGLUND, HENRY LEONARD. John Dewey's Moral Theory. Thesis (A.M.), University of Chicago, 1953.

SLEEPER, RALPH WILLIAM. Being and Value in the Axiology of John Dewey. American Catholic Philosophical Association, *Proceedings*, 1959, XXXIII, 83–96.

————. Dewey's Metaphysical Perspective: A Note on White, Geiger, and the Problem of Obligation. *Journal of Philosophy*, 4 Feb. 1960, LVII, 100–115.

Reply to interpretations of Dewey in Morton Gabriel White, *Social Thought in America*, and George Raymond Geiger, *John Dewey in Perspective*.

————. John Dewey's Empiricism and the Christian Experience. *Cross Currents*, Fall 1959, IX, 367–378.

————. Metaphysics and the Value Theories of Urban, Dewey, and Perry. Thesis (PH.D.), Columbia University, 1956.

SLOAN, PAUL W. Some Essentials of John Dewey's Progressivism. *Educational Administration and Supervision*, Dec. 1950, XXXVI, 501–504.

SLOCHOWER, HARRY. John Dewey. *Kant-studien*, 1930, XXXV, 398–402.

————. John Dewey: Philosopher of the Possible. *Sewanee Review*, Winter 1944, LII, 151–168.

Reprinted in his *No Voice Is Wholly Lost* (1945), 43–56.

————. John Dewey and Morris R. Cohen. *The Thinker*, Sept. 1931, IV, ii, 33–41.

————. Die Philosophie in den Vereinigten Staaten unter besonderer Berücksichtigung der Gegenwart. In *Reichls philosophischer Almanach*, Bd. 4. Darmstadt, 1927.

SLOSSON, EDWIN EMERY. John Dewey: Teacher of Teachers. *Independent*, 26 Mar. 1917, LXXXIX, 541–544.

Reprinted in his *Six Major Prophets* (1917), 234–275.

SMITH, FERRER, O.P. A Thomistic Appraisal of the Philosophy of John Dewey. *Thomist*, Apr. 1955, XVIII, 127–185.

SMITH, JAMES WARD. Pragmatism, Realism, and Positivism in the United States. *Mind*, Apr. 1952, LXI, 190–208.

———. Propædeutic to Value Theory.

Thesis (PH.D.), Princeton University, 1942.

SMITH, JOHN EDWIN. John Dewey: Philosopher of Experience. *Review of Metaphysics*, Sept. 1959, XIII, 60–78.

Reply by Richard J. Bernstein, DEWEY'S NATURALISM, *ib.*, Dec. 1959, XIII, 340–353.

SMITH, JOHN MILTON. A Critical Estimate of Plato's and Dewey's Educational Philosophies. *Educational Theory*, Apr. 1959, IX, 109 f.

———. John Dewey and Plato: The Foundations of Their Educational Philosophies. *Progressive Education*, Nov. 1949, XXVII, 33–37.

SMITH, MARTIN J., S.J. *John Dewey and Moral Education*. Washington: Guthrie Lithograph Co., 1939. [179 pp.]

"Submitted as a doctoral dissertation to the Philosophical faculty of the University of Munich in December, 1936."

SMITH, PHILIP G. Some Comments on Dewey's Theory of Valuation. Philosophy of Education Society, *Proceedings of 16th Annual Meeting*, 1960.

SMITH, THOMAS VERNOR. Dewey's Theory of Value. *Monist*, July 1922, XXXII, 339–354.

———. *The Philosophic Way of Life in America*. 2d ed. New York: F. S. Crofts & Co., 1943. xiii, 258 pp.

THE SOCIAL WAY OF LIFE WITH JOHN DEWEY AS GUIDE, 81–104.

———. The Promise of American Politics. *In* Progressive Education Association, Progressive Education Booklet No. 15, *Resources for Building America* (Columbus, Ohio, 1939), 5–19.

Delivered at the celebration of Dewey's eightieth birthday in New York, Oct. 1939.

SMITH, VINCENT EDWARD. Dewey's Discovery of the Instrument. In his *Idea-Men of Today* (Milwaukee: Bruce Publishing Company, 1950), 25–54.

SNETHLAGE, JACOB LEONARD. *De Schoolopvoeding in Amerika en het vraagstuk der Kennis*. Amsterdam: H. J. Paris [1923]. 104 pp.
Thesis (DR.PHIL.), Utrecht.
Dewey, *passim*.

SNODDY, E. E. John Dewey and Pragmatism. *College of the Bible Quarterly* (Lexington, Ky.), 1941, XVIII, ii.

SNYDERS, GEORGES. Le pédagogie de Dewey (Pédagogie nouvelle de Charybde en Dewey, II). *La pensée*, May-Aug. 1953, N.S. 48–49, 129–151.

SOSENSKY, IRVING. John Dewey's Theory of Warranted Assertibility.
Thesis (PH.D.), Columbia University, 1955.

SPAIN, CHARLES LYLE. Practical Aspects of John Dewey's Philosophy. *Platoon School*, Dec. 1929, III, 149.

SPERDUTI, G. Critica della educazione e della scuola tradizionale nella pedagogia di J. Dewey. *Nuova rivista pedagogica*, Dec. 1956.

———. Il naufragio della persona nella pedagogia del Dewey. *Ib.*, Dec. 1955, 30–36.

SPIELBERG, PAUL JAY. Problems of an Empirical Theory of Valuation—A Consideration of John Dewey and Charles Stevenson.
Thesis (A.M.), Columbia University, 1949.

SPIRITO, UGO. *Il pragmatismo nella filosofia contemporanea*. Firenze: Vallecchi, 1921. 222 pp.
Dewey, 41–42, 66–72.

STAFFELBACH, HUBERT W. Some Historical Backgrounds of the Principles and Purposes of Progressive Education.
Dewey, 79–82, 305–323.
Master's thesis, Leland Stanford, Jr., University, 1942.

STARR, ISIDORE. John Dewey, My Son, and Education for Human Freedom. *School Review*, Apr. 1954, LXII, 204–212.

STARR, MARK. John Dewey Attacked by the Communists. *Progressive Education*, Nov. 1951, XXIX, 58.

———. The Philosopher as a Man of Action. Editorial in *Saturday Review of Literature*, 22 Oct. 1949, XXXII, xliii, 18.

STEIBEL, GERALD LEE. John Dewey and the Belief in Communication. *Antioch Review*, Sept. 1955, XV, 286–299.

———. John Dewey, the Pragmatic Protagonist. *School Executive*, Dec. 1956, LXXVI, 53–54.

———. John Dewey's Philosophy of Democracy Applied in a Critique of Classical Liberalism.
Thesis (PH.D.), Columbia University, 1951.

STEIN, LUDWIG. "Der Pragmatismus." *Archiv für systematische Philosophie*, 1908, XIV, 143–188.

STEINBERG, CHARLES SIDE. Contemporary Aesthetic Theory: The Philosophy of Art of John Dewey and George Santayana.
Thesis (A.M.), New York University, 1939.

STERNFELD, ROBERT. Contemporary Philosophies of Experience: Philosophic Method in Dewey, Bradley, and Husserl.
Thesis (PH.D.), University of Chicago, 1948.

STEVENSON, CHARLES LESLIE. *Ethics and Language*. New Haven: Yale University Press, 1944. xi, 338 pp.
Dewey, 253–264 *et passim*.

STIERLIN, WILHELM PAUL. Der Begriff der Verantwortung. [Heidelberg], 1950. 170 leaves.
Inaugural dissertation, Heidelberg.
Carbon copy at Library of Congress.

STIERNOTTE, ALFRED. Dewey, Wieman and Marx. *Christian Register*, Feb. 1945, CXXIV, iii, 49–51.

STODDARD, GEORGE DINSMORE. On the Denigration of John Dewey. (The Princeton Unitarian Pulpit.) Princeton: The Unitarian Church of Princeton [1959]. 5 pp. Mimeographed.
Address delivered at the church, 22 Nov. 1959.
Copy in Princeton University Library.

STOLBERG, BENJAMIN. Degradation of American Psychology. *Nation*, 15 Oct. 1930, CXXXI, 395–398.

STORY, M. L. Dewey and Niebuhr: A Brief Juxtaposition. *Educational Theory*, Apr. 1953, III, 182–184.

———. Learning by Thinking. *Science Education*, Dec. 1953, XXXVII, 331–335.
Dewey and experimentalism.

STRAIGHT, WOOD C. Dewey and Our Inefficient Schools. *Brooklyn Daily Eagle*, 15 June 1922.

STRAIN, JOHN PAUL. An Answer to the Misconceptions of John Dewey's Philosophy of Education. *Educational Theory*, Oct. 1959, VIII, 269–274.

STRONG, EDWARD WILLIAM. John Dewey's Humanism: Man Making Himself. Part I. Man and Nature (*The Humanist*, Sept.-Oct. 1950, X, 203–207); Part II. Historical Humanism (*Ib.*, Nov.-Dec. 1950, 257–260).

———. Metaphors and Metaphysics. *International Journal of Ethics*, July 1937, XLVII, 461–471.

STROUT, CUSHING. *The Pragmatic Revolt in American History: Carl Becker and Charles Beard*. New Haven: Yale University Press [ᶜ1958]. 182 pp.

Dewey, *passim*.

SUGGS, WILLIAM A. Comparative Influence of Herbartism and Deweyism upon the Objectives of the Twentieth Century Education.

Master's thesis. Tennessee Agricultural and Industrial University, 1957.

SUITS, BERNARD HERBERT. The Aesthetic Object in Santayana and Dewey.

Thesis (PH.D.), University of Illinois, 1958.

———. Naturalism: Half-Hearted or Broken-Backed? *Journal of Philosophy*. 30 Mar. 1961, LVIII, 169–179.

SÜLEYMAN, ZEKIYE. A Study of the History and Development of Education in Turkey, with Special Emphasis upon the Influence of Professor Dewey's Theories of Education.

Thesis (A.M.), Smith College, 1934.

SUPPAN, A. A. The Making of Free, Responsible Citizens. 3. Participants in Life. *Saturday Review of Literature*, 22 Oct. 1949, XXXII, xliii, 14.

SURVEY. Among Ourselves: Ninetieth Birthday Celebration. *Survey*, Oct. 1949, LXXXV, 506.

———. John Dewey at 85. *Ib.*, Nov. 1944, LXXX, 323.

———. John Dewey in Russia. *Ib.*, 15 Dec. 1928, LXI, 348–349.

———. John Dewey Looks Ahead. *Ib.*, Nov. 1939, LXXV, 344.

SUSKY, JOHN E. How Would Dewey Answer Critics of Dewey-ism? *Phi Delta Kappan*, Oct. 1958, XL, 24–27.

SUTTELL, LLOYD. Intelligence in the Modern World (John Dewey, 1859–1952). *Pedagogia* (Colegia de Pedagogia, Universidad de Puerto Rico), June 1953, I, 70–84.

SWEENEY, FLORENCE. The Making of Free, Responsible Citizens. 2. Learning by Doing. *Saturday Review of Literature*, 22 Oct. 1949, XXXII, xliii, 13–14.

TABB, ANNIE LAURIE. From Pragmatism to the Instrumentalism of John Dewey in Contemporaneous Philosophy; the Course of Pragmatism.
Thesis (A.M.), University of Alabama, 1932.

TAKEDA, K. An Examination of Post-War Japanese Education Based on John Dewey's Theory. *Educational Forum*, Nov. 1961, XXVI, 53–61.

TAMME, ANNE MARY, SISTER. *A Critique of John Dewey's Theory of Fine Art in the Light of the Principles of Thomism*. Washington: Catholic University of America Press, 1956. xi, 131 pp.
Thesis (PH.D.), Catholic University of America.

TARELLO, GIOVANNI. Norma e giuridificazione nella logica di Dewey. *Rivista internazionale di filosofia del diritto* (Milano), 1960, XXXVII, 280–292.

TAYLOR, HAROLD. Modern Education and the Progressive Movement. *Antioch Review*, Sept. 1955, XV, 272–285.

TAYLOR, RICHARD WIRTH, ed. *Life, Language, Law: Essays in Honor of Arthur F. Bentley*. Yellow Springs, Ohio: Antioch Press [ᶜ1957]. xii, 223 pp.
Dewey, *passim*.

TEACHERS COLLEGE RECORD. Some Popular Appraisals of John Dewey. *Teachers College Record*, Dec. 1929, XXXI, 207–223.
Compiled by Clyde Raymond Miller; includes JOHN DEWEY, 70 TODAY: HONORED AS AMERICA'S FOREMOST TEACHER, from the *Springfield* (Mass.) *Union and Republican;* JOHN DEWEY AND OUR TIME, editorial from the New York *World;* JOHN DEWEY—PLATO'S KING, by Harry Elmer Barnes, from the *New York Telegram;* OUR FOREMOST PHILOSOPHER AT SEVENTY, by Irwin Edman, from the *New York Times Magazine;* HE MODERNIZED OUR SCHOOLS, by

Herbert Wallace Schneider, from the *New York Herald Tribune;* JOHN DEWEY AT SEVENTY, by Robert Morss Lovett, from the *New Republic;* JOHN DEWEY, editorial from the *New York Herald Tribune;* JOHN DEWEY, by Scott Buchanan, from *The Nation;* and SEVENTIETH BIRTHDAY OF JOHN DEWEY, by Harry Hansen, from the New York *World.*

TEBALDESCHI, IVANHOE. *Socialità e diritto nel pensiero di John Dewey.* Roma: Editoriale Arte e Storia [1957]. 75 pp.

TEIXEIRA, ANÍSIO. Dewey e a filosofia da educação. *CAPES, Boletim informativo de Campanha Nacional de Aperfeiçoamento de Pessoal de Nível Superior* (Rio de Janeiro), Dec. 1959, No. 85, 1–2.

TENENBAUM, SAMUEL. *William Heard Kilpatrick: Trail Blazer in Education.* New York: Harper & Brothers [°1951]. 318 pp.
Dewey, *passim.*

TERKEL, MEYER. John Dewey's Educational Principles and Contributions to Education in the United States.
Master's thesis, College of the City of New York, 1928.

THAYER, HORACE STANDISH. Critical Notes on Dewey's Theory of Propositions. *Journal of Philosophy,* 27 Sept. 1951, XLVIII, 607–613.
Apropos of Dewey's PROPOSITIONS, WARRANTED ASSERTIBILITY AND TRUTH, *ib.,* 27 Mar. 1941, XXXVIII, 169–186.

———. *The Logic of Pragmatism: An Examination of John Dewey's Logic.* New York: The Humanities Press, 1952. 222 pp.
Thesis (PH.D.), Columbia University.

———. Two Theories of Truth: The Relation between the Theories of John Dewey and Bertrand Russell. *Journal of Philosophy,* 11 Sept. 1947, XLIV, 516–527.
Thesis (A.M.), Columbia University.

T[HAYER], V[IVIAN] T[ROW]. John Dewey's Seventieth Anniversary. *Journal of Educational Research,* Dec. 1929, XX, 373–375.

THOMAS, WENDELL MARSHALL. Anglo-American Views: Dewey; Lloyd Morgan. In his *On the Resolution of Science and Faith* (New York: Island Press [1946]), 72–81.

THOMAS, WENDELL MARSHALL (*continued*). *A Democratic Philosophy*. New York: Correlated Enterprises [1938]. 148 pp.

"An attempt to clarify the goal and method of democracy through a study of John Dewey, Karl Marx, and the classic Hindu philosopher Sankara." PREFACE.

———. Reflections on Dewey's Philosophy. *Journal of Adult Education*, Jan. 1940, XII, 23–25.

THOMPSON, BETTY ANN. Implications of Reflective Thinking to Physical Education: An Interpretation of Dewey and Pragmatism to the Field.

Master's thesis, Ohio State University, 1954.

THORPE, LOUIS P., and ALLEN M. SCHMULLER. *Contemporary Theories of Learning, with Applications to Education and Psychology*. New York: The Ronald Press Company [ᶜ1954]. viii, 480 pp.

Chap. xi, PROBLEM SOLVING: DEWEY'S VIEW OF LEARNING AS EXPERIENCE, 362–383.

THRELKELD, ARCHIE LOYD. Dr. Dewey's Philosophy and the Curriculum. *Curriculum Journal*, Apr. 1937, VIII, 164–166.

TIME. Account Rendered [obituary]. *Time*, 9 June 1952, LIX, xxiii, 47–48.

———. Dewey at 80. *Ib.*, 30 Oct. 1939, XXXIV, xviii, 38–40.

Reprinted in John A. Beckwith and Geoffrey Gainsborough Coope, eds., *Contemporary American Biography* (New York: Harper & Brothers, 1941), 171–173.

———. The Long Shadow of John Dewey. *Time*, 31 Mar. 1958, LXXI, xiii, 44.

———. Perpetual Arriver. *Ib.*, 31 Oct. 1949, LIV, xviii, 35–36.

———. To Moscow. *Ib.*, 4 June 1928, XI, xxiii, 16–17.

TIMES LITERARY SUPPLEMENT (London). Humanism Revisited. *The Times Literary Supplement* (London), 20 Jan. 1961.

On the likenesses of Dewey and Irving Babbitt; an editorial.

TITONE, RENZO. Due libri, due fronti nella pedagogia dell' America contemporanea. *Salesianum*, Apr.-Sept. 1952, XIV, 328–342.

Dewey's *Democracy and Education* and Robert Maynard Hutchins' *The Higher Learning in America*.

————. Nota sull'attivismo pedagogico americano. *Salesianum*, Oct.-Dec. 1948, X, 673–677.

TOFIELD, AARON J. Dewey and Woodbridge on Tradition. New York, 1937.
Thesis (A.M.), Columbia University, 1937.

TORRES, JOSÉ ARSENIO. Philosophic Reconstruction and Social Reform in John Dewey and José Ortega y Gasset.
Thesis (PH.D.), University of Chicago, 1954.

TOWNSEND, HARVEY GATES. *Philosophical Ideas in the United States*. New York: American Book Company [ᶜ1934]. v, 293 pp.
Dewey, 233–250 *et passim*.

TURNER, ROBERT YONGUE. Dewey's and Kant's Classifications of the Arts.
Thesis (A.M.), University of Chicago, 1951.

TURNER, WILLIAM. Pragmatism. *Catholic Encyclopedia* (New York, 1911), XII, 333–338.
Dewey, 334.

TUTTLE, ELBERT PARR, JR. Individualism in Recent American Thought: William James, William Graham Sumner, and John Dewey.
Thesis (A.B.), Princeton University, 1942.

TUTTLE, ROBERT EUGENE. A Comparative Study of Basic Assumptions in the Philosophy of John Dewey.
Thesis (A.M.), Oberlin College, 1934.

ULBRICHT, ROBERT EMIL. A Study of John Dewey's Philosophy of Art.
Thesis (A.M.), University of Illinois, 1953.

ULICH, ROBERT. John Dewey. In his *History of Educational Thought* (New York: American Book Company [ᶜ1945]), 315–336.

————, ed. *Three Thousand Years of Educational Wisdom. Selections from Great Documents*. Second edition enlarged, with new chapters on John Dewey and the Judaic tradition. Cambridge, Massachusetts: Harvard University Press, 1954. 668 pp.
DEWEY 1859–1952 (615–640) includes the editor's comment, FROM ABSOLUTISM TO EXPERIMENTALISM (1930), *My Pedagogic Creed* (1897), and EVOLUTION AND ETHICS (1898).

União Cultural Brasil–Estados Unidos, São Paulo. John Dewey: Bio-bibliografia Comemorative ao 90º Aniversário (1859–1949), Organizada pela "Bibliothéca Thomas Jefferson." São Paulo [195–?]. ii, 7 pp.

Updegraff, Kathryn. History in Dewey's Theory of Education: A Critical Analysis.

Seminar study (A.M. IN ED.), University of California, 1952.

Ushenko, Andrew. Inquiry and Discourse. *Journal of Philosophy*, 29 Aug. 1940, XXXVII, 484–491.

Uyeda, Seiji, ed. *Ronri-Jissho-Shugi: Bunseki-Tetsugaku Kenhyu Ronshu*, Vol. I. Tokyo: Waseda University Press, 1954. 545 pp.

Logical Positivism: Essays in Analytic Philosophy. In Japanese. Includes the following essays on Dewey: Fukukama, J. Dewey's Semantics—Isono, J. Dewey's Theory of Evaluation—Takayagi, J. Dewey's Logic—Teshirogi, J. Dewey's Philosophic Naturalism—Uyeda, J. Dewey's Philosophy and Logical Positivism.

Van Acker, Leonardo. M. [Maurice] Blondel et "L'éducation nouvelle." *Les Études philosophiques*, Apr.-June 1954, N.S. IX, 163–173.

———. O naturalismo di John Dewey. *Revisita Brasiliera de filosofia* (São Paulo), 1957, VII, iv, 408–419.

———. Os valôres na filosofia de John Dewey. In *Anais do III Congreso Nacional di Filosofia* (São Paulo, 1959), 411–418.

Van Dusen, Henry Pitney. The Faith of John Dewey. *Religion in Life*, Winter 1935, IV, 123–132.

Reply by Marion John Bradshaw, A Comment on Van Dusen's Dismissal of Dewey, *Review of Religion*, Nov. 1938, III, 97–100.

Van Schalkwijk, Louis Marthinus Albertus Nicolas. *De soziale Paedagogiek van John Dewey en haar filosofiese Grondslag*. Amsterdam: M. J. Portielje, 1920. iv, 221 pp.

Thesis (DR.PHIL.), University of Amsterdam.

Van Til, William Andrew. John Dewey's Disciples. *Educational Leadership*, Dec. 1949, VII, 201–202.

Van Wesep, Henry B. (i.e., Hendrikus Boeve). *Seven Sages, The Story of American Philosophy: Franklin, Emerson, James,*

Dewey, Santayana, Peirce, Whitehead. New York, London, Toronto: Longmans, Green and Co., 1960. xiii, 450 pp. JOHN DEWEY: PROMETHEAN INSTRUMENTALIST, 181–247.

VASA, ANDREA. Epistemologia e sapere pragmatico nella logica del Dewey. *Rivista critica di storia della filosofia,* Oct.-Dec. 1951, VI, 304–318.

————. *Ricerche sul razionalismo della prassi.* Firenze: Sansoni, 1957. Dewey, vii, xii, 15, 122, 168, 171–192, 195.

VEGAS, FERDINANDO. Il pensiero politico e sociale di John Dewey. *Rivista critica di storia della filosofia,* Oct.-Dec. 1951, VI, 328–341.

VENTURA, LUIGI. A proposito di John Dewey. *Nuova rivista pedagogica,* 1952, II.

VERMONT CYNIC. John Dewey, Philosopher and Educator [University of] *Vermont Cynic,* 2 Nov. 1949, LXVII, xxvi, 2. The same issue includes UVM's FAVORITE ALUMNUS JOHN DEWEY FETED BY STUDENTS, FACULTY, by David Newhall, with interview (p. 1), and NOONTIME RECEPTION FOR JOHN DEWEY (p. 2).

VERRA, VALERIO, Naturalismo umanistico e sperimentale di John Dewey. *Filosofia,* Apr. 1950, I, 198–227.

VERSIANI VELLOSO, ARTHUR. Dewey e Santayana. *Kriterion,* 1953, VI, 220–225.

VESCOVINI, GRAZIELLA FEDERICI. La fortuna di John Dewey in Italia. *Rivista di filosofia,* Jan. 1961, LII, 52–96.

VIDARI, G. La pedagogia in Europa ed in America. *Annuario dei diritti della scuola* (Roma), 1931.

VILLEMAIN, FRANCIS TROWBRIDGE. Dewey and the Critical Faculty. *Saturday Review,* 21 Nov. 1959, XLII, xlvii, 26, 52.

————. Frontiers for an Experimentalist Philosophy of Education (with Nathaniel L. Champlin). *Antioch Review,* Fall 1959, XIX, 345–359.

————. The Qualitative Character of Intelligence. Report (ED.D.), Teachers College, 1952.

VIOLO, EVALDO. Il "religioso" di Dewey. *Aut Aut,* 1960, 54–60.

VISALBERGHI, ALDO. *Esperienza e valutazione.* Torino: Taylor Editore, 1958. 214 pp.
Dewey, 132 f.

————. Forma logica e contenuto empirico negli enunciati valutativi. I. La logica degli imperativi e delle norme (*Rivista di filosofia,* Oct. 1956, XLVII, 424–453); II. Valutazione e "transazione" (*Ib.,* Oct. 1957, XLVIII, 382–415; Jan. 1958, XLIX, 36–58).
Dewey is discussed in Part II.

————. *John Dewey.* Firenze: La Nuova Italia Editrice [1951]. viii, 152 pp. (Educatori antichi e moderni, 81.)
Reviewed in *Aut Aut 5,* Sept. 1951, 465–466 (Enzo Paci); *Rivista di filosofia,* Oct. 1952, XLIII, 452–455 (Valerio Verra).
Second edition. [1961]. viii, 148 pp.

————. John Dewey, maestro di umanità. *Scuola e città,* Apr. and June 1950, I, 54–59, 160–165.

————. John Dewey ovvero la consapevolezza critica dell'attivismo. *I problemi della pedagogia,* Dec. 1957.
Reprinted in his *Scuola aperte* (Firenze), 225–241.

————. Il mito della resipiscenza senile di Dewey. *Scuola e città,* 1954, V, 20–25.

————. Remarks on Dewey's Conception of Ends and Means. *Journal of Philosophy,* 3 Dec. 1953, L, 737–753.

————. La scuola progressiva e John Dewey. *Scuola e città,* Dec. 1950, I, 395–407.

————. La storia della filosofia nel pensiero di J. Dewey. *Rivista critica di storia della filosofia,* Oct.-Dec. 1951, VI, 373–397.

VIVAS, ELISEO. John Dewey's Achievement. *Partisan Review,* Spring 1939, VI, iii, 79–91.

————. *The Moral Life and the Ethical Life.* [Chicago:] University of Chicago Press [°1950]. xix, 390 pp.
See THE INSTRUMENTALIST MORAL THEORY, 100–137, and other references to Dewey, *passim.*

————. A Note on the Emotion in Mr. Dewey's Theory of Art. *Philosophical Review,* Sept. 1938, XLVII, 527–531.
Reprinted in his *Creation and Discovery: Essays in Criticism and Aesthetics* (New York: Noonday Press, 1955), 223–228.

VIVEIROS DE CASTRO, O. S. O conceito de finalidade en J. Dewey. *Verbum* (Rio de Janeiro), 1952, IX, 265–274.

WADE, FRANCIS C., S.J. The Child-Centered School: Dogma or Heresy? *National Catholic Education Association Bulletin*, 9 Aug. 1955, LII, 200–209; American Catholic Philosophical Association, *Proceedings*, 1955, XXIX, 263–274.

WAHL, JEAN. *Les Philosophies pluralistes d'Angleterre et d'Amerique*. Paris: Felix Alcan, 1920. 323 pp.
Dewey, *passim*.
English translation by Fred Rothwell, London: The Open Court Co., 1925.

WALCOTT, FRED GEORGE. Dewey's Theory of Social Progress. *Education*, Jan. 1960, LXXX, 319.

WALKER, LESLIE J. *Theories of Knowledge: Absolutism, Pragmatism, Realism*. (Stonyhurst Philosophical Series.) London: Longmans, Green & Co., 1910. xxxix, 696 pp.
Thesis (M.A.), University of London.
Dewey, *passim*.

WALLENROD, REUBEN. *John Dewey, édicateur*. Paris: Jouve et Cie, 1932. 227 pp.
Thèse (DR. DE L'UNIVERSITÉ), Paris.

WALLING, WILLIAM ENGLISH. *The Larger Aspects of Socialism*. New York: The Macmillan Company, 1913. xxi, 406 pp.
Dewey, 9–27, 34–40, 263–286, *et passim*.

WALLNER, NICO. John Dewey. *Neuphilologische Monatschrift*, July-Aug. 1934, V, 322–348.

WALTON, JOHN. Professional Jargon: A Remedy. *Peabody Journal of Education*, Nov. 1952, XXX, 161–165.

WANG, JO-SHUI. [Hu Shih and John Dewey in the May Fourth Movement.] *Jen Min Jih Pao* [Peking], 28 Dec. 1954, 3.
In Chinese. "One of a series of articles written in Communist China in the campaign to criticize the 'reactionary' thought of Hu Shih. Based on records of Dewey's lecture tour in China in 1919–21 at the time of the May Fourth movement...." (Abstract by T. S. Sun in *Historical Abstracts*, 1955, No. 1560.)

WARBEKE, JOHN M. Esthetic Form and Criteria in Croce and Dewey. *Journal of Philosophy*, 7 Dec. 1939, XXXVI, 679.
Abstract of a paper read before the American Philosophical Association at Columbia University, 28 Dec. 1939.

WARD, LEO RICHARD. John Dewey in Search of Himself. *Review of Politics* (University of Notre Dame), Apr. 1957, XIX, 205–213.

———. *Philosophy of Value: An Essay in Constructive Criticism.* New York: The Macmillan Company, 1930. x, 263 pp.
Thesis (PH.D.), Catholic University of America, 1929.
Dewey, *passim.*

———. *Values and Reality.* London and New York: Sheed & Ward, 1935. 331 pp.
Dewey, *passim.*

WARD, PAUL WILLIAM. The Doctrine of the Situation and the Method of Social Science. *Social Forces*, Oct. 1930, IX, 49–54.
Read before the session on the Philosophy of John Dewey at the meeting of the American Philosophical Association at Columbia University, 30 Dec. 1929.

WARREN, GUY H. M. Some Misinterpretations of John Dewey.
Master's thesis, Wisconsin State College (Superior), 1953.

WARREN, WILLIAM PRESTON. The Limits of Instrumentalism, or, John Dewey's Replies to His Critics. *Furman Bulletin* (Greenville, S.C.), Apr. 1940, 41–54.

WASSON, EVERETT LAWRENCE. Human Personality in the Philosophy of John Dewey.
Thesis (S.T.M.), Union Theological Seminary, 1933.

WATROUS, MARY W. A Comparative Study of John Dewey's *Democracy and Education* and *Experience and Education.*
Master's thesis, Gonzaga University, 1953.

WATSON, GENEVIEVE MARGARET. The Educational Philosophy of Froebel and Dewey Compared and Evaluated.
Thesis (PH.D.), New York University, 1931.

WATSON, GOODWIN. John Dewey as a Pioneer in Social Psychology. *Teachers College Record*, Dec. 1949, LI, 139–143.

WEBB, JOHN NYE. Three Score and Ten: Interview with John Dewey. *Columbia Varsity*, Oct. 1929, XI, i, 3–4.

WEBER, EDWARD LAWRENCE. The Beginnings of Progressive Education.
Thesis (A.B.), Princeton University, 1956.
JOHN DEWEY AND THE NEW EDUCATION, chap. iv.

WEGENER, FRANK C. Some Differences between the Organic Philosophy of Education and John Dewey's Experimentalism. *Educational Theory*, Oct. 1958, VIII, 239–248.

WELLS, HARRY K. *Pragmatism: Philosophy of Imperialism.* New York: International Publishers [°1954]. 221 pp.

Marxist critique of Charles S. S. Peirce, John Fiske, Oliver Wendell Holmes, Jr., William James, and John Dewey. The following chapters are on Dewey: VI. JOHN DEWEY: APOLOGETICS IN EDUCATION; IX. JOHN DEWEY'S INSTRUMENTALISM; X. DEWEY'S "HUMAN NATURE" THEORY OF SOCIETY; XI. DEWEY'S ETHICS OF GRADUALISM; XII. DEWEY'S RELIGION OF SUBMISSION.

WELSH, PAUL. Dewey's Theory of Inquiry.

Thesis (PH.D.), Cornell University, 1947.

———. Means and Ends in Dewey's Ethical Theory. *Journal of Philosophy*, 19 Nov. 1959, LVI, 960–961.

Abstract of a paper to be read at the meeting of the American Philosophical Association, Columbia University, 29 Dec. 1959.

———. Some Metaphysical Assumptions in Dewey's Philosophy. *Journal of Philosophy*, 23 Dec. 1954, LI, 861–867.

Reply by Elizabeth R. Eames, QUALITY AND RELATION AS METAPHYSICAL ASSUMPTIONS IN THE PHILOSOPHY OF JOHN DEWEY, *ib.*, 13 Feb. 1958, LV, 166–169.

WEN, LIEN CHUNG. The Conception of Culture, with Special Reference to the Educational Philosophy of John Dewey.

Thesis (PH.D.), Ohio State University, 1932.

WENLEY, ROBERT MARK. *The Life and Work of George Sylvester Morris.* New York: The Macmillan Company, 1917. xv, 332 pp.

Dewey, 312–321 *et passim.*

See Dewey's review of this book in *Philosophical Review*, Mar. 1919, XXVIII, 212–213.

WENTWORTH, EVA. Three Advanced Educational Reformers.

Thesis (A.M. IN ED.), University of Southern California, 1931.

WERKMEISTER, WILLIAM HENRY. *A History of Philosophical Ideas in America.* New York: The Ronald Press Company [°1949]. 599 pp.

THE EXPERIMENTALISM OF JOHN DEWEY, chap. xx, 541–561.

WEST, C. P. Pragmatism: The Logic of Capitalism. *New Essays* (United Workers Party, Chicago), Winter 1943, VI, iv.

WHALEN, WILLIS L. A Fifth Column in Catholic Education? *Homiletic and Pastoral Review*, May 1951, LI, 708–712.

WHEELER, JAMES E. The Thought of John Dewey in Its Historical Setting. *Educational Theory*, Apr. 1954, IV, 87–94.

WHITE, CARL MILTON. The Bearing of John Dewey's Philosophy of Education on Problems Confronting Librarians. *School and Society*, 10 Apr. 1937, XLV, 516–517.

WHITE, EDWARD A. *Science and Religion in American Thought: The Impact of Naturalism.* Stanford, California: Stanford University Press, 1952. 125 pp.
NATURALISM VERSUS SUPERNATURALISM: JOHN DEWEY, 90–109.

WHITE, HOWARD BURTON. The Political Faith of John Dewey. *Journal of Politics*, May 1958, XX, 353–367.

WHITE, MORTON GABRIEL, ed. *The Age of Analysis. Twentieth Century Philosophers.* (The Great Ages of Western Philosophy, VI.) Boston: Houghton Mifflin Company, 1955, and New York: New American Library of World Literature, Inc., 1955. 253 pp.
See chap. xi, SCIENCE AND MORALS: JOHN DEWEY (1859–1952), 173–189, with extract from *The Quest for Certainty, et passim.*

————. Experiment and Necessity in Dewey's Philosophy. *Antioch Review*, Fall 1959, XIX, 329–344.
Version of a paper delivered at Brandeis University in Apr. 1959 in a series on JOHN DEWEY IN THE LIGHT OF RECENT PHILOSOPHY.

————. *The Origin of Dewey's Instrumentalism.* (Columbia Studies in Philosophy, 4.) New York: Columbia University Press, 1943. 161 pp.
Thesis (PH.D.), Columbia University.
Reviewed in *The Humanist*, Summer 1943, III, 86–87 (Alfred Stiernotte); *Journal of Philosophy*, 29 Apr. 1943, XL, 250–252 (David Frederick Bowers).

————. The Revolt Against Formalism in American Social Thought of the Twentieth Century. *Journal of the History of Ideas*, Apr. 1947, VIII, 131–152.
JOHN DEWEY, 139–142.

————. *Social Thought in America: The Revolt against Formalism.* New York: The Viking Press, 1949. 260 pp.
"In [this book] I have tried to trace the development of the leading

ideas of Charles A. Beard, John Dewey, Oliver Wendell Holmes, Jr., James Harvey Robinson, and Thorstein Veblen, and to analyze critically some of their key philosophical views." PREFACE.

New edition, with a new preface and an epilogue, ORIGINAL SIN, NATURAL LAW, AND POLITICS, defending Dewey against the attacks of Reinhold Niebuhr and Walter Lippmann. Boston: Beacon Press (paperback), 1957. 301 pp.

See Ralph William Sleeper, DEWEY'S METAPHYSICAL PERSPECTIVE: A NOTE ON WHITE, GEIGER, AND THE PROBLEM OF OBLIGATION, *Journal of Philosophy*, 4 Feb. 1960, LVII, 100–115.

――――. Value and Obligation in Dewey and [Clarence Irving] Lewis. *Philosophical Review*, July 1949, LVIII, 321–329.

Reprinted in Wilfred Stalker Sellars and John Hospers, eds., *Readings in Ethical Theory* (New York: Appleton-Century-Crofts, Inc., 1952), 332–339.

Reply by John Ladd, "DESIRABILITY" AND "NORMATIVENESS" IN WHITE'S ARTICLE ON DEWEY, *Philosophical Review*, Jan. 1951, LX, 91–98.

WHITE, STEPHEN SOLOMON. *A Comparison of the Philosophies of F. C. S. Schiller and John Dewey.* [Chicago: University of Chicago Libraries], 1940. iv, 80 p.

Thesis (PH.D.), University of Chicago, 1938.

WHITEHEAD, ALFRED NORTH. John Dewey and His Influence. In his *Essays in Science and Philosophy* (New York: Philosophical Library [°1947]), 120–121.

Reprinted from Paul Arthur Schilpp, ed., *The Philosophy of John Dewey* (1939, 1951), 477–478.

German translation in *Der Monat*, Oct. 1949, II, xiii, 23–24.

WHITEHEAD, EUGENE S. J. Dewey's Educational Standards as Related to the Public Schools.

Master's thesis, University of Texas, 1928.

WICKHAM, HARVEY. *The Unrealists: James, Bergson, Santayana, Einstein, Bertrand Russell, John Dewey, Alexander and Whitehead.* New York: Lincoln MacVeagh, The Dial Press, 1930. 314 pp.

Dewey, 196–218.

WIELENGA, G. Didactics and a Philosophy of Life (John Dewey). *Free University Quarterly* (Amsterdam), 1953, II, 236–250.

Dutch version, Groningen: J. B. Wolters, 1953. 19 pp.

WIEMAN, HENRY NELSON. Philosophers' Dean: The Dual Dewey. *Christian Register*, Nov. 1949, CXXVIII, x, 22–24.

———. Religion in John Dewey's Philosophy. *Journal of Religion*, Jan. 1931, XI, 1–19.

WIENER, PHILIP PAUL, *Evolution and the Founders of Pragmatism*. Cambridge: Harvard University Press, 1949. xiv, 288 pp.
Dewey, *passim*. Foreword by Dewey, xiii–xiv.

WIGGINS, FORREST ORAN. William James and John Dewey. *The Personalist*, Spring 1942, XXIII, 182–198.

WILD, JOHN DANIEL, ed. *The Return to Realism: Essays in Realistic Philosophy*. Chicago: Henry Regnery Company, 1953. 373 pp.
Dewey, *passim*.

WILKINS, BURLEIGH TAYLOR. James, Dewey, and Hegelian Idealism. *Journal of the History of Ideas*, June 1956, XVII, 332–346.

WILLIAMS, CHESTER SIDNEY. *How Progressive Is John Dewey's Philosophy of Education?* (University of Wichita Bulletin, Vol. 39, No. 4, University Studies No. 43.) Wichita, Kansas: University of Wichita, 1959. 10 pp.

WILLIAMS, DONALD CARY. Mr. John Dewey on Problems and Men. *Harvard Educational Review*, Fall 1946, XVI, 297–308.

WILLIAMS, JAY. Dewey and the Idea of a Science of Education. *School Review*, Summer 1959, LXVII, 186–194.

WILSON, FRANCIS GRAHAM. The Foremost Philosopher of the Age. *Modern Age*, Winter 1957–58, II, 54–62.
Comments on the speeches at the dinners given in New York to Herbert Spencer, 9 Nov. 1882, and to Dewey, 20 Oct. 1949.

WILSON, HOWARD WOODROW. Some Implications of Dewey's Philosophy for the Teaching of Speech.
Thesis (A.M.), University of Illinois, 1940.

WILSON, NETTA WHITE. The Development of the Sociological Trend in John Dewey's Ethical Theory.
Thesis (A.M.), University of Minnesota, 1929.

WISCONSIN. UNIVERSITY. *In Honor of John Dewey on His Ninetieth Birthday* . . .‡ [Madison]: University of Wisconsin. The

School of Education and the Department of Philosophy [1951]. 40 pp.

Contents. John Dewey, by Max Carl Otto—John Dewey and Education, by Matthew H. Willing—John Dewey's Influence on the Arts and on Art Education by Frederick Manning Logan—John Dewey's Philosophy of Social Economy, by Fred A. Clarenbach—John Dewey and Science, by C. Leonard Huskins—John Dewey's Philosophy, by Horace Snyder Fries.

Papers presented at a convocation on the occasion of Dewey's ninetieth birthday, held at the university 19 and 20 Oct. 1949.

WOLFARD, HELEN M. What Dewey Means by Experience: Some Implications for Education.

Master's thesis, Reed College, 1954.

WOLSTEIN, BENJAMIN. Dewey's Theory of Human Nature. *Psychiatry*, Feb. 1949, XII, 77–85.

———. *Experience and Valuation: A Study in John Dewey's Naturalism.* New York City, 1949. 99, xxviii pp. lithographed.

Thesis (PH.D.), Columbia University.

WOOD, CHARLES W. Professor Dewey of Columbia on War's Social Results. New York *World*, 29 July 1917.

———. Professor John Dewey on the Hysteria Which Holds Teaching in Check. *Ib.*, 27 Aug. 1922.

Two interviews.

WOODBRIDGE, FREDERICK JAMES EUGENE. Experience and Dialectic. *Journal of Philosophy*, 8 May 1930, XXVII, 264–271.

Read before the session on the Philosophy of John Dewey at the meeting of the American Philosophical Association, Columbia University, 30 Dec. 1929.

Reprinted in his *Nature and Mind* (1937), pp. 230–239.

See Dewey's reply in *Journal of Philosophy*, 8 May 1937, XXVII, 271–277.

WOODRING, PAUL. *Let's Talk Sense about Our Schools.* New York, Toronto, London: McGraw-Hill Book Company, Inc. [ᶜ1953]. ix, 215 pp.

See chap. iii, THE SHADOW OF JOHN DEWEY, 27–48, *et passim.*

———. *A Fourth of a Nation.* New York, Toronto, London: McGraw-Hill Book Company, Inc. [ᶜ1957]. 255 pp.

Dewey, *passim.*

WORLD TOMORROW. Education in Action: The Story of John Dewey. *World Tomorrow*, Apr. 1931, XIV, 106–109.

WRIGHT, HENRY WILKES. Ethics and Social Philosophy. *In* Edward Leroy Schaub, ed., *Philosophy Today* (Chicago: The Open Court Publishing Company, 1928), 87–104.

WRIGHT, WARD WILBUR. The Psychology of John Dewey.
Thesis (A.M.), Oberlin College, 1936.

WYCKOFF, HARRY WILSON. A Study of the Esthetics of John Dewey.
Thesis (A.M.), Leland Stanford, Jr., University, 1936.

WYNNE, JOHN PETER. Mind and Education from the Standpoint of John Dewey and George Herbert Mead. *Educational Theory*, July 1952, II, 129–140.

YEAGER, IVER FRANKLIN. Personal-Social Values in John Macmurray and John Dewey: A Basis for a Creative Relationship between Religion and Higher Education.
Thesis (A.M.), University of Chicago, 1948.

YELLE, JOSEPH ROBERT. A Contextual Approach to the Problem of the Relation of Dewey's Theories of Value, Inquiry, and Experience.
Thesis (A.M.), University of Chicago, 1950.

YIN, FA-LU. [How Did Hu Shih, John Dewey and Bertrand Russell Start To Sabotage the New Cultural Movement in China?] *Shih-hsueh* (Supplement of *Kuang Ming Jih Pao*, Peking), 1955, No. 51.
In Chinese. Abstract by T. S. Sun in *Historical Abstracts*, 1955, No. 3366.

YOCUM, ALBERT DUNCAN. Dr. Dewey's "Liberalism" in Government and in Public Education. *School and Society*, 4 July 1936, XLIV, 1–5.

YOUNG, ELLA FLAGG. *Some Types of Modern Educational Theory*. (University of Chicago Contributions to Education, No. VI.) Chicago: University of Chicago Press, 1902. 67 pp.
THE PHILOSOPHY OF EDUCATION, 1895–1902, JOHN DEWEY, 53–67. Résumé of *School and Society*, THE INTERPRETATION SIDE OF CHILD STUDY, PRINCIPLES OF MENTAL DEVELOPMENT AS ILLUSTRATED IN EARLY INFANCY, and INTEREST AS RELATED TO WILL.

YOUNG, HOMER H. Contributions of John Dewey to American Education.

Master's thesis, Leland Stanford, Jr., University, 1937.

YOUNG, WARREN CAMERON. *The Influence of John Dewey in Religious Education.* Chicago, ᶜ1949. 54 leaves.

———. Nature and Naturalism in the Thought of Frederick J. E. Woodbridge and John Dewey.

Thesis (PH.D.), Boston University, 1947.

ZALLYS, RICHARD PAUL. Ideals or Experience—Santayana and Dewey.

Thesis (A.M.), University of Chicago, 1956.

ZAZZO, RENÉ. John Dewey et l'instrumentalisme. *Journal de psychologie normale et pathologique* (Paris), Apr.-June 1953, XLVI, 125–132.

ZEDLER, BEATRICE HOPE. John Dewey in Context. *In* Donald A. Gallagher, ed., *Some Philosophers on Education: Papers Concerning the Doctrines of Augustine, Aristotle, Aquinas, and Dewey* ([Milwaukee]: Marquette University Press, 1956), 1–25.

ZELTNER, HERMANN. Deutsche Philosophie und Deutsche Politik (In Auseinandersetzung mit John Dewey). *Kant-Studien,* 1956–7, XLVIII, 550–558.

Habilitationsvorlesung, gehalten am 9. 7. 1955, Erlangen.

Discussion of the German translation of Dewey's *German Philosophy and Politics* (Meisenheim/Glan, 1954).

ZENI, SILVIO. *Il pragmatismo americano: Peirce, James, Dewey.* Asti: La tipografo di Monticone, 1957. 221 pp.

ZINK, SIDNEY. The Concept of Continuity in Dewey's Theory of Esthetics. *Philosophical Review,* July 1943, LII, 392–400.

ZINMAN, MEYER E. John Dewey's Philosophy and the Classroom Teacher. *High Points* (New York City Board of Education), Nov. 1932, XIV, 31–36.

Compiler's Note

Selections from the Writings of George MacDonald; or, Helps for Weary Souls. Compiled by J. Dewey. New York: Thomas R. Knox & Co. [ᶜ1885], and later issued at Chicago by F. L. Dusenberry [ᶜ1889], 93 pp., was included in the 1929 edition of this bibliography as the work of John Dewey, the title having been taken from the Library of Congress card, which ascribes the item to him. The British Museum Catalogue more cautiously attributes it to Dewey with an interrogation-mark. Dewey's connection with the book of extracts from the British poet and novelist (1824–1905) was questioned, and since the authorship seemed doubtful, this entry was omitted from our 1939 edition, as stated in the Note on p. [204]. There the matter rested until 1960, when Dr. John Blewett reattributed the book to John Dewey in his *John Dewey: His Thought and Influence* (esp. note 14, p. 57). This has occasioned a re-examination of the evidence, and it is now possible to say definitely that John Dewey was not the compiler of the MacDonald volume. The catalogue of the Knox firm, bound in the *Publishers Trade List Annual for 1887*, lists the book as "Compiled by Miss J. Dewey."

We are satisfied that Miss J. Dewey is identical with Miss Jerusha Dewey, the daughter of Silas and Mary (Root) Dewey of Sheffield, Massachusetts, who was born 12 Nov. 1804 and died unmarried 6 July 1888 (A. M. Dewey and L. M. Dewey, *Life of George Dewey . . . and Dewey Family History*, 1898, p. 900). She was the compiler of *Helps to Devout Living*, listed as by J. Dewey, published in New Bedford, Massachusetts, by E. Anthony and Sons in 1879, and in a second edition by Lockwood, Brooks & Co. of Boston in 1881 (*American Catalogue*

1876–1884, p. 58; Orville Dewey, *Autobiography and Letters*, ed. by his daughter Mary Elizabeth Dewey, 1883, p. 349). Miss Jerusha Dewey was the sister of the Rev. Orville Dewey (Williams 1814), Unitarian minister in New Bedford, New York City, and Boston, who was born at Sheffield, 28 Mar. 1794, and died there, 21 Mar. 1882. Dr. Frederick Augustus Porter Barnard (Yale 1828), president of Columbia College from 1864 to 1889, was born in Sheffield, 5 May 1809, and first went to school there to Orville Dewey, then just out of college; they were lifelong friends (John Fulton, *Memoirs of Frederick A. P. Barnard*, 1896, pp. 14, 234). Barnard unquestionably knew his sister Jerusha in Sheffield. The Columbia University Library copy of *Selections from the Writings of George MacDonald* . . . was formerly owned by President Barnard and is recorded as his gift; it bears the inscription: "With the Compilers kind regards April 4/85."

"PRINCIPLES OF INSTRUMENTAL LOGIC, by John Dewey, Ph.D., Professor of Philosophy in the University of Michigan," announced for inclusion in the Library of Philosophy, 3d series, John Henry Muirhead, editor, was never published.

THE INTERNATIONAL CHARACTER OF MODERN PHILOSOPHY was reprinted in *Characters and Events*, II, 831–840, with the title PHILOSOPHY AND INTERNATIONALISM, from tear-sheets found in Dewey's office. It has not been possible to find the magazine in which this was originally published.

AN INTRODUCTION TO EDUCATIONAL PHILOSOPHY by Dewey has been published in Russian; this is probably an abridged translation of *Democracy and Education*.

DEMOKRATIE ALS AUFGABE UNSERER ZEIT, a Dewey title in *Bildung und Erziehung* (Stuttgart), 1948, I, ii, 1–6, has not been seen; it may be a translation of CREATIVE DEMOCRACY—THE TASK BEFORE US.

The Scientific Monthly, Jan. 1941, LII, 55, prints a three-paragraph quotation, SCIENCE AND DEMOCRACY, giving the citation: *John Dewey in "The Scientific Method and Study of Processes"*; this title is unknown to us.

UNPUBLISHED DEWEY ITEMS

A typescript of Dewey's LECTURES IN PSYCHOLOGY AT THE UNIVERSITY OF CHICAGO, 4 Apr.–20 June 1898 (175 pages), is in the Manuscript Department of Duke University Library; probably a stenographic report by a student.

The typescript of Dewey's lecture, PHILOSOPHY OF THE FINE ARTS, given before the Washington Dance Association at the Phillips Memorial Gallery in Washington, 13 Nov. 1938, is in the Fletcher Free Library at Burlington, Vermont; it runs to 17 pages.

Professor Houston Peterson of Rutgers University has in his personal possession a recording of an address made by Dewey at Cooper Union, Sunday evening, 7 Dec. 1941. Dewey was scheduled to speak in a series, LESSONS FROM THE WAR, his topic being IN PHILOSOPHY. Upon receipt of the news of the Pearl Harbor attack, he put aside his notes and spoke extemporaneously on the meaning of the attack for America.

The Oral History Research Office at Columbia University has a transcript of an interview with Dewey on his ninetieth birthday in 1949, made at New Alexandria, Pennsylvania, by Professor Richard Hope of the University of Pittsburgh. It runs to 8 pages. They also have a disc recording of ART AS OUR HERITAGE, the address made by Dewey over the N.B.C. network, 25 Apr. 1940, in honor of American artists who contributed toward decorations in Federal buildings; this address was printed in the *Congressional Record*, as listed on pp. 133–134, *ante*.

WORKS IN PREPARATION

The correspondence between Dewey and Arthur Fisher Bentley is being edited by Professor Sidney Ratner and Julius Altman for publication in two volumes by the Rutgers University Press in 1963.

Professor Gérard Deledalle of Sousse, Tunisia, has in preparation: L'IDÉE D'EXPÉRIENCE DANS LA PHILOSOPHIE DE JOHN DEWEY. I. POUR UNE PHILOSOPHIE DE L'EXPÉRIENCE; II. POUR UNE HISTOIRE DE L'IDÉE D'EXPÉRIENCE DANS LA PHILOSOPHIE DE JOHN DEWEY; a thesis for the *Doctorat d'état* at the Sorbonne. He is also making a French translation of Dewey's *Logic: The*

Theory of Inquiry. Several chapters of his biography of Dewey are completed.

Professor Max Harold Fisch of the University of Illinois is writing a biography of Charles Santiago Sanders Peirce which will include a chapter on Dewey and Bentley.

Mrs. Felix Kaufmann intends to publish the correspondence which passed between Dewey and her late husband, Professor Kaufmann of the New School for Social Research.

Professor Lewis Samuel Feuer of the University of California at Berkeley has a biography of Dewey in preparation. Some of his preliminary studies are listed in our section of Writings about Dewey.

ADDENDA TO WRITINGS ABOUT DEWEY

FROST, CORINNE CHISHOLM. John Dewey's Letters to Corinne Chisholm Frost. *Columbia Library Columns*, Feb. 1960, IX, ii, 34–36.

GUTMANN, JAMES. A Note on the Dewey-Frost Correspondence. *Ib.*, 32–33.

HAWORTH, LAWRENCE. Dewey's Philosophy of the Corporation. *Ethics*, Jan. 1962, LXXII, 120–131.

SCHMIDT, GEORGE PAUL. *The Liberal Arts College: A Chapter in American Cultural History*. New Brunswick: Rutgers University Press, 1957. 310 pp.

Chap. X, DEWEY VS. HUTCHINS.

Index

Wade, Francis C., 285
Wagner, Donald Owen, 90
Wagner Institute, 101
Wahl, Jean, 285
Walcott, Fred George, 285
Waldman, Joseph, 212
Walker, Leslie J., 285
Wallace, Henry Agard, 147
Wallace, William, 11
Wallas, Graham, 76
Wallenrod, Reuben, 285
Walling, William English, 285
Wallner, Nico, 285
Walton, John, 285
Wang, Jo-Shui, 285
Wanger, Ruth, 97
War: America and, 85
    Higher Learning and, The, 131
    If It Were Outlawed, 69, 85
    Outlawing Peace by Discussing,
        85
    Outlawry of, 55, 79, 82, 104,
        137, 259; What It Is Not, 69,
        85
    Social Possibilities of, The, 85
    Social Results of, 291
    Stay Out of, 131
    When America Goes to, 116
    Why Not Outlaw?, 85
    (World War II), 134, 297
    Activities for Civilians, 52
    and a Code of Law, 69, 85
    Debts, 98
War-System, International Law
    and the, 127–128
Warbeke, John M., 108, 285
Ward, Leo Richard, 253
Ward, Lester Frank, 10, 286
Ward, Paul William, 286
Wardwell, Mary Spargo, 131
Warranted Assertibility, Dewey's
    Theory of, 275
Warren, Guy M. H., 286
Warren, William Preston, 286

Wartime, Our Educational Ideal
    in, 48, 131
Washburne, Carleton, 135
Washington Conference on the
    Limitation of Armaments,
    61–63; The Issues at, 62
Washington Dance Association,
    297
Wasson, Everett Lawrence, 286
Waste in Education, 18, 43
Watrous, Mary W., 286
Watson, David Lindsay, 126
Watson, Genevieve Margaret, 286
Watson, Goodwin, 120, 286
Watson, John, 13
Watt, Robert J., 144
Way To Think, The, 84
Weaver, Raymond Melbourne, 59
Webb, John Nye, 286
Weber, Edward Lawrence, 286
Weber, Max, 235
Weber, Pearl, 89
Weeks, Raymond, 74
Wegener, Frank C., 287
Weinstock, Solomon, 147
Weiss, Paul, 99, 114, 121, 124,
    129, 268
Weller, Charles Frederick, 113
Welling, Richard Ward Greene,
    117
Wells, Harry K., 287
Wells, Herbert George, 84; Theo-
    logical Assembler, 51
Welsh, Paul, 124, 190, 287
Weltner, George, 226
Welton, James, 212
Wen, Lien Chung, 287
Wenley, Robert Mark, 4, 50, 57,
    287
Wentworth, Eva, 287
Werkmeister, William Henry, 124,
    128, 268, 287
West, C. P., 287
Western Drawing Teachers' As-
    sociation, 13, 57

PRINTED IN U.S.A.